Joltin' JOE DiMAGGIO

Edited by
Richard Gilliam

CARROLL & GRAF PUBLISHERS
NEW YORK

First Carroll & Graf edition 1999

Carroll & Graf Publishers, Inc.
19 West 21st Street
New York, NY 10010-6805

Library of Congress Cataloging-in-Publication Data is available.
ISBN: 0-7867-0686-4

Manufactured in the United States of America

Contents

A Few Words
about Joe DiMaggio

BY Allen H. Selig,
Baseball Commissioner

*J*OE DIMAGGIO IS my all-time hero. He had an aura about him that's hard to articulate. When you saw him you knew you were seeing a great player and a great person who was just different from anybody else.

I grew up a Cubs fan, so the first major league baseball games I saw were at Wrigley Field. Lots of Sunday doubleheaders. I was lucky my parents were willing to take me to so many games. From 1947 on I saw DiMaggio play almost every time the New York Yankees came to Chicago to old Comiskey Park. For my fifteenth birthday in 1949 my mother took me to New York to see Joe D play in Yankee Stadium. I also saw him play a couple of times in Cleveland, so I got to see him fairly often. He was amazing to watch. The films from that era only hint at the excitement he brought to the game.

In my opinion, he is the second most famous American athlete of all time, just an inch behind Babe Ruth, who to some extent has the advantage of being the first great baseball superstar. Joe

D retired after the 1951 season, almost forty-eight years ago, and yet he has continued to remain in the public spotlight more than any other player from his era.

Look at his career. From '36 to '42 his numbers are awesome—clanging the ball around in that huge, cavernous ballpark. And there's no question that losing '43, '44, and '45 to military service cost him greatly in his career stats, but also, I think, it was important what Joe and other baseball players did in helping the country's morale during World War II. Those three years were at the prime of his career.

After the 1951 season he turned down a six-figure paycheck and retired. What he said at the press conference told you about his standards. He had fought throughout his career for higher salaries, but once age and injury caught up with his skills, there was no amount of money he'd accept if it meant playing at less than what fans expected from Joe DiMaggio.

Even when I met him eighteen years later, it was a big thrill. He was a coach with Oakland then, and we brought the A's and the White Sox up to Milwaukee to play. It was a great thrill, I don't mind telling you, and also a great moment when he was my guest at the 1994 All-Star game. My whole family thought it was a great to meet him. It's a special memory for me.

But seeing Joe play was absolutely my biggest thrill as a baseball fan. In 1949 my father gave me an autographed baseball from Joe that he had gotten from a friend in New York. I still have it. It's difficult to explain why someone has the sort of impact on society that Joe had, but he did. His ability, his quietness, and his dignity formed a chemistry about him.

I was in San Francisco for Joe's funeral and it was, for me, a moment of great reflection. Sitting in the church and watching the thousands of people who had gathered outside to honor him. Thinking of my own childhood, and how much Joe had meant not just to me, but to the nation.

He was the most graceful baseball player I've ever seen. He never threw to the wrong base, never missed the cutoff man, and never made a baserunning error, or so it seemed. If he did make those kinds of mistakes, it was so seldom that his errors were absorbed into his overall greatness.

I watched the news the day he died and noticed how for nearly a week or so it was the dominant news story. I was with George Steinbrenner in Tampa, and my secretary called me on Sunday afternoon to say Dominic DiMaggio had called her to tell me that Joe was near his end. I felt so sad. I thought of all those memories that I had, and that so many other people had. There was something very special about Joe that passed from generation to generation, that went outside sports, that made him extraordinary to people too young to have seen him play.

I've heard the current Yankee players talk about how special it was when he entered the clubhouse. 'There's Joe DiMaggio' they would stop whatever they were doing and say. He was the most gracious person I've ever met. Just wonderful both to watch as a player, and later a privilege to know as a person.

Maybe I'm partial, but Joe may not have been even an inch behind Babe Ruth in fame. He was Joe DiMaggio—that's all you need to say!''

Joltin' JOE

The Silent Superstar

PAUL SIMON

*M*Y OPINIONS REGARDING the baseball legend Joe DiMaggio would be of no particular interest to the general public were it not for the fact that thirty years ago I wrote the song "Mrs. Robinson," whose lyric "Where have you gone, Joe DiMaggio? A nation turns its lonely eyes to you" alluded to and in turn probably enhanced Di-Maggio's stature in the American iconographic landscape.

A few years after "Mrs. Robinson" rose to No. 1 on the pop charts, I found myself dining at an Italian restaurant where DiMaggio was seated with a party of friends. I'd heard a rumor that he was upset with the song and had considered a lawsuit, so it was with some trepidation that I walked over and introduced myself as its composer. I needn't have worried: he was perfectly cordial and invited me to sit down, whereupon we immediately fell into conversation about the only subject we had in common.

"What I don't understand," he said, "is why you ask where

I've gone. I just did a Mr. Coffee commercial, I'm a spokesman for the Bowery Savings Bank and I haven't gone anywhere.''

I said that I didn't mean the lines literally, that I thought of him as an American hero and that genuine heroes were in short supply. He accepted the explanation and thanked me. We shook hands and said good night.

Now, in the shadow of his passing, I find myself wondering about that explanation. Yes, he was a cultural icon, a hero if you will, but not of my generation. He belonged to my father's youth: he was a World War II guy whose career began in the days of Babe Ruth and Lou Gehrig and ended with the arrival of the youthful Mickey Mantle (who was, in truth, my favorite ballplayer).

In the fifties and sixties, it was fashionable to refer to baseball as a metaphor for America, and DiMaggio represented the values of that America: excellence and fulfillment of duty (he often played in pain), combined with a grace that implied a purity of spirit, an off-the-field dignity, and a jealousy guarded private life. It was said that he still grieved for his former wife, Marilyn Monroe, and sent fresh flowers to her grave every week. Yet as a man who married one of America's most famous and famously neurotic women, he never spoke of her in public or in print. He understood the power of silence.

He was the antithesis of the iconoclastic, mind-expanding, authority-defying sixties, which is why I think he suspected a hidden meaning in my lyrics. The fact that the lines were sincere and that they've been embraced over the years as a yearning for heroes and heroism speaks to the subconscious desires of the culture. We need heroes, and we search for candidates to be anointed.

Why do we do this even as we know the attribution of heroic characteristics is almost always a distortion? Deconstructed and scrutinized, the hero turns out to be as petty and ego-driven as you and I. We know, but still we anoint. We deify, though we know the deification often kills, as in the cases of Elvis Presley,

Princess Diana, and John Lennon. Even when the recipient's life is spared, the fame and idolatry poison and injure. There is no doubt in my mind that DiMaggio suffered for being DiMaggio.

We inflict this damage without malice because we are enthralled by myths, stories and allegories. The son of Italian immigrants, the father a fisherman, grows up poor in San Francisco and becomes the greatest baseball player of his day, marries an American goddess and never in word or deed befouls his legend and greatness. He is "the Yankee Clipper," as proud and masculine as a battleship.

When the hero becomes larger than life, life itself is magnified, and we read with a new clarity our moral compass. The hero allows us to measure ourselves on the goodness scale: O.K., I'm not Mother Teresa, but hey, I'm no Jeffrey Dahmer. Better keep trying in the eyes of God.

What is the larger significance of DiMaggio's death? Is he a real hero? Let me quote the complete verse from "Mrs. Robinson":

Sitting on a sofa on a Sunday afternoon
Going to the candidates' debate
Laugh about it, shout about it
When you've got to choose
Every way you look at it you lose.
Where have you gone, Joe DiMaggio?
A nation turns its lonely eyes to you
What's that you say? Mrs. Robinson,
Joltin' Joe has left and gone away.

In these days of Presidential transgressions and apologies and prime-time interviews about private sexual matters, we grieve for Joe DiMaggio and mourn the loss of his grace and dignity, his fierce sense of privacy, his fidelity to the memory of his wife and the power of his silence.

Paul Simon is among the world's best known and best regarded singers and songwriters. This essay was first published in The New York Times *in 1999, shortly after the death of Joe DiMaggio.*

A Hitting Streak Not Soon Forgotten

GEORGE DE GREGORIO

ROM MID-MAY TO mid-July in 1941, Joe DiMaggio forestalled any onset of the American baseball fan's mid-season torpor, replacing day-to-day monotony with a state of day-to-day euphoria.

DiMaggio's streak—hitting safely in 56 straight games, a record that has never been matched—came at a time when Europe was already at war. Americans, filled with foreboding, stumbled faint-heartedly through civil defense drills. Roosevelt's fireside chats brought dire warnings of a blueprint by Hitler. The country wanted diversion from thoughts of war, and sought it in baseball games, Andy Hardy films, zoot suits, the ''Hit Parade,'' and the bobby-soxers' craze over a scrawny young crooner from Hoboken, New Jersey, named Frank Sinatra.

DiMaggio had been notified by the Selective Service Board that his draft number was 5,423 and that he would be registered in Class 3, assuring him of at least one more season in baseball. But there was anxiety in the New York Yankee front office as well. In mid-May the club was in fourth place; DiMaggio was batting .306, far below his career average, and the team lacked sparkle and élan in the field. The Yankees had lost four games in a row and seven of their last nine. They were five and a half games behind the league-leading Cleveland Indians. Edward G. Barrow, the Yankee president, feared a repetition of the team's poor start and loss of the title in 1940, when DiMaggio missed the first 30 games with a knee injury. Barrow issued broadsides to the effect that wholesale changes and the trading of star players, including DiMaggio, were not remote possibilities if the Yankees did not right their course.

As the heir to Babe Ruth and Lou Gehrig, DiMaggio was singled out as the figure most responsible for the apparent decline. He had won the league batting crown in 1939 with .381 and in 1940 with .352. He had been named the American League's most valuable player in 1939, his fourth straight year on a world championship team. No one else in baseball could boast such a ledger. DiMaggio had placed his stamp on this team as its leader, but now, though he was only twenty-six years old, the fans were beginning to wonder whether his reign as the monarch of the New York dynasty was nearing an end. If so, then surely the dynasty itself was in trouble.

Then, on May 15 at Yankee Stadium, DiMaggio began his streak with a seemingly inconsequential single off Edgar Smith, a left-handed pitcher for the Chicago White Sox, who routed the Yankees that day, 13–1 The team's tailspin was magnified in the columns of New York's newspapers.

No one could know, of course, that DiMaggio was now embarked on two months of the hottest batting in baseball history. In the seventh game of his streak, he went to the plate against the Detroit Tigers in the ninth inning with the winning run on third base and none out. In this situation, with a batter of his credentials, the baseball book usually dictates an intentional walk—all the more so since he had got two hits in the early innings. Now a long fly ball would be enough to bring in the winning run. But on this day Del Baker, the Tiger manager, did not hold him in such esteem. He ordered Al Benton, a right-hander, to pitch to DiMaggio, who grounded out.

The Yankees eventually won the game, in the tenth inning, but as the fans walked down the Stadium exit ramps, the prevailing sentiment was "They're not afraid of the Jolter anymore."

Baker was not alone in his strategy. Against the Boston Red Sox a few days later, the Yankees were trailing, 6–5, in the seventh inning. They had runners on second and third, DiMaggio going to bat.

"You can get him; don't walk him," Manager Joe Cronin told his left-hander Earl Johnson.

DiMaggio lined Johnson's first pitch for a single, driving in two runs for the victory. Now he had hit in 10 straight games. A mini-streak, nothing to be greatly excited about. It received only perfunctory mention in the sports pages.

Always prone to injuries and mild illnesses, DiMaggio had developed swelling in the neck that gave him enormous pain. He did not report it to Manager Joe McCarthy for fear he would be taken out of the lineup.

"This damn swollen neck is driving me crazy," he said to the pitcher Lefty Gomez, his roommate, a few days later. "But don't say anything about it."

The pain continued for two weeks, and, in a double-header on Memorial Day in Boston, DiMaggio made four woeful errors, dropping a fly ball, bobbling a grounder, and throwing wildly twice. A defensive performer of consummate grace and superb reflexes, he was dismayed over his lapse in the field.

"If you're not going to say anything about that neck, then I will," Gomez said to him.

"I get it every year," DiMaggio said. "It'll go away."

Finally the problem came to McCarthy's attention, and DiMaggio received treatment for it. On June 7, when the Yankees were in Sportsman's Park in St. Louis for a weekend series with the Browns, the pain disappeared. McCarthy, who always worried about the condition of his star player, sat back in the dugout and said, "The boys are just waiting for Joe to show 'em how to do it."

DiMaggio showed the way that day, with three hits. The next afternoon he belted three home runs and a double as the Yankees swept a doubleheader. Now they were riding an eight-game winning streak.

In mid-June, after DiMaggio had pushed his own streak to 25 games, the writers covering the Yankees began researching the record books. Forty-four years before, in 1897, a player named Willie Keeler, a trolley conductor's son from Brooklyn, had hit safely in 44 straight games. No other big league player had matched Keeler's streak, although in 1922 George Sisler of the St. Louis Browns had produced a string of 41, breaking Ty Cobb's American League record of 40, set in 1911.

The Yankee team record in this category was 29, held by Earle Combs and Roger Peckinpaugh. DiMaggio passed this milestone with a bad-hop single that struck the shoulder of Luke Appling, the White Sox shortstop. Lady Luck had not only kept his streak alive but also helped transform him into a national celebrity, not just another high-salaried, big-name ballplayer. She had helped him invade the nation's consciousness. He would become a symbol of cosmic masculinity; a creature of animal magnetism desired by women, approved by men; a subject to salute in song.

The drama of the hitting streak grew more intense with each game. Every pitcher worthy of his trade yearned for a chance to confront and defeat DiMaggio. Those who faced him summoned extra energy and grit and bore down on him even more than they did on other batters.

In his singleness of purpose, DiMaggio, too, summoned greater strength and tenacity. The central characters appeared to be waging a concentrated battle involving body, mind, and spirit.

Bob Muncrief, a twenty-five-year-old rookie right-hander

from the Texas League, became one of the first pitchers to get personally involved in the streak. It was in the 36th game. Muncrief, pitching for the Browns, had DiMaggio in trouble, having retired him three times in a row without a hit. But in the eighth inning, in what would have been his last time up, DiMaggio saved himself with a single.

Luke Sewell, the Browns' manager, was a hard-bitten competitor who hated to lose, a characteristic made more intense because the Browns were chronic losers. That DiMaggio got a hit his last time up incensed Sewell and he pursued Muncrief after the game.

"Why didn't you walk him the last time up to stop him?" Sewell barked, glaring at the rookie.

Muncrief answered brusquely. "I wasn't going to walk him," he said. "That wouldn't have been fair—to him or me. Hell, he's the greatest player I ever saw."

That generosity of spirit was not shared by Johnny Babich of the Athletics, a right-hander who tried to derail DiMaggio in game 40 of his streak at Shibe Park in Philadelphia on June 28. Babich had acquired his early baseball knowledge in the Yankee farm system. Like most players, he dreamed of being a Yankee. But whatever he had learned, the Yankees apparently did not think too highly of it and they traded him out of their system.

Babich never forgave them. He hooked on with the A's and in a short time he developed a reputation for being particularly tough on the New York team. In 1940, he had beaten the Yankees five times, contributing in a significant way to their failure to win the league title.

In the third inning DiMaggio had taken three wide pitches for a 3-and-0 count. Most batters would normally be given the take sign at 3 and 0, but DiMaggio was given the sign to swing away.

"He was out to get me," recalled DiMaggio, referring to Babich, "even if it meant walking me every time up. The next pitch was outside, too, but I caught it good and lined it right past Babich into center field for a hit."

The next stop was a double-header against the Washington Senators on a Sunday at Griffith Stadium. A crowd of 31,000 turned out to see whether DiMaggio could tie and break George Sisler's 41-game record.

During the between-games rest period, a fan jumped onto the field near the Yankee dugout and took DiMaggio's favorite bat as a souvenir. Tracked down in the stands with the bat, the fan adamantly refused to return it.

"Don't let it bother you, Joe," said Tommy Henrich, "you can use the one I've been using that you let me borrow. I've been doing pretty good with it."

Arnold Anderson, off whom DiMaggio had made two hits in a four-hit performance on May 27, was the Senators' pitcher for the second game. DiMaggio lined out twice and drove a long fly ball for another out his third time up.

When he went to bat in the seventh, the crowd sensed that the streak was in jeopardy. Anderson's first pitch almost knocked DiMaggio down. It is the ploy of every pitcher to brush back the batter, to make him so wary and tense that he will eventually defeat himself. The stands rumbled with boos. Even the Senators' rooters were backing DiMaggio.

DiMaggio moved into the batter's box again, his wide stance and bat creating a picture of power and concentration. Anderson's next pitch was a fastball. DiMaggio swung and sent a whistling liner into left field for a single. The fans stood and cheered DiMaggio for five minutes.

On the train back to New York, DiMaggio was in an expansive mood. He ordered beer for all of his teammates. But he was still worried about the loss of his favorite bat.

"I wish that guy would return that bat," he said to a reporter. "I need it more than he does. Most of my models are 32 inches long and weigh 36 ounces, but I had sandpapered the handle of this one to take off a half to three-quarters of an ounce. It was just right."

The next day, a Monday, was an off day for the teams.

DiMaggio learned that the fan who had taken his bat came from Newark, New Jersey. An ardent DiMaggio rooter, the fan had made the trip from New Jersey to Washington especially to see DiMaggio break the record. Having returned to Newark, he was boasting around town that he had the bat. DiMaggio had friends in Newark and made a few phone calls. They contacted the fan and persuaded him to give up the bat. It was returned to DiMaggio in time for his next assault, on Wee Willie Keeler's 44-game record.

The following day, a Tuesday afternoon at the height of summer, DiMaggio was the magnetic force that attracted 52,832 paying customers into Yankee Stadium for a doubleheader against the Boston Red Sox. When he failed to get a hit his first two times up in the first game, the silence that settled over the Stadium blended with the heat and humidity.

His third time up DiMaggio sent a choppy grounder, a tricky ball to handle, at Jim Tabor, the Boston third baseman. Tabor was known for his strong throwing arm. He had often thrown out runners from deep behind third, almost from short left field. This time Tabor rushed the play and threw a wild peg past first base. DiMaggio wound up at second base. Again the crowd became silent.

The official scorer of the game was Dan Daniel, a baseball authority who wrote for *The New York World-Telegram.* He had been the scorer at the Stadium for virtually all of the home games involving DiMaggio's streak, and the pressure on him to call the borderline plays was as intense as the pressure on DiMaggio to get a hit.

Daniel, aware that too long a delay in making a decision would place doubts in everyone's mind, shot up his right arm, indicating that DiMaggio was on second by virtue of a double. It was one of the few times DiMaggio had been given the benefit of a doubt during the streak. The crowd roared. He was one game from tying Keeler's record.

The next time DiMaggio went to bat in the first game, he

dispelled all doubts about whether his previous hit would taint his streak. He slammed a ringing single into left field for his second hit of the game.

Before the second game was an inning old, DiMaggio lifted the suspense. He belted a screaming liner for a hit to center field. Now only he and Keeler stood upon a baseball Everest that Ruth, Cobb, Gehrig, Hornsby, and even the great Sisler had not been able to reach.

The next day, in 95-degree heat, DiMaggio took sole possession of the record with his 18th home run of the season, his 13th of the streak, and his 100th hit of the campaign.

DiMaggio seemed to be hitting like a man possessed. In the next 11 games of the streak he rapped 23 hits in 44 times at bat for a .523 average, and in the first 5 of those 11 games he extended his streak in the first inning of each game.

Then on July 16, the Yankees arrived in Cleveland. Its huge stadium was foreboding. If DiMaggio was to meet his Waterloo, this could be the place. In the series opener DiMaggio notched No. 56 swiftly, slashing a first-inning single off Al Milnar's first pitch, and in the eighth, against Joe Krakauskas, he drove a 400-foot double.

Now, with an advance reserved-seat ticket sale of 40,000 already in the till, a large crowd for the July 17 night game was assured. The starting pitcher for the Indians was Al Smith, a veteran left-hander who had been cast off by the New York Giants.

By game time the crowd had swelled to 67,468, the largest to see a night game in the major leagues. DiMaggio had not bunted during the entire streak. But in the first inning Ken Keltner, the Indians' third baseman, was playing his position so deep, back to the edge of the outfield grass, that he seemed to dare DiMaggio to bunt his way to first base. With a 1-and-0 count. DiMaggio drove Smith's next pitch past the third-base bag. Keltner made a leaping lunge to his right for the ball, stopped it backhanded, and threw out DiMaggio from foul territory. Smith walked DiMaggio in the fourth, but in the seventh DiMaggio again sent a steaming grounder to Keltner, who again made a fine play and throw to nail him at first.

The tension heightened in the eighth as the Yankees staged a rally. They drove Smith to the showers with four hits and two runs, and as DiMaggio strode to the plate with the bases filled and one out, the Indians' manager, Roger Peckinpaugh, who had held the Yankee record for streak hitting at 29 games until DiMaggio broke it, brought in Jim Bagby, Jr., a right-hander whose father had posted 128 victories as a big-league pitcher with Cincinnati, Cleveland, and Pittsburgh.

DiMaggio worked Bagby for a ball and a strike and then slammed a grounder to Lou Boudreau at shortstop. The ball flitted on a bad hop to Boudreau, who picked it off his shoulder and threw to Ray Mack, who threw to Oscar Grimes for a double play. A roar went up in the stadium—DiMaggio's streak had finally come to an end.

Joe DiMaggio and the American Ideal

WILLIAM SIMONS

*F*OR MANY, THE mere mention of Joe DiMaggio's name conjures a series of indelible tableaux. His place in American culture far transcends baseball. DiMaggio personifies the ideal of American masculinity. Joseph Durso noted in *The New York Times*, "In a country that has idolized and even immortalized its Twentieth-Century heroes, from Charles A. Lindbergh to Elvis Presley, no one more embodied the American dream of fame and fortune or created a more enduring legend than Joe DiMaggio. He became a figure of unequaled romance and integrity in the national mind . . ." From the intense realism of Ernest Hemingway's *The Old Man and the Sea* to the whimsical satire of *Doonesbury*, DiMaggio is the standard by which others measure their masculinity.

Joe DiMaggio is a hero, an exemplar of American masculinity. More than any other player in baseball history, he symbolizes the masculine ideal. Honus Wagner, Christy Mathewson, Lou Gehrig, Bob Feller, Stan Musial, and Mark McGwire have been role models, but their place in the popular culture has neither been as prominent nor as enduring as that of DiMaggio. Caveats emerge when other baseball superstars are evaluated as male role models. Driven by inner demons, Ty Cobb, a racist and sociopath, trampled upon basic decencies. Joe Jackson and Pete Rose are forever linked to gambling scandals. Despite baseball and military heroics, Ted Williams too often lost control of his tempestuous emotions. And the eponymic sluggers who preceded and followed DiMaggio in the Yankee outfield, Babe Ruth and Mickey Mantle, were, according to *USA Today* reporter Erik Brady, ''overgrown adolescents.'' DiMaggio was an adult. If Ruth represented disreputable masculinity, DiMaggio epitomized masculine respectability.

And our racial protocols have impeded the emergence of a black DiMaggio in the American culture. Paternalism pervaded depictions of Joe Louis and Jesse Owens even as they were hailed as symbols of American democracy. Jack Johnson and Muhammad Ali polarized contemporaries. And Michael Jordan's prominence has yet to survive decades of retirement. Segregation deprived players in the Negro leagues of the recognition they merited. Before his premature death, Josh Gibson, arguably the greatest power hitter of all time, suffered from the recurrent delusion that Joe DiMaggio would not shake his hand. Circumstances rendered the courageous Jackie Robinson, who transformed baseball and America, a figure of controversy. Public perceptions of Willie Mays, perhaps even a better all-around player than DiMaggio, emphasized enthusiastic ebullience rather than heroic gravity. Milwaukee, distant from the nation's media centers, contributed to Hank Aaron's comparative obscurity during much of his career, and racism limited contemporary appreciation for the records set in his final seasons. Barry Bonds and Ken Griffey, Jr., excel in a game no longer the undisputed national pastime.

Indeed, the fact that DiMaggio was baseball's best player when it was the undisputed national pastime elevated his place in the national culture. So, too, did his good fortune in playing for sports' most storied franchise during its most successful era in the city that then dominated the nation's media. The fabled romance with Marilyn Monroe, appreciative prose by Ernest Hemingway and Paul Simon, official anointment as baseball's "greatest living ballplayer," and a dignified presence in highly visible Bowery Savings Bank and Mr. Coffee commercials kept the DiMaggio flame burning brightly throughout the years. Nearly a half-century after he played his last major-league game, DiMaggio's illness and death received the attention that the demise of a former president might receive. A *Newsweek* cover story, special thirty-plus-page wraparound tributes in both New York's *Daily News* and *Post*, the lead front-page story in nearly every other newspaper in the nation (including *The Wall Street Journal*), editorial tribute, commentary from intellectual and cultural authorities, television specials, many flags at half-staff, and the renaming of the West Side Highway marked DiMaggio's death.

In life DiMaggio perhaps endured longer than any other figure as a heroic symbol in the national consciousness. He even outlasted Jimmy Stewart. From his brilliant 1936 rookie season until his death more than sixty-two years later in 1999, Joe DiMaggio was a hero. Davy Crockett, Abraham Lincoln, Teddy Roosevelt, James Dean, Babe Ruth, Clark Gable, John Kennedy, Bobby Kennedy, Martin Luther King, Jr., and Elvis Presley, for example, did not even live sixty-two years. For Thomas Jefferson, Andrew Jackson, Robert E. Lee, Andrew Carnegie, Thomas Edison, Charles Lindbergh, Franklin Roosevelt, Dwight Eisenhower, John Wayne, Mickey Mantle, and Jonas Salk, the interval between apotheosis and death was far less than for DiMaggio. And so many tragic Audie Murphys and Jim Thorpes outlived their honor. But neither time nor physical decline diminished DiMaggio's appeal. In DiMaggio's final years, Americans still felt a chill as the final introduction at Old-Timers' games gave us one more glimpse of "the greatest living ballplayer."

In the final inning of his long life, DiMaggio retained his

heroic aura. Had illness and death not intervened, he would have thrown out the first ball at both the 1998 World Series and the 1999 Yankee home opener. As baby boomers entered middle age, they developed belated appreciation for the accomplishments of their parents, the generation that endured the Great Depression and defeated Hitler. And DiMaggio was one of the last remaining icons of that era. Director Steven Spielberg termed his popular 1998 film *Saving Private Ryan* a tribute to his father's generation. And Tom Brokaw's 1998 book *The Greatest Generation* rose to the top of the bestseller list extolling the virtues of the men and women who came of age during the Great Depression and World War II. As one of the last surviving icons of that era, DiMaggio's reputation benefitted by the renewed respect granted his generation. The Associated Press proclaimed "Current Yankees Awestruck by Joltin' Joe." So powerful a hold did DiMaggio have on American minds that a respondent to a survey taken by *The Daily Star* of Oneonta, New York, a week after the Yankee Clipper's death answered "Joe DiMaggio" to the query "Who do you think will be the most influential sports figure in 1999?"

It was not merely sports that DiMaggio influenced. He provided an ideal for respectable masculinity. In *Manhood in America: A Cultural History* (1996), sociologist Michael Kimmel argues that "the quest for manhood—the effort to achieve, to demonstrate, to prove our masculinity, has been one of the formative and persistent experiences in men's lives." Although a "multiplicity of masculinities . . . collectively define men's actual experiences," an idealized normative standard exists in the American consciousness. Although Kimmel is critical of the ideal, believing that devotion to it has rendered its adherents emotionally inarticulate, he emphasizes its prominence in American culture. Kimmel asserts that the dominant masculine ideal possesses the following attributes: not allowing domination by others, control over oneself, emotional autonomy, exemption from home and family, self-improvement and economic success, honor and morality, rendering the world safe for women and children, stoic confrontation of pain and hardship, recognition by others of one's achievements, protection of reputation, and serving as role model for others in an all-male domain. Classic American heroes—James Fenimore Cooper's frontiersman, John Wayne's cowboy, and Humphrey Bogart's urban detective possess these attributes. But none more so than Joe DiMaggio's baseball player.

DiMaggio possessed many admirable qualities, but his limitations received abbreviated attention. Introverted and insecure, DiMaggio, for example, suffered from ulcers and insomnia. And, according to various Monroe biographers, including Robert Slatzer, DiMaggio was so obsessed with Marilyn that he stalked his former wife for a time. Moreover, his inability to sustain relations led to estrangement from his only child. This is not to suggest that DiMaggio was a fraud, but our focus is the icon of popular culture, not that most private of men. A small coterie of revisionists and iconoclasts raised caveats. When DiMaggio held out for more money in the spring of 1938, it was one of the few times he was widely resented. But redemption came quickly. Yet a 1966 *Esquire* article by Gay Talese portrayed an aging DiMaggio as bored, lonely, and discontented. Furthermore, a *Newsday* article following DiMaggio's death bore the title "Joe Was a Hero to Many, but Not All." Likewise, Ottaway News Service columnist Ken Lovett wrote on March 20, 1999, "DiMaggio . . . certainly should not be held up as a role model." Moreover, a New York *Daily News* article by Bill Madden and Luke Cyphers claimed that in his final years DiMaggio could not protect himself from the exploitative machinations of his business manager. And *New York Times* pundit Robert Lipsyte gave this posthumous assessment of DiMaggio—"Private to the point of paranoia." Nonetheless, in the main currents of the American mind, DiMaggio is a peerless hero. The DiMaggio of popular culture meets Kimmel's eleven criteria of the masculine ideal.

Not Allowing Domination by Others

The ultimate test of an individual's capacity to avoid domination by others is to leave this life on one's own terms. In life Joe DiMaggio valued privacy, dignity, courage, and grace. He departed this world with his cherished virtues intact. During his ninety-nine-day hospitalization, he fought gallantly against pneumonia, cancer, and media intrusion. DiMaggio mounted several remarkable comebacks. The Yankee Clipper survived the last rites of the Catholic church and a premature announcement of his death by NBC. Emerging from a coma, he issued directives. DiMaggio's resilience amazed the doctors. At his insistence, the public was misled about the severity of his illness. And DiMaggio made the decision that he would die at his Hollywood, Florida, home. On March, 8, 1999, Joseph Paul DiMaggio died, as he lived, gracefully. With three family members, two friends, and hospice attendant Javier Ribe present, DiMaggio, radiant of face and lucid of mind, spoke his final words: "I love all of you." It was, recalled Ribe, "one of the most beautiful and peaceful deaths that I have ever seen."

DiMaggio had planned his funeral with meticulous detail, even down to where to get the cold cuts following the service. Attendance at the funeral was by invitation only. About eighty people, primarily family and friends, entered the vast cathedral. No celebrities. Commissioner Bud Selig and American League President Gene Budig were the only baseball representatives admitted. George Steinbrenner and Reggie Jackson were excluded. Police kept throngs of reporters and onlookers across the street. No baseball mementoes adorned SS Peter and Paul Roman Catholic Church. DiMaggio's brother Dominic, the last survivor amongst Joe's eight siblings and formerly the Red Sox center fielder, gave a simple yet moving eulogy. As the New York *Daily News* observed, "With a dignity that echoed his years as

a Yankee superstar and American icon, Joseph DiMaggio was
laid to rest . . .''

Control Over Oneself

DiMaggio's manner of death reflected the demeanor of his
life. His self-control was nearly absolute. Ty Cobb, Leo Durocher, Ted Williams, and Albert Belle are among the many as
noted for their emotional outbursts as for their baseball talents.
It is impossible to imagine DiMaggio taunting opponents, kicking an umpire in the shins, spitting at fans, or trying to run over
children. As to why he did not engage in dramatic displays of
emotion, Deadpan Joe explained, "I can't. It wouldn't look
right." As a baseball player, DiMaggio almost never lost control
of himself. The most atypical incident involved kicking the dirt
around second base when Brooklyn outfielder Al Gionfriddo's
spectacular catch deprived him of a home run during the 1947
World Series.

Thomas Jefferson envisioned God as the Supreme Architect.
In fashioning a perfect creation, Jefferson's God exhibited an
"economy of nature," wasting no energy and engaging in no
superfluous activity. It was, believed Jefferson, the task of humanity to emulate the Creator. That is how DiMaggio played
baseball, wasting no energy and engaging in no superfluous activity. Creating the illusion of slow motion through his balletic
grace, DiMaggio made the difficult look easy. A *New York Times*
editorial asserted, "The combination of proficiency and exquisite
grace which Joe DiMaggio brought to the art of playing center
field was something no baseball average can measure and that
must be seen to be believed." Honus Wagner's awkward mastery, Mickey Mantle's powerful but undisciplined swing, and
Willie Mays' dramatic catches with hat askew were all foreign
to DiMaggio's economy of energy. It was said that DiMaggio
made few theatrical plays in the field; his mastery and self-

control were such that he had no need for dramatics. DiMaggio "was the perfect Hemingway hero," observed David Halberstam. He exhibited stoic "grace under pressure." DiMaggio's self-control was so finely honed that he even conveyed quiet dignity endorsing Mr. Coffee.

Emotional Autonomy

Mr. Coffee was an appropriate endorsement for DiMaggio. He drank a good deal of coffee. He was also a moody, irritable, silent, chain-smoking loner. Like the frontiersman, cowboy, and urban detective, Joe DiMaggio was emotionally autonomous. He led the league in room service. "The essential American soul," wrote D. H. Lawrence, "is hard, isolate, stoic." That was DiMaggio's character. He was not a chatty middle infielder. DiMaggio's domain was the vast and remote frontier of Yankee Stadium's center field. As George F. Will observed, DiMaggio, like Charles Lindbergh, "wore an aura of remoteness." Inner directed, DiMaggio was not defined by others. When his wife Marilyn Monroe, fresh from entertaining troops in Korea, giddily announced, "Joe, you never heard such cheering!" DiMaggio quietly responded, "Yes, I have." Dave Anderson of *The New York Times* recognized that the Yankee Clipper maintained privacy "even better than he played." Sportswriter Jimmy Cannon knew that DiMaggio was both central to and apart from his Yankee teammates: "There were guys who played with him for years and considered him a stranger, but on the field he was the closest anyone ever came to them. His greatness was part of the whole of the team and the loneliness was defeated because this is where he belonged . . ."

Exemption from Home and Family

Emotionally autonomous frontiersmen, cowboys, and urban detectives were exempt from ties to home and family. So, too, was Joe DiMaggio. In his eulogy, his brother Dom noted that Joe never found a lifetime partner. His two marriages were brief. DiMaggio's discreet liaisons with anonymous showgirls created no ties that bind. He never truly inhabited the San Francisco house that his widowed sister Marie kept for him. A peripatetic bachelor by inclination, DiMaggio lived out of trains, airplanes, and hotel rooms.

Even from his few friends and relatives, including brother Dom, Joe went through periods of estrangement. Thus it is not surprising that DiMaggio did not form lasting connections to home and family. The most tragic estrangement was with his son Joe, Jr., who, in middle age, despite an Ivy League education, lived in a trailer park and worked in a junkyard. In 1946 Joe and Joe, Jr., then a child, posed together on the cover of *Sport*. Again, in 1961 when Joe, Jr., was a young man, they shared a *Sport* cover. Father and son wore Yankee uniforms in the *Sport* photographs. Baseball was not a sufficient bond, however. Feeling the burden of his name, Joe, Jr., a good player, quit baseball in adolescence. Baseball was the essence of the father. And an emotionally inarticulate father playing catch with his son finds generational communication tenuous when the father's legacy burdens the son. At the end of the movie *Shane,* a boy cries for the cowboy to return, but the man knows it is his destiny to live apart from home and family. Joe DiMaggio also knew.

Self-Improvement and Economic Success

Self-improvement and economic success are both quintessential American goals. Benjamin Franklin's *Autobiography* pays homage to those virtues as do subsequent generations of motivational literature. Joe DiMaggio was a self-made man. As a baseball player, DiMaggio drove himself relentlessly. A meritocracy sport produces an elite of talent. Remarkable ability and maximum effort brought DiMaggio to the top of his profession. He became, in David Halberstam's apt phrase, "the preeminent *athlete*" of his generation. DiMaggio's pursuit of self-improvement extended beyond his baseball craft.

DiMaggio reinvented himself. He learned to dress well, making Taub's list of ten best-dressed men in 1939. Through extensive dental work, DiMaggio further enhanced his appearance. He confronted his shyness and insecurities by attending the Dale Carnegie Institute. As host of a television baseball show in the early 1950s, he was awkward and wooden. By the 1970s, DiMaggio had transformed himself into a poised and polished commercial spokesman for Mr. Coffee and the Bowery Savings Bank.

DiMaggio, the son of an Italian immigrant fisherman, was a classic Horatio Alger hero. He rose from humble obscurity to fame and riches. Spectacular baseball success and tough contract negotiating made him the game's highest paid player. Baseball folklore is replete with tales of former stars like Grover Cleveland Alexander who squandered their money and died in poverty. In contrast, DiMaggio augmented his largess after retiring as a player. He invested his money wisely. DiMaggio was a well-paid commercial spokesman. And during his last years, DiMaggio earned millions of dollars in the sports memorabilia industry. His autograph commanded a higher price than that of any other living American.

Honor and Morality

DiMaggio pursued the American dream of economic success, but his honor was not for sale. In 1951 injuries and age diminished DiMaggio's baseball performance. Nonetheless, Di-Maggio's stature in the game was such that Yankee owners Don Topping and Del Webb offered him the same $100,000 contract he had received in 1951 to return for another season even if he chose to play only home games or limit his role to pinch-hitting. The Yankee owners told DiMaggio he would remain the game's highest paid player in the 1952 campaign. Topping confessed, "We tried everything we possibly could to get him to stay. But we couldn't convince him. I don't know why he had to quit. Sick as he was last season he did better than most of the players hanging around."

But "hanging around" would have violated DiMaggio's moral code. At the December 11, 1951, press conference announcing his retirement, DiMaggio spoke of honor: "I once made a solemn promise to myself that I wouldn't try to hang on once the end was in sight. I've seen too many beat-up players struggle to stay up there, and it's always a sad spectacle." An honorable man lives by a moral code. No matter how high the compensation or reduced the obligations, DiMaggio would not sacrifice his honor. DiMaggio's words made clear that he would retire on his own terms: "I feel that I reached the stage where I can no longer produce for my ball club, my manager, my teammates, and my fans."

DiMaggio's professional honor was not for sale, nor was his personal honor. Joe DiMaggio was a man of integrity. His life was not for sale. When DiMaggio died, Monica Lewinsky was on the cover of *Time* magazine. Promoting her book, Lewinsky gave explicit details about tawdry sexual encounters with President Bill Clinton. And Clinton himself, publicly engaging in strategic concessions and unpersuasive denials, embodies the sexual antithesis of DiMaggio.

As for DiMaggio, he dated a number of showgirls. He married Dorothy Arnold, an actress, and Marilyn Monroe, the woman every man desired. Comparing Frank Sinatra unfavorably to DiMaggio, Monroe revealed to a confidant Joe's great sexual prowess. But DiMaggio never spoke to a third party about private moments with Marilyn Monroe, Dorothy Arnold, or any other woman. An honorable man does not make public his romantic and physical intimacies. And Joe DiMaggio never violated his moral code. DiMaggio was outraged by the scene in *The Seven Year Itch* where the gust from a subway grate revealed more of his wife Monroe than he was willing to share with the public. A romantic hero, DiMaggio loved Monroe with a powerful emotional intensity. Through the years, he received several offers worth millions of dollars to write a book about his relationship with Monroe. DiMaggio always refused. A gentleman is discreet; he does not kiss-and-tell. It is immoral. Joe DiMaggio's integrity and memories were not for sale. Not at any price.

Rendering the World Safe for Women and Children

Joe DiMaggio helped render the world safe for women and children. His chivalry toward Marilyn Monroe was not confined to keeping her confidences inviolate. In the years after their divorce, Monroe, vulnerable and unstable, would repeatedly turn to DiMaggio's strength when overwhelmed by her emotions. Although tormented by her promiscuity, DiMaggio never refused Monroe's desperate pleas for help. DiMaggio was always there in her times of crisis. When a psychiatric hospital refused to discharge Monroe, DiMaggio won her release with the warning, from a man who did not make idle threats, that "if you don't give her to me, I will take this place apart, piece of wood by piece of wood." Then, DiMaggio, his playing career a decade in the past, took Monroe to the safety of the Yankee spring training camp. Long divorced, DiMaggio gallantly secured a separate hotel room for Monroe. Buoyed by DiMaggio's strength, Monroe felt better. For a time.

In the end, even DiMaggio could not save her. Stalked by her neuroses and celebrity, Monroe took her own life in August 1962. If DiMaggio could not protect Marilyn in life, he would shield her in death. Barring celebrities and the media, DiMaggio took control of her funeral. When DiMaggio was warned that important people were expected to attend Marilyn's funeral, he turned them away with a fierce retort: ''Tell them if it wasn't for them, she'd still be here.'' In death DiMaggio gave Monroe a poignant dignity that eluded her in life. For DiMaggio, the gallant romantic, even death did not end the tragic relationship with his beloved Marilyn. DiMaggio sent roses three times a week to her crypt.

Joe and Joe, Jr., never established a strong father-son relationship. The man and the boy both loved Marilyn, and their best times together were with her. And Monroe's death briefly brought father and son together again. At the time of DiMaggio's own death, he had not seen Joe, Jr., for years. In death, however, DiMaggio finally bridged the gap. Joe, Jr., served as pallbearer for his father. And DiMaggio's will established a trust fund that would grant his son $20,000 a year, a judicious sum to grant a man with a checkered occupational history. To have a comfortable life, Joe, Jr., would need to work to supplement the stipend. But $20,000 a year would provide a safety net.

DiMaggio, in death, through his will, made his only child's life more comfortable. In life, Joe DiMaggio rendered the world safer for many children. His brother Dom's eulogy said nothing gave Joe more pleasure than establishing the Joe DiMaggio Children's Hospital at Memorial Regional Hospital in Hollywood, Florida. About a week after the Yankee Clipper's death, a beautiful half-page photograph of Joe DiMaggio appeared in *The New York Times*. It was taken near the end of his life. In the photograph, DiMaggio tenderly holds a sick infant. Love radiates from DiMaggio's face. Beneath the photograph were the words ''Most Americans know Joe DiMaggio as the Yankee Clipper, the legend in baseball, the American Dream. For the kids at the Joe DiMaggio Children's Hospital he is all that and more . . . Joe

DiMaggio was always an inspiring visitor and a loving namesake to this nonprofit children's hospital. His support and commitment have helped to give many children that extra encouragement needed to promote healing and restore hope.''

Stoic Confrontation of Pain and Hardship

Joe DiMaggio felt the pain of children, but he stoically confronted his own pain and hardship. DiMaggio suffered numerous injuries during his career. But he mounted many remarkable comebacks, frequently playing while experiencing intense pain. Playing hard, DiMaggio repeatedly punished his body. Few other big men have ever slid into bases with such force. X rays revealed the toll DiMaggio's style of play inflicted on his back. And painful bone spurs, requiring multiple surgeries, made even walking excruciating. DiMaggio epitomized Hemingway's definition of courage as grace under pressure. After injury and surgery forced the aging DiMaggio to miss the first sixty-five games of the 1949 season, he waged one of the most exceptional personal comebacks in sports history. In his first three games after returning to active play, DiMaggio hit four home runs, knocked in nine runs, and made thirteen catches in the outfield. Then late in the 1949 campaign, DiMaggio contracted a virulent case of viral pneumonia. Weakened and suffering from nausea, he lost eighteen pounds. But a drawn, emaciated DiMaggio demanded that manager Casey Stengel play him in two crucial, late-September games against the Boston Red Sox. The measure of a man is what he does with what he has left. By that standard, DiMaggio was not simply a great athlete; he was a great man. Ashen, gaunt, and limping, a very ill DiMaggio singled and doubled, pacing the Yankees to victory over the Red Sox. And then in the final contest of the season, DiMaggio played eight innings before physical collapse on the field forced to exit. DiMaggio's courageous example and brilliant play ensured another Yankee pennant. Throughout his baseball career, DiMaggio never complained about the frequent illnesses and painful injuries he endured.

Nor did DiMaggio engage in self-pity away from the diamond. He did not bemoan hardship or pain. Even after the tragic loss of Monroe, the public saw only his stoic class. And when finally confronted by age and mortal illness, DiMaggio died with courage. Morris Engelberg, friend and attorney, witnessed the Yankee Clipper's demise: "DiMaggio fought his illness as hard as he played the game of baseball and with the same dignity, style, and grace with which he lived his life."

Recognition by Others of One's Achievements

Jimmy struts into the bar with a dog. He claims the dog can talk. Buster bets fifty dollars that Jimmy is a liar. Jimmy asks the dog how sandpaper feels. The dog answers, *"Rrrough!"* Buster laughs derisively. Jimmy immediately asks the dog what is on top of a house. The dog responds, *"Rrroof!"* Buster gestures contemptuously. Then Jimmy quickly asks the dog who was the greatest baseball player of all time. The dog growls, *"Rrruth!"* Buster snatches the money and tosses Jimmy and the dog out of the bar. The dog turns to Jimmy and says, "I should have said DiMaggio."

There are endless variations on the above story. Clearly, however, the punch line draws a laugh because many people believe that, despite the relative brevity of his career, Joe DiMaggio was baseball's preeminent player. DiMaggio did not labor in obscurity. A plethora of articles and books attest to the appreciative recognition by others of his achievements.

"There were more powerful hitters, flashier fielders, and speedier runners, but nobody combined these skills as efficiently, elegantly, and effortlessly as the Yankee Clipper," asserted baseball historian Robert W. Creamer. Casey Stengel termed Di-

Maggio "the greatest player I ever managed." Ted Williams contended, "I've never seen anyone who played the game with more perfection. He was the best player I ever saw." "He was," editorialized *The Daily Gazette* of Schenectady, New York, "a hero to children and adults for the way he played the game—with consummate skill, but also with grace and dignity." "Other players racked up better numbers. But no player," argued writer Glenn Stout, "ever, not even Ruth, played better when playing well meant the difference between his team winning and his team losing." "If you said to God, 'Create someone who was what a baseball player should be,' God would have created Joe Di-Maggio," mused ex-Dodger manager Tommy Lasorda. When DiMaggio died, the *Los Angeles Times* noted, "Many still consider him the best all-around player in baseball history."

DiMaggio's play in the field was peerless. His glove and arm were legendary. The art of base stealing languished in Di-Maggio's generation, but he was the best base runner of his era. And no one who ever saw it ever forgot DiMaggio's classic swing. He had a career batting average of .325, hitting .381 in 1939. In only 1,736 games, DiMaggio batted in 1,537 runs. Only five sluggers—Babe Ruth, Ted Williams, Lou Gehrig, Jimmie Foxx, and Hank Greenberg—retired with higher lifetime slugging percentages than DiMaggio, and none of them possessed DiMaggio's glove, arm, or base-running skills. Taking into account three prime seasons lost to World War II military service, numerous injuries, and that in DiMaggio's era the distance from home plate to the wall in his left-center field power alley at Yankee Stadium was 457 feet, his 361 home runs are impressive. Home-run hitters typically strike out frequently. DiMaggio, however, struck out only eight more times than he hit home runs. By contrast, Mickey Mantle hit 536 home runs but registered 1,710 strikeouts. A number of great players, including Ted Williams, Carl Yastrzemski, and Ernie Banks, never played on a team that won the World Series. As the heart of the Yankees, DiMaggio led New York to ten pennants and nine world championships during his thirteen-year career. DiMaggio's remarkable achievements earned him baseball's highest honors. Thrice he was named the American League's most valuable player. The Baseball Hall of Fame, the game's equivalent of Mount Olympus, proudly displays DiMaggio's plaque. And in 1969, sportswriters formally voted DiMaggio baseball's "greatest living ballplayer."

Moreover, many pundits regard DiMaggio's 1941 record fifty-six consecutive game hitting streak as sport's most remarkable record. Commentators often simply refer to it as *The Streak.* Harvard paleontologist, man of letters, and cultural guru Stephen Jay Gould asserts, "DiMaggio's streak is the most extraordinary thing that ever happened in American sports." According to Gould, DiMaggio's hitting streak is the only sports record that transcends the protocols of statistical probability. Sportswriter Bill Madden labels The Streak the "Feat to Top 'Em All." It inspired the Les Brown band to record the 1941 song, "Joltin' Joe DiMaggio," with the refrain, "Our kids will tell their kids his name, 'Joltin' Joe DiMaggio.' " *Time* called The Streak "a feat of consistency no other player has come close to matching." In a book, *Streak,* devoted to the feat, Michael Seidel wrote, "Amid the turmoil of world war and the preparation for our undetermined role in its conduct, the attention paid to Di-Maggio's streak . . . provided a heroic, factual focus for a land whose imagination seemed primed for increments of power."

Tributes to DiMaggio extend beyond his baseball triumphs. He was honored for his character. In 1977 the Yankee Clipper received America's highest civilian award, the Medal of Freedom. Former President Ronald Reagan called DiMaggio "a symbol of all that is good and decent." When former Secretary of State Henry Kissinger sat beside DiMaggio at the 1996 World Series, Kissinger said that the honor was his. Even the satiric *Doonesbury* identified DiMaggio as America's "moral authority." At DiMaggio's April 23, 1999, memorial service at St. Patrick's Cathedral in New York City, dignitaries from sports, entertainment, business, and government came to pay homage. And on Sunday, April 25, 1999, a granite and bronze tribute to DiMaggio was dedicated in Monument Park at Yankee Stadium.

The encomiums that followed DiMaggio's death celebrated the man more than the athlete. Bill Clinton observed, "When future generations look back at the Twentieth Century, they will think of the Yankee Clipper." *Time* columnist Roger Rosenblatt wrote, "DiMaggio's persona was wholly the product of abstracts: pride, fidelity, natural aristocracy and, above all, ability." Sportswriter David Kindred recognized DiMaggio's "majestic presence." Columnist George F. Will wrote that DiMaggio "proved that a healthy democracy knows and honors nobility when it sees it." Steve Campbell, *Albany Times-Union* sportswriter, referred to DiMaggio as "regal." Writing for *The Wall Street Journal*, Michael McCarthy claimed DiMaggio represented "a bedrock American ideal: that prosperity awaits he who will earnestly shoulder a day's work." In *The New York Times*, Bob Hebert pontificated that DiMaggio "became the designated hero of the colossus, the pre-eminent god of this secular creation myth." The Reverend Armand Oliveri asserted, "Joe had achieved greatness, but his real greatness was the way he carried himself."

Paul Simon wrote that DiMaggio was "as proud and masculine as a battleship." The lyrics to his song "Mrs. Robinson," explained Simon, acknowledge DiMaggio as a hero. And a hero, Simon ruminated, allows us to "read with a new clarity our moral compass." In the age of Clinton and Lewinsky, the lyrics of "Mrs. Robinson" possess even more poignant meaning than when they were composed thirty years ago:

Where have you gone, Joe DiMaggio?
A nation turns its lonely eyes to you.
What's that you say, Mrs. Robinson?
Joltin' Joe has left and gone away.

Protection of Reputation

Heroes protect their reputations. Natty Bumppo, Wyatt Earp, and Sam Spade did. So did Joe DiMaggio. In *Othello*, Shakespeare called reputation "the immortal part of myself" and wrote:

Who steals my purse steals trash; 'tis something, nothing;
'Twas mine,'tis his, and has been slave to thousands;
But he that fliches from me my good name
Robs me of that which not enriches him,
And makes me poor indeed.

Andrew Jackson's mother exhorted him to bypass legalisms in the case of slander and to settle the matter himself. Although we no longer fight formal duels, DiMaggio would have agreed with Shakespeare and Mrs. Jackson. As David Halberstam observed, Joe DiMaggio was the "keeper of his own flame." DiMaggio, wrote Halberstam, "guards his special status carefully, wary of doing anything that might tarnish his special reputation. He tends to avoid all those who might define him in some way other than the way he defined himself on the field."

The faux intimacy of television leaves no mystery. Taking place prior to the ubiquity of television, the prime of Joe DiMaggio lent itself to storytelling and epic legend. *Staten Island Advance* sportswriter Jerry Izenberg recognized that radio helped nurture the DiMaggio legend: "Then conjure up DiMaggio—as they did at their radios. Project—as they did—through the imagination that only radio could generate, the grace, the style, the magnificent tableau of DiMaggio's perfect timing." And DiMaggio was determined to give those who actually saw him play indelible memories. Asked why he always drove himself so hard, DiMaggio responded, "Because there might be somebody out there who's never seen me play before." DiMaggio retired from active play "because I don't want them [the fans] to remember me struggling." Sportswriter Marty Appell wrote, "He also knew when it was time to quit playing, and later, he knew when it was time to stop playing in Old-Timers' games, and even when to stop wearing a uniform." Proud and remote, DiMaggio protected his public image. DiMaggio, noted *New York Times* sportswriter George Vecsey, "set the conditions for his appearances on Old-Timers' Day. He was always described as the 'greatest living ballplayer...'" DiMaggio, observed Paul Simon, "understood the power of silence." The Yankee Clipper, wrote Simon, "never in word or deed befouls his legend and greatness...In these days of presidential transgressions and apologies and prime-time interviews, we grieve for Joe DiMaggio and mourn the loss of his grace and dignity."

Serving as a Role Model for Others

Serving as a role model for others is Michael Kimmel's final attribute of the ideal of American masculinity. And DiMaggio's fulfillment of all of Kimmel's other attributes rendered him a role model. Reacting to DiMaggio's death, New York Governor George Pataki said, "He was every American boy's hero, including mine." Wellington Mara, owner of the NFL's New York Giants, commented on DiMaggio: "I always felt that he was a model of professionalism that any athlete in any sport would do well to attempt to emulate." And countless American males have wished that they could play baseball, woo a beautiful woman, and display class like Joe DiMaggio. Even the film *Grease* cited DiMaggio as a role model.

Ernest Hemingway's novella *The Old Man and the Sea* provides the most memorable depiction of DiMaggio as a role model. Santiago, an old Cuban fisherman who does epic battle with a great fish, repeatedly evokes DiMaggio as the measure of a man. In talking to his young friend Manolin, Santiago implicitly evokes baseball as a metaphor for life. Manolin loyally considers Santiago the best of fishermen, and Santiago knows "the great DiMaggio" is the greatest baseball player. Santiago strives to emulate the masculine ideal DiMaggio represents. As he girds for heroic struggle, Santiago resolves, "I must be worthy of the great DiMaggio." Evoking DiMaggio as a masculine mantra, Santiago counsels Manolin to "think of the great DiMaggio." As a bond between himself and the great Yankee, Santiago notes that DiMaggio's "father was a fisherman." The old man dreams of taking "the great DiMaggio fishing." Since DiMaggio knew poverty in his youth, Santiago believes that the Yankee "would understand" his struggles. When the great fish nearly exhausts his endurance, Santiago reminds himself "of the great DiMaggio who does all things perfectly even with the pain of the bone spur in the heel." Santiago steels himself by asking, "Do you believe the great DiMaggio would stay with a fish as long as I will stay with this one?" Santiago is "sure" that DiMaggio would. And when Santiago finds dignity in his valiant struggle, he says, "I think the great DiMaggio would be proud of me today."

Americanization

Americanization is not one of Kimmel's attributes of the masculine ideal, but it merits consideration. The masculine ideal under discussion is American, and the United States is a nation of nations. Our dilemma concerns the need to balance ethnic/racial affiliations with a larger American identity. Although DiMaggio was obviously a standard bearer for Italian-Americans, he was also a symbol of a more generic process of Americanization.

During the 1930s baseball's ethnic composition changed substantially, and this highly visible transformation attracted extensive contemporary comment. A 1934 article in *Baseball Magazine* noted that "in recent years there had been a grand invasion of other nationalities," prominently featuring players with southern and eastern European antecedents. Italian-Americans, sons of immigrants who fled southern Italy between 1880 and the outbreak of World War I, contributed significantly to the ethnic recasting of baseball during the 1930s. As with their counterparts from other ethnic groups, Italian-American major leaguers confronted the universal dilemma of the second generation, resolving the conflict between the "Old World" values of their immigrant parents and those of the larger society, embodied in the "national pastime." Beyond the shared "marginal man" phenomena, however, Italian-American major leaguers of the 1930s faced additional anxieties not encountered by other athletes. By decade's end, Benito Mussolini, Italy's Fascist dictator, was on a collision course with the United States, raising questions about the loyalty of Italian-Americans. And domestic stereotypes about Italian-Americans often centered upon images of clownish, highly emotional simpletons and violent gangsters. Thus, given the ambience of the 1930s, the second generation's struggle to resolve the tension between ethnic and host society expectations assumed a special dimension for Italian athletes.

A number of Italian-Americans preceded Joe DiMaggio in the big leagues. Nor was DiMaggio the first Italian-American star. That distinction would belong to "Poosh 'Em Up" Tony Lazzeri, the Yankees' hard-hitting second baseman and future Hall of Famer who made his major league debut in 1926. But DiMaggio was baseball's first Italian-American superstar.

Sportswriters of the 1930s frequently noted DiMaggio's ethnic identity even in accounts of mundane incidents. Numerous ethnic sobriquets attached themselves to DiMaggio. Early in his career, a number of articles called DiMaggio "Giuseppe." A *New York World-Telegram* article stated that DiMaggio hailed "from the spaghetti society." Even the sedate *New York Times* referred to DiMaggio as "the coast Italian." And a *Time* magazine cover story claimed that DiMaggio was "like many young brothers in large Italian families."

It is instructive to examine the May 1, 1939, *Life* cover story on Joe DiMaggio by Noel Busch. At the time, *Life* was America's most widely read magazine, and Busch's eight-page article gave significant attention to DiMaggio's Italian background. The *Life* article teemed with ethnic references. DiMaggio's father, wrote Busch, "was a poor Italian crab fisherman," and the senior DiMaggio was "an expert at the Italian bowling game of boccie." Joe himself was referred to as "Giuseppe Paolo DiMaggio." The Yankee star was described as "the young Italian" and an "Italian youth." And Busch reinforced the association of Italian culture with food. In 1936, claimed the *Life* feature, DiMaggio's mother "rode to the World Series in a drawing room on a streamlined train carrying an armful of Italian sausage for Joe." At Joe DiMaggio's Grotto, the restaurant owned by the Yankee outfielder, Busch asserted that the "speciality of the house is cioppino, for which an alarming recipe is attached to menu." The writer further associated DiMaggio's ethnicity with food by commenting, "At home, Joe DiMaggio passes most of his days at the Grotto or in the DiMaggio kitchen."

The *Life* profile on DiMaggio shared the prevalent bias of that era that Italians were not very intelligent. "DiMaggio," wrote Busch, "is lazy, shy, and inarticulate." The magazine profile emphasized that DiMaggio was not cerebral: "It cannot be said . . . that he has ever worried his employer by an unbecoming interest in literature or the arts, nor does he wear himself down by unreasonable asceticism." Busch also linked DiMaggio to the common bias that Italians were lazy. According to the *Life* feature, DiMaggio's "inertia caused him to give up school after one year in high school." "Joe DiMaggio's rise in baseball," wrote Busch, "is a testimonial to the value of general shiftlessness." According to the article, "In laziness, DiMaggio is still a paragon." "On winter mornings," claimed Busch, DiMaggio "gets up at about eleven."

Busch even associated DiMaggio's baseball success with ethnic canards: "Italians, bad at war, are well-suited for milder competitions, and the number of top-notch Italian prize fighters, golfers, and baseball players is out of all proportion to the population.'' By denying that DiMaggio possessed either high intelligence or a strong work ethic, *Life* endorsed prevalent ethnic stereotypes. As portrayed by Busch, DiMaggio was not a self-made athlete; the Yankee star was instead depicted as a natural ballplayer. ''DiMaggio's reflexes,'' according to the *Life* article, ''are so fast that even a curve which breaks perfectly may not be effective.'' Busch wrote that the ''shiftlessness'' and ''lazy'' Italian outfielder possessed a ''mysterious quality called baseball instinct. In this respect Joe DiMaggio is without peer.''

Busch emphasized that DiMaggio was a standard bearer for other Italian-Americans: ''When in 1936 Joe DiMaggio gave unmistakable signs of being the greatest Italian star in the history of baseball, the effect upon New York's Italian population was amazing. Subway guards as far away as Coney Island were accosted by recent immigrants who wanted to know 'Which way da Yankee Stadium?' '' The *Life* article suggested that the Horatio Alger experience was open to Italian immigrants by commenting on ''Joe DiMaggio's sudden transformation from a penniless newsboy to a national celebrity.'' Despite his employment of patronizing stereotypes, Busch implied, albeit in paternalistic fashion, that DiMaggio provided fellow ethnics with a model of Americanization: ''Although he learned Italian first, Joe, now twenty-four, speaks English without an accent and is otherwise well adapted to most United States mores. Instead of olive oil or smelly grease, he keeps his hair slick with water. He never reeks of garlic and prefers chicken chow mein to spaghetti.''

In identifying the ethnicity of DiMaggio reporters were not treating him differently than players from other ethnic groups. A myriad of evidence, including such articles as *Baseball Magazine*'s ''An Italian Baseball Guide,'' illustrate the pervasiveness of ethnicity in the baseball literature of the Depression era. Sportswriters repeatedly portrayed baseball as the ''great American melting pot,'' which facilitated the assimilation of its heterogenous participants.

The press of the 1930s portrayed DiMaggio and other players with ethnic antecedents as symbols of the Americanization process at work. Although scribes thus viewed ethnic standard bearers such as DiMaggio as transitional figures, leading their co-ethnics to the figurative melting pot, writers enthusiastically approved of depicting DiMaggio and others as ethnic standard bearers to attract fans and increase baseball's profits.

Chico Marx (who ironically was Jewish), Jimmy Durante, Lou Costello, and other entertainers rendered the emotional, not too bright *paisan* a staple of American popular culture. And two of DiMaggio's Italian-American teammates, Phil Rizzuto and Yogi Berra, despite their immense athletic talents, catered to that image, perhaps making fun of themselves before others did. Even Fiorello La Guardia, former New York City mayor, reinforced perceptions about Italian emotionality. For many years, DiMaggio, with his reserved and dignified demeanor, largely alone provided a counterbalance to the stereotype of the Italian-American as clown. Only in the past generation did other Italian-Americans, including Lee Iacocca, A. Bartlett Giamatti, Mario Cuomo, and Rudolph Giuliani, with DiMaggio's emotional gravity garner extensive public visibility.

Likewise, DiMaggio, by his integrity, demonstrated that not all Italian-Americans were criminally inclined. During DiMaggio's era, Italian gangsters figured prominently in the American imagination. Al Capone and Lucky Luciano were household names. And most gangster movies of the period depicted organized crime as an Italian-American enterprise. Even non-Italian actors, such as Jewish film stars Edward G. Robinson and Paul Muni, portrayed Italian gangsters. It was rumored that boxer Primo Carnera, singer Frank Sinatra, and nearly every other celebrity of Italian background were mob connected. Not Joe DiMaggio. He was incorruptible. According to the New York *Daily News*, organized crime boss Albert Anastasia ''wanted idol of millions Joe DiMaggio to lend his name to a mob-backed hotel. But the Yankee Clipper wouldn't bite.'' And in *Me and DiMaggio: A Baseball Fan Goes in Search of His Gods*, author Christopher Lehmann-Haupt ultimately disproves DiMaggio's involvement in the business of an underworld gambler. Joe DiMaggio epitomized integrity at a time when the Italian-American gangster loomed large in the popular culture. Author Gay Talese wrote of DiMaggio's significance for Italian-Americans: "They had somebody who was making headlines who wasn't shooting somebody in dark alleys.''

As scholar Richard Gambino noted in *Blood of My Blood*, his informal history of Italian-American life, popular stereotypes of Italian-Americans distort reality. The buffoon and the gangster were the two most prevalent images of the Italian in American popular culture, but most Italians valued a very different ideal of masculinity. As their maxim "revenge is best cold" suggests, Italian immigrants believed that a real man kept his emotions under check. Italian immigrants felt that action taken without reflection would bring disaster. It was better to let emotions cool before preceding. The ideal man of Italian culture husbanded his resources for the appropriate occasion. Part of the appeal of "Deadpan Joe" to fellow Italian-Americans was that his controlled style of play and contained demeanor reflected their ethnic values. Likewise, according to Gambino, Italian culture upheld an ideal of masculinity that included an erect body, an impassive face, silence until addressed, courteous but brief responses to inquiries, and a wariness of the outside world. Italian-Americans saw those qualities in their standard bearer DiMaggio.

Joe DiMaggio had special meaning for Italian-Americans. Sportswriter Jerry Izenberg wrote in *The Staten Island Advance*, "Italian-Americans . . . would tell you DiMaggio was the ultimate rebuttal to names like *dago* and *wop*.'' They would tell you that his spectacular debut just nine years after the executions of [Nicola] Sacco and [Bartolomeo] Vanzetti was for many of them the first emotional dividend of their American dreams. They flocked to Yankee Stadium. Immigrants who spoke little English and knew less of baseball came to cheer their Joe, covertly carrying Italian flags and banners into Yankee Stadium. Early in DiMaggio's career, according to *Time,* "most of his [DiMaggio's] fan mail . . . comes from Italian well-wishers." Italian-Americans delighted in cheering one of their own. In 1941 residents of the Little Italy in Utica, New York, set up loudspeakers on the streets to better follow DiMaggio's fifty-six game hitting streak. Former New York Governor Mario Cuomo, an Italian-American, said of DiMaggio, "His life demonstrated to all the strivers and seekers—like me—that America would make a place for true excellence whatever its color or accent or origin." Sportswriter Mike Lupica said of Italian-Americans, "There was only one ballplayer for them, an Italian-American ballplayer of such talent and fierce pride that it made them fiercely proud."

It was important to those of Italian ancestry that Joe DiMaggio was a hero to all Americans, not simply to fellow ethnics. This took on great importance just prior to and during World War II, when Italy under the Fascist Benito Mussolini made common cause with Hitler, leading some to question whether Italian-Americans were loyal to the United States. By enlisting in the army, DiMaggio's patriotism provided a potent symbol of Italian-American loyalty. DiMaggio's commitment to the Allied cause, despite Italy's presence in the enemy camp, validated the melting pot. When Congress debated reclassifying Italian-American aliens as "enemies" and restricting their movement, a powerful argument, which contributed to the ultimate defeat of these proposals, was the recognition that their enforcement would discriminate against the parents of Joe DiMaggio.

After World War II, media references to DiMaggio's ethnicity declined dramatically. The advent of the Cold War, the growth of suburbia, and mass culture promoted assimilation. In post-1945 America, references to DiMaggio as an ethnic standard bearer were relatively rare. Instead, popular culture came to view

DiMaggio almost exclusively as the embodiment of baseball and American values. Postwar commentary about DiMaggio's ethnicity was essentially an exercise in nostalgia. In the film *A Bronx Tale,* its early scenes set in 1960, an Italian-American bus driver asks his son who is the greatest ballplayer. The ten-year-old never saw DiMaggio play and his hero is Mickey Mantle, but the boy dutifully gives the answer his father wants—Joe DiMaggio—"because he's Italian." In what author Max Rudin termed "the suburban, post-ethnic America," the transformation of Joe DiMaggio from Italian-American standard bearer to national icon was completed.

It is instructive to compare Joe DiMaggio to Hank Greenberg as an ethnic standard bearer. They was ballplayers during the same era. And DiMaggio's importance for Italian-Americans paralleled Greenberg's significance for Jewish-Americans.

Hank Greenberg, a first baseman-outfielder, ranks with the most powerful sluggers who ever played the game. Just as DiMaggio was the most significant Italian-American athlete of all time, Greenberg was the most significant Jewish-American athlete of all time. Runner Lon Myers, boxer Benny Leonard, and basketball star Dolph Schayes may have been as good or better athletes than Greenberg, but their sports did not have the status of the national pastime. A generation later, Sandy Koufax achieved at least as much in baseball, but Koufax played at a time when American Jews, feeling more at home with both their Jewish and American identities, did not respond to an ethnic standard bearer with the same intensity.

Neither Greenberg nor DiMaggio was the first of their ethnic group to reach the major leagues, but just as DiMaggio was the first great Italian ballplayer, Greenberg was baseball's first Jewish superstar. Aside from a final season with the Pittsburgh Pirates, Greenberg's major-league career (1933–1941, 1945–1947) was spent with the Detroit Tigers. The career statistics of both Greenberg and DiMaggio were circumscribed by injury and military service. Despite four and a half years lost to military service, Greenberg won four home-run and four RBI titles. Greenberg was the first Jewish-American to receive a Most Valuable Player award, and DiMaggio was the first Italian-American to receive that designation. Twice Greenberg received the American League's most valuable player accolade compared to DiMaggio's three selections. Both were the first of their respective ethnicity named to the Baseball Hall of Fame. Like DiMaggio, Greenberg countered negative stereotypes for fellow ethics. The actor Walter Matthau recalled the impact the six-foot-four, 215-pound Greenberg had on coreligionists, "When you're running around in the jungle of the Lower East Side you couldn't help but be exhilarated by the sight of one of our guys looking like a colossus. He eliminated for me all those jokes that start out: 'Did you hear the one about the little Jewish gentleman?' "

DiMaggio was clearly a better all-around player than Greenberg. DiMaggio's running, throwing, and fielding surpassed that of Greenberg. But Greenberg hit with more power. DiMaggio never hit more than forty-six home runs in a season. In contrast, no right-handed batter exceeded Greenberg's 1938 season total of fifty-eight home runs until 1998. Only four players have higher lifetime slugging percentage than Greenberg's .605; DiMaggio is sixth on the list with a mark of .579. In the category of RBIs per game, DiMaggio is fourth on the all-time career list with .89. Nonetheless, Greenberg averaged .92 RBI's per game, a mark that Lou Gehrig and Sam Thompson matched and no one has exceeded. DiMaggio's career batting average (.325), however, is higher than Greenberg's (.313). But the significance of these two great players clearly transcends their enormous athletic accomplishments.

As they did with DiMaggio, 1930s sportswriters frequently noted Greenberg's ethnic identity even in accounts of mundane incidents. Similar to DiMaggio, numerous ethnic sobriquets attached to Greenberg, including "Hebrew star," "the Tiger's great Jewish first baseman," "the Jewish slugger," and even "a conscientious Orthodox Jew." At times the press demonstrated imagination in its allusions to Greenberg's ethnicity as with the *Sporting News'* explanation that he "does everything in the Orthodox fashion." With repeated assertions that "Hank was born with a silver spoon in his mouth," the press of the Depression decade exaggerated the economic situation of Greenberg's parents, thus paralleling prevailing and erroneous stereotypes about Jewish wealth. Although Hank's father, a Rumanian immigrant, did own a cloth-shrinking plant, the Greenbergs were not wealthy. In contrast, journalists emphasized the humble circumstances of DiMaggio's Italian immigrant parents.

The 1930s press depicted the Italian Joe DiMaggio as a comic-book reader of modest intellect. Conversely, sportswriters depicted Greenberg as the quintessence of traditional Jewish respect for learning, which America transformed into a passion for secular knowledge. Commentators lingered over Hammerin' Hank's cerebral qualities. Some of the descriptions of Greenberg's intellect conjure up a Talmudic scholar more than an athlete: "put more thought into work than any other player," "has demonstrated . . . intelligence and imagination," "the most energetic . . . research," and "studied the best methods and practices as earnestly as a young physician."

Journalists depicted the Italian DiMaggio as a graceful, natural athlete who did not need to train very hard. By contrast, they depicted the Jewish Greenberg as an ungainly, self-made ballplayer. Numerous articles portrayed the young Tiger as "clumsy," "naturally slow," "awkward," and "[possessing] little natural ability." With near unanimity, however, pundits cast Greenberg as a Jewish Horatio Alger hero, who "overcame [his] glaring weakness" by "hard work and determination." Many writers repeated the refrain that "no ballplayer probably worked harder to prepare himself for success" than Greenberg. Both Greenberg and DiMaggio were portrayed by journalists as symbols of the rewards that athletic excellence could bring the sons of immigrants in baseball's melting pot.

Greenberg and DiMaggio provided counterbalances to negative stereotypes about their respective ethnic groups. During the Great Depression, DiMaggio gave Italian-Americans a hero to blunt stereotypes concerning Italian buffoons, gangsters, and Fascists. Likewise, Greenberg provided Jewish-Americans of the 1930s with a standard bearer to offset popular portrayals of Jews as weaklings, victims, and greedy shylocks. Greenberg was an especially potent symbol to second-generation Jewish-Americans, the children of East European immigrants. They wanted acceptance, and Greenberg became their role model. Like DiMaggio, Greenberg was the first of his ethnic group to become a hero to all Americans. Unlike the Jewish boxing champions of the era, Greenberg did not carry the legacy of the ghetto with him. In an era when second generation Jewish-Americans sought to distance themselves from the world of their parents and to make the American Dream a reality, Greenberg, like DiMaggio, offered an example of success that generally elicited approval, rather than resentment, from those beyond the ethnic group.

Just as Italian-Americans took special pride in Joe DiMaggio's fifty-six-game hitting streak, so Jewish-Americans delighted in Greenberg's assault on what was then baseball's most cherished record, Babe Ruth's season total of sixty home runs. In 1938 Greenberg came close, slugging fifty-eight home runs. Day by day, young Jews followed Hank Greenberg's 1938 home-run heroics. For Bert Gordon, baseball fan and the son of a rabbi, and other Jews of his generation, Greenberg was an epic figure: "I don't think anybody can imagine the terrific importance of Hank Greenberg to the whole Jewish community then . . . I can remember Rosh Hoshanah . . . in 1938, when Hank was going after Babe Ruth's record of sixty home runs in a season. Of course, nobody in the synagogue could go near a radio that day, but somebody came in late from the parking lot with a report about the game and the news went through the congregation like a wind."

World War II brought changes to portrayals of Greenberg's and DiMaggio's ethnicity. In the 1930s, they were repeatedly deemed ethnic standard bearers. During World War II, however, they were depicted as evidence of the Americanization and patriotism of their respective groups. The press commented favorably on the wartime military service of both ballplayers. During World War II American Jews proudly related the following apocryphal story: "A big fellow is weaving his way around a World War II embarkation point, saying in a loud voice 'Is there anybody here named Ginsberg or Goldberg? I'll kick the living daylights out of him.' A soldier stands up and says 'My name's Hank Greenberg, buddy.' The drunk looks him up and down and replies, 'I didn't say Greenberg. I said Ginsberg or Goldberg.'" The Jewish first baseman of the 1930s had become "Captain Henry."

After World War II, press references to DiMaggio and Greenberg as ethnic standard bearers virtually disappeared. The chronological distance from the era of mass immigration, the appearance of the third generation, the consensus created by World War II and sustained by the Cold War, and the growing mass culture, soon to be buttressed by the "new suburbs," interstate highways, franchises, and television, reduced the need for ethnic standard bearers. The relatively few post-World War II references to the ethnicity of DiMaggio and Greenberg were essentially exercises in nostalgia. But DiMaggio and Greenberg have lasting significance in American ethnic history. As historian G. Edward White recognizes, "Hank Greenberg and Joe DiMaggio were both ethnics and ballplayers, and there were things to celebrate about them in both capacities."

DiMaggio Versus the Pretenders

Joe DiMaggio more fully represents the masculine ideal as defined by sociologist Michael Kimmel than baseball's other eponymic figures. This assessment transcends arguments about playing skills and statistical accomplishments. Nor does it deny that there have been other great players who possess admirable character. But none so completely meet Kimmel's criteria. To illustrate this, it is instructive to compare DiMaggio to Babe Ruth, Mickey Mantle, Hank Aaron, Ted Williams, and Mark McGwire.

The name Babe Ruth is synonymous with baseball. Ruth's power hitting transformed the game's style of play. Prior to Ruth, "inside baseball" featured a cautious offense that produced low-scoring games. Abetted by a livelier baseball, Ruth rewrote the record book. In 1918 he led the American league with eleven home runs, a respectable total in an era in which John "Home Run" Baker paced the American league in home runs four times without ever accumulating more than twelve in a single season. In 1920, however, Ruth finished the season with fifty-four home runs, a figure that within historical context was far more re-markable than Mark McGwire's seventy in 1999. Others emu-lated Ruth's free swing, ushering in the age of the slugger. The dramatic increase in home runs during the 1920s saved baseball, helping fans to forget the 1919 Black Sox scandal. And Ruth, whose ebullience mirrored the iconoclastic Jazz Age, reigned supreme among long-ball hitters, leading the American League in home runs twelve times. Ruth's 1927 record of sixty stood for thirty-four years. Indeed, baseball Commissioner Ford Frick, Ruth's former ghostwriter and friend, sought to protect Ruth's record by ordering an asterisk besides Roger Maris' 1961 total of sixty-one home runs, noting that Maris had the advantage of an expanded 162 game schedule.

Despite his baseball heroics and genuine affection for the young, manifested by hospital visits with sick children, Ruth's image, as rendered by Robert Creamer, Marshall Smelser, and other biographers, was that of an emotional child. The Babe lacked the control over oneself central to the masculine ideal. Refusing Ruth's request to manage, Yankee owner Jacob Rup-pert told the Babe that a man who could not control himself could not manage others. Ruth drank excessively, chewed tobacco, violated curfew, ate in herculean quantities, reported out of shape to spring training, argued with umpires, feuded with manager Miller Huggins, engaged in shouting matches with fans, and endured suspensions. DiMaggio drank moderately, smoked, and disagreed with manager Casey Stengel, but he employed a discretion foreign to Ruth. While Ruth frequently failed to check his impulse for instant gratification, Joe DiMaggio embodied the self-control essential to the masculine ideal.

Babe Ruth preceded DiMaggio in the Yankee outfield and Mickey Mantle followed him. Mantle's life on and off the field paralleled Ruth's far more than DiMaggio's. Like Ruth, Mantle was a magnificent player and the preeminent Yankee of his era. Despite pain, illness, and injury, Mantle amassed Hall of Fame credentials. The switch-hitting center fielder was named the American League's most valuable player three times by sports-writers. The combination of speed and power possessed by the young Mantle inspired awe. Tape-measure home runs jumped off his bat. His Triple Crown season of 1956 encompassed a .353 batting average, 52 home runs, and 130 RBIs. Overall he connected for 536 home runs.

Yet Mantle could have been so much more given his immense gifts. With discipline, his career batting average might have been substantially higher than .298. Mantle lacked self-control. As depicted in Jim Bouton's *Ball Four,* Mantle was an emotional child. According to Bouton, Mantle roamed hotel fire escapes, searching for glimpses of women who failed to draw their curtains. Mantle abused alcohol, arriving at the ballpark on a number of occasions with a hangover. Although he demonstrated courage by playing despite pain, Mantle did not possess the self-control to follow the physical rehabilitation regimen mandated after injury.

Besides deficient self-control, Mantle, suggests Ken Burns' PBS *Baseball* series, lacked another of the attributes of Kimmel's masculine ideal—not allowing domination by others. Mutt Mantle, Mickey's father, was determined to make his son a great

baseball player. Mutt's expectations for his son were so great
that Mickey never felt confident about fulfilling them. In 1951
a frustrated nineteen-year-old Mickey contemplated quitting
baseball; Mutt retorted that apparently he had raised a girl.
Mutt's early death did not free Mickey from his father's expectations; instead, it spawned Mickey's fatalistic belief that he, too,
would die young. So Mickey drank heavily and destroyed his
liver. In contrast, DiMaggio, possessed of self-control and free
of domination by others, set his own expectations.

Given his historic achievements, it is appropriate to consider
Hank Aaron within the context of the masculine ideal. For most
of his twenty-three major league seasons, Aaron was a model of
excellence and consistency. A good defensive outfielder and an
effective base runner, he stole 240 bases and scored 2,174 runs
during his career. Registering a .305 lifetime batting average,
Aaron hit above .300 fourteen times. During fifteen seasons he
slugged more than thirty home runs. Aaron enjoyed eleven cam-
paigns with more than 100 RBIs. His 2,297 career RBIs constitute a career record. And, of course, Aaron holds the all-time
record for career home runs with 755. Moreover, Hank Aaron is
a good and honorable man.

How, then, does Aaron fail to conform to Kimmel's model of
the masculine ideal? Recognition by others of one's achievements is one of Kimmel's attributes, and Aaron, due to circumstances that are unfair, fails to meet this criterion. He does not
receive the recognition he merits. During Aaron's first twelve
major league seasons, he played in Milwaukee, distant from the
nation's media centers, but even after the Braves moved to Atlanta he did not receive his due. As the all-time career home-
run leader, Aaron should loom larger in the popular culture.
Bowie Kuhn, then commissioner of baseball, was conspicuously
absent, by design, when in 1974 Aaron hit home run 715, breaking Babe Ruth's record, and, for a time, near the main entrance
to the Baseball Hall of Fame a gratuitous sign noted that Aaron
had many more career at-bats than the Babe. Undoubtedly part

of the devaluing of Aaron's home-run record derives from the fact that the mark had belonged to the popular and mythic Bambino. Racism also played a role; there were those who were unhappy that a black player had supplanted Ruth. Others criticized Aaron by noting that he never hit more than forty-seven home runs in a single season. The laconic and somewhat aloof Aaron was not a charismatic personality; that, too, diminished his visibility as did other factors. The essential point though is that despite major league baseball's official twenty-fifth anniversary celebration of Aaron's achievements in 1999, attempting to right an old wrong, Hank Aaron does not occupy a DiMaggio-like presence in the American imagination. When Hank Aaron dies, the saturation media coverage that announced DiMaggio's passing will not occur.

With DiMaggio's death, numerous pundits believe that the title of greatest living player passes to Ted Williams. Many also term Williams the greatest hitter, living or dead, of all time. Despite losing nearly five seasons to military service and parts of others to injuries, the Splendid Splinter's accomplishments are remarkable. His .406 batting average in 1941 gives Williams the distinction of recording baseball's last .400 season. At thirty-nine years old in 1957, Williams hit .388; the next year, the forty-year-old Williams won still another batting title. Ted had a lifetime batting average of .344 and 521 career home runs. No one with a higher career batting average than Williams has more lifetime home runs. His career .634 slugging percentage is second only to Ruth's. With 2,019 walks added to his 2,654 hits, Williams possesses the highest lifetime on base percentage (.486). And, in one of baseball's most dramatic moments, the forty-two-year-old Williams hit a home run in his last major league at-bat on September 18, 1960. Moreover, Williams was a war hero and a strong supporter of the Jimmy Fund, a charity for pediatric victims of cancer.

Still, Williams, unlike DiMaggio, does not meet all of Kimmel's criteria of the masculine ideal. Williams experienced a

number of emotional outbursts—verbal tirades, obscene gestures, spitting, and throwing his bat in the air—which violate the
attribute of control over oneself. And Williams' periodic absence
of self-control made it difficult for him to fulfill the requirements
for another quality cited by Kimmel: protection of reputation.
Boston sportswriters, particularly Dave Egan, frequently
launched unfair assaults on Williams' baseball achievements and
character. Egan claimed that Williams choked in key situations.
In the "ten most important games of his life," contended Egan,
"Williams hit .232." Furthermore, Egan asserted that Williams,
aside from his obvious excellence as a hitter, was a mediocre
player who hurt the Boston Red Sox. "Ted Williams," wrote
Egan, "is not a team man, he is utterly lacking in anything that
even bears remote resemblance to team spirit." Stung by mali-
cious criticism, Williams frequently lashed out at journalists,
thus escalating the venom exchanged. The New York press
found dignity in DiMaggio's solitude; the Boston press found
arrogance in Williams' solitude. Whereas DiMaggio successfully
guarded his image; Williams, due to his volatile personality and
the pettiness of elements in the Boston press, was unable to protect his reputation.

In 1998 Mark McGwire and Sammy Sosa seized America's
imagination. The six-foot-five, 250-pound McGwire hit home
runs of prodigious proportion. Blasting seventy home runs, he
eclipsed Roger Maris' record of sixty-one by a wide margin.
McGwire's home-run battle with Sosa, who ended the season
with sixty-six home runs and the most valuable player award,
created renewed interest in baseball. Reporters generated significant controversy about McGwire's use of the legal and baseball-
permitted, strength-enhancing drug androsternedione, a
muscle-building substance banned by the NFL and many other
sports organizations. In contrast Sosa, standing in front of his
locker, charmed the media by proudly displaying the chewable
Flintstone vitamins he took before each game. And in his home-
land, the Dominican Republic, Sosa is regarded with a

DiMaggio-like veneration. Despite small perceived imperfections, the divorced McGwire enjoys a stellar reputation, enhanced by his close and loving relationship with his son, Matt. McGwire has overcome back pain and slumps, contributed large sums of money to assist sexually abused children, and refuses lucrative commercial endorsements that violate his values.

Still McGwire is unlikely to displace DiMaggio from his niche. Mystery contributes to the hero's mystique. McGwire's candor leaves little sense of mystery. "I opened up to talk about my divorce, and going through the problems I had injury-wise and going to see a psychologist," notes McGwire in an interview with Ken Burns. Such confessional sharing contradicts Kimmel's attribute of emotional autonomy. DiMaggio, understanding "the power of silence," did not share with the public marital problems or his emotional state. It is admirable that McGwire both sought help for his emotional problems and encourages others to do so. DiMaggio may well have lived a fuller life had he expressed his emotions more openly. Nevertheless, the most enduring masculine idols of the popular culture, the frontiersman, the cowboy, the detective, and DiMaggio, possesses an emotional autonomy absent from the media's portrayal of McGwire.

It is not clear if the appeal of Sammy Sosa and Mark McGwire will survive the decades. Joe DiMaggio's renown has met the test of time, and death will not erode his place in American culture. DiMaggio represents the ideal of American masculinity. He will remain the standard by which men measure themselves. Should anyone ever do the impossible and exceed DiMaggio's mark of hitting in fifty-six consecutive games, protection of his reputation will require no asterisk. For the qualities that made DiMaggio great are not quantifiable. Courage. Dignity. Grace.

William Simons is a professor of history at SUNY-Oneonta, where he teaches, among other things, the course "Athletics, Society, and History." His essays, reviews, and articles have appeared in such places as The National Pastime: A Review of Baseball History, Journal of Sport History, *and* Italian Americana. *In 1992 he received the Meckler Award for baseball writing and research. A former lecturer for the New York Council for the Humanities, Dr. Simons has given baseball talks under the auspices of the National Baseball Hall of Fame, Smithsonian Seminars, the Normal Rockwell Museum, and many other sponsors. His primary activity during the summer of 1999 was playing a historically accurate version of town ball.*

The DiMaggio Era:
Baseball from 1936–1951

JOHN HELFERS AND RUSSELL DAVIS

*A*NY SERIOUS DISCUSSION of the greatest baseball players of all time must include Joseph Paul DiMaggio. One of the best all-around players of the game, during his career the New York Yankees went to the World Series ten times and won nine of them. He was voted the American League's most valuable player three times, and set a record for safely batting in fifty-six games, a mark that may never be beaten. He was also the first baseball player to be paid $100,000 for a single season, a distinction not even Babe Ruth achieved. DiMaggio was voted into the Baseball Hall of Fame in 1955 and elected baseball's Greatest Living Player in 1969, joining that elite group of men who not only set the standard for others to live up to, but who gave to the game of baseball as much as they received from it.

DiMaggio set a benchmark during his career not only by his lifetime statistics, but also in the way he played, with honor, courage, and dignity that few, if any, have come close to matching. He understood what it meant to be a part of the team, and few professional ballplayers played for their team with more devotion or intensity.

The following summarizes all of DiMaggio's thirteen seasons, with an brief overview of the three years he missed while serving in the Air Force during World War II. With such an abundance of riches to work with, it would be impossible to simply boil down fifteen years of any man's life into a simple collection of statistics and anecdotes. However, through what has been chosen, it is hoped that a picture can be gleaned not only of Joe DiMaggio the athlete, but Joe DiMaggio the man.

1936

Joe DiMaggio's minor league career was nothing short of phenomenal. In his first full season of organized minor league baseball, playing in the Pacific Coast League with the San Francisco Seals in 1933, his statistics drew scouts from all sixteen major league teams: a .340 batting average, 259 hits in 187 games, 28 home runs, 45 doubles, 13 triples, 169 RBIs, and 129 runs scored. His record of hitting safely in 61 consecutive games still stands in the Pacific Coast League. He was eighteen years old at the start of the 1933 season.

The New York Yankees led the barrage of teams seriously interested in DiMaggio. The Yankees hadn't won the pennant in 1933, and were looking for fresh talent. Babe Ruth had retired, the majority of the team's strength lay in their first baseman, Lou Gehrig, and a power outfielder was needed. At the end of the 1933 season, the asking price for DiMaggio was $75,000.

In 1934, however, DiMaggio injured his leg getting off a bus, and was out of commission for six weeks. He returned to the lineup as strong as ever, and batted .341 in 101 games that season, but the damage had been done. Few major league teams wanted to take a chance on an injured phenomenon, even one with the numbers DiMaggio was posting. Bill Essick, the Yankees' chief scout on the West Coast, was one of the few still interested. He kept talking DiMaggio up to Edward G. Barrow, then the Yankees' business and general manager. Barrow, smelling a bargain, purchased DiMaggio's contract for $25,000, five players to be traded, and the provision that DiMaggio play the 1935 baseball season with the Seals. Years later, Barrow said, "It was the best deal I ever made."

It was a great deal for the Seals as well. In 1935, DiMaggio batted .398 for the season, missing the league batting title by a point. In 172 games he had 270 hits, with an amazing 456 total bases taken. He hit 34 home runs, 48 doubles, 18 triples, batted in 154 runs, scored 173, and stole 24 bases. Meanwhile, the Yankees limped through another disappointing season, losing the American League pennant to the Detroit Tigers while the management cursed the fact that they hadn't brought DiMaggio up right away.

Although DiMaggio's arrival in St. Petersburg for spring training sparked the most intense media scrutiny the Yankees had seen in years, DiMaggio preferred to keep his distance from the press, remaining tight-lipped about his prospects with the Yankees, himself, and anything else they might have asked him.

Due to simple bad luck, his professional-league career did not get off to the promising start his three seasons with the San Francisco Seals had indicated. During an exhibition game against the Boston Braves, DiMaggio injured his foot sliding into second base. While treating the stiff muscle, the diathermic heat lamp used by the team trainer blistered his foot. The Yankees had to announce that the player they had purchased for five players, $25,000, and an $8,500 salary would miss opening day and the first weeks of the season. New Yorkers speculated as to whether the kid from the West Coast, whom many insiders had hailed as "the greatest outfielder in Coast League history," would be able to fill the shoes of the Yankees' most esteemed slugger and outfielder, Babe Ruth.

After sitting out the first seventeen games, DiMaggio was ready to play by late spring, and made his debut on May fourth in left field in a game against the St. Louis Browns, where he went three for six with two singles and a triple, scoring three runs and driving another one home as the Yankees trounced the Browns 14–5.

DiMaggio hit his first major league home run, the first of 361, in a May 10 game against the Philadelphia Athletics. He drove in three runs and made the first of what would be many graceful catches in the outfield.

In the latter half of May and early June, DiMaggio had his first batting slump, going to the plate twelve times and walking away hitless. He broke out of the slide on June 8 with a home run, a triple, and a single. His reputation as a slugger began to grow, and improved with each game, like on June 24 against the Chicago White Sox, where DiMaggio became the fifth man in organized baseball to ever hit two home runs in an inning, tying a major league record. He also drove in five runs in one inning, tying another record.

Two weeks later, DiMaggio and six other Yankees suited up to represent their team in the All-Star game, where DiMaggio crashed to earth in a dismal 0-for-5 showing against the power pitchers of the National League, which consisted of Dizzy Dean, Carl Hubbell, Curt Davis, and Lon Warneke. DiMaggio's fielding wasn't much better. Trying for a shoestring catch, he missed a line drive that let two runs score. Then, in the fifth inning, he juggled a Billy Herman single, allowing Herman to move to second, and eventually score, setting up a 4–0 National League lead.

DiMaggio got a chance to redeem himself when he came up to bat in the seventh inning. The American League had closed to within one run, helped by a homer from Lou Gehrig. With the bases loaded and two outs, DiMaggio cracked a line drive between second and third, which was promptly grabbed by short-stop Leo Durocher, ending the rally. The National League would go on to win 4–3, taking its first All-Star game since the game's inception in 1933. Even after that humbling performance, DiMaggio's fame continued to grow, as evidenced by his appearance on the cover of *Time* magazine a week later.

That year was also DiMaggio's first of ten trips to the World Series. The Yankees crushed the highly regarded New York Giants four games to two. During the second game, President Franklin D. Roosevelt threw out the first ball and, unlike many photo-opportunity-seeking politicians, actually watched the entire game. In the bottom of the ninth, a request was made for all spectators to remain in their seats so the President could exit the field in his special car. DiMaggio caught the last out of the game, and as President Roosevelt was driven to the center-field exit gates, there was speculation that he saluted, waved, or otherwise spoke to the young DiMaggio, who had always maintained that he thought the President was waving to the fans in the stands. DiMaggio finished the Series with nine hits in twenty-seven at bats, with three doubles, three runs batted in, and a Series batting average of .346.

Overall, Joe DiMaggio's professional debut with the New York Yankees let the collective fans breathe a sigh of relief, and then an even greater cheer when they witnessed his prowess. In 637 at bats during 138 games, he posted a batting average of .323 and a slugging average of .576. He had 206 hits, including 44 doubles, 15 triples, 29 home runs, and 132 runs scored with 25 RBIs, 24 bases on balls, and four stolen bases.

1937

The start of DiMaggio's second season with the Yankees was also unfortunately marked by setbacks. After his stellar performance during the 1936 season, DiMaggio demanded a salary of $25,000. The Yankees' owner, Colonel Jake Ruppert, played hardball not only with DiMaggio, but with other Yankee greats such as Lou Gehrig and pitcher Vernon "Lefty" Gomez. Eventually they settled on a salary of $17,000, making DiMaggio the highest paid second-year man in baseball at the time. But DiMaggio's trials weren't over yet. In April, he had his infected tonsils and adenoids removed as part of a cure for a bout of neuritis plaguing his right shoulder. The operation effectively benched him for the start of the season.

Returning to the lineup on May 1, DiMaggio got three hits in a game against the Boston Red Sox and played a part in all three of the runs scored in the Yankees' 3–2 win.

During the first half of the season, DiMaggio hit thirty-one home runs in eighty-nine games, causing a hot debate as to whether he could beat Babe Ruth's record of sixty home runs in a single season, set in 1927. Even the Sultan of Swat had taken ninety games to reach the halfway point of his record. Speculation was rampant that this twenty-two-year-old kid could beat one of baseball's greatest legends in only his second year in the majors. But by the end of August, DiMaggio knew it wouldn't happen. That same month, Babe Ruth himself mentioned DiMaggio as a possible slugging successor, along with the Detroit Tigers' catcher Rudy York. DiMaggio ended the season with 46 homers, his last one a grand slam, which helped the Yankees secure their 102 wins.

The Yankees met the New York Giants again in that year's World Series. With almost nonchalant ease, the Yankees took the Series four games to one. DiMaggio went 6-for-22 with one home run and two runs scored, and four runs batted in. It was Lefty Gomez, with a lifetime batting average of .147, that drove in the winning run in Game 5. His pitching, however, was what kept the Giants down, allowing them to score just three runs in the first three games.

When the season was over, DiMaggio had lost the player of the year award by just four votes to Detroit second baseman Charlie Gehringer. He had been named player of the year by sportswriters in both New York City and Philadelphia, which he felt placed him in an excellent position to negotiate next season's contract.

DiMaggio's statistics seemed to bear him out as well. He played in 151 games and had 621 at bats, 215 hits, 35 doubles, 15 triples, 46 home runs, 151 runs scored, 167 RBIs, 64 bases on balls, and three stolen bases, with a batting average of .346 and a slugging average of .673, his career best.

1938

The 1938 season began with a replay of the contract negotiations of 1937, only this time DiMaggio was holding out for $40,000, which would have made him the highest-paid player in baseball (Lou Gehrig's salary in 1937 was $36,000, the highest in the major leagues). Ruppert countered with $25,000, equivalent to the salary of the President of the United States, and adamantly refused to go any higher.

DiMaggio refused to budge from his asking price, and sat out all of spring training, the exhibition season, and the first twelve games of the season, during which time the Yankees limped along around the .500 mark. Gehrig was in a batting slump, and the Yankees had lost two of their first three games of the season against the Red Sox.

After an acrimonious meeting in January, DiMaggio had been cooling his heels in San Francisco, running his restaurant and working out occasionally with his old minor league team, the San Francisco Seals. But as the days stretched into weeks, he began rethinking his position, and finally, on April 20, he sent a telegram to Ruppert that said, "Your terms accepted. Leave at 2:40 P.M. Arrive Saturday morning."

. Once there, DiMaggio quickly got into the swing of things, not always for his own good. Now playing center field, he made a lackluster debut in a game against the Washington Senators, which the Yankees won 8–4, in which his only contribution was a fluke single. Later in that same game, he collided with second baseman Joe Gordon, knocking them both unconscious, and sending both to the hospital overnight. Released the next day, DiMaggio hit his first home run of the season in a 4–3 defeat, also against the Senators. With DiMaggio's return, the Yankees snapped out of their doldrums, winning five out of the first six games with DiMaggio playing, and quickly reclaiming the No. 1 spot at the top of the American League.

But the fans did not forget so easily. Their resentment of DiMaggio's holdout dogged him throughout the season. On May 18 in St. Louis, where he had two home runs and five runs batted in during a 11–7 victory over the Browns, DiMaggio was roundly booed when he stepped up to the plate. The Depression had caused many to think that DiMaggio should have been more than satisfied with his $25,000 salary, rather than joining the eight million people who were unemployed.

DiMaggio accepted their taunts with his stoic implacability and concentrated on baseball, missing only seven games for the rest of the year. When the 1938 season ended, the Yankees had finished the season with ninety-nine wins, were nine-and-a-half games ahead of the Red Sox and looking to take a third World Series title.

The World Series that year was almost an anticlimax, with the Chicago Cubs surprising the Pittsburgh Pirates and winning the National League pennant. The Northsiders then dropped four straight to the Yankees. Newly acquired Cubs pitcher Dizzy Dean, who was fading as a power pitcher by this time, failed to hold off the New York onslaught. DiMaggio went four for fifteen with one home run, four runs scored, and two runs batted in. Charles "Red" Ruffing, New York's ace pitcher, led off the series by pitching a nine-hit game, and it was all downhill for the Cubs from there.

DiMaggio had obviously not let the season starting holdout get to him. He posted 194 hits in 599 at bats during 145 games, with 32 doubles, 13 triples, 32 home runs, 129 runs scored, 140

RBIs, 59 bases on balls, and 6 stolen bases. His batting average was .324, with a slugging average of .581.

1939

The 1939 season was one of growth and loss for Joe Di-Maggio and the New York Yankees.

First came the death of Colonel Jacob Ruppert, the fiery owner of the Yankees who had purchased the team with partner Captain Tillinghast L'Hommedieu Huston, in 1915 for $460,000. Ruppert bought out Huston in 1923 for $1.5 million, and transformed the Yankees from a down-and-out, debt-ridden team to the powerhouse that ruled baseball in the 1930s, 1940s, and early 1950s. With Ruppert's passing at age seventy-one, Ed Barrow, longtime Yankee executive, was elevated to the position of president.

This time DiMaggio didn't hold out for an extravagant raise, instead signing a contract that would pay him $27,500. Rumors abounded about what had caused his uncharacteristic acquiescence. With the acquisition of several promising rookie outfielders, including Charlie Keller, who would bat .334 and hit eleven home runs that year, Joe Gallagher, and Walt Judnich, DiMaggio may have felt that Barrow thought he was expendable. Or perhaps it was his budding romance with aspiring actress Dorothy Arnold that caused his mind to wander from his baseball contract. Whatever the reason, for the first time since signing with the New York Yankees, Joe DiMaggio would start with the team on opening day. Shortly thereafter, his engagement to Arnold became public knowledge.

On April 29, playing in a game against the Washington Senators, DiMaggio went after a line drive from Washington rookie Bobby Estalella. When the ball took a bad bounce, DiMaggio tried to stay with it and caught his spikes in the mud, causing him to collapse on the ground, writhing in pain. A hospital examination revealed that DiMaggio had separated several leg muscles from the bone, and would be out of commission for a week to ten days.

Then, on May 2, an era came to an end. Troubled by a increasing lack of coordination and power, Lou Gehrig took himself out of the Yankee lineup for the first time in 2,130 games. Babe Dahlgren, bought from the Newark Bears in 1938, would replace Gehrig at first base, the first time in more than a decade any other Yankee had started at that position.

DiMaggio was still recovering in the hospital when he heard the news. His response was loyal and encouraging. "There's plenty of baseball left in Lou Gehrig, and don't count him out because he's taking the first rest he's had in years."

Sadly, this time it was not to be. Eventually diagnosed with amyotrophic lateral sclerosis, a chronic form of poliomyelitis, Lou Gehrig's career as a baseball player was effectively over. On July 4, a day in honor of Gehrig was planned at Yankee Stadium. An overflow crowd packed the bleachers to see Gehrig next to baseball players such as Wally Pipp, the Yankee first baseman whom Lou had taken over for, and Everett Scott, whose record of 1,307 consecutive games played had been shattered by Gehrig.

Like the rest of the Yankee team, DiMaggio was saddened by the loss of their inimitable captain from the playing field. But he knew what had to be done. And when he returned on June 6, hitting a single, a double, and a home run during a 7–2 defeat of the Chicago White Sox, there was no doubt that DiMaggio was going to do his best to fill the void that would be left behind by Gehrig's absence.

DiMaggio made another appearance in the All-Star game this year, along with five other Yankees. He hit a home run off Bill Lee of the Cubs and led the American League team to a 3–1 victory.

For the last part of the season, DiMaggio's batting average had risen above .400, and the press and fans debated whether he could be one of the rarified few who completed a season above .400, the first since Bill Terry did so by hitting .401 in 1930. During a twelve-game road trip, of which the Yankees won ten, DiMaggio's average was .500, or twenty-seven hits in fifty-three at bats, with five home runs and twenty-eight RBIs. Then, during the last three weeks of the season, he caught a nagging cold. Combined with an allergic reaction in his left eye that hampered his vision for most of September, DiMaggio's batting average dropped to .380, and stayed there until the season ended.

Still, with a record of 106 wins and forty-five losses, the Yankees finished the pennant race with a seventeen-game lead and were the heavy favorite to win the World Series against the Cincinnati Reds. In their arsenal the Reds had double threat-pitchers Bucky Walters, who had won twenty-seven games during the season and had been voted the National League's most valuable player, and Paul Derringer, who had won twenty-five games.

As they had done with the Cubs in 1938, the Yankees swept the Reds in four straight games. The most notable of these was the fourth game, when Bill Myers muffed a double play that would have enabled the Reds to hold on to their two-run lead and force a fifth game. A single by DiMaggio set up the game-tying score and sent the game into extra innings.

In the tenth inning, DiMaggio was up again with runners Charlie Keller and Frank Crosetti on first and second respectively. He hit a single into right field, which was bobbled by Ival Goodman. Crosetti and Keller raced home, with Keller slamming into Reds catcher Ernie Lombardi so hard he knocked the ball loose from his glove. While Lombardi was still sitting there, the ball only a few feet from him, DiMaggio finished up his tour of the bases and crossed home plate, easily ahead of Lombardi's halfhearted attempt to tag him, and pounding the final nail in the Reds' coffin.

On October 23, DiMaggio received his first of three most valuable player awards, finishing well ahead of second-place nominee Jimmie Foxx.

Also that year, on November 10, after a two-year courtship, Joe DiMaggio and Dorothy Arnold were married in downtown San Francisco.

It has been said that the 1936–1939 New York Yankees may have been the best all-around team in baseball history, with multiple strengths and no weaknesses. Their record holds this to be very close to an absolute fact. The Yankees were the first team to ever win four consecutive World Series and win two consecutive Series with four-game sweeps. They were the first American League team to win four league pennants, with lead margins of nineteen and a half, thirteen, nine and a half, and seventeen games respectively.

In those four World Series, the Yankees lost just three games. Only in 1936 did the Series extend to six games, and the Yankees still won one of those games by a score of 18–4. Their standard crew consisted of Lefty Gomez and Red Ruffing pitching, with Johnny Murphy as their relief pitcher, Bill Dickey, perhaps the greatest catcher to ever play the game, behind the plate, Lou Gehrig at first base until 1938, afterward replaced by Babe Dahlgren, Tony Lazzeri, and later Joe Gordon at second, Frank Crosetti at shortstop, the often underrated Red Rolfe at third base, and several excellent outfielders including George Selkirk, Tommy Henrich, Jake Powell, Charlie Keller, and Ben Chapman. Of course, the Yankees also had Joe DiMaggio.

They also had a superb manager in Joe McCarthy, who knew how to get the most out of a baseball team. He never let the Yankees become complacent, and always treated everyone, including DiMaggio, Dickey, and Gehrig, equally. Along with Ruffing, Gomez, DiMaggio, Gehrig, and Dickey, Joe McCarthy was later inducted into the Baseball Hall of Fame.

DiMaggio's statistics for 1939, the last year of the Yankee dynasty: 462 at bats in 120 games with 176 hits, 32 doubles, 6 triples, 30 home runs, 108 runs scored, 126 RBIs, 52 bases on balls, 3 stolen bases, a batting average of .381 and a slugging average of .671.

1940

The baseball season of 1940 began with an unusually loquacious DiMaggio accepting the Golden Laurel award for his accomplishments during the 1939 baseball season. It was during several press conferences that he announced his goal of winning baseball's triple crown—home runs, batting average, and RBIs.

Across town, rumors were spreading that the Yankees' management was secretly planning to limit DiMaggio's salary to $30,000 for the upcoming season. Although President Ed Barrow denied such a meeting ever took place, by the time March rolled around, DiMaggio had signed a contract worth $30,000, although he had been asking for $35,000.

The opening day curse continued to rear its ugly head, with a strained tendon during an April 14 exhibition game against the Dodgers sidelining DiMaggio for the season opener against Philadelphia. DiMaggio was out for more than two weeks, and eventually consulted a specialist at Johns Hopkins University to get him back in action.

With DiMaggio sidelined, the Yankees, once favorites to make it five World Series in a row, slid into a last-place tie with the Chicago White Sox, losing eight straight home games. Lefty Gomez was out with a bad back, and the rest of the pitching staff couldn't take up the slack. As a whole, the team was batting .250. Even DiMaggio's return in a game against Detroit wasn't the spark it should have been, as he popped out against the eighteen-year-old pitching sensation Hal Newhouser.

The Yankees' decline continued, and on August 8 they were 50–51 and eleven games out of first place. All bets were off where the Yankees were concerned, and the fans began to wonder if their team had what it took. But in late August, they started a drive back to the top, with DiMaggio leading off with a grand slam against Cleveland on the way to a 15–2 rout. But two days later, he pulled a muscle running a triple, pulling himself back out of the lineup.

Despite all of the problems, by September 10 DiMaggio was back and hitting his usual .350, the Yankees had won twenty-five of their last thirty-one games, and they trailed the Indians by a half-game. The two teams slugged it out during a wet doubleheader in Cleveland, where the Yankees held first place in their hands for an afternoon, only to see it slip away as they split the two games 3–1, 3–5.

After that, they could never regain the lost ground, although they certainly tried. Two games dropped to Detroit and a three-game slaughter by the usually hapless St. Louis Browns put the Yankees four games out of first place, from which they never recovered.

The Yankees finished the season with a record of 94–60 and had to settle for third place, two games out. Detroit won the pennant and was defeated by Cincinnati in seven games.

One final note about the 1940 baseball season is that it was the first to have the three youngest DiMaggio brothers playing in the major leagues. DiMaggio's older brother Vince had been in the National League since 1937, first with the Boston Braves, then Cincinnati, and finally traded to Pittsburgh in 1940. He was the league leader in strikeouts for six out of his ten seasons, with a .249 batting average and 125 home runs, but distinguished himself as an outfielder.

That year was also the rookie year for Dom DiMaggio, the youngest brother of the DiMaggio clan. Dom started with the Boston Red Sox, played for eleven years, and in many ways proved himself DiMaggio's equal in the outfield. But although all three DiMaggios were excellent defensive players, there was only one slugger in the family, and that was Joe Di-Maggio.

DiMaggio fell ten home runs and seventeen RBIs short of his triple crown. His statistics for the year were: 508 at bats in 132 games with 179 hits, 28 doubles, 9 triples, 31 home runs, 93 runs scored, 133 RBIs, 61 bases on balls, 1 stolen base, with a batting average of .352 and a slugging average of .626.

1941

Baseball experienced a watershed year in 1941. Lefty Grove won his three hundredth game. Mel Ott hit his four hundredth home run. Ted Williams batted .406 for the season. Bob Feller had his third consecutive season of more than twenty-four wins. Rookies Stan Musial and Phil Rizzuto made their debuts. But there is no doubt in any baseball fan's mind that 1941 will always belong to Joseph Paul DiMaggio and his fifty-six-game hitting streak.

The season had started out as usual, with the now-familiar negotiation between DiMaggio and Barrow ending up with a signed contract for $7,500. DiMaggio missed the first week of training camp and came into the lineup as the Yankees began one of their worst starts in the past five years. The Streak began during a game against the Chicago White Sox with an innocuous single to left field that drove in Rizzuto. The Yankees dropped that game and the next four, placing them well below .500. But DiMaggio kept hitting.

Singles, doubles, triples, home runs, DiMaggio connected for all of them. He had close calls, like the game against the Senators when he almost got beaten by the throw to first. That hit extended The Streak to fourteen games.

After DiMaggio had hit safely in nineteen games, he and the rest of the Yankee team got the news that they had been dreading for the past two years. After a valiant struggle, Lou Gehrig, the Iron Horse, was dead at age thirty-six. Current Yankees, including DiMaggio, Lefty Gomez, and Red Ruffing, paid tribute to Gehrig over the NBC radio network.

During this time, DiMaggio wasn't the only one with a hitting streak going. Ted Williams had a streak of twenty-two games.

He would be stopped a few days later at twenty-three games, the longest of his career, but his batting average that month was .487, an impressive feat regardless.

Meanwhile, DiMaggio kept on hitting. His streak was now attracting attention from both the media and the fans. DiMaggio's next challenge was to break the Yankee club record of twenty-nine games, held by both Earl Combs and Roger Peckinpaugh, who was managing the Indians. Exactly 44,161 fans packed Yankee Stadium to watch the Yankees beat the Indians 4–1, and DiMaggio's streak stretch to twenty-seven games.

A bad hop almost ended DiMaggio's streak at twenty-nine games. During a loss to the Chicago White Sox, DiMaggio hit a single toward shortstop Luke Appling. Just before it reached Appling, it bounced, careened off his shoulder, and skipped into left field. If the scorer, Dan Daniel, called it an error, then the streak was over. After a few tense seconds, he held up one finger, signifying a single, and the streak rolled on.

The next record to fall was George Sisler's forty-one-game streak set in 1922. DiMaggio passed this one on June 29 in a doubleheader against the Senators. It seemed that it would be smooth sailing for the Yankee Clipper, but then an enterprising sportswriter dug up a report that a player named Willie Keeler had hit safely in *forty-four* consecutive games in 1897. This was the next marker DiMaggio had to pass, and he did so on July 2 with a home run in Yankee Stadium against the Boston Red Sox.

With DiMaggio's streak at forty-five, the Yankees had won their last six outings and led the American League by three games. Everyone was wondering: How long could he go?

DiMaggio went for eleven more hits, until, on July 17, with 67,468 fans watching in Municipal Stadium, the Yankees took on the Cleveland Indians. One walk, two fantastic defensive plays by third baseman Ken Keltner, and one double play started by shortstop Lou Boudreau later, The Streak was over, frozen at fifty-six games, where it will most likely remain forever.

DiMaggio is reported to have felt relieved. But the next day he started another streak, where he hit safely in sixteen more games. From May 3 to August 16 he hit safely in seventy-two out of seventy-three games. Here are the statistics of The Streak:

- DiMaggio went to bat 223 times.
- He had ninety-one total hits, including sixteen doubles, four triples, and fifteen home runs.
- He batted .408.
- He walked twenty-one times and was hit by two pitches.
- He struck out seven times.
- He scored fifty-six runs in fifty-six games.
- He had fifty-five runs batted in in fifty-six games.

The Yankees rode DiMaggio's streak into first place and headed for the World Series against the Brooklyn Dodgers, whom they defeated four games to one. One of DiMaggio's contributions in his five hits for nineteen at bats was a home run that knocked in a run in the first game, helping the Yankees to a 3–2 victory. The Yankees were never in serious trouble, even after a close call in the fourth game when the Dodgers led 4–3 in the bottom of the ninth but a muffed third strike allowed Tommy Henrich to score, bringing DiMaggio up to single and ultimately be driven in by Charlie Keller for an eventual 7–4 win. From there on the Dodgers did everything wrong, and dropped the fifth game 3–1.

Even with Ted Williams' amazing accomplishment of batting .406 for the season, DiMaggio was elected the American League's most valuable player again. He also had a personal accomplishment when Dorothy gave birth to his son, Joe, Jr., on October 23.

DiMaggio's statistics for the incredible year of 1941: 541 at bats in 139 games with 193 hits, 43 doubles, 11 triples, 30 home runs, 122 runs scored, 125 RBIs, 76 bases on balls, and 4 stolen bases. His batting average was .357, with a slugging average of .643. And of course, The Streak.

1942

The 1942 season was a year of unexpected surprises for DiMaggio. He experienced his first serious batting slump, and lost the Yankees the World Series to the St. Louis Cardinals, the only World Series loss during DiMaggio's career. The Yankees finished the season with 103 wins and 51 losses.

After holding out for a salary of $42,000, DiMaggio signed his contract for the 1942 season during the middle of spring training. After a noticeably slow start, he snapped out of his batting slump in early May during a game against the White Sox, hitting two home runs, and a tenth-inning triple. The Yankees won that game by the narrow margin of 5–4, marking their fourth straight win of the season.

By mid-July, DiMaggio had regained much of his struggling average, mostly by a series of base hits. At that point in the season, DiMaggio was batting .300, and was hoping to average .330 for the season. At the end of June, he was hitting .268, but in the 28 games during July, he tallied 42 hits in 111 at bats for a .378 average, including 6 home runs and 3 triples.

The 1942 World Series was seemingly a mismatch. Odds-makers were favoring the New York Yankees by two-to-one, but the end result was much different. In the ninth inning of the opening game, the St. Louis Cardinals rallied, and took command of the Series from that point on. In the fifth game, on October 5, with the Yankees struggling to make up lost ground, the Cardinals stumbled through the game with four errors, but each time their defense rose to the occasion, helped by their Golden Glove pitcher Johnny Beazley. When the Yankees threatened in the fifth with the bases loaded on two of the Cardinals' errors, Beazley retired Roy Cullenbine and DiMaggio himself to halt the rally. Then in the ninth, the Yankees had men on first and second and were threatening the Cardinals' lead when Beazley again retired the last two batters. The St. Louis Cardinals beat the Yankees four games to one, the first time the Yankees had lost a series since 1926. During the Series, DiMaggio batted .333 with three runs batted in. He also set a World Series record with twenty putouts for five games. He had seven hits, all of which were singles.

In December, DiMaggio's wife, Dorothy Arnold, a former radio and nightclub performer, began the process of filing for a divorce in Reno, Nevada, which became final in 1944. They had been married for just more than three years. In January 1943, DiMaggio announced he would enlist in the Air Force. His brother Dom DiMaggio, who was still with the Red Sox at the time, enlisted as well, only he went to the Coast Guard.

World War II was breaking up many teams, and cutting short the professional careers of many players. Additionally, it wasn't until October 12 that President Roosevelt declared that Italians living in the United States were no longer considered enemy aliens. Many baseball scholars feel, and rightly so, that DiMaggio's participation in the military certainly robbed him of what may have been his prime years. Even he mused what he would have been able to accomplish had he not been interrupted with military service.

The 1942 baseball season ended with statistics that weren't quite what DiMaggio had hoped for. In a total of 154 games (the first time he played the entire season) and 610 at bats, DiMaggio had 123 runs, 186 hits, 29 doubles, 13 triples, 21 home runs, 114 RBIs, 68 bases on balls, and 4 stolen bases for a season average of .305, and an slugging average of .498.

1943-1945

In January DiMaggio announced he was enlisting in the Army Air Force to serve during World War II. After a brief stint playing for the Santa Ana baseball team, DiMaggio was conscripted by Brigadier General William Flood as the center fielder for the Seventh Air Force team, joining other professional baseball players including Mike McCormick of the Cincinnati Reds, Walt Judnich of the St. Louis Browns, and Gerry Priddy of the Washington Senators. The Seventh Air Force team drew a crowd of 20,000 when it played against the Navy team, which featured a roster that included first baseman Johnny Mize and shortstop Pee Wee Reese. DiMaggio hit a home run during that game that eyewitnesses claim traveled 450 feet.

Many of baseball's great players traded their team uniforms for military stripes during the war. Ted Williams, Hank Greenberg, Joe Gordon, Phil Rizzuto, Dom DiMaggio, Luke Appling, and Mickey Vernon all served at least two-year terms.

Back in baseball, team owners, desperate to keep the sport alive when many of the stars were serving their country, turned to baseball veterans, some of whom were in their forties. The St. Louis Browns were so needy for players—any players—that they signed a one-armed man, Pete Gray, as an outfielder. Gray's throwing technique, although unorthodox, was effective; when he caught the ball, he would throw it back into the air, throw off his glove, catch the ball again, and throw it in.

Two notable players would emerge during this time. Slugger Dick Wakefield, a rising star in the minor leagues, was headed for a career in the majors when he was called into the service. When he returned, all of the major pitching talent had come back with him, and he couldn't handle the strong pitchers. Eventually he sank into obscurity.

The other player of note was Hal Newhouser, who would later face DiMaggio. The eighteen-year-old prodigy loyally signed with Detroit for a pittance—$400, turning down a $15,000 offer from Cleveland. After getting his fastball under control, he became a hot young pitcher until a sore shoulder sidetracked his career in 1948. Although he pitched until 1955, he was never as good afterward.

In 1943, the Yankees went to the World Series again, defeating the St. Louis Cardinals four games to two. The Cardinals capitalized on the weakened rosters of the other teams and made it to the World Series again in 1944, this time winning against the St. Louis Browns four games to two. The Detroit Tigers were back on top in 1945, beating the Chicago Cubs in a best-of-seven World Series.

And what of DiMaggio? Although he played on several military baseball teams, he was plagued by recurring stomach ulcers during his stint in the Air Force. In 1944, recurring he was assigned to the Redistribution Center in Atlantic City, where, as luck (or maybe a higher power, such as the Yankee management office) had it, the Yankees were booked for spring training. DiMaggio spent the next six months holding a bat instead of a rifle.

Finally, as his term of service was winding down, DiMaggio received a transfer to the pink palace on St. Petersburg Beach in Florida, ostensibly to be isolated from the temptations of downtown St. Petersburg. On September 14, DiMaggio was discharged from the Air Force, and on November 20, DiMaggio signed his first baseball contract in three years.

1946

Upon returning from his military duty during World War II, DiMaggio resumed his interrupted baseball career with the New York Yankees. The Yankees finished in third place in 1946, and DiMaggio spent the majority of the season trying to sharpen his rusty skills. By season's end, he had slumped to a batting average of only .290, down from a prewar, seven-season average of .337. Conversely, season attendance was high, and DiMaggio had developed a new appreciation for the game and the fans, signing more autographs during the 1946 spring training camp than he did during entire seasons prior to entering the military.

The 1946 spring training camp set a record by picking up $150,000 in box-office fees, enough money to actually pay for the training period. Most of the 316,846 fans who attended came to watch the return of DiMaggio. It was also during spring training that DiMaggio and Charlie Keller bet a Coke to see if DiMaggio's rusty swing could outdistance Keller's. DiMaggio accepted the bet and hit the first of three pitches about 375 feet over the center-field fence. Keller's second swing took the ball over the right field wall about an equal distance. They called it a tie.

The 1946 season also brought a series of changes on the Yankees' management staff. In the second month of the season, Joe McCarthy resigned as manager, and was replaced by Bill Dickey, who in turn was replaced by Johnny Neun, the Yankees' third manager in that season.

By this time, DiMaggio was beginning to show signs of wear, and a series of nagging injuries kept him off the field for twenty-two games. The worst of them, a knee sprain from a slide into second base during a game in Philadelphia, happened just prior to the All-Star game, and caused him to miss two weeks of the season.

It was during this time that DiMaggio also began feeling pain in his right heel. Caused by calcium deposits, the pain forced him to take some of the controlled heat away from his at bats and his fielding. In August, DiMaggio threw out his arm in a game against the Red Sox while trying to get Bobby Doerr out. In the sixth inning, he batted and hit a home run, and then Bill Dickey, the manager, agreed to take him out of the game. With little hope left for a great comeback season, DiMaggio had a late drive in his quest to finish the season over .300, but failed by a small margin. The Yankees finished the 1946 season with eighty-seven wins and sixty-seven losses.

The Yankees finished the season in third place, behind Detroit and Boston. Boston appeared in the World Series against St. Louis, with the Cards winning the Series four games to three.

His final statistics for 1946 in 132 games played were: 503 at bats, 81 runs, 146 hits, 20 doubles, 8 triples, 25 home runs, 95 RBIs, 59 bases on balls, 1 stolen base, for a season average of .290, and an slugging average of .511.

1947

DiMaggio and the Yankees experienced something of a comeback year in 1947, though DiMaggio was still troubled by injuries. It was also the year that the phrase "as DiMaggio goes, so go the Yankees" (a phrase originally coined when speaking about Babe Ruth) began to truly apply to Joe DiMaggio. It was also the first year that a young man named Jackie Robinson began playing baseball for the Brooklyn Dodgers, stealing twenty-nine bases in his rookie season.

During spring training, many people questioned DiMaggio's ability to stage a successful comeback, and the team doctor announced in mid-February that DiMaggio would be unable to practice for six weeks. In late February, DiMaggio returned from the Puerto Rico training camp for a second heel operation to hasten recovery.

In May, DiMaggio reportedly led a team "revolt" in refusing to pose for a previously agreed to team promotion with the Army Signal Corps. While he was hardly leading anyone, as soon as DiMaggio bowed out of the photo shoot, Keller followed his lead, and was quickly mirrored by Johnny Lindell and Aaron Robinson. Shortly thereafter, several other players, apparently persuaded by Lindell, and Robinson also refused to attend. DiMaggio told news reporters that "the management wanted me to pose for the Army newsreel shots during batting practice last Monday and I said I wouldn't because I needed the batting practice badly and did not want to give up that time to anything else." Larry MacPhail, the president of the Yankees, fined DiMaggio and four other players, including Lindell, Robinson, Keller, and Don Johnson.

The heel pain that DiMaggio had complained of during the 1946 season kept plaguing him, and was eventually diagnosed as bone spurs. He underwent an operation that kept him out of the lineup until April, and he was limited to pinch-hitting duties in the season opener. During a July doubleheader in Detroit, DiMaggio pulled a leg muscle, and in August, he tore a neck muscle. Interestingly, he underwent his heel operation at the same time as Babe Ruth, who was also hospitalized for sinus surgery.

Early in the season, the Yanks dropped to sixth place before a five-game winning streak moved them back up to second, behind the Detroit Tigers. In an early June game, the Yankees beat the Tigers to draw within two games of the division lead—due mostly to the batting of DiMaggio, who hit four straight, and brought his season average to .368.

After a nail-biting pennant race against the Boston Red Sox, DiMaggio led the Yankees to victory in a highly competitive World Series against Brooklyn. The first-televised World Series went seven games, with three of the games decided by a single run. The rights to the broadcast were reportedly sold for $65,000 after a brewing company had offered $100,000 and was turned down by Baseball Commissioner A. B. Chandler.

DiMaggio made his presence felt in the fifth game by scoring the winning home run. In the sixth game, with two men on and the Yankees needing three runs to tie, DiMaggio smashed a long fly to deep left field that seemed to be heading out of the park. But Dodger left fielder Al Gionfriddo, a man only five feet six inches tall, followed the ball back and made a leaping catch that *The New York Times* described as "breathtaking." DiMaggio is said to have kicked the dirt near second base when he saw the ball caught, reportedly the only display of emotion he ever showed in a ball game.

The Yankees pulled the Series out four games to three, with the final game ending 5–2 in the Yankees' favor. DiMaggio hit two of the four Yankee home runs, with a Series batting average of .231. Immediately after clinching the World Series, President Larry MacPhail resigned from the team. It was the eleventh championship for the Yankees in fifteen World Series, and their first since 1943.

Despite the nagging injuries, DiMaggio had a fine season, earning his third most valuable player award by a one-vote margin over Ted Williams. Williams, who won his fourth American League batting crown that year, finished the season with a batting average of .343, higher than DiMaggio's. The Yankees completed the season with a record of ninety-seven wins and fifty-seven losses. On the public side of the field, DiMaggio was making headlines for spending time with his fans. In particular, an eight-year-old boy, named Patty Ciccarelli, dying of leukemia, received a visit from Joltin' Joe just two weeks before passing away.

DiMaggio's final statistics for 1947 were: 141 games, 534 at bats, 97 runs, 168 hits, 21 doubles, 10 triples, 20 home runs, 97 RBIs, 64 bases on balls, and 3 stolen bases, for a season average of .315, and a slugging average of .522.

1948

Despite continued problems with his knees and feet, 1948 was another good year for DiMaggio. He made it to the All-Star team for the tenth time, and led the American League in home runs and RBIs. Yet on the field, DiMaggio continued to struggle with injury, and the Yankees failed to make an appearance at the World Series.

Still, there were several career highlights for DiMaggio during this season, including his three hundredth career home-run hit in September, and three home runs in the season opener against the Cleveland Indians (the second such game in his career). In April, DiMaggio received the Landis Memorial Trophy. On June 13, Babe Ruth appeared at Yankee Stadium for his uniform and number-retirement ceremony while the current Yankee team and 49,641 fans looked on.

By mid-July, DiMaggio's trouble with his legs and feet were becoming more apparent. The pain in his heel was constant, making him even more guarded and reticient than ever. He had been playing baseball for seventeen years, and was thirty-four years old. Still, he missed only one game during the season. Joe Trimble of the New York *Daily News* suggested that if DiMaggio wanted to continue to play, he'd need to make the transition to first base, where speed and agility were not as important. Yet in August, after Babe Ruth's death, the *Daily News* called DiMaggio "... the spark and spirit of the Yankees ..."

The summer of 1948 was also a sad time, as baseball legend Babe Ruth succumbed to a two-year battle with cancer on August 16. Ruth's body lay in state at Yankee Stadium, "the House That Ruth Built" for two days while more than 100,000 people paid their respects. He was then taken to New York City's St. Patrick's Cathedral, which was packed with 6,000 mourners while 80,000 people stood outside the church. DiMaggio was one of the honorary pallbearers at the funeral, the only active player to take part in the services.

Immediately after Babe Ruth's funeral, DiMaggio flew to where the Yankees were playing, and losing, against the Washington Senators. In his first at bat during the fourth inning, he singled to start a six-run rally that helped the Yankees win the game 8–1 and sweep the three-game series.

In mid-September, a single game separated the Boston Red Sox, the Cleveland Indians, and the Yankees, all contending for a spot in the World Series. Playing in severe pain, DiMaggio helped split a doubleheader in St. Louis by hitting his thirty-seventh and thirty-eighth home runs of the season. The next day, virtually hobbling on one leg, DiMaggio hit his thirty-ninth home run. In Boston, during the last game of the season, DiMaggio made four straight hits before he was taken out, and the Boston fans gave him a standing ovation.

In October, the Yankees fired Bucky Harris, and Casey Stengel was named as the new general manager of the team, even though the Yankees posted a season of ninety-four wins and sixty losses. Yet by the end of the season, it was obvious that DiMaggio had been playing in a great deal of pain, when the Yankees were taken out of the quest for the World Series on the next-to-last day of the season. That year it was the Cleveland Indians who defeated the Boston Braves four games to two.

DiMaggio posted excellent statistics in 1948, including: 153 games played, 594 at bats, 110 runs, 190 hits, 26 doubles, 11 triples, 39 home runs, 155 RBIs, 67 bases on balls, and 1 stolen base with a season average of .320 and a slugging average of .598.

1949

Despite seventy-one team injuries during the season, in 1949 the Yankees still managed to win the pennant, and defeat the Brooklyn Dodgers in the fifth game of the World Series 10–6 to clinch the championship. DiMaggio appeared in only 76 of the 154 game schedule, still hampered by various injuries and ill-nesses, including the continuing problems with his heel, which had been operated on to remove the troublesome bone spurs last season.

Spring training was harder than ever on DiMaggio, and it was soon apparent that he wasn't going to start this season as well. Not being in the lineup bothered DiMaggio, as evidenced by his short temper with the constant swarm of reporters that dogged his every move, whether it was at spring training camp, the hospital, or back in Yankee Stadium. For several weeks after spring training, DiMaggio sequestered himself in his hotel room, wondering if his career was over.

The challenges of the 1949 season were intensified by the death of DiMaggio's father in May, just one month after he had passed the test for U.S. naturalization.

For the Yankees, not having DiMaggio on the field was like letting loose a dozen black cats on Friday the thirteenth. The backbone of the hitting crew, including Tommy Henrich, Yogi Berra, and Charlie Keller, were all out with various ailments. Seven different men played first base during the first sixty-five games of the 1949 season. Even trainer August Mauch broke two ribs in a bizarre accident when he walked into a parking meter. The Yankees' hopes of winning the pennant, much less the World Series, appeared to be dashed.

Then, on one magical June morning, DiMaggio got out of bed, stood on his feet, and felt no pain. The bothersome right heel was pain-free, and DiMaggio wasted no time getting back in the game.

In his first game of the season, on June 28, DiMaggio hit both a home run and a single to lead the Yankees to a 5–4 win against the Red Sox. A crowd of 36,228 gave him an ovation the first time he came to the plate. He hit his home run in the third inning, driving in a run, and essentially won the game. During the three-game sweep, DiMaggio hit a total of four home runs and drove in nine runs. One month later, he appeared on the cover of *Life* magazine with the title "It's great to be back" below his picture.

During the 1949 season, DiMaggio was named to his eleventh All-Star game, but as manager Lou Boudreau's special selection, rather than by fan ballot. Health problems, including a viral infection in September, kept him in and out of the lineup from day to day.

Manager Casey Stengel juggled players throughout the season

and somehow achieved the impossible. By clutch-hitting and with Mauch's magic in the training room, the Yankees turned the second half of their season around and were tied with the Boston Red Sox with a week left. The showdown for the lead, which Boston won 7–6 on a controversial slide into home by Johnny Pesky, was played out before 66,156 fans in Yankee Stadium. Four days later, the Yankees and Red Sox met again in New York City for a two-game series that would decide the fate of the American League leaders.

The first game started badly for the Yankees, with pitcher Allie Reynolds giving up four runs in the first three innings. But the Bombers kept clawing their way back from the deficits, with Johnny Page cracking an eighth-inning home run to give the Yankees a 5–4 lead. Relief pitcher Joe Page, while trying to stave off the Red Sox hitters, looked out at center field and the weary figure standing there and thought, *If he can play the way he feels, I can pitch forever.* He did, and the Yankees won.

It all came down to one game, on Sunday, October 2, before 68,055 fans, the Yankees and the Red Sox, DiMaggio against his brother Dom, fought with bat and glove to clinch the pennant.

It was 1–0 Yankees until the bottom of the eighth, when the Yankees scored four more to seemingly wrap up the game. But in the top of the ninth the Red Sox answered the challenge with three runs of their own, including a Bobby Doerr triple, which DiMaggio had to chase down, allowing two of those runs to score. DiMaggio called for a time-out, then took himself off the field, knowing he had given the game everything he had. The Yankees held on to their lead and won, 5–3.

The Yankees met the Brooklyn Dodgers in the 1949 World Series, and swept them four games to one. The first two games were a duel of pitchers, and the Yankees and Dodgers each took one with identical scores of 1–0. In the third game, the Yankees and Dodgers scored all but two of their runs in the ninth inning as the Yankees won 4–3. The fourth game saw the Yankees leap out to a six-run lead in the first five innings, then let the Dodgers score four runs and almost take the game, only to be stopped by pitcher Allie Reynolds, who finished the game by striking out four of the last seven batters he faced. DiMaggio hit a home run in the fifth and deciding game and the Yankees won 10–6. As the Dodgers lost to the Yankees in the final game of the Series, they tried a total of six pitchers, setting a record for the most ever used in a single World Series game.

In October 1949, New York City Mayor William O'Dwyer and thousands of baseball fans honored DiMaggio during Joe DiMaggio Day. He received more than sixty gifts, including a Cadillac sedan from the people of New York City, a four-year scholarship for a boy of DiMaggio's choice to a New York City college or university, a speedboat from the fans of New Haven, and $7,500 cash, all of which was donated to various heart and cancer funds in his name. Among the strangest gifts sent was three hundred gallons of ice cream. It was during this event that DiMaggio said his famous quote, "I thank the good Lord that He made me a Yankee."

The Associated Press' annual year-end poll voted Joe DiMaggio as the greatest comeback for 1949, beating the Yankee team as a whole by one vote. During the same poll, Yankee Manager Casey Stengel received six votes, tying in third place with the LSU football team.

Statistics for 1949 include appearances in 76 games, with 272 at bats, 58 runs, 94 hits, 14 doubles, 6 triples, 14 home runs, 67 RBIs, 55 bases on balls, no stolen bases, a .346 batting average, and a .596 slugging average, which led the American League for the season.

1950

In 1950, DiMaggio signed with the Yankees for $100,000— baseball's highest salary figure. He started the season by telling reporters that he felt better than he had at any time since World War II. DiMaggio also said he wanted to play throughout the season and on at least two more championship teams before retiring.

At the beginning of the season, the Yankees' office sent a questionnaire asking players who their baseball model was and which player they most admired. More than half responded Joe DiMaggio. Tommy Henrich replied, "He does everything better than anybody else." "He puts his heart into every inning more than any other player I've ever seen," said Billy Johnson. "He is grace, strength, power, all of it effortless," said Jerry Coleman. Such was the devotion among DiMaggio teammates to the Yankee Clipper.

DiMaggio's performance at the beginning of the season, however, betrayed his body's true condition; thirteen at bats without a hit, ten games without an extra base hit, a .243 batting average, and a strained muscle in his back.

On June 21, against the Indians, DiMaggio hit his two thousandth ball in an 8–2 victory that drove home the seventh Yankee run of the game. He gave the ball to his son, Joe, Jr., as a souvenir. By July, DiMaggio was playing first base, and looking good in that position. In a game with the Washington Senators, he fielded the ball thirteen times without an error (eleven throws and two grounders). He did not, however, stay in that position long, returning to his customary spot in center field the next day. Unfortunately, in July, DiMaggio was unable to play in the All-Star game due to a groin injury.

In August, DiMaggio was once again in a hitting slump (his worst ever), and Casey Stengel was forced to put him on the bench. During May DiMaggio's average had been .220, in June it was .253, but by August, he had made only four hits in thirty-eight times at bat—a dismal average of .103. By September, however, DiMaggio was hitting homers again. In a game at Washington's Griffith Stadium against the Senators, he hit three home runs in a single game—the first player ever to do so. All three home runs cleared the left-field bleachers, more than 405 feet from home plate.

DiMaggio finished September the same way he'd begun it. From August 18 to September 30, he batted an average of .376, hitting safely in nineteen straight games. It was also during the 1950 season that the seeming imbalance in baseball salaries began to be noticed by the press. A comparison was drawn between Jackie Robinson, who signed for $35,000 for 1950, and DiMaggio, who signed for $100,000. In a late January news article, the assertion was made that Robinson was the best hitter in his league and the best base-stealer, as well as being a large box-office draw and having the ability to play every day. Conversely, DiMaggio was frequently injured and unable to play, yet drew a larger salary. This may have been the beginning of the salary wars that continue to this day in professional baseball.

The Yankees returned to the World Series against the Philadelphia Athletics in October. While DiMaggio was certainly not playing as he had in previous Series, he nevertheless made an impact. During Game 2, he hit a home run that won the game for the Yankees. The Yanks went on to win the Series, their thirteenth World Series championship, in a four-game sweep. DiMaggio batted .308, the highest average of the team, and the Yankees' pitching squad (Reynolds, Raschi, Ford, Lopat, and Ferrick) combined for an amazing earned run average of 0.73.

DiMaggio's statistics for 1950 were: 139 games, 525 at bats, 114 runs, 158 hits, 33 doubles, 10 triples, 32 home runs, 122 RBIs, 80 bases on balls, 0 stolen bases, for a batting average of .301, and a slugging average of .585.

1951

Even at the beginning of the 1951 season, people knew that Joe DiMaggio was considering retirement at the end of the year.

Though he initially indicated he would wait until the end of the season to announce his decision, in late March DiMaggio announced that 1951 would be his last season. His primary concern was to "quit while I'm on top." The saying "as DiMaggio goes, so go the Yankees"—a rallying cry that had followed DiMaggio since his early days with the team—continued to be true even in his last season.

In the season opener, DiMaggio hit two home runs, and batted in five runs. The next day, he made a horrendous error in miscounting the outs in a game against Detroit. With George Kell at second, DiMaggio went back for a long fly ball hit by Steve Souchock. After catching it, he started to trot to the infield, thinking he'd caught the third out. By the time he realized his mistake, Kell had scored, and Detroit was leading 4–2. The Yankees came back, and DiMaggio himself singled in the ninth to drive the winning run home, but it was obvious that his era was coming to an end.

In July, during a game against the Red Sox at Fenway Park, DiMaggio, Phil Rizzuto, Gerry Coleman, and Allie Reynolds were benched (DiMaggio in the second inning). The Yankees lost the game in a 10–4 rout that cost them possession of first place. It was also in July that he was selected for the thirteenth time to the All-Star team, again he was unable to play due to an injury—a torn muscle in the back of his left leg.

Prior to the World Series, a scouting report of the New York Yankees was written by Andy High for the Dodgers and turned over to the New York Giants. Published in *Life* magazine twelve days after the Series ended, it became one of the most famous scouting reports ever. In a scathing report on DiMaggio, High said, "He can't stop quickly and throw hard . . . You can take the extra base on him . . . He can't run and won't bunt . . . His reflexes are very slow and he can't pull a good fastball at all." Many sportswriters and players, as well as DiMaggio and his teammates, were angered by the report, though DiMaggio later said it had little to do with his decision to make 1951 his last season.

The New York Giants, who had climbed from nearly total oblivion to the championship series, made it to the 1951 World Series via an amazing run of thirty-seven wins in forty-four games. During the pennant race, they faced the Dodgers in a best-of-three-game playoff. After splitting the first two games, the "shot heard round the world"—a two-out, three-run home run by Bobby Thomson off Ralph Branca—secured the pennant for the Giants.

The Yankees managed to return to the World Series, beating their crosstown rival, the Giants, in six games, including the fifth game, in which the Giants took a 13–1 beating, the worst loss in a World Series game in fifteen years. After starting slow with no hits in the first three games of the Series, DiMaggio came to life in the fourth game, hitting a single in the third inning, and following it with a two-run homer into the left-field stands. In the fifth game of the Series, he hit two singles, drew an intentional walk, and a two-run double. In the sixth and final game, the Giants' pitcher intentionally walked him twice. Finally, during his last time at bat, his one hundred ninety-ninth appearance at the plate in fifty-one World Series games, DiMaggio hit a double, but was tagged out while trying to reach third on a bunt by the next batter. As he jogged to the dugout, the crowd gave him a five-minute standing ovation.

Joe DiMaggio's final statistics for 1951 were: 116 games played, 415 at bats, 72 runs, 109 hits, 22 doubles, 4 triples, 12 home runs, 71 runs batted in, 61 bases on balls, no stolen bases, for a batting average of .263, and a slugging average of .422.

For his career, Joe DiMaggio compiled the following regular season statistics: 1,736 games, 6,821 at bats, 2,214 hits, 389 doubles, 131 triples, 361 home runs (a 5.3 percent), 1,390 runs, 1,537 RBIs, 790 bases on balls, 369 stolen bases, with a batting average of .325, and a slugging average of .579.

John Helfers is a writer and editor currently living in Green Bay, Wisconsin. A graduate of the University of Wisconsin–Green Bay, his fiction appears in more than a dozen anthologies, including Future Net, Once Upon a Crime, *and* The UFO Files, *among others. His first anthology project,* Black Cats and Broken Mirrors, *was published by DAW Books in 1998. Future projects include more edited fiction anthologies as well as a novel in progress.*

Russell Davis currently resides in Green Bay, Wisconsin, with his very patient wife, Monica, and his beautiful daughter, Morgan Storm. He holds a B.A. in English from the University of Wisconsin, and writes nonfiction, fiction, and poetry. His current projects include a book-length manuscript of poems entitled In the Absence of Language *and several novel projects that may never see the light of day.*

DiMaggio's Ten Greatest Games

PHIL MINTZ

*J*OE DiMAGGIO PLAYED in 1,736 regular season games over thirteen years, each one adding to his reputation as the consummate ballplayer. His spread stance and quick swing, his daring base running, and his loping stride as he patrolled center field thrilled fans in Yankee Stadium and ballparks throughout the American League.

There were the frequent days that his name filled the headlines of the newspapers, and the rare days that opposing pitchers had the good fortune to get him out. There were the days that he won the game with his bat, others with his skill and speed, and still others by just being Joe DiMaggio.

Still, for the slugger known as Joltin' Joe, there are games that stand out in the DiMaggio legend, games that will be talked about for as long as baseball fans talk about Joe DiMaggio. Here are ten of DiMaggio's greatest games:

May 3, 1936: DiMaggio's Major League Debut

Joe DiMaggio, tagged as the "Boy Wonder" and the star who was to fill Babe Ruth's ample shoes, was expected to start the 1936 season in left field for the Yankees, but a burned foot resulting from a spring training accident with a diathermic heat lamp kept the celebrated rookie out of the lineup for the first seventeen games of the campaign.

Not that the Yankees missed him much, winning 11 of those contests and sitting just a hair behind the Boston Red Sox in the early season standings. So it wasn't until the first Sunday in May, with the last-place St. Louis Browns as the opponent, that manager Joe McCarthy put DiMaggio's name on the lineup card, batting third behind Frank Crosetti and Red Rolfe and ahead of Lou Gehrig. About 25,000 fans showed up at Yankee Stadium, many of them drawn by DiMaggio's debut. On the mound for the Browns was Jack Knott, a rangy right-hander, while the Yankees sent out Lefty Gomez.

Crosetti opened the bottom of the first with a triple, and Rolfe walked, setting the stage for the first plate appearance by the twenty-one-year-old DiMaggio, who was wearing No. 9 on his back, not the familiar No. 5 that clubhouse keeper Pete Sheehy bestowed on him in 1937. DiMaggio grounded back to Knott, but the pitcher, flummoxed by Crosetti's break from third, threw the ball away, allowing Crosetti to score. DiMaggio crossed the plate after Gehrig walked and Ben Chapman doubled. Knott, who gave up four runs, got only one out before being replaced by Earl Caldwell, who shut down the Yankees—but only temporarily.

In the second inning, DiMaggio came up again and sent a fly ball to center field that dropped in for a hit—the first of 2,214 that he would collect in his career. "Some of the experts were disposed to castigate Roy Pepper for lazy work on that hit, but as a matter of fact, [DiMaggio] hit a sinker, which the outfielder could not judge,'' sportswriter Dan Daniel, DiMaggio's biggest booster in the press, opined in *The New York World-Telegram*. DiMaggio scored on Bill Dickey's fly to center field—one of three runs the Yankees added in the second inning.

In the fourth, DiMaggio struck out, but in the sixth, facing left-hander Elon Hogsett, he lashed a triple to deep center field. ''Giuseppe raced as fast as he could. But it was seen that he was dragging his left foot a bit,'' Daniel gushed in his game report. ''When Joe recovers fully from the injury, he will turn such drives into home runs.'' DiMaggio scored again—one of four runs the Yankees posted in the sixth—on a single. A fifteen-minute rain delay threatened to wash out the triple, but the rain let up and the game went on.

The Browns, meanwhile, gathered five runs off Gomez, who was knocked out in the fifth. But reliever Johnny Murphy held the Browns at bay for the rest of the afternoon.

But the day's main event continued to be the Yankee rookie. In the seventh, he popped out to second baseman Tommy Carey. But he added another single in the eighth off Russ Van Atta to finish the day 3-for-6 as the Yankees beat the Browns 14–5. And although Chapman had batted 4-for-4, with two triples, a double, and a single, it was DiMaggio's name that filled the headlines in the New York papers the next day.

''Joe DiMaggio is our regular left fielder for now on, and will be in there every day,'' manager Joe McCarthy pronounced after the game.

A week later, DiMaggio smacked his first home run off George Turbeville of the Philadelphia Athletics, at Yankee Stadium. In June, after the Yankees traded Chapman, DiMaggio moved to center field. He went on to hit twenty-nine home runs in his rookie season, and he batted .323 with 206 hits and 125 RBIs. The Yankees, meanwhile, took the American League pennant with a record of 102–51, leading the league by nineteen and a half games.

In the World Series, DiMaggio rapped out another nine hits

as the Yankees defeated their cross-river rivals, the Giants, four games to two. In the seven seasons before DiMaggio was to leave for the U.S. Army Air Force, the Yankees would win six pennants and five World Series.

June 13, 1937: DiMaggio's First Three-Home-Run Game

DiMaggio, who earned $8,500 in his standout rookie season, spurned the Yankees' offer of a $1,000 raise the next year, and fired back his own demand—$17,500 for the season. The stand-off continued until March 12, when DiMaggio accepted a revised offer of $15,000 from Yankee owner Jacob Ruppert. The next month, DiMaggio had his tonsils and adenoids removed, in an effort to cure a problem with his right shoulder. For the second straight season he didn't make his first start until early May.

The slow start didn't hurt DiMaggio, however, particularly on June 13, when the Yankees squared off against the Browns in St Louis' Sportsman's Park for a Sunday doubleheader. In the opener, he produced only one single as the Yankees came back from a 9-to-7 deficit by scoring two in the eighth and seven in the ninth to trample the Browns 16–9. Still, the hit was good enough to give DiMaggio a fourteen-game hitting streak.

But DiMaggio, who had already hit eleven homers in his injury-shortened season, really got going in the second game, clouting home runs in three successive times at bat off St. Louis pitcher Julio Bonetti.

The Browns struck first, getting three runs off Yankee starter Bump Hadley in the bottom of the fourth. In the fifth, the Yankees got that back and more, as the Yankees scored six runs— three of them on DiMaggio's first home run of the game. But the Browns scored five in the bottom of the inning, chasing Hadley and roughing up reliever Pat Malone.

So it was up to DiMaggio to even the score. In the seventh, he launched a solo shot, bringing the Yankees to within one run of the Browns. With two out in the ninth, he hit his third, also with the bases empty, knotting the score at eight runs apiece. DiMaggio had one more chance in the eleventh, coming up with one man on and one out. But he hit into a double play.

The game, played before lights were installed in the St. Louis stadium, was called following the eleventh inning because it was getting dark and both teams needed to make trains. Although the game was a tie, the home runs counted, and added to DiMaggio's season-end total of forty-six, the most he ever hit in a single campaign, and still the most ever by a Yankee right-handed hitter.

On that day, the Yankees scored twenty-four runs, made thirty-one hits, including five home runs, three triples, and five doubles. But they still lost ground to the Chicago White Sox, and, heading back to Yankee Stadium, held only a half-game lead in the standings.

July 9, 1937: DiMaggio Hits for the Cycle

It was a steamy ninety-five degrees in New York, and only about 5,625 fans showed up at Yankee Stadium on a Friday afternoon to watch the Yankees post their second sixteen-run game of the season, as they trampled the Senators 16–2, paced by a 5-for-5 day from DiMaggio. DiMaggio hit for the cycle, and added a second home run for good measure, knocking in a total of seven runs in the process.

The homers were numbers twenty-one and twenty-two for the season, and prompted speculation that DiMaggio might make a run at Babe Ruth's home-run record.

The Yankees backed complete-game pitcher Monte Pearson with seventeen hits, shelling left-hander Carl Fischer and his replacement, Ed Linke. Lou Gehrig had his fourteenth home run in the game, and even Pearson got three hits, including a double, knocking in two RBIs. The victory gave the Yanks, who went on to win the pennant and the World Series, a five and a half game lead over the Tigers.

DiMaggio began his rampage in the first, with the Yankees trailing 1–0. He homered into the left-field stands with two outs and the bases empty, tying the score at one apiece. In the third, Pearson singled, Red Rolfe tripled, DiMaggio tripled to left-center, and Gehrig singled, resulting in four runs for the home team. In the fourth, when the Yankees scored four more runs, DiMaggio drew an intentional pass. The Yankees added one in the fifth and two in the sixth, when DiMaggio and Gehrig homered in succession. In the seventh, DiMaggio beat out an infield hit, and he completed the cycle in the eighth with a double to left.

For many in the sparse crowd, however, the highlight of the contest was a short-lived free-for-all between the two teams sparked by a fistfight between Yankee left fielder Jake Powell and Joe Kuhel, the Washington first baseman. A week earlier, in Washington, Powell had barged into Kuhel on a play at first base, leading to a shower of soda bottles from the stands. Now, Kuhel, after retiring Powell on a ground ball, tagged the Yankee as he sped over the bag. There were words, a slight push, and a quick right-hand punch that missed the Washington player by a foot. A brief brawl followed, ending with the umpires tossing both Kuhel and Powell out of the game.

June 29, 1941: DiMaggio Breaks George Sisler's Hitting Streak Record

It's known simply as The Streak. By the time it was over, DiMaggio had hit safely in fifty-six consecutive games, a record that may never be seriously challenged.

On this sweltering day in Washington's Griffith Stadium, DiMaggio's attention was focused on a doubleheader. A hit in the first game would tie him with George Sisler's 1922 record streak of hits in 41 straight games. A hit in the second game would give DiMaggio the record all to himself.

In 1941, DiMaggio had once again started the season in a contract squabble. He reported two weeks late for spring training after Yankee general manager Ed Barrow trimmed his contract by $2,500. DiMaggio got the team to increase his pay to $37,500. By mid-May, however, DiMaggio had been in a three-week batting slump. The Yankees were also in a funk and five and a half games out of first place. On May 15, DiMaggio singled to center off Chicago White Sox left-hander Edgar Smith to begin the streak. Day after day, the hits kept coming. By June 17, he had hit in thirty consecutive games, and The Streak had become a national obsession.

The stress on DiMaggio grew as he approached Sisler's mark. He drew within one of the record on June 28 with two hits against the Athletics in Philadelphia's Shibe Park. The next day, an eager crowd of 31,000 packed into steaming Griffith Stadium to see if DiMaggio could surpass Sisler.

In the first game, Red Ruffing took the mound for the Yankees. The Senators sent out knuckleballer Dutch Leonard. Leonard got DiMaggio to line to center in the second inning and pop out to George Archie in the fourth. But in the sixth, with the Yankees ahead 3–0, Leonard threw a low fastball to DiMaggio, who knocked the ball into left center, rolling to the 422-foot sign on the bleacher wall. DiMaggio streaked to second with a double. Sisler's streak was tied.

Between games, DiMaggio told reporters that he was jubilant but embarrassed over all the commotion. "Sure, I'm tickled. Who wouldn't be?" he said as he changed uniforms. "It's a great thing I've realized an ambition." But DiMaggio also thanked his manager, Joe McCarthy, who gave him the green light to go after pitches with three balls and no strikes. "It brought me many a good ball to swing at," DiMaggio said. "You know, he's got to give you the signal on '3 and 0' pitches and he was right with me all the time."

When DiMaggio returned to the field to go after the record, there was a problem. Between games, a fan had reached into the bat rack in the Yankee dugout and had taken his favorite bat.

Years later, Tommy Henrich still recalled the incident. "He said, 'Tom, what the heck is this? You got my bat?' " Henrich replied that he had some other bats that DiMaggio had used, but not the "lucky" one. And he offered to let DiMaggio use his. "I said, 'Joe look at my bat.' He picked it up and said, 'Yeah, that feels pretty good.' "

With the borrowed bat, DiMaggio went hitless for his first three at bats in the second game. Facing Sid Hudson, he lined to right field in the first, and hit another shot on the nose in the third, but straight at shortstop Cecil Travis. In the fifth, he came up against reliever Arnold "Red" Anderson, a big right-hander, and lofted a fly to Doc Cramer in center field. Then in the seventh, Anderson almost knocked DiMaggio down with his first pitch, a high fastball. The second was another fastball, waist high and over the middle of the plate. DiMaggio smacked a clean single to left field, with the newsreel cameras whirling and the fans roaring their approval. He came in to score on Charlie Keller's triple.

Almost incidental in the hoopla over DiMaggio's feat was the fact that the Yankees swept the Senators by scores of 9–4 and 7–5, giving them a game and half lead over the second-place Cleveland Indians. For DiMaggio, the next goal was Willie Keeler's all-time hitting streak mark of forty-four consecutive games

June 3, 1947: Four Hits Against the Tigers

DiMaggio spent the 1943, 1944, and 1945 seasons in the U.S. Army Air Force. He returned to the Yankees in 1946, but that season was disappointing. DiMaggio hit only .290, his lowest to date, with 25 homers and 95 RBIs. The 1946 season was also a bust for the Yankees, who ended the season third, seventeen games behind the pennant-winning Red Sox.

The next season, 1947, started out inauspiciously as well. In January, DiMaggio underwent surgery at Beth David Hospital to have a bone spur removed from his left heel. When the season began, the Yankees were slumping, and slipped into sixth place. In May, DiMaggio was fined for the first time—$100—for allegedly leading a "revolt" by failing to pose for an Army Signal Corps newsreel. DiMaggio complained that he needed the time for batting practice.

But, as New York *Daily News* sportswriter Joe Trimble wrote that year about DiMaggio, as DiMaggio goes, so goes the Yankees. When DiMaggio began a hitting tear, the Yankees began to pull closer to the first-place Tigers.

They were three games out of first place when they took the field on June 3 at Briggs Stadium in Detroit. DiMaggio whacked three singles and a double in the 3–0 victory, as the Yankee pitcher, Frank Shea, held Detroit to five hits.

The Yankees got their first run in the opening frame when an error by Detroit shortstop Eddie Lake on a grounder by Snuffy Stirnweiss got Detroit left-hander Hal Newhouser in trouble. With one out, Newhouser walked Charlie Keller. DiMaggio then smacked a solid single to left, scoring Stirnweiss.

In the third, DiMaggio singled to left, and took second as left-fielder Dick Wakefield fumbled the ball. Newhouser walked George McQuinn and DiMaggio scored the Yankees' second run on Bill Johnson's single. DiMaggio doubled with two out in the fifth, but ended up stranded. DiMaggio's single in the seventh was also wasted.

Only in the ninth was DiMaggio stopped, when reliever Hal White got him to hit into a double play. Still, DiMaggio's outburst gave him a sixteen-game hitting streak.

October 4, 1947: Home Run Wins Fifth Game of World Series

With DiMaggio continuing to hit, the Yankees overtook the Tigers and won the pennant by twelve games. The World Series, the first ever to be televised, was another crosstown contest with the Brooklyn Dodgers.

Games 1 and 2 of the series went to the Yankees in the Bronx. The Dodgers came back and won the next two games at Ebbets Field.

Game 5, also in Brooklyn, pitted Yankee hurler Spec Shea against Brooklyn's surprise starter, Rex Barney. Barney proceeded to walk the first batter, Snuffy Stirnweiss, on five pitches and, after two strikes and a ball, gave up a double to Tommy Henrich. Johnny Lindell walked, filling the bases, setting the stage for DiMaggio, who struck out swinging. A force-out on Stirnweiss and a Billy Johnson strikeout ended the inning.

In the third inning, Stirnweiss flied to center-fielder Carl Furillo for the first out. Then Henrich and Lindell walked, bringing DiMaggio up again. With the count three and one, DiMaggio banged a grounder to Pee Wee Reese, who turned a double play.

The Yankees got a run in the fourth, knocked in by Shea's single to left. In the fifth, a frustrated DiMaggio came to the plate again, this time with the bases empty. He looked at one ball, then another. He fouled a pitch in back of the plate. The next pitch was a fastball. He launched it into the third row of the upper-left-field deck, about 400 feet from home plate. It was his fifth home run in the series.

"It was high and inside and right where I could lose it. Into the upper tier too," DiMaggio said after the game. "Well, I like 'em better that way. Don't like to have any doubt about it."

The Dodgers attempted to come back in the sixth. Al Gionfriddo, who was to rob DiMaggio of a possible Series-winning home run in Game 6, batted for Joe Hatten, who had relieved Barney in the fifth. Gionfriddo walked. Eddie Stanky fanned.

Reese walked. Working the count to two and two, Jackie Robinson knocked a single over Shea's head to center field, scoring Gionfriddo with the first Dodger run.

The Dodgers got the tying run on second base in the bottom of the ninth, but the Yankees came away with a 2–1 victory after Shea fanned pinch-hitter Cookie Lavagetto on a 3–2 count.

The next day, Brooklyn took Game 6 at Yankee Stadium in a game famous not for a DiMaggio feat, but frustration. In the sixth inning, with the Yankees trailing 8–5, DiMaggio came up with two men on and two men out. He hit a long drive that Gionfriddo grabbed by the 415-foot sign, saving the game for the Dodgers, who went on to win 8–6. DiMaggio, in his disappointment, kicked the dirt between first and second base. It was, DiMaggio's teammates said, one of the few times he ever showed emotion during the game.

The Brooklyn euphoria was short-lived, however. The following day the Yankees took Game 7 of the series, 5–2.

May 23, 1948: DiMaggio vs. Feller

Cleveland Indians pitching ace Bob "Rapid Robert" Feller and DiMaggio both came up as rookies in 1936, and anytime they squared off against each other it was an eagerly anticipated baseball event.

"Joe was the toughest right-handed batter I ever faced," Feller told sportswriter Maury Allen years later. "I really did enjoy the confrontations with him. He hit me good, sure, but I got him plenty of times, too. That's the way it worked."

It was no different on this day in 1948, when 78,431 fans, at the time the second-largest crowd to see a baseball game, packed Cleveland's Municipal Stadium for a doubleheader and saw DiMaggio hit three home runs against the Indians in three successive at bats.

Feller got the Yankees in order in the first.

Allie Reynolds—nicknamed "The Chief" because of his part-Indian blood—took the mound for the Yanks and immediately was nicked for four runs: Thurman Tucker beat out a slow roller to Billy Johnson at third and went to second on Johnson's throwing error. Larry Doby struck out, and the Indians' player-manager, Lou Boudreau, grounded to Bobby Brown at shortstop. But after Eddie Robinson walked, Joe Gordon singled, driving in the Indians' first run. Ken Keltner—the third baseman whose spectacular fielding plays stopped DiMaggio's fifty-six-game hitting streak in 1941—then blasted his thirteenth home run of the season, making it a 4–0 game.

It stayed that way until the top of the fourth. Tommy Henrich walked, and DiMaggio, who had singled in the second, took a high inside pitch and drove it 350 feet into the stands. The game was now 4–2.

Henrich walked again in the Yankee sixth, followed by a Charlie Keller single to right center. DiMaggio then slammed a ball over the fence in left-center field. The three-run shot made the score 5–4 Yankees.

Feller was lifted for a pinch-hitter in the seventh, and Bob Muncrief took the mound for Cleveland in the top of the eighth. He became DiMaggio's next victim, as the Yankee slugger launched a solo shot to left.

Meanwhile, Reynolds, who gave up just two hits after the Cleveland first, began to falter. In the bottom of the ninth, he walked Dale Mitchell. Boudreau sent Hal Peck to hit for catcher Jim Hegan. With a 2–0 count, Yankee manager Bucky Harris decided to bring in lefty Joe Page. Peck greeted Page with a single to left. Joe Tipton, batting for Muncrief, sacrificed, and the tying run was on second. Boudreau sent right-hander Allie Clark, a Yankee cast-off, to pinch-hit for Thurman Tucker. Page pitched carefully to Clark, and walked him. Up came Pat Seerey, hitting for Larry Doby. Page struck him out. Boudreau was next, and he walked, forcing in Mitchell and sending the huge crowd into a frenzy. The score was 6–5 and Eddie Robinson was at the plate.

"Page looked around at his outfield," James P. Dawson wrote in the next day's *New York Times*. "He gave his infield a cursory glance. He looked over at the Yankee bench. He fanned Robinson." Game over.

DiMaggio had apparently shot his wad in the first game. DiMaggio went hitless in the second game, which Cleveland won 5–1 behind the pitching of Don Black and Russ Christopher.

More than three decades later, writer Christopher Lehmann-Haupt ran into a story about the three-homer game. The tale, transmitted to Lehmann-Haupt secondhand, was that DiMaggio, seeking a good time on a Saturday night, spent the night before the game drinking and gambling at a mob-run nightclub—drinking so much, in fact, that the Yankee center fielder was poured into his bed at the Hotel Cleveland sometime around dawn on the day of the game. According to the story, the mobster who brought DiMaggio back to his hotel was so convinced that DiMaggio couldn't play that day, he called his bookie and bet heavily on the Indians.

Lehmann-Haupt began checking into the story, which even drew the attention of baseball commissioner Bowie Kuhn. Ultimately, he confronted DiMaggio himself with what he heard. DiMaggio, whose memory of the events was uncertain, agreed that he had on occasion visited the nightclub, and maybe even missed curfew, but insisted he never drank heavily enough that it would impair his ability to play the game.

"I wasn't the kind of guy that was going to go out and raise a lot of hell if I had known I was gonna play a doubleheader the next day," DiMaggio told Lehmann-Haupt. "I never raised a hell of a lot of hell. I mean, we had rules on our ballclub and we had a manager that was pretty strict in those days. Twelve o'clock was 'all in.' I mean we had to be in. Sorry to throw a hole in your story."

June 28, 1949: DiMaggio Returns from a Bum Heel

DiMaggio played in 1948 with an extremely painful bone spur in his right heel. A month after the season ended, he had surgery to rectify the problem, and the Yankees signed their thirty-four-year-old star to a 1949 contract worth between $90,000 and $100,000, making him, at the time, the highest-paid ballplayer ever. But by spring training, the heel injury flared up again, and DiMaggio played only forty-three innings during the exhibition season for the Yankees' new manager, Casey Stengel.

Once again, the Yankees started their season without Di-Maggio in the lineup. He missed the first sixty-five days of the season, and there was concern that DiMaggio was washed up as a baseball player. While the Yankees went about their business, DiMaggio worked out, tried special shoes, and waited for the heel to get better. Finally, one morning in June, he woke up in his hotel room without pain. On June 27, with the Yankees scheduled to play the Mayor's Trophy exhibition game against the Giants, he went to Stengel and said he'd like to play. Stengel put him in the lineup.

The next day, the Yankees left for Boston and a three-game series with the Red Sox. DiMaggio stayed behind, ate lunch in Manhattan, then caught a 3:15 P.M. plane to Boston. He got to Fenway Park two hours later, and began dressing for that night's game.

At Fenway, 36,228 fans packed the stadium. Later, it was estimated that 100,000 would have come if the stadium could hold them. On the mound for the Red Sox was Maurice "Mickey" McDermott, a twenty-year-old, hard-throwing left-hander recently called up from Louisville. Leading off the second inning, DiMaggio singled to left center. The next two Yankees struck out, but Johnny Lindell walked and Hank Bauer homered, giving the Yankees a 3–0 lead

In the third, with Phil Rizzuto on base, DiMaggio slammed

an authoritative home run into the screen above Fenway's high left-field wall. It was 5–0 Yanks.

The Red Sox began nibbling their way back against Yankee pitcher Allie Reynolds. They got two in the fourth and tacked on another in the eighth. Matt Batts led off the Boston ninth with a triple. Pinch-hitter Birdie Tebbets singled, scoring Batts and making it a one-run game. Lou Stringer ran for Tebbets as Joe Page came in to relieve Reynolds.

Dom DiMaggio sacrificed Stringer to second, and Stringer moved to third on Johnny Pesky's ground out. It was up to the Red Sox slugging star, Ted Williams. Williams smacked the ball hard, 400 feet to deep center field. But DiMaggio made the catch look easy, and the Yankees held on for a 5–4 victory. "It was a tremendous night for the returning hero," Louis Effrat declared in *The Times* the next day.

But if that was a tremendous night, the next afternoon was just as exhilarating. DiMaggio smacked two more home runs, the first igniting the Yankee team when it was down 7–1, and the second providing the margin of victory as the Yankees won 9–7. And the next day, DiMaggio hit another home run, giving him four homers and nine RBIs for the series.

DiMaggio's comeback galvanized the nation, and the Yankee star soon made the cover of *Life* magazine. In September, DiMaggio fell victim to pneumonia, but was back in the lineup as the Yankees won the pennant by beating the Red Sox 5–3 on the last day of the season. In seventy-six games, DiMaggio batted .346, with fourteen home runs and sixty-seven RBIs.

As the *New York Herald Tribune*'s Rud Rennie wrote with serious understatement after that momentous first game back: "For a cripple who missed sixty-five games, Joltin' Joe did all right."

September 10, 1950: DiMaggio Hits Three Homers

Washington's Griffith Stadium measured 402 feet down the left-field line, and from the time it was remodeled in 1920, no ballplayer had hit three home runs in the roomy ballpark during a single game. That is, until the first game of a scheduled late-season doubleheader in 1950, when DiMaggio put three shots into the left-field bleachers, and added a walk and a double for a perfect afternoon in a game that was delayed twice by rain. It was the third time in DiMaggio's career that he hit three homers in a game.

The Sunday twin-bill opened with the Yankees trailing the first-place Detroit Tigers by a single game, and DiMaggio coming off a weak showing against the Boston Red Sox. Leading off the second inning, DiMaggio, batting cleanup, took a pitch from veteran side-armer Sid Hudson and rocked it into the bleachers for the Yankees' first run. The Yankees scored two more in the third, on two two-out singles by Johnny Hopp and Hank Bauer, followed by a walk and a throwing error by Hudson.

In the sixth, DiMaggio came up against Hudson, again with the bases empty, and the Yankee slugger sent his second home run of the day into the stands. In the bottom of the inning, the Senators scored a run off Yankee pitcher Vic Raschi, by way of two hits and a walk. But that was all they were to get.

Meanwhile, DiMaggio opened the eighth inning with a hot double down the left-field line, and he breezed home on Tommy Henrich's triple off the right-field wall.

The Yankees continued to pour it on in the ninth. Bauer knocked in Phil Rizzuto from second base with a single off reliever Mickey Harris. DiMaggio then made it 8–1 with his third home run. The round-trippers were numbers twenty-five, twenty-six, and twenty-seven of the season, and pushed DiMaggio's RBI count over 100 for the ninth and final time in his thirteen-year career. It was DiMaggio's final great season.

The scheduled second game of the Washington doubleheader was washed out by rain, so the victory, coupled with a Tiger split in Chicago, brought the Yankees within a half-game of the league lead. They finished the season with a three-game lead over the Tigers, setting them up for a World Series confrontation with the "Whiz Kids" of the Philadelphia Phillies.

October 5, 1950: DiMaggio Home Run Wins Game 2 of Series

Robin Roberts of the Philadelphia Phillies said it was a fastball. DiMaggio said it was a low, inside slider.

Whatever it was, DiMaggio, who had been held hitless until the tenth inning of Game 2 of the 1950 World Series, rocketed a 2–1 pitch from Roberts into the left-field upper deck at Shibe Park to give the Yankees a 2–1 victory and take a 2–0 lead over the Phillies, who were in their first World Series since 1915.

The Yankees had taken the first game of the series 1–0, behind a two-hit performance by Vic Raschi. The Yanks themselves managed only five hits off relief ace Jim Konstanty, who had been called in to start for the Phillies' depleted pitching staff.

The next day, a Thursday, 32,660 fans filled Shibe Park to see what promised to be another great pitching matchup—Phillies' ace Roberts against the Yanks' Allie Reynolds.

The Yankees got at least one hit off Roberts in each of the first four innings, but managed to draw blood only in the second, when a walk to Jerry Coleman, followed by singles by Reynolds and Gene Woodling, brought in a Yankee run. The Phillies, for their part, managed a triple and two doubles in the first three innings, but couldn't score. Finally, in the fifth, singles by Mike Goliat and Eddie Waitkus, followed by Richie Ashburn's fly to left field, brought in the tying run.

It stayed knotted at one until the tenth, when DiMaggio

stepped to the plate. Roberts got behind DiMaggio, two balls and one strike, when he threw that pitch he regretted over the plate, allowing DiMaggio to swat his seventh World Series home run.

"It streaked over second base on a rising line," Red Smith recounted in the *New York Herald Tribune*. "Richie Ashburn, playing center field for the Phillies, turned and started toward the double-decked bleachers. He ran a few yards, stopped, and watched. He saw a customer several rows back in the upper stands rise, catch the ball and sit down.

"It was an old gentleman's hit, an old professional gentleman's. The old professional gentleman went creaking around the bases, and the Yankees got ready to catch a train for New York, where they will endeavor to beat the Phillies for a third and fourth time tomorrow and Sunday."

"I never hit a better one in my life," DiMaggio exulted after the game. "That was the greatest homer of my career. Any four-bagger that wins a ball game carries a thrill. But this one tops any that I can remember."

Roberts, then the twenty-five-year-old ace of the Philadelphia staff, wanted that pitch back. "I get the guy out all afternoon, and then I get behind him the last time and have to come in with that fastball," Roberts said, shaking his head in the clubhouse. "I go nine innings without any trouble, and then, wham, there it is."

The Yankees went on to sweep the series, taking Game 3 by a score of 3–2, and Game 4 by a score of 5–2. It was DiMaggio's next-to-last World Championship.

Phil Mintz is a veteran writer and editor at Long Island, New York's Newsday, *where he has won several major journalism awards. He was born in the Bronx in the closing weeks of the 1949 pennant race and was exposed to his first televised World Series that year on the lap of his fa-*

*ther, Lou, a devoted Yankees fan. He went to his first base-
ball games at Yankee Stadium and rode the IRT Woodlawn
line past the ballpark every day on his way to high school.
Despite a Little League career marked by an inability to
hit for power, he remains an avid baseball fan, and, even
with the advent of interleague play, manages to split his
loyalties between the Yankees and the Mets. As a journalist,
Mintz has covered many major national stories, and was
on the team of* Newsday *reporters and editors awarded a
1997 Pultizer Prize for the paper's coverage of the crash
of TWA Flight 800 off the South Shore of Long Island. His
poetry has appeared in many general and literary
publications, including* The Nation *and* The Village Voice.
*He holds a B.A. from Queens College of the City University
of New York and lives in Huntington Station, New York,
with his wife, Dale, his son, Dan, and his daughter, Emily—
who still hasn't forgiven the Yankees for trading David
Wells to Toronto.*

The Price of the Game

ROBERT STAUFFER

"I played baseball because I could make more money doing that
than I could doing anything else."
—BILL TERRY (GIANTS FIRST BASEMAN 1923–1936)

HE BATTER STEPS up to the plate—his first at bat of
the year despite the fact that it's April 30—and the fans
start to boo. They boo, not because they expect him to
fail at the plate, not because they think he's not carrying his
weight for the team. Quite the contrary, they expect him to lead
the team to the pennant. Why then do they boo? They boo because he held out—refused to play for the month of April,
watched his defending World Championship team begin to fade.
And for what? He held out for lousy money. A young man and
he wants more money than anyone could possibly use in ten
lifetimes, let alone one year. And to top it all off, later that day,
he collides with another star of the team, knocking them both
out of the game and causing them both to miss several more
starts. All the while this guy's still making some crazy sum of
money. The fans boo even more the next time he's able to play.

Who is this disfavored star whose arrogance alienated the local fans? Is it Mike ''For-the-love-of-the-contract'' Piazza or Al-

bert "Don't-call-me-Joey" Belle deigning to take an at bat between stints on the Disabled List, or even Bobby "I-don't-wanna-pinch-hit" Bonilla. No, this is actually a scene from the Golden Era of baseball, and the player is none other than Joe DiMaggio.

Joltin' Joe sat out the beginning of his third season with the Yanks, 1938, over a salary dispute. The fans and the press sided with Colonel Ruppert, the owner of the Yanks, when he came out and said what he'd offered this young athlete. Twenty-five thousand dollars was a lot of money in the latter days of the Great Depression. A $1500 salary was considered enough to keep a roof over one's head and the heads of one's family, and to insure that they'd eat extremely well. And young DiMaggio had turned the colonel down—not satisfied with a $10,000 pay raise. He wanted the unheard-of sum of $40,000 when it was well known that the Iron Horse, Lou Gehrig, made only around $30,000.

There was speculation at the time, first that he was deluded by his fine performance of 1937 when he batted .346, drove in 167 runs, and crushed an amazing 46 home runs, and then that he was operating under the advice of Joe Gould, a famous boxing promoter. But even more astounding was the rumor that Ruppert and DiMaggio had agreed and signed a contract the previous summer and that this was some kind of publicity stunt to build a fervor among the fans to see DiMaggio play. Not since Babe Ruth had signed with the Yanks for an overwhelming $80,000 in 1930 had salary piqued the fans' interest and actually driven their disapproval.

What made this even worse was that after all the hype and anger and frustration, DiMaggio had not even gotten what he'd asked for. After missing spring training (for his third consecutive year) and the opening month of the season, DiMaggio still had no recourse for his demands. He could play for the Yanks for the sum they offered or he could go back to the docks in San Francisco and take up fishing for crabs with his father. Baseball's reserve clause made sure that no other owner would even consider this talented ballplayer. Though the St. Louis Browns were said to have offered $150,000 to buy DiMaggio from the Yanks, none of this money would have gone to him—and they were probably less likely to pay him $40,000 a year once they had him.

Green Is the Color of the Game

"Accept this and I'll take care of you."
—Branch Rickey to Marty Marion

"Give me what I want and I'll take care of myself."
—Marion's reply

We all know that baseball was different before the advent of players' unions and free agency. Not a day goes by when the fans aren't reminded that their favorite player plays elsewhere because the rival team was able to offer more money. Even small children seem to know how much a player is worth. It's surprising that a salary column hasn't been added to the list of stats on the backs of baseball cards yet.

But that doesn't mean that the game was not about money before the spiraling salaries or spiraling ticket prices. Players didn't play solely for the love of the game any more than they do now; owners weren't altruistic old family men who just wanted their teams to win one for the home crowd. It's just that it's all out in the open now. The age of innocence for the fan is over, and eating the apple from the tree of free agency has cast us out of our imagined Eden.

Salaries in every industry are driven by the competition for employees and the amount of money an owner might make off their work: the old law of supply and demand. This is why in a free-trade society ruled by capitalism our government has seen fit to openly break any business that threatens the individual's rights to make as much money as he can by monopolizing all the opportunities that individual might have. Idealized as the "all-American game," major league baseball has managed to dodge the antitrust laws time and time again, each time carving its niche a little deeper into the American soul.

Yes, baseball is America's game. To the innocent American fan of the pre-free-agency era, that meant it was a game that focused on the individual's talents while he was being used for the good of a team. Out of many (players), one (team). But now that salaries are out in the open, we can see that it is also America's game because it follows the economic structure of our people. In these last few years of the Twentieth Century we talk about the squeezing of the middle class, the rich getting richer, and the disparity of the distribution of wealth both in our country and on our baseball teams. *Baseball Weekly* has taken to listing overall team salaries in a grid that resembles the standings box, and oddly the teams are nearly in the same order in both boxes. But is this something new, or just a peek behind the wizard's curtain?

The National League owners of early baseball squabbled among themselves, wanting the best players for their teams so as to draw the best crowds. But the best player couldn't play for every team at the same time. As a result the great players were offered more and more money as the teams tried to outbid one another. The owners decided there had to be a rule of order and compromise. And so the reserve clause was enjoined, an actual clause in a player's contract that restricts him from dealing with any other team until his current team has passed him up. It served as a gentleman's agreement between the owners, to keep the players from merely negotiating with every team at the beginning of each season and going to the highest bidder. At first the reserve was only on the very best players the owners wanted to protect—just five players on each team. But a team needed more stability, or so the owners felt, so during the 1880s they extended the clause to cover every player. No player could determine his own fate once he signed with a team or, even worse, another team had bought out his contract.

What made the reserve clause so onerous was not the salaries it induced. Baseball players were usually paid well above the average pay of the time, and while there were players who did not merit even the average pay, many were well accommodated. The real trouble was that players had no negotiating power for when they were no longer able to play the game, either through injury or old age. No pensions had been planned for, let alone provisions for a player facing job-related illness or injury. And with the owners in such tight collusion, a player dropped from one team would probably not find work among the others.

One must consider with ballplayers that their career is finite even beyond the usual limitations of work. We live in an era when people mourn others who are forced into retirement at the age of sixty-two but we think nothing of calling a forty-year-old baseball player an old man. The number of times it was said of Rickey Henderson in the late 1990s that he was still playing well (the "for an old man" usually unsaid, but never very far from the speaker's mind) is petty praise considering that he led the majors in stolen bases in 1998. And that's just the player who remains healthy and lucky throughout his career. There's always a danger of illness (as in DiMaggio's case with his bone spurs) or other oddities of human history (like a war, which also affected DiMaggio's career) shaping the player's ability to earn. With all the things that can happen to a player along the way, both he and the owner must consult oracles to see what may lie ahead. And that's not even considering reimbursement for all the years it might take a player to reach the bigs.

But the owners insured that a player could not think about such things with the institution of the reserve clause. All he was allowed to think about was the present.

The biggest threat to the reserve clause in its early years came from outside the leagues. In its earliest years, the National

League had to contend with the American Association and the Union Association. Higher salaries and split fan interest made the National League clamp tighter to the reserve clause, expanding it to cover every player. It also instituted a rent for the players' uniforms.

Inspired by this, the Brotherhood of Professional Base Ball Player was organized to combat the owners. When that did nothing to break the reserve clause, the Players' League was set up as a rival to the National League in 1885 by a group of players who felt that they were being ill used by the owners. Led by John Ward Montgomery (a player for the New York Giants), the Players' League was the first to put forth that baseball was no longer about a good, clean contest of athletes, but about money. The National League put a swift end to the Players' League by blackballing any player who played for the league and offering outrageous salaries to keep the players it had. With so much division among the fans' dollars, the Union Association collapsed after one year. Despite support from major players like King Kelly and labor leaders like Samuel Gompers, the Players' League folded after two.

Next, it was the American Association, which the National League drove out of business by slashing its own ticket prices. Of course, the minute the American Association folded its tent, the high prices were back and it was the players' salaries that were slashed.

When the American League (formerly the Western League) was brought east by Ban Johnson in 1899, promising higher salaries, the National League owners tried to simply ignore him. He snapped up players from the struggling National League, including such luminaries as Cy Young and Willie Keeler; created a cleaner game by banning alcohol from his stadiums for the fans; and all in all, "furnished a better article of baseball than the National League," as Spalding's *Guide to Baseball* put it. It was clear that the American League could not be put down as easily as the American Association had been. Quite the contrary, the American League was succeeding where the National League was failing. Rather than risking its bottom line again, the National League proposed a merger, deigning to recognize the American League as a major league. In later days this led to an even more profitable game with the invention of the World Series and proved the age-old adage "if you can't beat 'em, join 'em." (Note also that the World Series was named for the sponsor of the Series—the New York *World* newspaper—and not the domination of one team over the entire world. Money strikes again.)

The Federal League would be the next challenge for the newly formed major leagues, not only because it offered competition to the majors, but also because it challenged the legitimacy of the reserve clause. By offering players the possibility of free agency and the recognition of the lately organized Fraternity of Professional Base Ball Players, the Federal League managed the defection of eighty-one players from the majors. Once again the majors would use the two-pronged approach of higher salaries and cheaper tickets. It even tried appealing to the fans' innocence as well by claiming that the Federal League was just a greedy band of pirates. When that didn't work and fans still packed the Federal League parks (including Chicago's Weeghman Park, now known as Wrigley Field), the owners conceded the Fraternity of Professional Base Ball Players demands that the owners would pay for uniforms and make small changes like painting the outfield walls green so batters would be in less danger of being hit by pitches. Lastly the major league owners offered the players even more money. Ty Cobb's salary jumped from $9,000 in 1910 to $20,000 by 1915.

When the Federal League sued the majors for antitrust under the Sherman Act, the new league made the mistake of not researching the judge assigned to hear the case thoroughly, for while he was death on trusts, he was a diehard baseball fan. The judge held the case up as long as possible, afraid to be the arbiter who might bring the game he loved down, and the Federal

League settled out of court rather than face bankruptcy, leaving the majors with protection from the antitrust laws for nearly the rest of the century. A couple of years later, that judge, Kenesaw Mountain Landis, would become baseball's first commissioner.

In two years of existence, the Federal League gave baseball such treasures as Wrigley Field, the first-ever players' union, and affordable ticket prices. Its collapse immediately brought baseball a government-sanctioned monopoly, slashed players' wages, and put an end to unions altogether in the majors until the latter half of the century.

In 1919, one of the greatest moral threats to baseball occurred when several players of the Chicago White Sox took money from big-time gamblers to throw the World Series. It didn't matter that they were found innocent of all wrongdoing by the courts; what mattered was that the fans were now led to question the integrity of the game. Disillusionment prevailed among fans, their spokesman the little boy who begged Joe Jackson to say it wasn't so. The newly appointed Kenesaw Mountain Landis, who had already been unwilling to convict the major leagues on antitrust charges, now felt he had to defend the game by barring the players involved. Still, eighty years later, fans wonder what the game would have been like had Joe Jackson played out his career—where might the game have gone?

Incidentally, one might wonder if the real Black Sox scandal lies in this dark nickname. The team was not called this because of the thrown World Series in 1919, but because of how Charles Comiskey began charging his ballplayers for their laundry. To demonstrate his cheapness, the players refused to have their uniforms washed and thus could hardly live up to the name White Sox. Perhaps the players would not have been driven to whatever deceit was involved during the 1919 World Series had Comiskey been a little more forthcoming with his employees, but dismissing the tarnished players must have seemed easier than fixing the owners' attitudes toward their stars.

During the 1940s the Yankees paid nearly a quarter of all their expenditures to cover their players while taking in nearly three quarters of their income at the gate. One cannot deny that the owners provided a place to play, the promotion, the concessions, and the tickets, but it was the players who drew the fans. As the Yankees discovered during the quiet between Ruth and Di-Maggio, the fans need a reason to come to the games. Maybe Ruth had spoiled New York, granting them winners nearly every year, and the jaded New York fans needed to have the best teams. But with salaries kept quiet, the players dissuaded from becoming a union or even having agents by threats of black-balling, and promises of higher pay to a select few, players had no idea how much they were really worth to the owners. It is told that Bill Veeck in the late '40s offered his Indians a chance to fill in the amounts on their own contracts, offering blank con-tracts to the players, and leaving the room. When he returned he argued only with Ken Keltner (a .276 hitter who played at least 140 games at third base in all but three years of his thirteen-year career—who later became famous for robbing DiMaggio of two hits on a warm night in Cleveland to end The Streak) who had asked for too little.

In 1946, a liquor magnate attempting to form a rival league in Mexico, succeeded in luring several ballplayers away from the majors with offers of outrageous salaries—doubling, even tripling, the best the majors offered. (In his Hall of Fame accep-tance speech, Phil Rizzuto spoke of how he was almost tricked by the large sum of money, and how luckily his wife talked him out of it.) When the league collapsed under the weight of its own poorly thought out finance, a confrontation was forced between the returning players and the owners who wanted to blackball them. Branch Rickey, then owner of the Dodgers, went so far as to claim that players who jumped to escape the reserve clause demonstrated "Communistic tendencies." For the next decade a bill was bandied about the Senate to confirm baseball's (as well as every other organized sport's) exemption from the antitrust laws until finally there was an actual hearing in front of the

Senate Subcommittee on Anti-Trust and Monopoly in 1958. Casey Stengel made his famous forty-five-minute speech that made no points (but used the word *baseball* more times than any other speech ever made before the Senate) and the bill died, leaving baseball's reserve clause completely intact.

Also in 1946, a lawyer named Robert Francis Murphy attempted to start a union among the baseball players. He was astounded by the poor pay for a number of the players and the scarcity of protection for retired men. But strong antiunion sentiment and the right salaries in the hands of a few key players defeated the union by a narrow margin.

The owners, realizing that this might be a really serious problem, threw the players a bone by creating a pension with a percentage of the monies made from the broadcast rights of the World Series and the All-Star games. It covered only players who had retired after 1941 with at least ten years' experience. Of course the plan would kick in only if the player achieved ten years (in 1968, the Braves would sign Satchel Paige at age sixty-two so that he could qualify for the pension) in the big leagues and was paid out only once the player was fifty years old. Originally it would cost a player two dollars for each day he played in the bigs. Marty Marion (a Cardinal shortstop) and Dick Wakefield (a Detroit outfielder) were credited with the concept, but it was generally considered to have been pushed through once Walter O'Malley got behind it. Because of the stipulation that it was retroactive only to 1941, many players were not covered, and certainly no players from the Negro League would qualify until 1997, when both groups were voted a pension of about $7,500 to $10,000 by baseball's owners—by which time there were only about sixty-five living players from the two groups. They also pledged twenty-five dollars a week for spring training (now called Murphy money)—time that had previously been unpaid—and that no player's salary could be slashed by more than twenty-five percent from the previous year.

And while the major leagues were distracted by the postwar

social issues such as integration and the booming economy, it would also be challenged financially with the rise of other sports and the changing technology of broadcasting games via television. Even the new federal program of taxation would have an effect on the game. Revenues would have to be acquired and protected with new strategies, and the variation in market size became a real issue. Sponsors paid more in areas that would reach more viewers and as a result teams would afford better players and higher salaries in bigger-market towns. New York, already the center of baseball, would capture quite a large share of both advertising dollars and championships—though that lack of competition could only hurt the other markets. Once again we see America in the owners' shortsighted struggles with one another. Revenue sharing could only be good for a sport, but how could you get a successful owner to give up those dollars to help a fading team?—a question that still plagues the sport.

Nothing further would develop until Marvin Miller came along in the mid-1950s and after many, many years of patience and hard work, finally broke through with a strong Players' Association. It would also take the supreme sacrifice of Curt Flood to finally break the curse of the reserve clause and set the stage for the free-agency era, which would create even more troubles between the owners, fans, and players.

The Hundred-Thousand-Dollar Man

> "For all his greatness DiMaggio wasn't altogether popular around here. This was probably due to his repeated holdouts and the manner in which he went about them."
> —Joe Williams, 1943

Joe DiMaggio was not the highest-paid ballplayer who ever lived. He was not even the highest paid of his own time—although that is not as easy to determine as one might think. Nowadays when his name is mentioned, it is rarely alongside a discussion of salaries or huge bonuses. No, DiMaggio was a ballplayer from a time before such petty questions of money entered the game of baseball, when great men did great things for the sheer love of the game.

Or was he?

The Yankee Clipper played in a day before there were such things as free agency, ESPN (let alone cable), or a players' union. Even the baseball card had yet to come into its own. There were only ticket sales, concessions, and, sometimes, World Series bonuses. And then Kenesaw Mountain Landis had managed to suppress—if not completely stifle—the idea of the night game, limiting even that form of income.

DiMaggio began his professional baseball career during the height of the Great Depression, when unemployment was at an all-time high and wages at an all-time low. He was not flashy or boisterous or wildly eccentric like the Babe, didn't have the sturdy health of Gehrig. He wasn't a big-town savvy or small-town country boy with a smile to steal hearts, but still he managed to come to the biggest city in the country and become one of the highest-paid men in the country.

Right from the start he knew what he was worth. When the San Francisco Seals of the Pacific Coast League (PCL) offered him the usual $150-per-month salary, DiMaggio sent his brother Tom in to help with negotiations to raise that number to $225 per month. But it was an absolute bargain. The Seals had already cut some expenses by dropping many veterans (including Joe's older brother Vince). Saving money was the key with the Depression in full swing and the demise of the league imminent. Attendance was a serious problem in every one of the PCL's parks. But what the owners never expected was that in his first complete season Joe would embark on a sixty-one-game hitting streak that would single-handedly save the Seals and the PCL. He increased attendance by such a large percentage that it was later said that scorekeepers and infielders had helped him out to keep the people coming.

In 1935, the New York Yankees found themselves in a similar bind. The legacy of Babe Ruth was swiftly fading, and the Yanks hadn't even managed to make it a close pennant race since the Babe wandered off in a vain attempt to make a name for himself as a manager with the Braves. Gehrig was still the Iron Horse, but could not carry the team on his work ethic, as Ruth had on his bat. With attendance sagging to an all-time low, the Yanks needed a new hero. The Yanks had already paid the Seals off for Joe DiMaggio, with five players, a hefty $25,000, and, the real kicker to the deal, the use of DiMaggio for the 1935 season. Even at this young age, DiMaggio was plagued with injuries, particularly in his legs, and the Yankees wisely wanted to make sure he'd be okay before they pinned their hopes and wallets to him.

After capping off the 1935 season by carrying the Seals into a playoff with the Los Angeles Angels and capturing the PCL crown, the Yankees were ready to make their rookie a hero. After a bit of wrangling, they paid him the princely sum of $8,500 for the 1936 season, and this in an era when the average veteran made only $7,000 and while the country remained embroiled in the Depression. A New York newspaper noted that the Yankees were worried that their new acquisition would be too shy to play in the Big Apple, but they were relieved because "when he became a holdout last night, they decided he had plenty of nerve—too much in fact." DiMaggio quickly signed when he was offered not only the $8,500 but also some money for advertising for Camel cigarettes. The Yanks would have a great season with their young slugger, sweeping their way to 102 victories, another pennant, and once again winning the World Series.

It was tradition in 1937 (and probably good business sense, considering how overpaid the teams made the players feel) to offer the player the money he'd made in the previous contract.

As expected, DiMaggio turned it down. He knew that the Yankees were drawing like in the good ol' days, because they contracted out to build new stands in right field to expand the total accommodations to fit 75,000 fans per game. The team had broken a million in their attendance in 1936 and nearly that much on the road. But that didn't mean they were ready to give the youngster anything he wanted. The Yankees were glad to double his salary in 1937 to $17,000, though he asked for $25,000. The reserve clause still held sway over the majors, and players could either take what they were offered or go find a new profession, so there was nothing to worry about here. But when he slugged 46 home runs, crossed the plate a league-leading 151 times, and earned himself the nickname of the Yankee Clipper with his smooth fielding, DiMaggio knew they had gotten a sweet deal.

But Colonel Ruppert was not in the business to pay players what they were worth. Though he would later claim that he always gave the players what they asked for because he "did not want the issue of money to interfere with a player's performance," he was actually a real bargain hunter. In 1937 he paid Gehrig a measly $31,000 though the Iron Horse had asked for $50,000. Gehrig had even offered to take the difference as a bonus if he played in more than 100 games—a sure bet for the Iron Horse. The colonel responded by asking why he should pay a man extra for doing the job he was contracted for. He even sliced Lefty Gomez's pay from $20,000 to $7,500 citing the pitcher's drop in wins and complete games from Gomez's amazing campaign in 1934. Ruppert made it clear that the Depression was still on and anyone who didn't like what they were making could go try and find a job in the hurting economy.

Just for some perspective, the Yanks weren't the only ones to be tightening the belts. The Red Sox were paying hero Jimmie Foxx only $18,000 and the Detroit Tigers were paying Mickey Cochrane (who would later have to be supported by a fund Ty Cobb set up for him and several other not-so-fortunate players, because of an injury he received this same year) $28,000 for catching *and* managing the team. While none could deny that this was still a lot of money for the time, it was not even a dent on the monies the teams were taking in.

In 1938, Joe bucked Jack Ruppert and Ed Barrow, the president of the Yankees, by trying to make his claim on a $40,000 salary stick. When the owners retorted that that was more than even Gehrig made, the young man reportedly replied, "Then Mr. Gehrig is a badly underpaid player." He even sat out the first few weeks of the season trying to make them see what he meant to the ball club, but he only earned the disdain of the media and the fans. An article that ran in *Life* magazine chastised his greed—although they passed it off as bad advice from his brother Tom, and sympathized that baseball was "run according to strictly Fascist lines." The article describes a "violent antipathy" at home that they could ascribe only to fans siding with the owners over the matter of salary. After all, $25,000, the papers had urged, was enough for anyone to live out their lives comfortably, let alone as a yearly salary.

For the most part, salaries were not bandied about by the press much before the coming of free agency. Eddie Lopat would later joke that nobody talked about salaries because they "didn't want anybody to know how little we were making."

But there had been a few who knew what the players were worth, if not to the game, then to the owners. Ty Cobb knew that when Detroit's storied dynasty of 1907–1909 was over, the fans were still coming out to see *him*. It is no coincidence that he was one of the highest-paid players of his day. If it had been solely merit that made the player's salaries there would have been many more like him. But players asking for more money was a rarity and the owners weren't going to do much to change that.

Ruth in his day was able to pull down the unheard-of sum of $80,000. In one of the most retold stories about salary from the era before free agency, the Babe was asked by a reporter if he did not think it was unseemly to be making more than the President of the United States. Ruth replied simply, "I had a better year."

Nowadays it seems that when a player gets all the money he's asked for, he tends to relax and his performance tails off a bit. Of course a player gets a whole lot of money because he's just had a record season and it is likely he won't be able to match those numbers. But when the slugger strikes out in the ninth with two men on and the team down by two, the fans are rarely thinking economics and stats.

And so fans booed Joe DiMaggio for asking what he thought himself worth. Never mind that he was hitting .324 or that he drove 140 runs in ahead of him as he crossed the plate 129 times himself. Ruppert had called him greedy and that was enough to make the fans wary. Even carrying the team to the pennant and then helping to win the World Series would not be enough.

At the beginning of 1939, DiMaggio was healthy and under contract: both firsts for him. The Yankee Clipper attended spring training for the first time and started in the lineup on opening day for the first time. His contract had been settled unusually fast mainly because Colonel Ruppert had passed away during the off season. Barrow, now sole custodian of the Yankees, was not willing to take any guff from the young player, was not the big-hearted man Ruppert had purported him to be, and DiMaggio was still in a state from the poor response he had from the fans over his previous salary negotiations.

In DiMaggio's day there were no long-term contracts with options for both the players and the teams to extend. The Yankees had to deal with contracting every player every year. Of course they had the only option thanks to the reserve clause, but it still left the team up in the air as to who would sign for what money and who would finally decide they'd had enough. Agents were not allowed and any suggestion that an agent was involved in the negotiations between the team and the player was vehemently denied by both sides. In 1940, DiMaggio was reported to have a big meeting with Kenesaw Mountain Landis and manager Joe McCarthy with the expressed purpose of denying that Joe Gould, a famous boxing promoter, was giving DiMaggio career advice and getting a cut of his salary to boot. Such a thing would not be tolerated by the league. Again, by keeping the players away from people who could be knowledgeable about contract negotiations, baseball kept itself away from the worries of a union or salary inflation. They also kept baseball clean of the dubious interests that had ruled boxing.

DiMaggio saw small increases in salary until 1942, when the government imposed a nationwide salary freeze in order to slow spiraling wartime inflation. DiMaggio had become dissatisfied with the yearly contract negotiations, arguing that the team would offer the same as the previous year knowing that it would be unacceptable and then call him a holdout. The press in the early 1940s noted several of the bigger-name holdouts such as DiMaggio, Ted Williams, Johnny Mize, and Mickey Owen, under the headline: BIG LEAGUE HOLDOUT LIST IS BECOMING IMPRESSIVE. The Cardinals were said to be short twenty-three players as late as mid-February, the Cubs thirteen, the Yankees fourteen, the Giants eleven, and the Reds eight, and the explanation given was that some were angry about the cuts they were being asked to take and some were just testing the water.

Attendance had been down for major league baseball as a whole for a decade, but in 1940 and 1941 the fans were back in droves, topping ten million in 1940 and quite near that mark the next year. This was still a time when a major share of the team's revenues was made from attendance and concessions, and without fans in the seats, there would be no money to pay the players. DiMaggio was an important factor in bringing the fans out both at home and on the road, and 1941 would serve to underline that fact once again. His streak fired up fans across the country and brought thousands of them to the ballpark. About 52,000 saw the mark tied at Yankee Stadium; 50,000 saw the mark advanced to fifty-three at Comiskey Park; and 67,468 saw it stopped in Cleveland. His rivalry with Ted Williams (who would bat more than .400 that season for what might be the last time anyone has hit .400 in the Twentieth Century) for the spotlight of the American League led to a summer that would never be forgotten. So while the Yanks didn't want to give up on contracts without a struggle, they knew they could not afford to let this one go.

Though the war with Germany and Japan would depress baseball attendance once again and steal away some of the biggest-drawing players, the memory of seeing DiMaggio and Williams carried through their absences made their return that much more phenomenal in the 1946 season. The Yankees would attract 2.2 million fans that year by themselves, and considering that the entire American League entertained only five million in 1945, this number was quite staggering. The Yanks entered a boom time, as the salary freeze was still on, but the fans were pouring in with their dollars.

During 1946, the first concession to ballplayers' futures was made. The players and owners agreed to make matching contributions to a pension fund that would serve players who had at least five years' experience going back to 1941. DiMaggio, at one point the highest-paid Yankee, was now insured of one hundred dollars a month after he turned fifty. It would not be until the Players' Association got going that the players' contributions would be eliminated and more money would be squeezed from the owners (who were able to pay based on the monies received for the television and radio rights to the All-Star and World Series games).

Larry MacPhail became the leader of a syndicate who bought the Yankees in 1945 knowing full well that baseball would have a revival in the postwar economy. MacPhail was not interested in the long tradition of the game, but the grandeur of his new role as both owner and general manager. He wanted to make money and he saw many opportunities right up front. He introduced air travel to cut down on the team's travel time, promotional gimmicks such as Ladies' Night, and he wanted a young ball club who would do just as he told them. As a result he traded Hank Borowy, one of the Yanks' best pitchers, chased Ed Barrow into retirement, forced Joe McCarthy into retirement, and in 1947 nearly traded DiMaggio to the Washington Senators for Mickey Vernon, the 1946 batting champion.

It wouldn't be until 1948 that the Yankees would give DiMaggio another raise in reward for a return to form in 1947. MacPhail had retired, and DiMaggio had picked up his third MVP award from the Base Ball Writers of America (despite the fact that Ted Williams had won the triple crown). Though his MVP award was sullied years later during a controversy involving gambling and the writers' votes, there are still many who argue that DiMaggio's role went beyond that which his statistics might show. He was now a leader, no longer the bright new rookie in a sea of sluggers and Hall of Famers. His postwar role, thanks largely to the ineptitude of MacPhail as general manager, became that of an elder statesman teaching, cajoling, and advising a group of new faces into the heavy mantle of World Champions.

This time DiMaggio's salary was a princely $65,000 and while it trailed both Bob Feller's and Ted Williams' pay, it was very close to that magic number, $80,000, that Ruth had made headlines with nearly twenty years before. As Roger Maris and Hank Aaron would learn in the decades to come, baseball fans were very wary of the memory of the Babe being surpassed. The Babe had passed into legend so long ago—even while he was still playing—that no one liked to contemplate the fact that he might ever be superseded in any way. But if anyone should surpass him, Joe DiMaggio was the man to do it.

And while 1947 had not been quite injury-free, it seemed that when DiMaggio was in he was hitting—always when the team needed him most. His postwar averages were nothing like his prewar stardom, but he was a clutch performer and contributed with nearly every at bat to the Yanks' triumphant return to the World Series. Their paltry third-place finish in 1946 was thought to be the setting of the Yanks' sun, but neither the Yanks nor

DiMaggio were through yet. Of course, even when he was playing he had not really been injury free and maybe it was that
resolve and spirit that kept the Yanks battling right to the end.
But playing hurt may have been a major factor in the career-
shortening injuries that would plague him through his final seasons. The bone spurs and the muscle tears in his legs and feet
would eventually be his downfall.

The secrecy involved in salary negotiations, kept strictly between the player and his owner, makes the first $100,000 player
in history tough to figure out. While it is generally accepted that
Hank Greenberg of the Pittsburgh Pirates was in 1947 the first
to be paid this salary, there is some evidence about players like
Stan Musial, Ted Williams, Bob Feller, and of course Joltin' Joe.
Greenberg was paid $80,000 or so, but allegedly had attendance
bonuses built into his contract, which boosted him over the
$100,000 mark. Some have recollected Augustus Busch paying
Stan "The Man" $100,000 because he thought it would be great
for publicity, but since he was not an owner in 1947 that claim
can probably be dismissed. Ted Williams and Bob Feller both
lay claims to being the first to actually have $100,000 written
into their contracts, but there is no evidence of this dating before
1950, which leaves DiMaggio's contract as the first substantiated. DiMaggio was originally offered $90,000 with an atten-
dance bonus that might have netted him somewhere near
$140,000 when the season was over, but he took the advice of
some friends (most notably Toots Shor, the famous New York
restaurateur) and turned it down.

Regardless of who was the first to reach this lofty number
(well below the league minimum in our current era, but so far
above the average worker's salary of the time), the leap over
Babe Ruth's salary was noted everywhere in the New York papers.

But 1949 would be a hard year for DiMaggio. The bone spur
in his heel and the death of his father in May would keep him
out of the game nearly through June, just in time for a very

important series in Boston. DiMaggio would call it his best series ever as he hit three game-winning home runs, four home runs all told. The Yanks even came back from a 7–1 deficit in the second game with DiMaggio driving in seven of the nine runs with two of his homers. The series would also see his brother Dominic's hitting streak halted at thirty-four games. The afternoon of the second game a plane tugging a sign that read THE GREAT DIMAGGIO might have been intended for Dom, but by the end of the weekend, it was Joe DiMaggio who was the acknowledged great one.

In the August 1, 1949, issue of *Life* magazine, a piece appeared said to be written by the Great DiMaggio himself discussing the hardships he had endured in the beginning of the year. He described his depression watching the Yanks win without him, the pain from his injuries, even tried to explain and apologize for a fight he had had with some reporters. "When a check came from the ball club," he wrote, "I would look at it and think, *I've certainly done a swell job of earning this money.*" Though he played only seventy-six games that year, Joe did rise from his sickbed whenever the chips were down, playing in considerable pain, but he always brought the victory home to New York.

The season ended with the Yanks battling Boston at the stadium, but the Yankees stacked the deck by declaring the first game Joe DiMaggio Day. Playing before a crowd of 70,000 fans, the Yanks won a squeaker 5–4. The next day DiMaggio, completely spent, had to take himself out of the game, after Bobby Doerr hit a ball over his head. It had been playable for the DiMaggio of old, but he had already given everything he had. DiMaggio played in the World Series against the Dodgers but he hit only twice. His contribution was more as the team's spiritual leader. By dragging himself out to play, he showed his teammates what true spirit was and as a result they all played better and they went on to beat what had been considered the better team for the championship.

In 1950, George Weiss, the new president of the Yanks, matched the $100,000 of the previous year. He also reportedly told his star center fielder that he expected more than seventy-six games out of him this year. It was initially reported that Weiss offered DiMaggio $75,000 (since players could be cut only twenty-five percent by the 1946 agreement with the difference if he played in more than 130 games, but DiMaggio was not one to fall for something like that. DiMaggio assured Weiss and then the media that he was feeling fine and was ready to play a full season. He wanted to win at least two more titles for the Yanks. When asked by the press about what would come after that, he said, "Why don't you write the ticket for me?" launching all kinds of speculation that he would succeed Stengel as manager.

DiMaggio wasn't the only one who was handsomely paid that year, though. Weiss opened the vault and shelled out money to Tommy Henrich ($40,000), Phil Rizzuto ($40,000), Joe Page ($35,000), and Allie Reynolds ($25,000). Though these sums were not anywhere near DiMaggio's money, they were well above the league average, which still stood somewhere around $15,000. The Yanks were touted as the most expensive club in the league and in history as far as anyone could tell, and the press was sure that this team would nab yet another championship just on the bucks spent. DiMaggio would put up another creditable season smacking 32 home runs and driving in 122, but his average would drop nearly 50 points.

The newspapers credited Weiss' generosity to the new income-tax laws. By paying the players, perhaps it was thought the Yankees might lower their income liability. Since they were in the habit of drawing more than two million fans a year now, perhaps they were getting too wealthy.

By 1951, DiMaggio's salary was not newsworthy. Ted Williams had already moved on to $125,000. What was newsworthy was that DiMaggio began to hint around that this would be his last season as a player. The Yanks gave him $100,000 for a third straight year. Though he played in more than a hundred games, his batting average would dip below .300 for the first time. With Mantle waiting in the wings, as storied in the minors as DiMaggio himself had been, DiMaggio knew it was time to retire. Of course the Yanks swept ahead of their archrivals, the Red Sox, and finished five games out in front of Cleveland, and then conquered their crosstown menace, the Giants. It had become rote, and, at age thirty-six, DiMaggio wisely knew it was time to go.

The Yanks would have DiMaggio back in 1952 as a broadcaster for yet another $100,000. His job was to conduct pregame and postgame interviews, but his shyness and awkwardness in front of the cameras made this job much harder than his work in center field and he gave up after only a year. He didn't return to manage or coach and did not hold another baseball job until his years with the Oakland A's in the late sixties.

When adding up the salaries DiMaggio earned throughout his years, the papers always came up with a figure somewhere around $650,000 and compared it with the Babe's $840,000 lifetime. Of course you have to throw in his World Series' earnings, which probably amounted to another $50,000, and his endorsement money, which is anybody's guess. Without cracking the million-dollar figure that would not even approach the average salary for one year for a big-league player today, he did all right for his day. Never fabulously wealthy, but always comfortable.

What covered DiMaggio in his later years would not be the pension plans of the mid-forties, but trading on his own name. In 1972, he launched his most famous advertising work both locally (for the Bowery Savings Bank in New York) and nationally (for Mr. Coffee). Later he entered the memorabilia market, selling autographs and pictures. Both created an income that far surpassed his lifetime earnings in baseball. But he always managed to maintain his quiet dignity and his privacy, turning down most offers for ads. And though he was accused of egotism when he asked to be announced last on occasions such as Old-Timers' games, it always seemed like just good business sense for everyone involved.

Was He Worth It?

"Great baseball players in general fall into two classes: specialists like Ruth, who made home runs, or Walter Johnson, who pitched the game's greatest fastball; and all-around players like Ty Cobb, Tris Speaker, Napoleon Lajoie, and Honus Wagner, who did everything superbly. DiMaggio falls into the second category."

—Noel F. Busch in *Life* magazine

There is a danger looking at stats alone to decide whether a player is worth the salary he is being paid. While the old saying is "numbers don't lie," the caution, "but they can be misunderstood" never seems to be added. Of course they are a great benchmark for comparison and do have some merit. In 1961, when Roger Maris broke the single-season home-run record, there was talk about adding an asterisk to the record, noting that while Maris did indeed hit sixty-one he had five more games with which to hit that last run than Ruth did. Of course no one has ever suggested that the quality or use of pitching at the times of both batters, the fact that 1961 was an expansion year for the majors, and that Maris hit .269 that year while Ruth had hit .356 be noted, let alone the effects of modern medicine and nutrition on the game.

In honor of the Babe, Maris accepted the asterisk, but the truth was that Maris didn't have the charisma to hold the record and the asterisk was just a way of saying that stats don't make the player. If all factors were always taken into account every time a record was broken, then there would be no record today without the dreaded asterisk.

There are many factors that go into making a baseball player, which is why there will never be a definitive list of the hundred or even thousand greatest players to ever play the game, let alone a list of the top nine. But the reason DiMaggio will always be in the upper echelons of this list is simply that he met the qualifications for hero in so many different ways.

First off, he did have the stats on his side, not always the key to a trip to the Hall of Fame, but certainly a good foundation. He was a slugger, no question about it. If his 361 home runs or his lifetime .325 average aren't enough to satisfy, perhaps the fifty-six-game hitting streak could help, or the fact that he led the majors in total bases three times, set the record for most hits by a rookie, or was elected American League MVP three times. And while many speculate on the number of homers he might have hit in a park built for right-handed batters, or how much bigger his lifetime totals would have been had he not served three years in the military during World War II, no one ever adds "for a guy who played only thirteen years" to the statement "he was one of the greatest to ever play the game." There was no question that his individual accomplishments spoke loudly enough for a trip to Cooperstown.

Second, he was a team leader. During his thirteen years the Yanks drove to the World Series ten times. And while he himself scored only—only?—fifty-five RBIs and crossed the plate fifty-six times during his fifty-six-game hitting streak, his teammates exploded, scoring an impressive 301—an average of more than five a game—runs and setting a record of twenty-six straight games where at least one homer was hit in that same stretch.

The year 1949 will always be pointed to as the one DiMaggio won the pennant for the Yanks on the strength of his will even though he played in only seventy-six games. He was ill most of the year, having horrible pain in his legs. But whenever the Yanks needed him, he was there, giving everything he had.

In 1998, Sammy Sosa said he was willing to concede the home-run race to Mark McGwire if Sammy could get his team into the playoffs. The fans had loved the home-run race, but Sosa recognized that it could only distract him from an even more amazing feat—namely the Cubs with a chance at the World Series. Just by allowing the team to focus on the real goal of the playoffs, Sosa earned his MVP award. On the other hand, in the waning years of Cal Ripken's streak many people thought that he was playing just for the streak and not because he was the best qualified. And while people came from all over to see the new Iron Horse complete the streak, it was the Baltimore fans who suffered as their overqualified team was defeated year after year in the standings. It is not at all easy to balance individual feats with team leadership. But even after Ripken's remarkable consecutive-game streak was ended, questions of leadership tended to vanish, at least for a while, after Ripken posted a six-hit game on national television against the pitching-strong Atlanta Braves.

DiMaggio was a team leader and a role model for the other players and could be counted on to show good sense both on and off the field. Red Smith would remark that while the Babe's personality and crazy antics in his baseball career and his private life were all part of the reason the fans loved him, DiMaggio was paid strictly for his professional ability. He was no publicity stunt; as the song advises, "He's just a man, and not a freak."

Thirdly, he was an asset to the owners. Much as Mark McGwire helped an ailing baseball in the nineties by becoming a one-man show, DiMaggio's streak brought the fans out to cheer him on, no matter what park the Yanks were playing in, to sound baseball's return from the Great Depression. The conflict of emotions—wanting to see DiMaggio hit, wanting to see one's own team win—was what baseball is all about. The triumph of the individual was worth a few bucks to a fan, and those few bucks repeated several thousand times insured the owners of a successful business.

In those days, owners did everything in their power to put fans in the seats on a regular basis, even pay their ballplayers more money. Nowadays, owners realize that they can charge more for their seats when they have great ballplayers on the field.

It seems a fan will be willing to pay anything, and corporations will think it a great asset for clients, if they can just get seats to see the great players. Either way, the owners can only gain when they have greatness on their side.

But DiMaggio transcended even his own playing time. Fans flocked every year to see the aging DiMaggio in extragame activities. He was still slugging home runs at Old-Timers' Day games in front of full houses. The 1998 scorebook sold at Yankee Stadium even had a full-page picture of DiMaggio's distinguished figure, dressed in a great suit and throwing a ball, with the caption ''The baseball season doesn't start until Joe D throws out the first pitch at Yankee Stadium.'' Even after he died, the Yanks were able to pack the house for a memorial at which a new monument was placed in left-center field alongside those of the Babe, Miller Huggins, Lou Gehrig, and Mickey Mantle. The legend of the Yankee Clipper is one that the owners of the Yankee ball club will continue to be able to trade on.

Maybe it is impossible to tell how much a player is worth. And that's after he's had a long storied career, a distinguished post-glory life, and a dignified, stately death. Nowadays it seems that the owners and the fans have to guess beforehand who will be the great legends of the future, and so far not even the best analysts or most arcane fortune-tellers have managed to come close. Just looking at the recent careers of players like Hideo Nomo, Kerry Wood, and even the great Mark McGwire, we have magnificent examples of obscured futures. Nomo and Wood, both rookies of the year in their time, have a long row to hoe before they reach the potential imagined for them. On the other hand, it was not long ago that the money would have been on Ken Griffey to be the first to shatter Maris' home-run record, when it was thought that McGwire would be too injury-riddled to make it.

But even beyond their playing time, who can tell what other fortunes lie ahead in backing a player. Casey Stengel and Tommy Lasorda, while decent players, were never what one would call heroes, and yet their managing careers made them superstars. Ruth and Cobb, on the other hand, were superstars as players and would find it an uphill battle to maintain their roles in a community whose motto has always been ''What have you done for me lately?''

Yes, some of what makes the hero is marketing—whether it's putting a face on a T-shirt, or building a stadium for a player. The greats of the game have to be afforded the opportunities to become the greats. That is where the symbiosis with the owners comes in. Especially with the recent events in baseball, both the strikes and the spectacular history-making year in 1998, there has been a lot of stress put on the conflict between the owners and the players. The truth is that there must be some symbiosis or the game would have fallen into disgrace so long ago. Owners are charged with the role of giving the players the chance to shine, the difficult task of keeping the fans happy, and the nearly impossible chore of looking into a dim future and trying to suss out what will be good for the game. But it is the player who must fulfill the potential the owners provide day after day, year after year, or face the boos of the crowd.

In examining a career from the lofty heights of hindsight, we must examine the player in all his roles, as an individual, as a team leader, and as a charismatic fan magnet, in order to discover his true worth. And with those kinds of guidelines it can be easily said that Joe DiMaggio was underpaid, that probably no amount of mere dollars would ever be enough to pay back what he gave his teams, the fans, and the magnates of baseball, let alone the legend he left behind for the game itself.

Robert Stauffer spent the first fifteen years of his life as a Yankee fan, but the death of his boyhood hero, Thurman Munson, and his rebellious adolescence showed him the light. He now follows the New York Mets. In the mid-1990s he discovered minor league baseball, Wrigley Field, and the love of his life (star-crossed, as she is a Cubs fan) and in 1996 he managed to touch the Green Monster at Boston's Fenway Park. Though usually a fiction writer, much of his writing contains baseball in one form or another, as he finds the game to be an allegory for life.

Joe's Stats: Good, Better, and Best

BY ANDY LEFKOWITZ

HERE IS NO question Joe DiMaggio was one of the best pure hitters of his era and while the numbers stand out on their own merit—a major league record 56 game hitting streak, 361 career homers against only 369 career strikeouts, and a three-time MVP—a large part of his success was dictated by who he was.

But keep in mind, when DiMaggio played, the statistics that so many media rely on and fans take for granted when reading the box scores in their local newspapers or on the Internet just were not available. For all intents and purposes, sacrifice flies did not exist. Neither did intentional walks.

DiMaggio on a hot streak? We'll never know if after going 4-for-4 with two homers and two extra base hits in a game whether he was given an intentional pass the fifth time up. You'd be surprised at how often newspaper and other accounts of a particular game contradict one another. DiMaggio played long before pitch-by-pitch game records were kept, and in some cases important stats are not available.

But let's look in depth at what we know he did accomplish.

To use a phrase so common in describing up-and-corners today, DiMaggio was the quintessential "five-tool" player. The five tools are: hitting for power, hitting for average, speed, throwing arm, and overall defense.

Some of today's players who have had this term grafted to their names include Seattle's Ken Griffey, Jr.; who is one, Atlanta's Andruw Jones, who has shown flashes of being one; and Milwaukee's Alex Ochoa, who is already on the fourth team of his young career.

When it comes to hitting for power and average, there is little doubt that DiMaggio was one of the best players of his or any era despite leading the league in homers just twice and never hitting fifty homers in a season.

The Yankee Clipper made his major league debut on May 3, 1936, and from that point, the torch was passed. DiMaggio quickly supplanted Babe Ruth and Lou Gehrig to become the next link in the chain of great Yankee players.

In that first season, DiMaggio batted .323, rapping 206 hits, 88 for extra bases. The forty-four doubles would be into a career high and the fifteen triples were both major league and career bests.

Just months after being named the American League Rookie of the Year, things would only get better. In 1937, his power numbers improved dramatically as he set career highs with 46 homers and 167 RBIs to go along with 35 doubles and 15 triples.

He also led the league 27 road homers, 418 total bases, 151 runs scored, and a .673 slugging percentage. Not horrible.

By 1939, DiMaggio had a season that ensured his place as one of the best baseball players of all time. Joltin' Joe had just 176 hits—the lowest total of his career to that point—but he recorded a league high and career high .381 average with 30 homers and 126 RBIs en route to his first American League MVP award.

Two years later, DiMaggio's .357 average was 49 points less than that of Boston's Ted Williams. But while the Splendid Splinter had the lofty average, DiMaggio had other numbers to back him up: .348 total bases, 125 RBIs, and 5 double plays, all league highs.

By today's standards, imagine Griffey, Tony Gwynn, or Jeff Bagwell being drafted to serve in the Gulf War or as part of a peacekeeping force in Kosovo. Unfathomable. But by the time the United States entered World War II—taking baseball's brightest stars into battle with it—DiMaggio would miss three years right at the heart of his greatness.

Had he not gone to war, and averaging his career stats to that point, DiMaggio may have easily put up three more MVP awards. His projected numbers per season are:

140 games played
193 hits
.341 batting average
35 doubles
12 triples
31 homers
123 RBIs
133 runs scored

Throw in that he may have been facing watered-down pitching and those numbers may easily go up ten percent or more.

At first blush, it doesn't appear DiMaggio had the speed necessary to call him a five-tool player. In his fifteen-year career, he stole just thirty bases in thirty-nine attempts in an era when the stolen base was not considered a viable weapon to manufacture runs. Moreover, the New York Yankees were a power-hitting lineup that seldom needed to manufacture a run. Why risk a stolen base when the likes of Phil Rizzuto, Tommy Henrich, and Yogi Berra were there to help drive in runs? Di-Maggio's absence during the war years and diluted overall talent allowed the Yankees base-running specialist Snuffy Stirnweiss to lead the American League in stolen bases twice. But once the war ended and the regular stars returned, both Stirnweiss and the stolen base became seldom-used parts of the Yankees' attack.

It was when DiMaggio roamed the outfield that he showed his speed. Consider in his first season, he led the American League with twenty-two assists. He followed that up in 1937 by posting a league high 413 putouts. But he was not perfect. In two of his first three seasons, DiMaggio recorded double digits in errors, including a league worst seventeen in 1937.

In the four seasons before World War II, DiMaggio posted double digits in assists three times and totaled thirty assists and twelve double plays.

When DiMaggio returned to the major leagues in 1946, it seemed as if he needed a season to reacclimate himself to the game. His .290 batting average was the lowest of his career to that point and he did not lead the league in a single category.

The one-year "layoff" was just what he needed.

DiMaggio won his third MVP award in 1947 despite leading the league in just one category—he made one error in 316 chances for a near-perfect .997 fielding percentage.

In 1948, DiMaggio had the last great year of his career, leading the American League in homers (39), RBIs (155), and total bases (355). The only blemish was he had nearly twice as many errors (13) as assists (8).

His final three seasons were marked by injury and he led the league in just two categories—twenty-three road homers and a .585 slugging percentage in 1950, the year he played one game at first base, cleanly fielding all thirteen chances.

Several factors keep DiMaggio's career stats from ranking higher. First, he played only thirteen major league seasons. By comparison, Babe Ruth played twenty-two seasons and Hank Aaron played twenty-three. Three prime years of DiMaggio's career were lost to World War II, while injuries shortened several of his seasons. Aaron and Ruth chose to play long past their glory days. DiMaggio retired comparatively early rather than play at less than his hard-earned reputation. Aaron, for example, batted only .234 and .229 during his final two seasons with the Milwaukee Brewers, and Ruth's .181 with Boston in his final year is an unsightly blemish on a superb overall record. Di-Maggio retired in 1951 after seeing his batting average drop to .263, where only the year before he had batted .301 and led the American League with a .585 slugging percentage. DiMaggio had standards that went beyond money. He wasn't hesitant to demand substantial contracts when he was baseball's greatest player. And when he was no longer baseball's greatest player, he retired. Likewise it should be mentioned that Yankee Stadium was designed for the left-handed-hitting Ruth, making the power numbers of the right-handed-hitting DiMaggio all the more impressive.

Only in slugging percentage does Joe DiMaggio rank among the Top 10 in baseball's major career stats, with a .579 mark that ranks as the sixth highest of all time. His World Series career stats are quite a bit better, ranking in the Top 10 in games played, at bats, hits, home runs, runs, RBIs and walks. Moreover, DiMaggio's .993 World Series fielding percentage (one error in 150 chances) is considerably higher than his .978 regular season career percentage—yet more evidence that DiMaggio was at his best when it mattered most.

Think of Joltin' Joe the next time the term *five-tool player* is touted. The numbers may be better in the long run, but they will never stack up to the one of the game's first.

Andy Lefkowitz, who grew up in the shadow of Shea Stadium, was an associate editor for ESPN SportsTicker *and the sports editor at the* Daily Ardmoreite *in Ardmore, Oklahoma. He lives in Bayside, New York.*

Joe D, the Kid, and Stan the Man

GEORGE MITROVICH

*J*OE DIMAGGIO'S DEATH did not come as a shock. He had been hospitalized for ninety-nine days. There were almost daily media updates on his condition.

The passing of the Yankee Clipper occasioned a flood of stories and memories of one of the most graceful ballplayers who ever lived. The day after he died, the front pages of *The New York Times, The Washington Post, Chicago Tribune, The Denver Post, The Wall Street Journal,* and *The Boston Globe* (in the heart of the Red Sox nation) carried stories and lengthy profiles on DiMaggio. They were not alone. It was a major story in every American newspaper. *The Times,* America's newspaper of record, devoted more than four pages to DiMaggio's life. In addition, most newspapers carried editorials honoring DiMaggio.

I found the coverage given DiMaggio's death amazing. By profession and habit I am a person who pays close attention to the print media in America—and there have been foreign heads of state whose demise received less attention than Joe D's. In addition, there have been substantial public figures in the life of our country—business leaders, powerful publishers, scientists, architects, artists, writers—whose obituaries didn't come close to rivaling the coverage given DiMaggio. Indeed, there have been movie stars whose passing was hardly more than a footnote; DiMaggio's was the whole book.

Joe DiMaggio, almost every newspaper agreed, was an American icon.

I learned of DiMaggio's death from one of my brothers, Mike Mitrovich. Twenty-two years younger than I, he knows only the DiMaggio of legend, but the great man's death touched him. "I teared up," he said when he called. "I don't why, I just did." His reaction didn't surprise me. I'm sure that every person with a heart, soul, and feeling was touched by the death of the quiet, private man from San Francisco.

Why? What was it about DiMaggio that made him so different from other great athletes, from other persons of fame and celebrity? Why did we care so much about DiMaggio, while barely noticing the passing of other persons of prominence? Why did time seem to stop when number 5 died?

When his greatness is recalled, as it was over and over following his death, two records are cited, records that border on the unbelievable, especially to anyone who has ever tried to play the game, from sandlot to pro.

The first record, hitting in fifty-six consecutive games before his great streak was stopped in a game against Cleveland. Every time I think about that streak, another statistic comes to mind: his proceeding to hit in the next sixteen games. But you can't think about that without remembering The Streak ended because of two brilliant fielding plays by Ken Keltner, the Indians' third baseman. Save for those plays DiMaggio would have hit seventy-three consecutive games!

But I remember something else about those fifty-six games, something that preceded them. It occurred when DiMaggio was playing for the San Francisco Seals of the Pacific Coast League

(PCL), the minor league I grew up with. At a very young age, in a league many considered just a step below the majors, he hit safely in sixty-one straight games.

The second record, striking out only 369 times. Which means, in his thirteen years with the Yankees, he averaged fewer than thirty strikeouts a season. His home-run total—361—was only eight fewer than his strikeouts. An incredible achievement, one that never fails to impress other players, both then and now.

Tony Gwynn of the San Diego Padres, arguably baseball's best hitter today, said on ESPN on the day DiMaggio died that he considered his strikeout–to–home-run ratio the most amazing statistic of all. Gwynn, the eight-time National League batting champion whose own strikeout ratio is among the lowest of today's players, is hardly alone in his amazement at how seldom DiMaggio struck out. Gwynn's comment reminded me of Ted Williams' famous line, "The hardest thing to do in sports is hit a baseball."

But like many fans, I can't think of DiMaggio's 361 home runs—thirty-seventh on the all-time list—without wondering what might have happened had he played with another team in a ballpark friendly to right-handed hitters, like the Red Sox and Fenway, or the Tigers and Briggs Stadium. When you think about DiMaggio playing more than half his games at Yankee Stadium, with its vast distances in left and left-center field, his home-run total becomes more than a statistic.

One of the unforgettable images of my youth was the catch Al Gionfriddo of the Dodgers made against DiMaggio in the '47 World Series. Racing madly across the outfield grass at the stadium he ran the Clipper's long drive down at the bullpen gate in left center. The sign read: 415 feet. It was the kind of play that sticks in a twelve-year-old's memory. "The Catch" caused DiMaggio to display an element of conduct no one remembers witnessing before with the Clipper: public emotion. You see it in the old newsreels. As he rounds second base, out of frustration over Gionfriddo's amazing play, he kicks at the dirt.

But his thirteen-year career, a lifetime batting average of .325, eleven All-Star games, and ten World Series appearances do not explain DiMaggio's mystique, his hold on our imaginations—a grip still tight after forty-nine years.

My wife, La Verle, smart about baseball and a lot of other things, asked me the night DiMaggio died if I had rooted for the Yankees when I was growing up in San Diego. I said I was never a Yankee fan. It was hard to root for a team that seemed so superior—and was—to the fifteen other teams that made up the major leagues. But DiMaggio, I told her, belonged to more than New York. She knew what I meant. She felt it too, even as a young girl enduring the icy cold winters of Spokane, on the eastern edge of Washington State, she knew DiMaggio's name.

As we talked that night, after watching a series of television tributes to DiMaggio, I reminded her of my favorite baseball story. A story involving the Clipper's marriage to Marilyn Monroe. It's a story I find irresistible. It has great appeal, even if I have sometimes wondered if it is merely apocryphal.

DiMaggio and Monroe. Wow. Have two greater stars from two different constellations ever been joined, however briefly? Anthony and Cleopatra? Maybe.

The story about Joe D and Monroe concerns their honeymoon in Tokyo. Monroe was asked by the U.S. Army if she would entertain America's soldiers in Korea. DiMaggio wasn't sure he wanted her to go. This was their time to be alone. But she told him it would be a quick trip and, after all, it was for "our boys." When she returned she excitedly told DiMaggio about her great experience, the thrill of entertaining more than a 100,000 troops. "Joe," she said, "You've never heard such cheering." There was a pause, and then DiMaggio said quietly, "Yes, I have."

As my wife and I continued to chat, I said DiMaggio was one of the three greatest players of my generation, which meant growing up in San Diego in the late 1940s and early 1950s. The other two were Ted Williams and Stan Musial.

When DiMaggio retired in 1951, I was sixteen. Baseball was

big in my life. I played the game almost every day. I exhausted the sports pages of *The San Diego Union* and the *Los Angeles Herald-Examiner.* The kids I played with at San Diego's University Heights and Golden Hill recreation centers accused me of memorizing *The Sporting News,* the weekly "baseball bible."

Every Tuesday I walked five blocks from my home to the drugstore on the corner of Upas and Thirtieth. I put down my quarter and took home *The Sporting News.* It was a depressing Tuesday when it was late. I read it cover to cover. I had splendid recall, but memorize it? No, that didn't happen. But then, as now, I start each day by reading the sports section of three newspapers. For me the worst period of the year is from the end of the World Series to the beginning of spring training. Life without box scores is hard.

Of the three, DiMaggio, Williams, and Musial, I saw only two play in person. For me Joe D was never more than an image on television, on a black-and-white screen.

Williams I saw play once. It happened during an exhibition game at Westgate Park, the home of the Pacific Coast League (PCL) Padres (it was the only time the Red Sox trained in Arizona, far from their normal training camp in Sarasota, Florida).

On the night the Kid came home to San Diego to play at Westgate—he had grown up in the community of North Park, a couple of miles south of the ballpark—I went to the game with a friend. By chance and good fortune we sat near a reporter— Ed Rumill, the sports editor of *The Christian Science Monitor.* He was a fine gentleman and we had a wonderful time talking with him during the game. Afterward we offered Rumill a ride to his hotel, the El Cortez in downtown San Diego. He invited us to join him for a late dinner.

While we ate hamburgers (our choice) and Rumill put away a swordfish steak, he told us fascinating stories about Williams. Stories at odds with Williams' image, an image arising out of his reputation among sportswriters, especially with Boston writers who covered the Red Sox, a rather virulent breed. To them

Williams was abrasive and arrogant, an exceedingly difficult human being. But to Rumill, Williams was a kind, thoughtful, caring person. He shared with us that night many instances where Williams had befriended him. Rumill thought the Kid was one of the most misunderstood ballplayers of his time.

I have never met Williams. But when he broke in with the PCL Padres, fresh out of Hoover High School, he often ate at a diner across the train tracks that looped behind the grandstand at San Diego's Lane Field, a WPA creation. My dad was the short-order cook at the diner and frequently served Williams and another young Padre player, Bobby Doerr, who would also star with the Red Sox.

Teddy Ballgame was the game's greatest hitter—ever. It is amazing what he accomplished, especially when you consider that during the prime of his career, he lost five years to the U.S. military. It's conceivable, except for the years he lost, that Williams, not Henry Aaron or Babe Ruth, would have been the game's home-run champion.

But growing up I never felt any particular affinity for Williams other than our sharing the same hometown. Boston, the Red Sox, and Fenway Park were far away, on another coast, a place I had never been. Plus, Williams, the product of an unhappy home, seldom came back. The memories were too painful, the embarrassments too great. San Diego was where he was from, but that was the beginning and end of the connection.

Affinity for the immortal number 9 would come later—and it started that night with Ed Rumill.

In many ways Musial was my favorite. I had played for an American Legion team called the Cardinals. Our coach, Lee Singleton, had played in their farm system. He was able to get us old Cardinal uniforms. Mine had been worn by Johnny Hopp. It carried number 42. I was six foot two and weighed 130 pounds. Hopp's uniform shirt was big enough for three of me, but it was the real thing. The Cardinals, both American Legion and major league, were my teams—and Musial was my favorite player.

One of my prized possessions is an authentic Cardinals jersey with number 6 on the back, identical to the one Musial wore with St. Louis. (I also have DiMaggio's number 5 jersey and Williams' number 9, but Musial's is the one I treasure the most.)

The first time I saw Musial play was at the Los Angeles Coliseum, that huge "converted" football stadium near the University of Southern California where the Dodgers played when they arrived from Brooklyn. The place with the infamous "Chinese Wall" and the 250-foot foul line in left field. Musial was 4-for-4. He scored twice and twice was thrown out trying to score. He was everything I expected. It was a memorable night, attesting for me to Stan the Man's greatness.

When DiMaggio died, the media was quick to seek comments from Williams and Musial about Joe D. To the Kid, "He was the best player I ever saw. He seemed to do everything right." Stan the Man called Joe D "the pride of the Yankees, but he was much more than that. Really, he was the pride of baseball."

Three wonderfully talented players—DiMaggio, Musial, and Williams. All three among the eight or nine most gifted players in the history of baseball. All three a part of my youth, of growing up, of loving the game. Each different in their personas but equal in the consummate nature of their brilliant athletic skills. God's gift to them—and to us.

But of the three, I have no doubt it is Joe DiMaggio, the Yankee Clipper, who will be remembered the longest.

At the beginning of this essay I raised a question of why, among all the post–Babe Ruth players, was it DiMaggio who gained such a hold on our attention, our imagination? In answering you cannot avoid the fact that he played in New York, the media capital—then and now—of the world. In the most public of ages, in a city that sanctifies celebrity, he was placed upon the high altar of fame. A fame that grew in almost direct proportion to the privacy he sought. His privacy, however, was not contrived. It is who he was. But by keeping his privacy and limiting his public appearances, there arose about him a mystery—and out of that mystery came the great DiMaggio mystique.

But it was more than that. He had an undeniable grace, defined by a playing style so fluid that it seemed effortless. It is the image that people had during his playing days; it remains today the image of Joe D. An image not confined to the playing field, but to how he carried himself away from it as well.

In the old royal courts of Europe and Great Britain kings and queens understood that limited public appearances resulted in a mystique beneficial to their reign, to the authority of their realm.

In a real sense DiMaggio, serene, dignified, distant, rising to levels greater than those accorded most athletes, achieved a state of being beyond that of a mere baseball player. He became, in a profound sense, a king of his realm. And so he shall always be.

Not bad for a fisherman's kid from San Francisco.

George Mitrovich is president of the City Club of San Diego and the Denver Forum, two nationally respected public forums. He also serves as chairman of the Committee of 2000, an independent committee of San Diego citizens that successfully supported, in the November 1998 election, a new ballpark for the Padres. He has written for some of America's leading newspapers, including articles on Fenway Park and the Cape Cod Baseball League for The Boston Globe.

He'll Live in Baseball's Hall of Fame

PAMELA HODGSON

*W*HETHER BASEBALL HAD its beginnings in the tiny central New York community of Cooperstown is open to some question. That doesn't matter—the legend has taken hold, and this town in the midst of green hills dotted with fields and Holstein cattle has become a synonym for baseball greatness. Whether or not baseball started here, there's no question that the history of baseball—and the legacy of greats like Joe DiMaggio—has its home today in Cooperstown.

Main Street in Cooperstown is a Norman Rockwell vision of an American town, lined with neatly trimmed brick storefronts and wrought-iron lamps. (Instead of dry goods and hardware and linens, though, many of these quaint store windows feature baseball cards and memorabilia and souvenir T-shirts. You can find just about any baseball souvenir imaginable here if you're willing to pay the price.) In winter, the street is snow-muffled, the white blanket covering any modernities that might remind you that this isn't the setting for a warm-and-fuzzy 1940s movie. In summer, it teems with visitors, becoming more like Main Street, Disney World.

The National Baseball Hall of Fame and Museum's long red-brick facade presides over the street with the clean-lined importance of a courthouse or college. It is a centerpiece kind of building, one that draws your attention and expects you to take it seriously. It is almost surprising upon entering to see how sleek and modern the inside is.

The Hall of Fame itself is a long, airy room paneled in golden wood and lined with small bronze plaques honoring each man voted into the Hall, none more prominent than another, each plaque about the size of a coffee-table book. They are arranged in chronological order of election to the Hall. Benches in the center of the room let visitors linger and contemplate the baseball greats, which many—clad in jerseys or T-shirts emblazoned with the name or number of a favorite player or team—take time to do. Some stop in front of a particular plaque and their gazes retreat into memory—you can almost see them reliving a favorite game: remembering a great play or victory, corners of the mouth twitch upward; recollecting a disappointment, defeat, brings on a blink and a sigh. Parents point out the plaques of heroes of their youth to their children, who reach up to feel the lettering on the plaque as if they, too, could live the moment by touching the words.

Joe DiMaggio's plaque is about halfway along on the right-hand side, along with those of the five others named to the Hall in 1955. On the day DiMaggio died, a small spray of flowers was placed on the corner of the plaque, as is done for any Hall of Famer who dies. His plaque, just like all the others, bears a raised likeness of the player's face; beneath the image is his name, team affiliations, and a few terse (for space reasons) lines reporting his key accomplishments. DiMaggio's plaque reads:

JOSEPH PAUL DI MAGGIO

NEW YORK A.L. 1936 TO 1951

HIT SAFELY IN 56 CONSECUTIVE GAMES FOR MAJOR LEAGUE
RECORD 1941. HIT 2 HOME RUNS IN ONE INNING 1936. HIT 3
HOME RUNS IN ONE GAME (3 TIMES). HOLDS NUMEROUS
BATTING RECORDS. PLAYED IN 10 WORLD SERIES (51 GAMES)
AND 11 ALL STAR GAMES. MOST VALUABLE PLAYER A.L. 1939,
1941, 1947.

(Lest an accomplishment noted on a plaque be exceeded—or, as
occasionally happens with players from the pre-World War II
era, a statistic or record is changed by new research or a change
in rules about how those numbers are calculated—there is a
small disclaimer posted near the entrance to the Hall: "The data
on all plaques was taken from reliable sources at the time the
plaques were made." However, the plaques stay away from mentioning broken records—because they can be equaled or exceeded—in favor of the actual numbers.)

At the end of the Hall is a sunlit, high-ceilinged exhibit area.
The current exhibit is about single-season home-run records, and
features as its centerpiece Mark McGwire's uniform, bat, and the
baseball he hit to break Roger Maris' 1961 record. (McGwire's
and Sammy Sosa's uniforms, etc., had occupied a place of honor
in the entrance to the building at the end of 1998, until this
exhibit was created.) McGwire's jersey, encased in glass, appears
crisply pristine. Sosa's, nearby, is streaked with Wrigley Field
dirt; rather than sullying it, the stain makes it look more real.

But the exhibit isn't just about McGwire and Sosa, or even
McGwire and Roger Maris and Babe Ruth. It describes home-
run record chases through history. "We like to tell stories of
baseball in historical context," says Ted Spencer, curator of exhibits. The exhibit discusses the challengers that drove each
record-holder on: Gehrig for Ruth, Mantle for Maris, and Sosa
for McGwire. (Ruth predicted in a letter written in 1941 that his
record would certainly be broken: "All it will take is a good
home run hitter to be followed by another good home run hitter
like I was with Gehrig for all those years." One imagines

DiMaggio might have agreed: The Clipper's hitting streak of that year is often paired with Ted Williams' season average of .406.) In addition, such lesser-known stories as Joe Bauman's seventy-two home-run season for the minor league Roswell, New Mexico, team are told—a baseball from Bauman's 1954 campaign is here, too.

The exhibit notes that the record Roger Maris set in 1961 stood uncontested for thirty-seven years; it doesn't mention that Maris is not honored with a plaque in the adjacent Hall.

It isn't making or breaking a record that gets a player elected to the Hall of Fame. Players are named to the Hall by a group of baseball writers, members of the Baseball Writers Association of America, each with at least ten years' tenure writing about the sport. The voting is subjective—intentionally so, says Jeff Idelson, executive director for communications and education at the Hall. "The rules are designed on purpose for that anybody the writers feel is a potential Hall of Famer can be elected. There are no automatics for .300 seasons or twenty wins or five hundred home runs. The one area we do ask the writers to examine is character, integrity, and sportsmanship, and there is no doubt"—enthusiasm rises in Idelson's voice and he breaks into a smile—"that DiMaggio embodied all three of those qualities." Idelson is probably a generation too young to have seen DiMaggio play, but his admiration for the Yankee Clipper is nonetheless apparent.

The first Hall of Fame election was 1936, the same year Joe DiMaggio began his major league career. DiMaggio received one vote in 1945's voting, while he was still an active player (and therefore ineligible). DiMaggio was first formally considered for induction into the Hall of Fame on the ballot for the 1953 induction. One hundred ninety-eight of the 254 ballots were needed to win a place in the Hall that year. DiMaggio received 117 votes. At the time, it was assumed that DiMaggio would win a place in the Hall in due course, but many voters were first casting their ballots for pre-World War II greats who had yet to be inducted: among those inducted that year were Harry Wright, whose career ended in 1877, and Chief Bender, who played from 1903 until 1925.

In addition to honoring players whose careers predated the Hall of Fame, the sense prevailed that the perspective of time was required to assess a career adequately. That sense was about to be formalized: Effective with the ballot for 1954, the rule was adopted that a player would not be considered for induction into the Hall until five years after his retirement. However, any player who had received at least a hundred votes in the previous year's balloting was grandfathered, and could be considered whether or not his five years were up. DiMaggio, under that exemption, was once again considered and fell short, with 175 of the 252 ballots cast. Among those who did make the cut that year were Bill Dickey, star catcher for the Yankees until 1946. Dickey caught a hundred or more games in thirteen successive seasons, played on eight All-Star teams and eight World Series teams. He ended his career with a respectable .313 batting average. Although his numbers don't quite match DiMaggio's, there is no question of the significance of the contributions Dickey made to his team, and, given that he had begun and ended his career before DiMaggio, it isn't surprising that he was honored before the Yankee Clipper.

Finally, in 1955's voting, DiMaggio received 223 of the 251 votes cast, and was inducted that summer. Only two of his five fellow inductees had major league careers that overlapped DiMaggio's, and both ended their careers before DiMaggio (Gabby Hartnett, 1922–1941, whose mark of catching a hundred or more games for each of eight consecutive seasons had been a record, as were his 7,292 putouts; and Ted Lyons, 1923–46, best known for pitching a twenty-one-inning complete game in 1929, and for pitching twenty complete games in 1942 with an ERA of 2.10). The other inductees that year (Frank Baker, 1908–1922; Ray Schalk, 1912–1929; and Dazzy Vance, 1915–1935) had all waited quite a bit longer to be recognized by the sports-writers. To be inducted into the Hall in this company, relatively quickly after the end of his career, demonstrates the great respect the voters had for DiMaggio's accomplishments.

"Posterity needs a single transcendant event to fix [a man] in permanent memory," Stephen Jay Gould wrote about Di-Maggio's fifty-six-game hitting streak in a 1988 essay. Certainly, that 1941 streak was an accomplishment that the Hall of Fame voters recognized—it's the first thing mentioned on the plaque. The mark still stands, having been approached only by Pete Rose with hits in forty-four consecutive games (DiMaggio opined that Rose might have extended his streak if he hadn't bunted). DiMaggio himself had exceeded his own mark in 1933 with the minor league San Francisco Seals, when he hit safely in sixty-one consecutive games. And after the fifty-six-game streak lapsed, DiMaggio again hit in sixteen consecutive games.

During The Streak, DiMaggio's average was .408. (Ted Williams made history the same year with a full season batting average of .406.) DiMaggio ended the season with a .357 average, third in the league.

But those are just numbers. Ty Cobb had a better take on what made Joe DiMaggio a sure-thing Hall of Famer: "Joe DiMaggio is one of the greatest hitters, quickest fielders, surest throwers, and fastest runners I've ever seen. He would be a star at any time in the history of the game." Likewise, that great scholar of hitting and DiMaggio contemporary Ted Williams rated DiMaggio best among hitters. When comparing DiMaggio with his successor Mantle after both their careers were complete, Williams considered Mantle his all-around favorite, but as a hitter found Mantle wanting for being less selective than DiMaggio when he had two strikes against him.

And so often, DiMaggio performed with apparent effortless-ness, something of a feat when, for example, covering the vast expanse of center field at Yankee Stadium. Yet he did it with a minimum of drama. As his manager, Joe McCarthy, said in 1936,

"He does what you're supposed to do. The idea is to catch the ball, not make catches that look exciting."

Indeed, the Hall of Fame's Idelson focuses on DiMaggio's contribution to his team as a whole: "For what he did individually, but more so for what he contributed to the success of the Yankees, going to ten World Series in thirteen years, and their winning nine of them, he's an important part of our time line." Still, there's no denying his individual popularity (and accompanying economic impact): On the day in Cleveland that The Streak ended, 67,468 fans attended the game. Throughout the latter part of The Streak, attendance at games where Joe DiMaggio appeared skyrocketed. Much as with McGwire in 1998, even fans of opposing teams cheered for DiMaggio to hit.

But what so many remember about Joe DiMaggio transcends such quantifiables as individual and team performance. Author E. L. Doctorow introduced the Yankee Clipper as DiMaggio received an honorary degree from New York University in 1994 by saying, "His appeal has not to do with statistics, but with grace. It has to do with playing the ball, not the crowd." Indeed, grace is probably the most frequently used adjective by people who saw DiMaggio play. He played smoothly, apparently effortlessly, moving with the fluid ease of the ship whose nickname he carries. Grace isn't something that can be measured, or captured, but it is certainly a piece of why DiMaggio is remembered with such affection and admiration.

Adjacent to the Hall itself is the museum. The entire history of baseball is a story told in about sixty thousand square feet of display space. That story is told in no small part with the artifacts of the game.

There's no better way to capture and preserve a moment in time—a particular hit or win, a great player or team—than to keep hold of a piece of it. The leather of gloves and the wood of bats, the paper of scorecards and the wool of uniforms, all will deteriorate in due course. But for as long as we can prevent that, we can lock into place a tangible memory of a specific day or summer. If we can't hold in our hands Babe Ruth's bat or try on Lou Gehrig's uniform for size, we can at least look at them and remember (or imagine—depending on age) what it was like to see these men play.

Peter Clark, curator of collections for the National Baseball Hall of Fame and Museum, is the man responsible for seizing those objects and keeping them from dissipating. He's been with the Hall for about thirty years. He is soft-spoken in the way you might expect a man who spends his days in the bowels of a museum to be, as if he cradles the artifacts in his care with gentle speech. His office is a bright, modern but crowded space in the basement, reached by a long, sterile corridor off which are a few baseball fields' worth of climate-controlled storage space. Two colleagues share the cramped office space with Clark. He steps over a stack of baseball bats to get to his desk; worn gloves for the collection are heaped off to one side of the room. A World Series trophy is tucked away on top of a file cabinet.

"You cannot measure a man by what we have here," says Clark with regard to the Hall's holdings of DiMaggio-related items. The Hall depends on teams, players, and others to donate items for their collections. DiMaggio himself didn't donate any of the items that the Hall has; most came from the Yankees organization, with which staff members have had an excellent relationship through the years.

Indeed, relationships between the Hall and all the major league teams today are excellent. Jeff Idelson and his colleagues are in constant touch with the organizations as teams or players approach landmark numbers, arranging to obtain mementos that are likely to have historical importance. Idelson reinforces those relationships with spring training trips, introducing himself to players and team staff, thanking them for anything they've given the Hall, encouraging them to keep the Hall and history in mind.

Historical importance is a key consideration today, as space becomes an issue. Initially, the Hall began with only a handful of staff, and acquisitions were limited. Initiatives were made through the fifties, sixties, and seventies to build a collection. "The geography question raises its ugly head," Clark says, noting that the Hall's upstate New York location has meant that New York teams were likely to be better represented in the collections. Keep in mind, too, that until 1958 there was no major league baseball west of Kansas City. With the Yankees, Dodgers, and Giants, New York was for all practical purposes the center of the baseball universe in the early years of the Hall of Fame.

Geography is not much of a concern in today's acquisitions of bats, balls, uniforms, and other artifacts of the game, but it still may be an issue with the clipping files maintained in the Hall's library.

The recently opened Giamatti Research Center provides facilities for researchers like the members of the Society for American Baseball Research, scholars, journalists, and fans to look at files, books, video, and audiotapes relating to anything about baseball. On this busy spring Friday, tourists wander in just to see what this room at the rear of the building is. Frank Vito, a staff researcher, welcomes them, tells them it's fine if they'd like to just look around, and mentions that the library has files on every player who has ever played in the majors. One visitor admits that a guy he knows played a few games in the bigs; Vito assures the man that there is a file on his friend, and invites him to wait a moment while he fetches it.

Meanwhile, researchers sit at a long table, wearing cotton gloves if they will be poring over old papers. Several doors open off the main reading room, one with equipment for reviewing audio- and videotapes. In another, a crew is preparing a television program about greats of the Twentieth Century. Next to the reference desk, a window lined with baseballs (including one inscribed GO THE DISTANCE.—BILL KINSELLA) looks into the office of director of research, Tim Wiles.

Wiles returns from an errand wearing the hat of his favorite team, the Chicago Cubs. (Jeff Idelson is a former Yankee staffer;

Ted Spencer lets his Boston accent speak for itself; Peter Clark
says that after thirty years at the Hall, he's really a fan of all
teams, but when pressed admits that he roots for the Mets.) Some
days, the Internet-audio broadcast of a Cubs day game filters
from his computer. Here, a baseball cap seems like appropriate
business attire. In his office are photos of him dressed in another
job-related outfit: he periodically dons a Mudville uniform and
handlebar mustache to play Casey of the poem for events around
Cooperstown.

Leaning on a wooden chair back, Wiles chats with researchers
about their projects, or about baseball in general. He tells about
Padres star Tony Gwynn's visit to the research center (many
players visit the Hall; only a few make their way to the library,
and Wiles can probably name them all). "There's a file on everyone? Even me?" Wiles says Gwynn asked. Wiles brought him
the file. Perusing it, Gwynn commented that most of the newspaper clippings were from East Coast newspapers. Wiles explained that the staff depends on volunteers to provide materials
from outside the Hall's immediate area; yes, there is a bit of East
Coast bias in what is in the clipping files. Without a volunteer
in San Diego to send the library clippings, Gwynn and his teammates are to some degree represented in the files with a different
perspective than their contemporaries playing in the East. As
Wiles tells it, Gwynn asked whether it would be okay if he cut
out and sent along a few things for the file himself.

When Wiles brings the DiMaggio clip file down from the
stacks, he takes a cart along to do it, there are so many bulging
manila folders. And that's not counting the books and audiovi-
sual materials, which would have required another trip.

The library is able to keep large quantities of print and au-
diovisual material because those aren't very space-intensive, but
as far as the artifacts in curator Peter Clark's care, an accessions
committee reviews potential donations to decide whether they
are of sufficient historical interest and display value to justify
the temperature- and humidity-controlled storage space and the

periodic restoration that will be required. In addition, each item must be carefully authenticated by the Hall staff—the museum must be confident that the items it showcases are what they are represented to be—which entails a great deal of time and effort.

In addition, Bill Guilfoyle, who retired as vice president of the Hall in 1996, works to obtain items to fill specific gaps in the museum's collections. Word of mouth—and publicity generated by such events as Hall of Fame officials arriving with Roger Maris' bat at the game where Mark McGwire hit number sixty-two, and leaving with everything McGwire was wearing that day—brings items to the Hall as well. The Hall acquires at a steady rate of about three hundred to five hundred new items per year.

Some acquisitions are no-brainers. Although the Hall's relationship with Major League Baseball is "non-financial," as Jeff Idelson puts it, Major League Baseball has been key in obtaining items for the museum. Prominent is the purchase (at a price reported to be between five million and seven and a half million dollars) of about two hundred items from noted baseball memorabilia collector Barry Halper, which will be housed in their own gallery within the museum. Included in the Halper collection are the contract finalizing the sale of Babe Ruth to the Yankees; a Honus Wagner T-206 baseball card, the rarest card there is; and an 1872 National Association scorebook completed by Henry Chadwick. (Chadwick is generally credited with the invention of the box score—a plaque at the Hall says so. However, according to author Paul Dickson, crude examples of the box score appeared in print in 1845 and 1853. Nevertheless, Dickson notes, there's no question that it was Chadwick who developed and improved the box score, so that scores appeared routinely in newspapers by the 1870s.) Halper is scheduled to auction much of his multimillion-dollar collection, but Jeff Idelson says that the Hall has been fortunate enough to acquire what they most wanted from the Halper treasure trove.

There isn't much the Hall wishes it had. "Covet? Not really,"

says Idelson. The only items Idelson can name are the bat and
ball from home-run number 715 by Henry Aaron, which Aaron
owns and which are displayed at the Atlanta Braves' museum.
He is quick to add that Aaron has been very generous to the
Hall over the years. This year, in recognition of the twenty-fifth
anniversary of that home-run swing, an exhibit honors Aaron.

In 1991, the Hall recognized the fiftieth anniversary of Joe
DiMaggio's fifty-six-game hitting streak. That's the last time
DiMaggio visited Cooperstown. Peter Clark reports that when
DiMaggio did visit, there were conversations about the possibility of his donating some items, but they never resulted in anything coming to the Hall. "Some players don't keep things from
their careers," Clark says. "They give them to friends or family,
or just don't keep them."

"What we have is not in proportion to a player's importance," Clark reiterates. "DiMaggio was certainly one of the
greats of the game." He ticks off a list of DiMaggio items in
the collection:

1951 home uniform
two caps
two jerseys
two pairs of pants
one pair of shoes
two pairs of socks
two gloves
one game-used bat
DiMaggio's Yankees locker
the pen DiMaggio used to sign the $100,000 contract

He also mentions several "tangential" items, including the
glove Al Gionfriddo used to make the famous catch of Di-
Maggio's fly ball in the 1947 World Series; a wristwatch given
to Yankee owner George Weiss by DiMaggio; autographed base-

balls; bats of the same model that DiMaggio used, but not themselves used by him; baseball cards; and a matchbook cover from DiMaggio's restaurant.

In the first-floor gallery that features record-setting performances (as well as currently active leaders in several hitting and pitching categories), DiMaggio's hit streak isn't featured. His name appears in several all-time lists, but nowhere is The Streak mentioned here. But that's part of the philosophy of the museum: to tell the bigger story of all of baseball. In the lists that make up the records display, it's clear where DiMaggio—and so many others—fit into the larger picture of the game. There are intentionally no superstars in this display.

The largest canvas for painting the picture of baseball is the series of galleries that follow the history of the game through a time line. Even here there are only a few superstars, and the emphasis remains on baseball as a team sport. The bulk of the DiMaggio items Clark mentions are displayed as part of an exhibit case honoring the entire Yankees team of the DiMaggio era.

The centerpiece of that case is a team photo. The two players in that photo who could be named by even the most casual fan of the game—DiMaggio and Gehrig—are represented by several items surrounding the photo, but so are names that are less well remembered outside baseball, like Bill Dickey and Joe Gordon and Red Ruffing.

On display in the case are a glove and bat belonging to Joe DiMaggio, and his 1938 road uniform, cap, and shoes. They're placed off to one side, next to a photo of DiMaggio, manager Joe McCarthy, and several teammates after the Cleveland game in which DiMaggio's streak was ended. Everyone is smiling— even though The Streak ended, the Yankees beat their rivals, the Indians, and that was the main thing. These items, each captioned in small white letters, like everything else in the case, frame the team photo. (Slightly more central in circling the photo than the DiMaggio memorabilia are the Gehrig items, including Gehrig's

1942 New York license plate reading 1-LG, the glove from his last game, a bronze shoe, and a plaque. After all, Gehrig—playing seventeen years of the thirty-eight years he lived—had a longer streak.) Baseball is a team sport, and DiMaggio and Gehrig and Dickey and all the others—great as each may have been—were part of a spectacular team, the display implies.

Of course DiMaggio was part of a great team, but he had an important role in driving them, according to sportswriter Dan Daniel, who had this to say on July 18, 1941, following the end of DiMaggio's consecutive game hit streak: "While DiMaggio was on his streak, the Yankees did some amazing hitting. They got homers in such cloisers [sic], and with such profusion, as never before had been seen in the major leagues. Pitchers turned in deeds of derring-do, fielders went daffy, as a club which had been seven lengths behind the Indians dashed into an incredible lead in so short a time." Would the streak have been so important had it happened on a losing team?

The comparison to the 1998 Yankees is inevitable. That, too, was a stellar team, marching to a record number of victories and a World Series championship. (They're honored in the Hall, too, as the most recent World Series champions always are.) The difference is, as we think of them today, no one or two of the players on the 1998 team stand above their teammates as names that will be remembered so much longer and with so much greater reverence than their fellows. As Daniel continued in 1941, ". . . all these feats were submerged under the wave of popular excitement over the DiMaggio streak. Now the spotlight can be trained on this New York club as a machine. That DiMaggio mark is high enough. Perhaps no other hitter ever again will poke baseballs safely in fifty-six straight games."

The spotlight is trained on DiMaggio in a life-size picture of the Yankee Clipper opposite the Yankees display case. Next to that picture is a baseball bearing the faded signatures of all three DiMaggio brothers who played in the bigs. Even standing alone, he is in the context of his family.

Just around the corner is Joe DiMaggio's Yankee locker, acquired from the team during the stadium renovation of the 1970s. Inside are DiMaggio's 1951 uniform, belt, and cap. The uniform looks fresh and clean, so new as to seem unremarkable, with DIMAGGIO 51 neatly scripted in black ink near the hem. The lettering on the glass front of the locker casts a shadow of the word *DiMaggio* onto the front of the cap. That's where he looms large.

The locker was also used, the caption tells us, by DiMaggio's "heir apparent" Mickey Mantle. Peter Clark tells me that when the locker first came to the Hall, they didn't know that it had also been Mantle's. When they learned that, the caption was changed to reflect that fact.

The Streak itself is named twice in the Hall, once among a list of items in the printed time line that introduces each section of the history display (it's the second item listed for 1941), and again in the display honoring great hitting and pitching performances in the minor leagues. The latter reads: "There are many followers of baseball statistics who believe the most remarkable of all records is the 56-game hitting streak by Joe DiMaggio with the New York Yankees of 1941. And yet a longer streak was already in the books by Joe DiMaggio, who hit in 61 consecutive games with San Francisco Seals in 1933." It goes on to tell us of Joe Wilhoit's 1919 streak of sixty-nine games, although it is also noted that in Wilhoit's day foul balls didn't count as strikes.

Will the streak ever be broken? DiMaggio thought so. In 1996, he told the New York *Daily News* that in his view the unbreakable record was Johnny Vander Meer's double no-hitter. But he added that "the record I thought would last forever was the one Ripken just broke, a shortstop, a man who is getting knocked over by sliding players. Unbelievable."

Reading the later volumes of his clipping file in the Hall's library, one wonders at the frequent description of DiMaggio as shy. DiMaggio appears to have become an unofficial—and frequently interviewed—spokesman for baseball. Although he limited his public appearances and interviews, he didn't end them, and he was often sought out for his thoughts on free agency and salaries ("The owners are paying the players too much. I wish I'd have had that chance"), the DH ("I was 100 percent for it. Hitting was in the doldrums. Now I think it should be a thing of the past. They tried to encourage more hitting with the DH and they're getting it"), long-ball hitters ("The batting averages are having the hell knocked out of them. I don't care how light their bats are and how fast they can swing them around. If only they would stop swinging away on every pitch"), and assorted other baseball-related issues.

That's no doubt because he remained a source of awe within baseball. In 1974, longtime Yankee clubhouse manager Pete Sheehy—the man who assigned DiMaggio's old locker to Mickey Mantle—told *The Sporting News:* "Even now when he comes back for Old-Timers' Day and he walks into the clubhouse, he makes the room light up."

DiMaggio still had that effect on former Yankee player and broadcaster Phil Rizzuto in 1985: "When Joe walks into a locker room—even an all-star locker room—it's like a senator or a President coming in. There's a big hush. The respect for this man is amazing."

When the Hall's Jeff Idelson remembers the Sheehy story, he tells it as: "When DiMaggio would walk through the door, the lights would flicker." Maybe Sheehy told the story differently to Idelson, maybe Idelson simply remembered it in the light of his own awe. It doesn't matter which: as with any story of legend, the point is not the recording of facts and exact quotations; the story is about how the legend is remembered.

"DiMaggio is very much part of the fabric that makes up our culture, and much of that developed after his career," says Idelson. Ted Spencer agrees, noting that during their careers Ted Williams was the more heroic, likable figure, but their roles reversed after retirement.

In 1969 a poll named Joe DiMaggio the game's greatest living player.

There are no special exhibits on Joe DiMaggio. There are no statues of him at the Hall of Fame. (There *are* realistic-looking statues of larger-than-life slugger Babe Ruth and legendary hitter Ted Williams greeting visitors just inside the entrance, back in their customary place after temporary relocation for the Mc-Gwire and Sosa items late in 1998.) That's not to say that the Hall has given DiMaggio short shrift by any means. But the Hall of Fame is about baseball and its times, and the legacy of Joe DiMaggio is perhaps about more than that.

During his career, it almost goes without saying that Joe DiMaggio was vastly famous. He was known for his grace on the field and articulation off. It didn't hurt that reporters covering DiMaggio's Yankees had all their travel expenses covered by the team, as was the custom at the time; DiMaggio himself was known to pick up the meal tab for a new reporter, and he developed friendships with some members of the press corps. Even leaving the personal relationships aside, it is hard for any reporter who lives with a team through the season not to begin to see the world from inside that team's world, looking out. (Reporters traveling with candidates on the campaign trail have to deal with a similar shift in perspective.) It didn't hurt, either, that DiMaggio came to fame as the nation clambered out of The Depression and teetered on the edge of war, when a hero was definitely called for; nor that he married and divorced a beautiful actress (and after his retirement married another, more famous, one). No question, Joe DiMaggio was famous. But despite the name, fame isn't exactly what the Hall is about, either.

You'll literally hear the name Joe DiMaggio in the Hall if you listen to the music of baseball that pours from speakers near a display of baseball-related sheet music, across from a wall of baseball cards (there are two DiMaggio cards there, which you will be hard pressed to pick out among the rows and rows of them). Particularly well known is "Joltin' Joe DiMaggio" by Les Brown and his orchestra. Countless other songs that list names of baseball greats mention his prominently. What you won't hear is the one that is probably the most remembered today, because it's not actually a baseball song: Simon & Garfunkel's "Mrs. Robinson."

The mention of DiMaggio in that song, though, is an indicator of the DiMaggio legacy beyond the Baseball Hall of Fame, indeed beyond baseball. "I haven't tried to create or maintain an image," DiMaggio told the *San Francisco Examiner*'s Dwight Chapin in 1987. Whether or not that's the case—DiMaggio did, for example, work hard as a young player to become more articulate than his limited education afforded, and throughout his life reporters relied on him for the kind of quote that in the pre-television era we might think of as a word bite—Joe DiMaggio *had* an image, a vivid one. He didn't tarnish it with creaky play in Old-Timers' games too late in life, and his ads for a coffee-maker and a bank didn't mar the image. (In fact, when he was replaced in 1992 after eighteen years as the Bowery Savings Bank's spokesman, a result of the acquisition of the bank by another financial institution, fans raised sufficient stir for there to be substantial media coverage. It didn't, however, change the bank's new owners' minds.) Negatives, like first wife Dorothy Arnold's tearful testimony at their divorce hearing (which DiMaggio didn't attend), or the fans who booed him over his salary demands, made the news at the time but with years' passing have slid away, leaving the image unmarked. Elegantly attired, well spoken and graceful, a nation might indeed turn its lonely eyes to this graciously heroic character, and sigh its disappointment to find him absent from his place in center field.

Thanks perhaps to that song, but also to the image that created the song lyric, DiMaggio is among the handful of players who would be cited if you asked people who never followed baseball to name some big names of the game. Beyond simply being identified with and known beyond the game, as Babe Ruth or Mickey Mantle or Lou Gehrig were, the DiMaggio image and legacy seeped into many other aspects of the culture. Hemingway's mention of his name in *The Old Man and the Sea* was of course a reflection of the friendship between the two men, but also spoke to DiMaggio as part of the cultural establishment— when Hemingway says, "the great DiMaggio," we know what he means. In 1988, DiMaggio was photographed holding a baseball signed by President Ronald Reagan and Soviet Premier Mikhail Gorbachev at their summit meeting. What does a retired baseball player have to do with international politics? Nothing, unless he is not merely a retired athlete, but has been elevated to the status of American icon.

His hitting streak may indeed be surpassed, and as with Maris it will draw new attention to DiMaggio's record and his career accomplishments. Possibly, the old questions about whether certain rulings by official scorekeepers were made in DiMaggio's favor to keep The Streak alive will resurface. But they'll be rapidly dismissed, with little or no investigation, as they were at the time. More like Ruth, when Henry Aaron surpassed the career home-run record, his successor will more likely stand beside DiMaggio than above him in reputation.

The strongest memory many of us have about someone whose major accomplishments happened before we were born, or at least before we were old enough to be paying attention, is the manner of the person's dying. The death sets the tone for the recollection of the life; for those who didn't know much about the person, the events surrounding the death become the image in its entirety—the death is what becomes the legacy. For some famous people, that's just fine, because they die much as they lived—or at least what we see of their deaths serves as a summary of what we know of their lives.

Joe DiMaggio's death is one such.

Compare DiMaggio's death, for example, with that of fellow

Hall of Famer Mickey Mantle, whose name is paired so often
with DiMaggio's—in talking about the Yankees, in comparing
baseball greats, even (as we've seen in the galleries of the Hall)
in the locker that they shared that bears the legend of both their
names. Both were famous, glamorous, and great. But their deaths
were as different as it is possible for them to be. The Mick's
dramatic struggle with liver disease, scandalous with the mea
culpa of his alcoholism, and rife with (unsubstantiated) rumors
that his fame had bumped him to the top of the list of potential
recipients for donor organs for transplant—Mantle's was a brash,
larger-than-life, made-for-tabloid way of dying. Perhaps it's not
surprising, then, that Mantle is, as far as anyone at the Hall
remembers, the only baseball player whose death moved fans to
leave mounds of flowers and trinkets and mementos at his plaque
in the National Baseball Hall of Fame.

Then there's Joe DiMaggio. Our kids will tell their kids his
name, says the song.

Predecessor in life and successor in death to Mantle, Joe
DiMaggio's dying had the gravitas that Mantle's didn't. It was
silent, private, marred only by the erroneous announcement of
his departure weeks before the actual event (and if we didn't
know better, we might suspect the false announcement to be a
ruse to draw our attention both toward and away from DiMaggio:
toward his importance and his legend and his past, and therefore
away from the man himself lying abed suffering the ugly, graceless details of dying). Indeed, long before his demise, DiMaggio
limited his participation in Old-Timers' games lest the creakiness
of age devalue the immaculate memory of his playing days. (Ty
Cobb had done the same.) Where Mantle ended his days an open
book—or perhaps on the front of the *New York Post*—DiMaggio
finished his life more like a finely decorated leather-bound volume with gold-edged pages, displayed on a shelf barely out of
reach.

Image doesn't define the man, of course; it isn't even short-
hand. But it does help to define legacy.

DiMaggio once ran into former third baseman for the White Sox and then the Indians Willie Kamm, whose .967 fielding percentage places him seventh on the all-time list for his position. Kamm was weak and obviously in poor health. Said Kamm to DiMaggio, then seventy-three: "I'm eighty-seven. Joe, don't get that old." Kamm died the following year.

DiMaggio never did get that old. Whether through careful intent or a natural inclination to grace, we never saw him—or even imagined him—doddering and pathetic. Whatever the actual moment of his death may have been like (and death from the constellation of related ailments that finally ended his life is seldom anything but hideous), we will always have the illusion of him passing away gently and quietly in his sleep, and the mental image of him either as the gangly youngster sailing across center field or as the dapper silver-haired gentleman on television. Our collective recollection of him, his legacy, may well be magnified beyond the fragments of history sealed in display cases or storage rooms in Cooperstown. But it's a good place to start.

Pamela Hodgson is a freelance writer of fiction and nonfiction, a baseball fan, and a die-hard Cubs fan. Her work has appeared in magazines as diverse as Chicago History *and* Fantasy and Science Fiction. *She is a frequent contributor to* Techniques *magazine.*

Ted Williams and Joe DiMaggio: Most Valuable Players

RANDY MILLER

"Ted Williams was the best hitter I ever saw. There was nobody
like him."

—JOE DIMAGGIO

"In my heart, I've always felt that I was a better hitter than Joe,
which was always my first consideration. But I have to say he
was the greatest player of our time. He could do it all."

—TED WILLIAMS

SO WHICH WOULD you choose? Ted or Joe?
DiMaggio and Williams, rival American League batting kings for ten seasons (1939–1942, 1946–1951),
were frequently compared and contrasted. Each stood on his own
as a baseball legend. It is known that the Yankees and the Red
Sox considered a trade in 1946 that would have sent DiMaggio
to Fenway with its inviting left-field wall and given Williams a
shot at that right-field porch at Yankee Stadium. The proposed
trade was perceived by many as a fair swap, one for one.

Williams studied the science of batting and was famed for his
batting eye, which kept him from ever recording a two-hundred-
hit season because he received a large number of walks through
his prime. Defensively, he worked to master the caroms of Fenway's Green Monster. He was also noted for a fiery temper and
the willingness to display it publicly when fickle fans would jeer
at him.

DiMaggio was better in the outfield, better at baserunning, and could handle the bat almost as well as Williams. If Williams were a volcano, erupting at the slightest of slights, DiMaggio was a glacier, hiding movement beneath the surface. DiMaggio was known for few displays of emotion on the field during his career, the best known exception being his celebrated kick of the infield dirt after Al Gionfriddo's miraculous catch in the '47 Series.

For those who watched them closely from the press box, the sports journalists, a slight nod went to DiMaggio.

The MVP awards are decided by totaling votes from the Baseball Writers' Association of America. Voters receive a ballot on which they may rank ten candidates. A first-place vote equals ten points, a second-place vote equals nine points, and so on. Separate votes are taken for the American League and the National League. Since both Ted Williams and Joe DiMaggio played their entire careers in the American League, this article will deal with the American League MVP award, except where noted otherwise.

In six of the ten years that both were reasonably eligible for the American League MVP award, DiMaggio received more points than Williams. Even more telling, in seasons when each had truly outstanding seasons, DiMaggio always received more points than his Red Sox rival did.

In 1939, for example, Williams finished fourth in the voting after hitting .327 and driving in a league-leading 145 RBI. However, DiMaggio won his first MVP award that season by leading the American League with a .381 average for a pennant-winning team.

Remarkably, DiMaggio earned the award despite missing more than a month of the season. On April 29, Washington's Bobby Estalella smacked a single into left field at Yankee Stadium. As DiMaggio moved to cut off the hit, his spikes caught and he fell, injuring his ankle.

"I heard a loud crack," DiMaggio said. "I thought my bone was gone."

He would be more fortunate than the Yankees' next star center fielder, Mickey Mantle, who never completely recovered his speed from a knee injury suffered in a similar manner.

DiMaggio was still recovering—not even at the ballpark—on the day when Lou Gehrig concluded his remarkable 2,130-game hit streak. When Joe did come back, he dominated the league and in the last month of the season had a real chance to achieve one milestone that eluded him, the .400 mark. He was hitting .408 when he sustained an eye injury. Yankee manager Joe McCarthy kept putting him in the lineup and DiMaggio's average dropped twenty-seven points down the stretch, still good enough to lead the American League.

Two years later, DiMaggio and Williams each achieved superb performances, which still stand, at the plate.

DiMaggio, of course, compiled his celebrated hitting streak in a year that saw him lead the league in RBIs with 125. During the season, Williams had hit safely in twenty-three straight games (in fact, during DiMaggio's streak), but watched his rival's performance from afar. "Left field in Fenway Park," he is quoted in Joseph Durso's biography of DiMaggio, "is where the scoreboard is. I got to be buddies with the guy who operated it, Bill Daley. He'd give the word on what was going on around the league, all the scores and everything. When DiMaggio was on his hitting streak, Bill would keep track. He'd call out to me from the window in the scoreboard and say: 'Joe just got a double,' and I'd pass it on to Dom DiMaggio in center field."

Williams became the last Twentieth-Century batter in the major leagues to break the .400 mark by hitting .406 while also finishing first in home runs, runs, and, of course, walks. He had to scuffle down the stretch to get there, not an easy task since he faced a cadre of unfamiliar pitchers up from the minors for a late-season look. On the final day of the season, Williams entered a doubleheader against Philadelphia with a .3995 average, just barely .400. He chose to play rather than sitting it out and in the first game hammered farmhand Dick Fowler and reliever

Porter Vaughan for three hits to raise his average to .404. Williams then racked up two more hits against Philadelphia A's farmhand Fred Caligiuri in the nightcap.

Both DiMaggio and Williams had great 1941 seasons. Both had achieved stardom and were recognized by their peers as the best in the game. (Williams hit one of the most famous homers in All-Star game history off Claude Passeau that season.)

But the MVP vote went to DiMaggio, who received 291 points to Williams' 245. The difference is explained by their teams' respective performance: The Yankees won the league, as usual, while the '41 Red Sox finished seventeen games out. In some seasons, journalists sometimes justify their first-place votes as rewards for the player who led a team to a title. As quoted in Durso's biography, Williams agreed with the writers' decision. "In 1941, when I hit .406, Joe DiMaggio was named the MVP and I didn't feel robbed or cheated because DiMaggio had that 56-game hitting streak and he was a great player on a great team that won the pennant."

Williams may not have felt the same way six years later. Williams won the Triple Crown in 1947 with 32 home runs, 114 RBIs and a .343 average. But in the MVP balloting, Williams finished one point behind DiMaggio's 202 points. DiMaggio had a strong year that season as well, hitting .315 with 20 homers and 97 RBIs for another world championship team. Had Williams received the single point given to such figures as Jeff Heath, who hit 27 homers for the lowly St. Louis Browns; future teammate Vern Stephens, who batted .279 for the Browns; or Taffy Wright, a .324 hitter for the White Sox, he would have tied DiMaggio.

It became a small tempest in the Boston teapot when it was revealed that *Boston Globe* writer Melville Webb didn't list Williams in any of the ten slots on his ballot. The slight was intentional and only somewhat surprising given the long-standing venomous relationship between Boston sportswriters and Williams. Famed *New York Herald Tribune* sports editor Stanley

Woodward once dichotomized the sports journalists into the "gee-whiz" school and the "aw-nuts" school. During those days, the aw-nuts school was headquartered in Boston. New York writers tended toward the gee-whiz mentality.

Current New York players would be shocked to learn that the New York sportswriting community, in those days, treated most athletes, and especially DiMaggio, very well. The New York press, for the most part, projected an image of Babe Ruth that may not have matched the reality. And DiMaggio was equally protected by the press corps, notably beat writer Dan Daniel and *New York Times* writer Arthur Daley. DiMaggio's only real tiff with the press came in 1949 when they hounded him during his convalescence from a serious heel injury.

However, in Boston, the writers started out ripping Williams during his rookie season and he bristled at their printed jibes. Michael Seidel's excellent biography, *Ted Williams: A Baseball Life,* notes throughout his career the various jabs taken at Williams. In one case, a *Sport* magazine story was titled "Why We Pick on Williams." In it, Harold Kaese said, "In Boston, a man does not qualify as a baseball writer until he has psychoanalyzed Williams."

In an award determined by the sports journalism community, it would seem that DiMaggio's reputation and image were considered by the writers as factors in the voting.

DiMaggio also outpointed Williams 213–171 in 1948, when the Yankee Clipper led the American League in homers and RBIs to finish second in the voting behind Cleveland player-manager Lou Boudreau. The Indians knocked off the Red Sox in a one-game playoff before beating the Boston Braves in the World Series. Williams topped the league in batting average, doubles, and walks, but finished third in MVP voting, not bad considering he spent much of the season battling rib problems that began in a horseplay wrestling tussle with teammate Sam Mele.

DiMaggio also got the nod over Williams in 1940, when he

led the league with a .352 average and finished third in MVP voting behind award-winner Hank Greenberg of Detroit. Williams was a distant fourteenth, tied with Washington's Sid Hudson. The Yankees started slowly that season and could not climb back. But DiMaggio, by then, was a city celebrity and a fixture among the nightclub circuit. Williams, on the other hand, went through a year marked by critical comments in the press. In his second season with the Red Sox, Williams ranted to one writer about the grief he had taken throughout the season. "Maybe I should have been a fireman," he said, and sparked bench jockeying throughout the league. White Sox manager Jimmie Dykes, for one, needled Ted: "Fireman, fireman, save my child." Ted was as much an outsider as DiMaggio was a fixture in the system by then.

The other DiMaggio MVP points victory came in 1950 when Williams' season was curtailed by a broken arm sustained in the All-Star game. DiMaggio finished ninth that season with fifty-four points, well behind the winner, teammate Phil Rizzuto. Williams received seven points, but missed forty games down the stretch after he chipped his elbow running into the Comiskey Park outfield wall chasing a Ralph Kiner hit during the All-Star game. While Williams was out, the Sox climbed into the race, but after Williams' return, could manage to finish only third.

DiMaggio had his own problems in 1950. Casey Stengel asked him to give first base a try during a July game at Fenway. Seidel reports that Williams teased his rival: "Hey, Jolter, they come at one a lot faster than they do in the outfield." DiMaggio met with Stengel after the game and returned to the pastoral setting of center field.

Williams won MVP honors twice over DiMaggio, but those happened in down seasons for the Yankee star. In 1946, Williams led a strong Red Sox team to the American League championship while DiMaggio played hurt for much of the season and finished with a .290 average and only six MVP points.

But even in that season, Williams wound up overshadowed

when newspapers reported on the eve of the World Series that New York planned to trade Joe DiMaggio to Boston for Williams. Then, St. Louis' pitching staff stifled Williams and the Sox to win the Series.

In 1949, Williams won the American League MVP easily for a season in which he led in homers, RBIs, doubles, walks, and runs (even then, the National League MVP gathered his share of attention as Jackie Robinson became his league's best player in his third major league season). But even that award was small consolation. DiMaggio finished twelfth in the voting in a year in which he batted .346, but was most known for his recovery from physical problems to help the Yankees defeat the Red Sox to reach the World Series.

The 1949 season is still remembered for the heated pennant race between the Yankees and Red Sox. DiMaggio missed the first sixty-five games of the season with a heel injury that threatened to end his career. His almost mythic comeback made him, Durso noted, a hero beyond even his earlier status. The Yankees sustained numerous injuries and DiMaggio, down the stretch, had to play through a viral infection.

Still, the Yankees won. Despite Williams, despite the injuries and infection, they swept the final two games of the season at Yankee Stadium. The first came on Joe DiMaggio Day, when the guest of honor received $50,000 worth of gifts from the fans. The second came a day later with a worn-out DiMaggio playing center until a ninth-inning Bobby Doerr triple-sailed over his head to make the score 5–3

DiMaggio, the team player, took himself out of the game.

In 1942, Williams won the Triple Crown to place second in the MVP balloting ahead of DiMaggio, who placed seventh. This time, New York's Joe Gordon defeated Williams in the voting by twenty-one points. It was DiMaggio's worst year in his early career and Williams' best. But both should have been ready for peak seasons when they spent three years in the military; Williams seeing action as a pilot, DiMaggio playing baseball and then working with the Air Transit Command.

Williams also finished ahead of DiMaggio in the 1951 MVP balloting by placing thirteenth while DiMaggio, in his final season, received no votes for the only time in his career. It was clear that the Yankee Clipper had been surpassed by Rizzuto and the season's MVP, Yogi Berra, who would go on to be named MVP in 1954 and 1955. Williams would continue as a Top 10 finisher in the voting throughout most of the 1950s.

DiMaggio finished in the Top 10 in the balloting during his first three major league seasons. In 1936, the rookie led the American League with fifteen triples to finish eighth behind Lou Gehrig. A year later, he led the league with forty-six homers and narrowly lost the MVP to Detroit second baseman Charlie Gehringer. He placed sixth in 1938, with his 108 points well behind Boston's Jimmie Foxx.

But then came the first of three awards in 1939 and, as Jack Moore said in *Joe DiMaggio: A Bio-Biography*, the Yankee Clipper went "beyond being another star performer, to the status of national hero with class." DiMaggio achieved a status that not even Ruth could attain. Williams would eventually be recognized at this level as a senior statesman for the game long after his run-ins with the Boston press and fans were forgotten.

That difference might be why you'd pick DiMaggio.

AMERICAN LEAGUE MVP PLACE TOTALS

	DIMAGGIO	WILLIAMS	MVP
1936	8th	DNP	Lou Gehrig, NY
1937	2nd	DNP	Charlie Gehringer, Det
1938	6th	DNP	Jimmie Foxx, Bos
1939	1st	4th	DIMAGGIO
1940	3rd	14th	Hank Greenberg, Det
1941	1st	2nd	DIMAGGIO
1942	7th	2nd	Joe Gordon, NY

1943	DNP	DNP	Spud Chandler, NY
1944	DNP	DNP	Hal Newhouser, Det
1945	DNP	DNP	Hal Newhouser, Det
1946	20th	1st	WILLIAMS
1947	1st	2nd	DIMAGGIO
1948	2nd	3rd	Lou Boudreau, Cle
1949	12th	1st	WILLIAMS
1950	9th	22nd	Phil Rizzuto, NY
1951	no votes	13th	Yogi Berra, NY

AMERICAN LEAGUE MVP PLACE TOTALS (WITH POINTS)

	DiMaggio	Williams	MVP
1936	8th (26)	DNP	Lou Gehrig, NY (73)
1937	2nd (74)	DNP	Charlie Gehringer, Det (75)
1938	6th (106)	DNP	Jimmie Foxx, Bos (305)
1939	1st (280)	4th (126)	DIMAGGIO
1940	3rd (151)	14th (16)	Hank Greenberg, Det (292)
1941	1st (291)	2nd (254)	DIMAGGIO
1942	7th (86)	2nd (248)	Joe Gordon, NY (270)
1943	DNP	DNP	Spud Chandler, NY (246)
1944	DNP	DNP	Hal Newhouser, Det (236)
1945	DNP	DNP	Hal Newhouser, Det (236)
1946	20th (6)	1st (224)	WILLIAMS
1947	1st (202)	2nd (201)	DIMAGGIO
1948	2nd (213)	3rd (171)	Lou Boudreau, Cle (324)
1949	12th (18)	1st (272)	WILLIAMS
1950	9th (54)	22nd (7)	Phil Rizzuto, NY
1951	—(0)	13th (35)	Yogi Berra, NY

Randy Miller is a lifelong baseball fan who entertained his father's Marine coworkers by reading them scores from the newspaper at age four. He is an associate professor of journalism at the University of South Florida (USF) in

Tampa, where he avidly follows the USF Bulls' baseball team. Before earning a Ph.D. at the University of Texas, he worked as an award-winning sportswriter and sports columnist for six years. His favorite stint came one spring at the Waco Tribune-Herald *when he covered NCAA baseball, junior college baseball, two high school baseball leagues, and no track. His short stories have appeared in such critically praised anthologies as* Excalibur, Phantoms of the Night, *and the Bram Stoker Award–winning* Horrors! 365 Scary Stories.

For a Memory

PAMELA HODGSON

EOPLE SAY MEMORIES are priceless. Certainly that's true for fans who had the opportunity to see Joe DiMaggio play. But those of us who aren't old enough to have seen the Yankee Clipper in action seek access to those memories in other ways. Ways that have a definite price tag attached.

I held a moon rock once. It looked just like a rock you might pick up in the alley or on a nature trail; if I hadn't been studying meteorites in my college class, I probably wouldn't have even noticed anything distinctive about it. As it was, I picked out colors and lines I'd learned to identify, indicative of certain elements and processes; but it was still pretty much a rock. But what made me catch my breath as I ran my fingers over the jagged surfaces of that pyrite-studded hunk of igneous matter, what made that moment unforgettable, was the sense that I was cradling in my two small hands a piece of the sky.

You can't buy a moon rock—but if you could, no doubt the

price would be less related to the actual, measurable cost that
NASA incurred in acquiring those rocks than it would be to the
limited supply, and the degree of interest in owning a moon rock.
Moon rocks would probably be sold with certificates of authenticity from NASA experts. You'd need that assurance, because,
if the desire to touch the sky in the form of a moon rock was
strong, there would probably be fakes out there—which you
would need to be a rocket scientist to identify. It's likely a moon
rock brought back by Neil Armstrong after that one small step
would be more valuable than one retrieved on a later moon mission. Perhaps astronauts would even autograph moon rocks.

You may want the moon, but you will have to settle for something a little more accessible. If you had three million dollars
late in 1998, you could have gotten a pretty famous sphere of a
different sort.

The ball Mark McGwire hit for his record-setting seventieth
home run of that season was bought for that kind of money. The
McGwire ball is a special case (although many dealers in sports
collectibles are hoping that case and the publicity it received will
drive other prices upward), but baseball memorabilia in general
still represents an enormous and often pricey market. If you're
after Joe DiMaggio memorabilia, there are only a limited number
of items to be had and his popularity means that there are few
bargains.

Why do collectors collect? Renowned collector and DiMaggio
friend Barry Halper—whose collection of baseball memorabilia
was appraised in 1995 at a value of forty-three million dollars,
and who is in the process of selling off much of that collection—
told *Sports Illustrated* that Sandy Koufax once asked him why
he filled his house with what Koufax termed junk. "I haven't
lived the game," Halper told Koufax. "Maybe that's the reason." Like holding a moon rock in place of walking on the
moon, holding Joe DiMaggio's bat will let you imagine for a
moment what it was like to be the Yankee Clipper poised at the
plate with a World Series on the line. Halper has had the op-

portunity to hold more than DiMaggio's bat: his collection includes fifty-six baseballs autographed by DiMaggio in honor of the 1941 hitting streak, and a baseball signed by DiMaggio and "Norma Jean DiMaggio," better known to most of us as Marilyn Monroe.

The celebrity of DiMaggio and certain other players contributes to the desire of many people to collect baseball memorabilia: as well as a brush with greatness, owning a DiMaggio item is a brush with fame. Baseball players became popular celebrities early in the history of the game, before there were movie stars, and for many years rivaled them for public recognition. As a measure of that star factor, consider this: one of the earliest incidents of what today we call celebrity stalking happened to Eddie Waitkus of the Philadelphia Phillies. In 1949, Ruth Steinhagen, obsessed with Waitkus and distressed that he had been traded from the Chicago Cubs, tracked the player to his hotel, bribed a bellman to give him a note luring him to a room, and shot him.

Waitkus survived the injury and returned to the game. One of his later baseball cards lists as his greatest thrill in baseball: "I was shot by a deranged girl."

But baseball celebrity began well before 1949. As early as the 1880s, the makers of Old Judge cigarettes thought to dispel the impression that machine-made cigarettes were unmanly by enclosing in each package a picture of a famous ballplayer. The connection between cigarette companies and baseball players remained strong until health concerns about cigarette smoking were raised in the 1960s. Joe DiMaggio appeared in ads for Camel cigarettes—including a cartoon series featuring DiMaggio—for several years of his playing career.

Candy and snack companies used baseball cards as promotional items as well (Cracker Jack even did a series), but the most famous and popular cards for many years were produced by tobacco companies. Today's most valuable baseball card, the T-206 card of Hall of Fame Pittsburgh shortstop Honus Wagner, was produced by the American Tobacco Company and included with Sweet Caporal cigarettes in 1909. The card is sufficiently famous that one hangs in the Metropolitan Museum of Art.

That card is valuable because it is extremely rare. Wagner objected to the use of his image on the cards—some say because he opposed tobacco, others suggest it was because the company didn't pay him for the use of his image—and the card was withdrawn. No one knows exactly how many of the cards made it into circulation, but the highest estimate is 150. Memorabilia expert Don Flanagan guesses there are no more than sixty known examples of the card today.

The value of a T-206 Wagner card varies widely according to condition. Two widely reported sales at auction involved examples that were well preserved and in excellent condition: in 1991, hockey star Wayne Gretzky and team owner Bruce McNall partnered to purchase one for $451,000, and in 1996 another was sold for $640,500. However in a recent sale, a T-206 Wagner in poor condition sold for $62,000—less than a tenth of the price. To compare, the 1949 Leaf card of Joe DiMaggio lists at $2,500 in mint or near-mint condition; it is hard to find in that condition because it was the No. 1 card in the '49 Leaf series. In very good condition, the price goes down to $800.

As part of the Barry Halper collection, Sotheby's will be offering for auction an uncut strip of T-206 cards, including a Wagner. The strip is expected to sell in the range of $50,000 to $100,000.

No matter how much you may admire Mr. Wagner (although if you're not an avid fan of the game, you may not even have heard of Wagner except in connection with this card), even at the relative bargain price of $62,000, owning a T-206 Wagner is out of the league of most people. That didn't used to be the case.

Collector Bill Mastro, head of Mastro's Fine Sports Auctions, owned his T-206 Wagner—and a number of other highly prized cards—by the time he was nineteen years old. That's because

Mastro was nineteen in 1971, before the market for sports collectibles began to boom.

The market for baseball cards—originally collected in large part by kids, but gradually becoming popular with adults as well—skyrocketed in the later 1970s and the 1980s, taking all baseball collectibles with it. "The underlying economic foundation of the whole sports memorabilia market is cards," says memorabilia expert Don Flanagan, who appraised the Halper collection in 1995. That boom was driven by the economic conditions in the United States in general. He continues: "People were putting their money into hard assets, whether it was precious metals or collectibles."

Although the boom has leveled a little in recent years, the sports memorabilia market remains strong, and cards remain a large part of it. Flanagan mentions a recent sports memorabilia auction that took in five and a half million dollars. Half of that was cards.

Meanwhile, Matt Robbins of Sotheby's says that it has been several years since the famous auction house handled a sports auction. But the Halper collection is sufficiently attractive to them, and high-profile enough (thanks in part to Halper's well-known friendship with DiMaggio, among others), that part of it will be used to launch Sotheby's Internet auctions.

Businesspeople were quick to see the opportunities in baseball and other sports cards. Although cards were not produced around World War II, they returned in force thereafter. The Bowman Gum Company, Topps, and Red Man Tobacco were active producers of cards in the late 1940s and through the 1950s. As card companies insisted that players sign exclusive agreements to appear on their cards, the competition became fiercer, and Topps bought out Bowman in 1955. Topps had what amounted to a monopoly on baseball cards until 1981.

In a 1981 court action, Topps lost its monopoly. Numerous competitors sprung up or revived in the 1980s, including Fleer, Donruss, Upper Deck, and Score. In addition, each company

introduced a variety of lines and designs, including commemorative cards for players of previous years, like the 1992 set of
Joe DiMaggio cards produced by Score. Card sales went from
250 million cards a year in the 1970s to 5 billion cards in 1988.
The Major League Baseball Players Association, which collects
licensing revenues, collected about $2 million for cards in 1981.
The figure in 1992 was near $70 million. Prices—for *all* cards—
have risen accordingly.

That's created a new generation of collectors who do it from
the start with an eye toward value. Not to say they aren't fans
of the game—just that the investment angle is never far from
sight. The older generation—and still, some of the new—do it
for love.

Barbara Wilson describes herself as her father's only son. "He
had two daughters, and I was the one who loved baseball. He
used to take me to Ebbets Field and I became a Brooklyn Dodger
fanatic." Wilson started collecting Dodger cards, as well as articles from the local papers, and put together a scrapbook of
articles and pictures of her favorite, Pee Wee Reese, which Reese
signed for her at the ballpark. She left that scrapbook at her
parents' house when she went to college; when her mother sold
the house after her father's death, the scrapbook was left behind.
"I was heartbroken," she says, "but I hope that someone found
it and had many pleasant memories."

In 1978 an Old-Timers' game between the Brooklyn Dodgers
and New York Giants took place in Wilson's new hometown of
San Diego. She was able to get Reese's attention and tell him
about her lost scrapbook, and ask for an autograph. "I was the
only one he signed anything for and I treasure it," she says. "I
saw him again at an autograph signing in L.A. and believe it or
not he remembered the incident."

Wilson is a grandmother now, and gives each of her three
grandchildren a complete Topps set every year.

Collectibles like the ones Barbara Wilson has come with a
story. There are lots of those. Joe DiMaggio fan Stanley Modrak

was in the hospital in North Korea in 1950 when Joe DiMaggio and Lefty O'Doul visited injured soldiers there. DiMaggio signed a baseball for Modrak, who asked a corpsman to mail it to his father in Pittsburgh for safekeeping.

The ball never made it there.

Modrak was living in California in 1991 when DiMaggio visited Oakland to commemorate his 1941 fifty-six-game hitting streak. Modrak's wife contacted the A's, told them her husband's story, and asked for their help in getting an autographed baseball for her husband. Modrak received the ball on his sixty-second birthday, inscribed, ''To Stanley—A replacement. Best wishes, Joe DiMaggio.''

Stories like these help to assure authenticity of a memorabilia item, should the owner ever decide to sell it or trade with another collector for something of comparable value. (Card trading has always been a common practice; swapping other baseball collectibles is much less frequent.) Even collectors who love the items they own will sometimes sell, in order to upgrade to a more expensive item, or because they need the money, or for reasons of estate planning. Don Flanagan reports that, if Barry Halper died suddenly before selling his collection, his heirs would owe about half its value in estate taxes. By selling the collection himself, he can manage resources for his family more effectively.

Players often decide to sell items themselves, for similar types of reasons. Pitcher Steve Carlton recently sold two of his four Cy Young awards at auction. Since his diagnosis with Lou Gehrig's disease, Jim ''Catfish'' Hunter has placed some of his memorabilia on the block.

The value of items that are intrinsic to the game—awards, game-used bats, uniforms, lineup cards, and the like—is increased by the fact that there are a very limited number of them. The other factors that drive value of those intrinsic items are the age and condition of the items, the popularity of the player, and—above all—numbers. If it belonged to a player who set a record, or put up Hall of Fame numbers, it will have value. But long-term numbers are worth more than one-time numbers. For example, the lineup card from the game in which Cubs pitcher Kerry Wood struck out twenty batters is estimated to be worth about sixteen hundred dollars; were he not out for a year or more with elbow surgery with a questionable future, experts say the card would probably go for two or three times that amount.

Personality plays a role, too. Just about anything Babe Ruth touched—during his playing days or not—will go for top dollar. As an example, Upper Deck packaged *slivers* of a Babe Ruth bat with a few of its baseball cards. Those slivers are being sold on the open market for $2,000 to $3,000. Mickey Mantle is also popular enough that ancillary items remain highly sought; his passport was recently purchased for $11,000. Collectors and dealers agree that DiMaggio is in the top ten for popularity, although the supply of items from his playing days is very limited. His 1947 road jersey recently sold for about $60,000.

After their playing days are over, many players continue to thrive on the market for anything associated with their names. They may sell some of their own memorabilia. The better-known names make money through appearances to autograph at card and memorabilia shows, and many have realized the immense earning potential in creating limited-edition collectibles.

The sports card convention circuit is a great source of authentic autographs for collectors (there's no better guarantee of authenticity than having the player sign the item himself, in front of you), as well as a chance to meet a favorite player, if only for a moment. The economics from the players' standpoint are appealing, especially since they are sometimes compensated in cash. As long as they don't run afoul of the law: In July 1995, Duke Snider pleaded guilty in federal court for failing to report $100,000 in income from show appearances to the IRS.

Joe DiMaggio earned as much as $150,000 for a single appearance at a sports card convention—more than he ever earned in a year as a player. But in the early eighties he stopped signing bats for fans at shows and elsewhere, because he was aware of the profit being turned when those signed bats were resold by dealers. Instead, in 1993, with the demand for DiMaggio-signed bats artificially high because of his moratorium, the Yankee Clipper made a deal with two marketing firms, Pro-Sports Services and Madison Sports & Entertainment, to sign 1,941 bats, in commemoration of the season of his 56-game hit streak. DiMaggio asked that his compensation be kept private, but media reports estimated it to be between $3 million and $4 million. That works out to approximately $1,500 to $2,000 per autograph. The bats originally sold for $3,000 to $4,000 each. Today, they can be found for anywhere from $2,000 to $4,000. (Possibly of more value—if you could get hold of it—is the videotape of DiMaggio signing the bats. Originally, the tape was intended as part of the promotion of the bats, but DiMaggio blocked its release because the hot day of signing made his appearance unflattering.)

For purposes of comparison, a pre-World War II baseball bat used by Joe DiMaggio—unsigned—may go for $5,000 or so today.

DiMaggio signed an enormous number of bats, balls, and other items in the last twenty years of his life; as a result, those autographs are less valuable than anything signed during his playing career. They've held a certain amount of value, though, not only because of his lasting popularity both as a baseball player and as a public figure (for example, items relating to the brief DiMaggio-Monroe marriage are rare and extremely coveted), but also because in many cases the recently signed items are easily authenticated.

Authenticity is a huge concern for collectors and dealers in all types of baseball memorabilia, but most especially autographs. "A lot of the autographs you see for sale on eBay [the online auction service, which takes no responsibility for the items offered on its site] are fake," says Don Flanagan, formerly of Christie's. And most serious autograph collectors will tell you that a certificate of authenticity is hardly worth the paper it is printed on.

Some fakes are done for profit; others are the result of popular players having spouses, friends, or clubhouse attendants or other team employees help fill the many requests they receive by mail for autographed photos, etc. If you don't know what the real autograph looks like, it is easy to get burned.

Even the people who should know get burned. One widely circulated magazine for collectors publishes an autographed player photo on its cover. In 1998, it published one of Mark McGwire. McGwire himself pointed out that the signature printed on the cover bore no resemblance to his real John Hancock.

The best documentation for an autograph is getting it yourself, face-to-face. (And you get the memory of meeting the player, at no extra charge. Although Joe DiMaggio guarded his privacy carefully, he was known to oblige fans who approached him politely.) The next best thing is acquiring the autograph from the person who did get the autograph, and documenting that fact with a photo of the player signing the item. Also generally safe are items, like the 1,941 DiMaggio-signed baseball bats, that have been provided by reputable companies with the player's participation—special autographed cards distributed by the major baseball card companies are an example. (DiMaggio had a deal in the early 1990s with Score Board, a memorabilia and card company, for which he was paid $4 million a year for signing cards, balls, and other items.) Although those items aren't directly connected with the player's playing days, they at least can be easily documented as to authenticity, should you choose to sell them at any point.

Certain players have taken authenticity concerns into their own hands. Ted Williams Family Enterprises markets items with an authentic autograph from DiMaggio contemporary and competitor Ted Williams. Williams' son, John Henry Williams, found that nine of ten Williams autographs he saw advertised turned out to be fakes. To prevent forgeries, his company now attaches holographic labels to authentic items.

Authenticating items other than autographs is an even tougher problem. There's a wonderful thread in Don DeLillo's novel *Underworld* about the provenance of the baseball from Bobby Thomson's 1951 "shot heard round the world" home run, as the author tracks the numerous owners of the baseball over several decades—from the father of the young man in the novel who struggles with other fans for the prize, to another father who gives it to his son, through numerous sales and gifts until it is owned by a leading character in the novel. That kind of detective work is dramatic, but almost impossible for the average collector.

Recently, DiMaggio successor Mickey Mantle's five hundredth home-run ball was removed from auction by Guernsey's, a well-regarded New York auction house, to allow time to dig deeper into its history and authenticity. Owner Dale Cicero reported purchasing the ball from a collector who is said to have purchased it from a baseball museum, which in turn would have received it from a Mantle friend—the provenance appeared to be clear. The questions arose when the player's widow, Merlyn Mantle, claimed that the Mantle friend had actually returned the ball to the Mick, who then gave it to her. Experts who have seen photos say Mrs. Mantle's ball does not have the American League stamp, but both balls have Mantle's signature. If both Mrs. Mantle and Mr. Cicero agree, the two balls will be compared by authentication experts to determine which is most likely the real one.

How collectibles come into circulation is often the subject of question, and even during the forties, dubious methods were employed. On the day that DiMaggio's hitting streak matched that of George Sisler at forty-one, his bat was stolen (although it was later returned to him, and after the streak he donated it to the USO for a benefit auction). He also lost the only glove he had kept from his San Francisco Seals days to theft. More recently, according to the New York *Daily News,* DiMaggio attorney Morris Engelberg suggested that the player's 1951 World Series ring, which Barry Halper purchased from a dealer, had been stolen from the Yankee Clipper. Halper says his friend DiMaggio told him the ring had been given away, and certified its authenticity. (In the months since DiMaggio's death, *Daily News* writers Bill Madden and Luke Cypher have reported that Engelberg as DiMaggio's trustee may have sought to profit inappropriately from DiMaggio and his legacy, through unreported compensation in the form of memorabilia, among other means.)

As far as collectors and dealers know, balls hit by Joe DiMaggio during his fifty-six-game hitting streak have not made their way onto the market. If someone turned up with one today, the owner would be hard pressed to provide sufficient evidence of its specific origin. While its approximate age could be derived by forensic methods, proving that it was actually hit by DiMaggio, and during the specific period of his streak, would be more problematic. Today, the technology to assure authenticity of record-making balls (like McGwire's number sixty-two) exists; so far, Major League Baseball has chosen to go only to the expense of using the special marking for those balls for the 1998 home-run chase (and in fact Sammy Sosa's number sixty-two was not tagged for identification), but given the attention Diamondback outfielder Luis Gonzalez received during his 1999 hitting streak of thirty games, it seems likely that a serious challenge to the DiMaggio record would warrant the marked baseballs. Programs, ticket stubs, and other items from the games of DiMaggio's streak are easier to date and authenticate and have found their way into the memorabilia market over the years.

Jerseys would seem to be straightforward in terms of authenticity, what with the player's name and number on the back, but replicas and outright fakes abound. For prewar players, jerseys were often recycled, the names and logos removed and new ones (particularly for the team's minor league affiliates) added. Even if the jerseys weren't recycled in that manner, few people were saving or collecting uniforms in the first half of the century, and even fewer preserved them from deterioration, so few have survived. As a result, the genuine article, especially for a player for whom few uniform items have come to light, can command huge prices. But it's important that the item indeed be genuine; rumors have abounded that some of the jerseys to be auctioned as part of the Halper collection will be withdrawn from the September 1999 sale because, under expert scrutiny, their authenticity has been questioned. A spokesman for Sotheby's, which is handling the auction, declined to comment.

There are only a handful of true experts on autographs, jerseys, bats, and other baseball-related memorabilia, according to Don Flanagan, currently with Mastro's Fine Sports Auctions, and there are a lot of people who claim to have expertise that they don't. The major auction houses and dealers work closely with the top experts, either sending items to the specialists for evaluation or, in the case of a large sale, bringing the experts in to evaluate the items that have been consigned to them. They will look for such features as the set number tag on old jerseys (players were generally issued a limited number of uniform ''sets''), composition and wear appropriate to the age of the item, and fine details in pen pressure and letter formation in signatures.

The experts used by the large auction houses are costly. The average collector of DiMaggio memorabilia will have to rely on the source of his item to be satisfied that someone, somewhere, has rigorously examined its bona fides.

That's if it's important to you to know. Certainly, if you ever expect to resell an item, the importance is critical. If not, if the value for you resides in having something that *you* believe is special, that belonged to or was associated with DiMaggio, then perhaps it doesn't matter whether extensive forensic analysis has been conducted to reassure you that your money has been well spent.

Some expertise, like that of Peter Clark, curator of collections for the National Baseball Hall of Fame, isn't routinely available.

Clark has custody of some of the finest items from Joe Di-Maggio's career, including uniform items, gloves, a bat, assorted signed baseballs from the Yankee Clipper's playing days, and even a matchbook from DiMaggio's restaurant.

A matchbook is hardly the oddest DiMaggio item someone has sought to keep. During the 1950 World Series, DiMaggio slipped out for a cigarette. He hadn't finished the smoke when it was his turn to bat. Joltin' Joe (who was a spokesman for Camel cigarettes, but many years later signed a Camel ad with the notation that he hadn't had a cigarette in thirty-six years) asked a Philadelphia police officer on duty at the ballpark to hold his cigarette. When DiMaggio came back to finish his smoke, the officer declined to return it, keeping it as a souvenir.

Philadelphians will recognize the name of that officer. He went on to become the city's mayor, Frank Rizzo. Rizzo never sold the cigarette butt; he kept it until it disintegrated.

What's still available for the rest of the DiMaggio collectors? And what will it cost? Some examples of DiMaggio items, and what they went for, when:

What	When	How Much
1985 "Cracker Jack All-Star" Old-Timer's game uniform worn and signed by DiMaggio	1991	$4,000
DiMaggio glove	1991	$25,000
DiMaggio home jersey	1994	$130,000
1939 Play Ball R334 DiMaggio baseball card	1998	$2,500
Commemorative baseball issued by the Yankees for Joe DiMaggio Day September 28, 1998	1999	$20–$25
One of 160 baseballs signed in 1998 with DiMaggio's stats	1999	$2000–$2400
1947 DiMaggio road jersey	1999	$60,000

Of course a large number of DiMaggio items, including uniforms, autographs, and photos, will enter the market in September 1999 in the Halper collection auction. Sotheby's estimates, as one example, that DiMaggio's 1933 San Francisco Seals uniform will go for between $50,000 and $100,000.

How good is baseball memorabilia in general as an investment? Speculating in current or recent players is always risky. For example: In late 1993 author Paul Green speculated that the $30 price tag on a 1992 Fleer Update card of Mike Piazza was the most that card would ever be worth, and owners of the card should sell it while they could. In 1999, *Beckett's Official Price Guide* lists that card at $100. However, at the same time in 1993, the 1990 Donruss King of Kings card of Nolan Ryan with errors on the back sold for $9 to $10. Today those cards list between 40 cents and $1.50. Card prices are certainly more volatile than the prices of game-used items like bats and jerseys, but one can never know for sure whether a promising rookie will become a DiMaggio-quality future Hall of Famer or just a brief listing in *The Baseball Encyclopedia.*

Memorabilia from superstar players like Joe DiMaggio will always be popular, but how popular—in dollars and cents—is just as hard to predict. If supply were the only issue, the value would certainly stay high, as there are no more DiMaggio items to be had than what exists today. But demand is more fickle. As long as there are baseball fans, there will be people interested in greats of the game like Joe DiMaggio; the open question is whether those fans will continue to be able and willing to spend thousands of dollars to own a piece of baseball history.

Ultimately, the worth of any item is dictated by the collector. If it means a lot to you to own something, then it's worth a high price. The happiest collectors will always be the ones who buy items because they prize them because they are close to their hearts. If the appraised value goes up, so much the better. But if it doesn't, they will have had the chance to treasure something that brings them closer to a game and a player they have loved and admired, and that in itself will be every bit as valuable as having the chance to hold a piece of the sky.

The Home Runs of Joe DiMaggio

ROBERT STAUFFER

A Rightie in the House that Ruth Built

THE GAME OF baseball has always been a game of what-ifs. Make tiny changes in the history of the game and see how huge a difference they could have made. In 1938, Joe DiMaggio sat out the month of April over a contract dispute with Colonel Jacob Ruppert. During that time, the St. Louis Browns were said to have made an offer to buy the straying young ballplayer from the Yanks. If Ruppert had in exasperation made the foolhardy move to sell his difficult holdout, what effect might that have had on DiMaggio's home-run total?

DiMaggio hit 148 of his 361 dingers at Yankee Stadium, which certainly is not a bad total. The deep, deep left field (490 feet at left-center) of the stadium before the renovation in the seventies—remnants of which still haunt right-handed hitters today, even though the field has been turned ever so slightly to equalize the corners a little—was something of a menace to

DiMaggio. One of the most memorable of DiMaggio's big flies was hit deep to left, 415 feet or so, right into the mitt of waiting outfielder Al Gionfriddo. It came in the sixth game of the 1947 World Series and despite the fact that the Yanks came back and won the series the next day, that catch will live on like Carlton Fisk's waving a ball fair for a home run in the 1975 World Series. Had DiMaggio been a switch-hitter, that ball would have been out of there; the Dodgers finished for the season.

Of course many of the parks that DiMaggio played in were built against the righties. Right-handedness is more common and thus the more defended against. In parks that tended to be a little more balanced depthwise, walls or overhangs were constructed to keep the home-run totals lower for the righties. Shibe Park had a twelve-foot-high wall in left, although the A's later built a thirty-one-foot wall in right to keep people from getting a free view of the game. Detroit's Tiger Stadium, then known as Briggs Stadium, has an overhang in left field that tends to catch the higher fly balls, rendering them home runs. Boston, of course, still has the Green Monster to rein the righties in—nineteen feet of railroad ties covered in tin on top of eighteen feet of concrete.

But Ruth's House was so lopsided in favor of the left-handed hitter that one might say that the proof of DiMaggio's greatness was that he could hit even the 148 homers he did hit there. Lou Gehrig, Reggie Jackson, Yogi Berra, Graig Nettles, Tino Martinez, Roger Maris—all the great home-run hitters of the Yankees were lefties. Even Mickey Mantle hit the bulk of his homers as a leftie at Yankee Stadium. Of the top five home-run hitters at Yankee Stadium, DiMaggio is the only rightie.

Not one of DiMaggio's eight World Series homers came at Yankee Stadium. As a matter of fact, when DiMaggio joked that his first World Series homer would have landed in the upper deck at Yankee Stadium, the reporter responded in his column by saying, it "also might have been a foul. He hit it with a tremendous pull and, traveling the greater distance, it might have hooked out of fair territory." His only All-Star game home run did come at Yankee Stadium, but then, DiMaggio did always come through when he had to. Playing against the best of the best would have only made him stronger.

What *if* Joe DiMaggio had become a St. Louis Brown in 1938? While hitting home runs out of Sportsman's Park in St. Louis was not easy, there were no outrageous obstacles either. No mile-high walls or death valleys in left field. If you shift the balance from Yankee Stadium as a home field to Sportsman, DiMaggio might have hit another hundred home runs or so. Who knows, maybe he would have lasted as an outfielder a little longer if he didn't have to cover quite so much ground.

THE PARKS:

TEAM	PARK	LF	CF	RF	HR	NOTES
Boston	Fenway Park	321	488	314	29	The Green Monster in left field stands 37 feet.
Chicago	Comiskey Park	362	420	362	30	Designed with the help of a pitcher.
Cleveland	League Park/ Municipal Stadium	385 322	462 470	290 322	22	Cleveland split their home games between two parks.
Detroit	Briggs Stadium	345	467	370	30	Overhang in right field catches high flies hit there.
New York	Yankee Stadium	281	490	295	148	Deep alley in left field called Death Valley.
Philadelphia	Shibe Park	334	468	331	27	Left has a twelve-foot-high wall.

| St. Louis | Sportsman's Park | 353 | 430 | 320 | 45 | Most evenly shaped diamond of the time. |
| Washington | Griffith Stadium | 407 | 421 | 320 | 30 | Deep left field wall. |

What Price, War?

Another what-if certainly has to be about World War II. A lot of players settle in so well after that first blush as a rookie and early journeymanship that it is easy to think that after seven seasons, a player is locked into his career. By 1942 DiMaggio was a regular .300 hitter, settling in to thirty or so homers a year, and though it would not be a great year for him slugging-wise, he was settling into a routine of being the hero. The Yankees moved on to their seventh World Series in as many years, as right as rain.

But 1943 would be the beginning of the war for baseball. After declaring that baseball should continue in order to keep up the morale of the American people, Franklin Delano Roosevelt began drafting the boys of summer and sending them off to fight, or, rather, in many cases, play baseball for the troops.

Joe DiMaggio was no dodger in any sense of the word, and in a lot of ways had more to prove in the war effort, being the son of an Italian immigrant. So while his father suffered such indignities as not being allowed near the San Francisco docks where he had worked since coming to the United States DiMaggio went off to begin a new career as a soldier in the Army Air Force.

So how many more home runs would DiMaggio have hit had he stayed away from the draft? Well, that's not so easy to figure. Before the war he pounded out 219 home runs in seven seasons, afterward, 142 in six seasons. Maybe it slowed him down to have to start over again, but then, he was playing quite a bit during the war, too. How do you determine what he might have hit in the years he missed?

DiMaggio's favorite victim, Bob Feller, also served the 1943, 1944, and 1945 seasons in the war, so one could argue that DiMaggio's numbers might have gone down, but on the other hand, a lot of pitchers of the time were serving, which means DiMaggio would have faced a lot younger, less experienced brand of pitcher, which would make his numbers go up.

DiMaggio's replacements in center field hit twenty-eight homers total the three years the Clipper was at war. As a matter of fact, Tuck Stainback hit a career-high five homers in 1945, accounting for nearly a third of his thirteen-year-career total of seventeen. I think it's safe to say that DiMaggio would have managed more than that.

But what if there hadn't been any war and baseball had continued on the way it was going? Perhaps DiMaggio and the Yankees would have grabbed another three titles. Maybe one of the men killed overseas was the next Cy Young and DiMaggio would have had a real nemesis. So many things might have happened, so that number will have to remain a what-if.

Rapid Robert

Bob Feller was one of the best pitchers of the 1940s and 1950s. He led the league in wins in six of his years, in ERA once, and in shutouts and complete games numerous times. He and the Cleveland Indians were a perennial thorn in the side of the Yankees, constantly squeezing the champs, making them sweat out what could have been runaway seasons. DiMaggio's famous streak was halted in Cleveland, and the year the Yanks climbed to 103 wins in 1954, the Indians were there to top them by winning 111.

Many people consider the Yanks' greatest rivals to be the Red

Sox, but that was born of an ill-advised sale on the part of the Beantowners in 1920, and fostered on the constant contest between the DiMaggio brothers during the 1940s, to say nothing of the DiMaggio-Ted Williams struggle for dominance in the headlines. But these were rivalries of the nobler sort. What the Yanks and Indians had was more gritty and down-to-earth, a struggle for team dominance.

But there's no question that Feller was dominated by the Clipper. There's even a photo of the two together autographed by both to each other. Feller wrote: "You almost keep me out of Cooperstown with all your hits." In DiMaggio's last season, the greatest slight he received from the Indians was to have Feller walk Berra in front of him with a man already on second. In essence the Indians were saying that the Clipper was sunk. DiMaggio responded by hitting the ball 457 feet to straightaway center over the head of the center fielder (but still in the park) to bring the two runners home.

The Big Cut

From the beginning of the game's history, baseball has been fraught with what were affectionately known as freaks. These were men who could do one thing so well that their names have become nearly synonymous with the deed. Cy Young's name is uttered forever before pitchers who know what it takes to win. Ruth's home-run capability seems to be all that's remembered of his storied and multifaceted career.

If Joe DiMaggio is remembered in this way for anything, it's his ability to do everything.

Many times, particularly with the kind of offense DiMaggio could offer, a player's defense is forgotten. But the Yankee Clipper earned his nickname with his graceful plays in the outfield, never making anything look very difficult. Critics called him icy, while fans called him cool.

His grace extended to the plate, of course. While Ruth would crush the ball, or tear the cover off it, DiMaggio would ease the ball over the wall, or lift it gently to left. No hacking, no destroying, only grace.

The proof of this lies not in his home-run total but in his strikeout total. Generally power hitters have to strike with such force and timing that they can be fooled by pitches. As in everything, the higher the profit, the more numerous the risks that need to be taken. But DiMaggio's stylish approach to swinging led to less wiffs. His good eye and strong back and arms minimized the risk of strikeout despite his power. The majority of his yearly totals show his number of homers greater than that of his strikeouts. In the years where he struck out more, the difference exceeds ten only four times: his rookie year, his first two years back from war, and his final year.

Of the men who hold the Top 10 spots for home-run bashing, only Ted Williams comes close in the strikeout department, striking out merely twice as many times as DiMaggio did or nearly three strikeouts for every two homers. Every other leader in the home-run department struck out at least 1,300 times. Reggie Jackson managed to strike out 2,597 times—nearly a five-to-one ratio of strikeouts to homers—on his way to the sixth spot in lifetime home runs.

DiMaggio's meager 369—pretty much a one-to-one ratio to his homers—is truly an incredible mark. Even Ted Williams, probably the century's last .400 hitter, admired how well DiMaggio chose his pitches with two strikes on him.

TOP 10 HOME-RUN HITTERS AND JOE DIMAGGIO:

PLAYER	# OF HRs	# OF Ks	CAREER GAMES	LIFETIME AVG.
Hank Aaron	755	1383	3298	.305
Babe Ruth	714	1330	2503	.342
Willie Mays	660	1526	2992	.302
Frank Robinson	586	1532	2808	.294

Harmon Killebrew	573	1699	2435	.256
Reggie Jackson	563	2597	2820	.262
Mike Schmidt	548	1883	2404	.267
Mickey Mantle	536	1710	2401	.298
Jimmie Foxx	534	1311	2317	.325
Ted Williams	521	709	2292	.344
Joe DiMaggio	361	369	1736	.325

We Want Them on Our Side

As all great hitters know, one hitter does not a winning ball club make. A great team, certainly one that can win nine World Series in a mere sixteen years, is a club that can provide a united offense and a strong defense, year after year. The Yankees of the '20s,'40s,'50s,'70s, and '90s have shown that repeating a championship is a lot easier when you have the right mix of talent and everyone works together.

When one looks back at the team Joe DiMaggio inherited from his spiritual ancestor, Babe Ruth, maybe there aren't a lot of names recognizable to us today. Lou Gehrig was approaching the end of his career, though he still managed forty-nine homers and a marvelous .354 average while leading the league in runs, homers, walks, and slugging percentage in DiMaggio's rookie year. Red Rolfe was in the prime of his career, leading the league in triples with fifteen. George Selkirk, Bill Dickey, Tony Lazzeri, as well as Gehrig and DiMaggio all finished with more than one hundred RBIs. And that's not even talking about the pitching. This was a powerhouse team that rolled to 102 victories— nineteen and a half games in front of the second-place Tigers.

During that rookie year, DiMaggio would perform the astounding feat of hitting two home runs in one inning, but I think it says a lot about the team that it was not the lead for the article for the next day's *New York Times*. The headline starts off instead noting the most important thing: YANKS WIN, and then notes that DiMaggio tied the record for homers in an inning—not that he led the team to victory. As a matter of fact, Gehrig's 101 hits (and this was only the end of June) and Jake Powell's grand slam were reported first in the article, and even Tony Lazzeri's "badly damaged" finger came ahead of this rookie feat.

And all through his career, DiMaggio would be surrounded by a core of great players. Sometimes one would move on and leave the team for one reason or another, but the Yanks always managed to pick up another slugger just in time. Gehrig out, Tommy Henrich in; Frank Crosetti out, Phil Rizzuto in; Charlie Keller out, Yogi Berra in. Eventually it would be DiMaggio out, Mantle in. This was the true strength of the Yankees, always a core to which was added those who would someday be at the center for the next generation.

When there are no safe batters in the lineup to pitch to, each batter helps another. Nobody is walked or fed garbage or pitched around. You can't afford to put another runner on base when the next guy up is going to knock him in. But, also, the players can learn from one another, can protect one another, and enjoy one another's successes. In nearly all the years that DiMaggio was in the Top 5 for home runs in the American League, the Yankees also led the league in homers as a team.

Years from now, maybe people won't be able to name all of the current New York Yankees, but they'll certainly remember a team that inspired one another to victory, each taking his share and making the wins—no one great hero who won every game. The Yanks of the thirties and forties were also of this variety. While many looked to DiMaggio at first to be a rookie phenom and then to be a role model for the younger players, there was never any expectation that he would score every run, make every catch, hit a home run every time he came to the plate. That is a luxury that makes a great ballplayer even greater. He can take the time he needs to hit the ball well, to play when he's strong, and rest when he's not.

In his autobiographical *Life* article in 1949, DiMaggio talks about how hard it is to sit back and watch his team hold first place without him, not because he felt passed by or forgotten, but because he wanted to be out there playing the game. When a team can fuel itself with its own victories and revel in its own strengths, it makes every player that much better.

So while DiMaggio was not the greatest home-run hitter ever, he certainly qualifies to be near the top of any list. He was sixth in homers for the decade spanning 1941 to 1950 (behind Ted Williams, Ralph Kiner, Vern Stephens, Johnny Mize, and Bill Nicholson). He is second for players whose last name begin with *D* (behind Andre Dawson), and just off the Top 5 for players who hail from California.

He might have hit more if circumstances were different, but then, he might have hit less as well. He was without a doubt one of the greatest hitters the game has ever seen and deserves his place in the annals of Yankee and baseball history.

JOE DIMAGGIO'S REGULAR SEASON HOME RUNS:

Cr#	Yr#	Date	Pitcher	Team	R/L	H/A	#oB	Inn	Final
1	1	05/10/36	Turbeville	Philadelphia	R	H	1	1	7–2
2	2	05/20/36	Rowe	Detroit	R	A	0	6	3–4
3	3	05/24/36		Philadelphia		A	0	6	25–2
4	4	05/27/36	Walberg	Boston	L	A		2	9–8
5	5	06/08/36	Knott	St. Louis	R	H	1	5	12–3
6	6	06/21/36	Rowe	Detroit	R	A	1	2	7–8
7	7	06/24/36	Phelps	Chicago	R	A	1	5	18–11
8	8	06/24/36	Evans	Chicago	R	A	2	5	18–11
9	9	06/27/36	Thomas	St. Louis	R	A	0	7	10–6
10	10	06/28/36a	Hogsett	St. Louis	L	A	1	8	3–6
11	11	07/04/36b	Newsom	Washington	R	A	1	3	4–3
12	12	07/10/36	Uhle	Cleveland	R	H	1	8	18–0
13	13	07/22/36	Andrews	St. Louis	R	A	1	7	5–6
14	14	07/23/36	Hogsett	St. Louis	L	A	0	1	15–3
15	15	07/23/36	Hogsett	St. Louis	L	A	0	3	15–3

16	16	07/26/36a	Chelini	Chicago	L	A	1	7	12–3
17	17	08/05/36	Marcum	Boston	R	A	0	1	7–2
18	18	08/09/36a	Kelley	Philadelphia	R	H	0	8	7–6
19	19	08/16/36a	Fink	Philadelphia	R	A		1	10–2
20	20	08/17/36	Cohen	Washington	L	A	0	9	5–7
21	21	08/19/36	DeShong	Washington	R	A	0	5	7–4
22	22	08/23/36a	Marcum	Boston	R	H	0	8	5–3
23	23	08/25/36	Thomas	St. Louis	R	H	0	3	13–1
24	24	08/28/36b		Detroit	R	H		2	19–4
25	25	08/31/36	Dietrich	Chicago	R	H	1	1	5–1
26	26	09/09/36b	Lee	Cleveland	L	A	0	8	11–3
27	27	09/13/36a	Hogsett	St. Louis	L	A	0	3	10–7
28	28	09/13/36a	Knott	St. Louis	R	A		7	10–7
29	29	09/13/36b	Andrews	St. Louis	R	A		7	13–1
30	1	05/10/37	Lyons	Chicago	R	A	0	6	7–0
31	2	05/10/37	Chelini	Chicago	L	A	0	8	7–0
32	3	05/23/37	Galehouse	Cleveland	R	H	0	5	7–3
33	4	05/25/37	Rowe	Detroit	R	H	1	5	4–3
34	5	05/29/37a	Turbeville	Philadelphia	R	H	0	6	9–4
35	6	06/05/37	Gill	Detroit	R	A	0	8	6–5
36	7	06/06/37	Russell	Detroit	R	A	1	8	4–5
37	8	06/07/37	Wade	Detroit	L	A	0	9	3–4
38	9	06/08/37	Lee	Chicago	L	A	0	4	4–5
39	10	06/11/37	Knott	St. Louis	R	A	1	3	10–0
40	11	06/11/37	Knott	St. Louis	R	A	0	5	10–0
41	12	06/13/37b	Bonetti	St. Louis	R	A	2	5	8–8
42	13	06/13/37b	Bonetti	St. Louis	R	A	0	7	8–8
43	14	06/13/37b	Bonetti	St. Louis	R	A	0	9	8–8
44	15	06/20/37a	Lyons	Chicago	R	H	1	7	8–4
45	16	07/01/37	Ross	Philadelphia	R	A	1	5	12–7
46	17	07/02/37	Fischer	Washington	L	A	1	6	3–8
47	18	07/03/37	Weaver	Washington	R	A	0	6	5–4
48	19	07/04/37	W. Ferrell	Washington	R	A	0	1	7–0
49	20	07/05/37b	Walberg	Boston	L	H	3	6	8–4
50	21	07/09/37	Fischer	Washington	L	H	0	1	16–2

51	22	07/09/37	Linke	Washington	R	H	0	6	16–2
52	23	07/14/37	Coffman	Detroit	R	A	0	7	10–2
53	24	07/18/37	Feller	Cleveland	R	A	3	9	5–1
54	25	07/20/37a	Hildebrand	St. Louis	R	A	2	5	5–4
55	26	07/23/37	Whitehead	Chicago	R	A	1	1	6–9
56	27	07/25/37a	Lyons	Chicago	R	A	0	1	12–11
57	28	07/27/37	Wade	Detroit	L	H	1	6	6–5
58	29	07/31/37	Knott	St. Louis	R	H	0	8	6–9
59	30	07/31/37	Knott	St. Louis	R	H	2	9	6–9
60	31	08/01/37	Bonetti	St. Louis	R	H	1	7	14–5
61	32	08/03/37a	Lee	Chicago	L	H	2	7	7–2
62	33	08/11/37a	Grove	Boston	L	A	1	1	8–5
63	34	08/12/37b	McKain	Boston	L	A	0	8	5–3
64	35	08/18/37	Appleton	Washington	R	H	0	9	7–6
65	36	08/22/37	Thomas	Philadelphia	R	H	1	3	4–1
66	37	08/26/37	Knott	St. Louis	R	A	0	6	5–1
67	38	08/28/37	Walkup	St. Louis	R	A	1	4	5–9
68	39	09/02/37	Feller	Cleveland	R	A	0	8	2–4
69	40	09/06/37a	Ross	Philadelphia	R	A	2	4	6–3
70	41	09/11/37	DeShong	Washington	R	H	1	5	6–4
71	42	09/12/37b	Phebus	Washington	R	H	0	1	2–1
72	43	09/18/37b	Dietrich	Chicago	R	H	0	8	4–0
73	44	09/20/37	Wade	Detroit	L	H	1	5	5–0
74	45	09/28/37a	Weaver	Washington	R	A	2	5	9–0
75	46	10/03/37	Gonzales	Boston	R	H	3	7	6–1
76	1	05/01/38	Hogsett	Washington	L	A	0	6	3–4
77	2	05/02/38	DeShong	Washington	R	A	0	4	3–2
78	3	05/05/38	Tietje	St. Louis	R	H	1	5	12–10
79	4	05/08/38	Dietrich	Chicago	R	H	0	6	7–3
80	5	05/18/38	Newsom	St. Louis	R	A	1	5	11–7
81	6	05/18/38	Newsom	St. Louis	R	A	2	8	11–7
82	7	06/03/38	Coffman	Detroit	R	H	0	8	5–1
83	8	06/06/38	Knott	St. Louis	R	H	1	7	6–5
84	9	06/24/38	Eisenstat	Detroit	L	A	0	5	8–12
85	10	06/25/38	Lawson	Detroit	R	A	1	6	9–3

86	11	06/30/38	Rose	Philadelphia	R	H	2	1	13–1
87	12	07/02/38	Kraukauskas	Washington	L	H	1	7	12–2
88	13	07/04/38b	Hogsett	Washington	L	A	0	4	4–4
89	14	07/12/38b	L. Mills	St. Louis	L	H	0	3	10–5
90	15	07/13/38	Cole	St. Louis	R	H	1	7	15–12
91	16	07/13/38	Walkup	St. Louis	R	H	2	10	15–12
92	17	07/26/38a	Linke	St. Louis	R	A	2	4	10–5
93	18	07/28/38	Hildebrand	St. Louis	R	A	0	4	3–4
94	19	07/30/38	Stratton	Chicago	R	A	0	3	9–6
95	20	08/04/38	Coffman	Detroit	R	A	0	7	8–4
96	21	08/11/38	Krakauskas	Washington	L	H	2	3	9–6
97	22	08/12/38a	Nelson	Philadelphia	R	H	1	1	4–5
98	23	08/16/38b	Krakauskas	Washington	L	A	1	7	16–1
99	24	08/21/38b	Caster	Philadelphia	R	A	1	4	8–4
100	25	08/25/38b	Galehouse	Cleveland	R	H	1	8	15–3
101	26	08/26/38a	Feller	Cleveland	R	H	1	7	15–9
102	27	09/02/38	Wilson	Boston	R	H	2	1	6–4
103	28	09/04/38	Hogsett	Washington	L	H	1	3	7–4
104	29	09/07/38	Heving	Boston	R	A	0	4	4–11
105	30	09/10/38	Monteagudo	Washington	L	A	1	7	6–5
106	31	09/17/38	Benton	Detroit	R	A	1	4	3–7
107	32	10/02/38	Dickman	Boston	R	A	2	8	6–1
108	1	04/21/39	Krakauskas	Washington	L	A	1	3	6–3
109	2	06/08/39	Smith	Chicago	L	A	0	5	7–2
110	3	06/18/39	Rowe	Detroit	R	H	0	8	5–6
111	4	06/28/39a	Nelson	Philadelphia	R	A	0	3	23–2
112	5	06/28/39a	Beckman	Philadelphia	R	A	1	4	23–2
113	6	06/28/39b	Caster	Philadelphia	R	A	0	5	10–0
114	7	07/02/39	Wade	Boston	L	A	1	6	3–7
115	8	07/05/39	Chase	Washington	L	H	1	6	6–4
116	9	07/25/39	Mills	St. Louis	L	H	0	7	5–1
117	10	08/03/39	Newsom	Detroit	R	H	2	1	12–3
118	11	08/03/39	Benton	Detroit	R	H	0	8	12–3
119	12	08/05/39	Eisenstat	Cleveland	L	H	2	7	6–1
120	13	08/06/39a	Feller	Cleveland	R	H	0	2	4–5

121	14	08/09/39	Chase	Washington	L	A	2	2	13–8
122	15	08/13/39b	Potter	Philadelphia	R	A	2	6	21–0
123	16	08/13/39b	Potter	Philadelphia	R	A	0	8	21–0
124	17	08/16/39	Leonard	Washington	R	H	1	7	4–0
125	18	08/17/39	Krakauskas	Washington	L	H	2	3	9–8
126	19	08/22/39	Marcum	Chicago	R	A	1	8	14–5
127	20	08/23/39b	Lee	Chicago	L	A	0	5	16–4
128	21	08/28/39	Bridges	Detroit	R	A	3	3	18–2
129	22	08/28/39	Coffman	Detroit	R	A	2	9	18–2
130	23	08/29/39	Newsom	Detroit	R	A	2	9	6–7
131	24	09/02/39	Ostermueller	Boston	L	A	1	6	7–12
132	25	09/03/39b	Auker	Boston	R	A	1	6	5–5
133	26	09/06/39	Grove	Boston	L	H	0	8	2–1
134	27	09/07/39	Ostermueller	Boston	L	H	0	1	5–2
135	28	09/16/39	Pippen	Detroit	R	H	0	2	8–5
136	29	09/23/39	Leonard	Washington	R	A	1	7	7–1
137	30	09/24/39	Chase	Washington	L	A	0	9	3–2
138	1	05/17/40	Smith	Chicago	L	A	1	1	6–1
139	2	05/23/40	Newsom	Detroit	R	A	1	1	2–3
140	3	05/27/40	Chase	Washington	L	H	0	2	5–0
141	4	05/30/40b	Hash	Boston	R	H	1	4	4–11
142	5	06/02/40a	Harris	St. Louis	R	H	0	4	13–4
143	6	06/04/40	Smith	Chicago	L	H	1	9	3–7
144	7	06/09/40	Smith	Cleveland	L	H	1	6	4–3
145	8	06/16/40a	Kennedy	St. Louis	R	A		8	6–12
146	9	06/16/40b	Bildilli	St. Louis	L	A	2	6	5–6
147	10	06/18/40	Smith	Chicago	L	A	1	9	3–5
148	11	06/29/40	Heusser	Philadelphia	R	H	0	5	12–9
149	12	07/01/40	Chase	Washington	L	A	1	3	8–4
150	13	07/05/40	Babich	Philadelphia	R	A	0	6	3–6
151	14	07/13/40a	Niggeling	St. Louis	R	H	1	1	10–4
152	15	07/13/40a	Cox	St. Louis	R	H	2	8	10–4
153	16	07/13/40b	Trotter	St. Louis	R	H	1	7	12–6
154	17	07/18/40	Eisenstat	Cleveland	L	H	0	7	4–3
155	18	07/24/40	Mills	St. Louis	L	A	0	3	12–14

156	19	07/28/40a	Lyons	Chicago	R	A	2	3	10–9
157	20	07/28/40a	Dietrich	Chicago	R	A	0	9	10–9
158	21	08/06/40	Dickman	Boston	R	A	0	4	3–8
159	22	08/07/40a	Bagby	Boston	R	A	1	3	7–10
160	23	08/10/40	Beckman	Philadelphia	R	H	1	8	13–0
161	24	08/13/40b	Dickman	Boston	R	H	2	1	19–8
162	25	08/13/40b	Hash	Boston	R	H	3	4	19–8
163	26	08/22/40	Milnar	Cleveland	L	H	3	2	15–2
164	27	08/23/40	Smith	Cleveland	L	H	0	4	5–3
165	28	08/29/40b	Auker	St. Louis	R	H	2	9	6–5
166	29	09/07/40	Heving	Boston	R	A	1	4	4–3
167	30	09/15/40a	Niggeling	St. Louis	R	A	2	5	1–2
168	31	09/16/40	Kennedy	St. Louis	R	A	0	4	4–16
169	1	04/16/41	Potter	Philadelphia	R	H	0	9	7–10
170	2	04/19/41	Leonard	Washington	R	A	1	10	5–2
171	3	04/20/41	Besse	Philadelphia	L	A	3	9	19–5
172	4	04/21/41	Ross	Philadelphia	R	A	0	2	14–4
173	5	04/27/41	Sundra	Washington	R	H	0	9	3–6
174	6	05/16/41	Lee	Chicago	L	H	0	3	6–5
175	7	05/27/41	Anderson	Washington	R	A	2	4	10–8
176	8	06/03/41	Trout	Detroit	R	A	0	4	2–4
177	9	06/08/41	Auker	St. Louis	R	A	2	3	9–3
178	10	06/08/41a	Auker	St. Louis	R	A	0	6	9–3
179	11	06/08/41b	Kramer	St. Louis	R	A	0	7	8–3
180	12	06/12/41	Lee	Chicago	L	A	0	10	3–2
181	13	06/15/41	Bagby	Cleveland	R	H	0	3	3–2
182	14	06/19/41	Ross	Chicago	R	H	0	8	7–2
183	15	06/22/41	Newhouser	Detroit	L	H	0	6	5–4
184	16	06/25/41	Galehouse	St. Louis	R	H	1	4	7–5
185	17	06/27/41	Dean	Philadelphia	L	A	0	7	6–7
186	18	07/02/41	D. Newsome	Boston	R	H	1	5	8–4
187	19	07/05/41	Marchildon	Philadelphia	R	H	1	1	10–5
188	20	07/11/41	Kramer	St. Louis	R	A	1	9	6–2
189	21	07/20/41	Bridges	Detroit	R	A	0	5	12–6
190	22	07/23/41	Smith	Cleveland	L	H	0	4	3–2

191	23	07/27/41b	Lee	Chicago	L	H	0	2	3–7
192	24	07/29/41	Newhouser	Detroit	L	H	1	6	3–6
193	25	07/31/41b	Benton	Detroit	L	H	0	2	5–0
194	26	08/06/41a	Ryba	Boston	R	A	0	8	3–6
195	27	08/09/41	Hadley	Philadelphia	R	A	0	9	8–3
196	28	09/23/41	Vaughan	Philadelphia	L	H	0	4	8–9
197	29	09/24/41	Marchildon	Philadelphia	R	H	1	1	7–2
198	30	09/24/41	Marchildon	Philadelphia	R	H	0	5	7–2
199	1	04/15/42	Newsom	Washington	R	A	2	5	9–3
200	2	04/22/42	Beckman	Philadelphia	R	H	0	3	11–5
201	3	05/05/42	Rigney	Chicago	R	H	0	4	5–4
202	4	05/05/42	Rigney	Chicago	R	H	1	6	5–4
203	5	05/10/42a	Hudson	Washington	R	H	1	4	4–3
204	6	05/13/42	Dean	Cleveland	L	A	0	7	2–7
205	7	05/13/42	Dean	Cleveland	L	A	0	9	2–7
206	8	05/16/42b	Trout	Detroit	R	A	0	2	2–1
207	9	05/29/42	Masterson	Washington	R	H	0	6	16–1
208	10	06/03/42	Dietrich	Chicago	R	H	2	3	4–1
209	11	07/01/42	B. Harris	Philadelphia	R	A	0	4	4–5
210	12	07/04/42b	Hughson	Boston	R	A	0	2	4–6
211	13	07/18/42	Wade	Chicago	L	H	1	7	7–6
212	14	07/19/42a	Dietrich	Chicago	R	H	1	1	9–2
213	15	07/28/42	Haynes	Chicago	R	A	0	5	8–3
214	16	07/29/42a	Ross	Chicago	R	A	1	3	5–6
215	17	08/16/42	Christopher	Philadelphia	R	A	1	3	11–2
216	18	08/17/42	Knott	Philadelphia	R	A	1	4	15–0
217	19	09/14/42	Smith	Cleveland	L	A	0	7	8–3
218	20	09/17/42	Trout	Detroit	R	A	2	5	7–4
219	21	09/27/42	Hughson	Boston	R	A	1	3	6–7
220	1	04/16/46	Christopher	Philadelphia	R	A	1	6	5–9
221	2	04/21/46	Haefner	Washington	L	H	0	7	6–1
222	3	04/26/46	Hudson	Washington	R	A	0	2	11–7
223	4	04/26/46	Pieretti	Washington	R	A	0	5	11–7
224	5	05/04/46	Overmire	Detroit	L	H	1	4	4–3
225	6	05/10/46	Dobson	Boston	R	H	3	5	4–5

226	7	05/14/46	Potter	St. Louis	R	A	2	9	6–2
227	8	05/19/46b	Ferrick	Cleveland	R	A	1	8	7–1
228	9	05/23/46	Trucks	Detroit	R	A	1	5	12–6
229	10	05/26/46b	Harris	Boston	L	A	0	4	4–1
230	11	05/30/46a	Harris	Philadelphia	R	H	1	8	6–1
231	12	06/16/46a	Miller	St. Louis	R	A	2	6	9–2
232	13	06/21/46	Newhouser	Detroit	L	A	1	9	2–6
233	14	06/23/46	Trucks	Detroit	R	A	0	5	10–8
234	15	06/23/46	Newhouser	Detroit	L	A	0	9	10–8
235	16	06/25/46	Feller	Cleveland	R	A	1	8	3–8
236	17	07/06/46	Fagan	Philadelphia	R	A	2	5	8–5
237	18	08/11/46b	Zuber	Boston	R	H	0	6	9–1
238	19	08/16/46	Harris	Boston	L	A	0	6	1–4
239	20	08/20/46	Lopat	Chicago	L	A	0	6	2–9
240	21	08/21/46a	Rigney	Chicago	R	H	1	5	10–1
241	22	08/21/46b	Haynes	Chicago	R	H	0	7	5–4
242	23	09/04/46	Marchildon	Philadelphia	R	A	1	3	3–4
243	24	09/13/46	Newhouser	Detroit	L	A	1	7	5–4
244	25	09/14/46	Hutchinson	Detroit	R	A	1	7	4–7
245	1	04/20/47a	Flores	Philadelphia	R	A	2	3	6–2
246	2	05/13/47	Sanford	St. Louis	R	H	0	6	9–1
247	3	05/17/47a	Maltzberger	Chicago	R	H	0	9	4–3
248	4	05/26/47	Dobson	Boston	R	H	2	5	9–3
249	5	06/01/47	Gromek	Cleveland	R	A	0	5	11–9
250	6	06/01/47	Wolff	Cleveland	R	A	3	8	11–9
251	7	06/06/47	Sanford	St. Louis	R	A	0	3	3–4
252	8	06/07/47	Potter	St. Louis	R	A	0	4	3–1
253	9	06/26/47	Coleman	Philadelphia	R	A	0	8	2–4
254	10	07/02/47	Haefner	Washington	L	H	1	3	8–1
255	11	07/06/47a	Scheib	Philadelphia	R	H	2	1	8–2
256	12	07/12/47a		St. Louis		A	2		12–2
257	13	07/15/47a		Cleveland		A			9–4
258	14	07/27/47b	Lee	Chicago	L	H	0	4	4–5
259	15	08/24/47b	Ruffing	Chicago	R	A	2	1	16–6
260	16	08/30/47	Scarborough	Washington	R	H	1	3	6–5

261	17	09/01/47b	Johnson	Boston	L	A	0	8	1–4
262	18	09/04/47	Masterson	Washington	R	A	0	7	2–3
263	19	09/11/47b	Overmire	Detroit	L	H	2	3	11–5
264	20	09/23/47b	Haefner	Washington	L	H	0	4	3–1
265	1	04/21/48	Haefner	Washington	L	A	1	1	3–6
266	2	04/25/48	McCall	Boston	L	H	2	1	5–4
267	3	05/01/48	Kramer	Boston	R	A	2	5	6–8
268	4	05/10/48	Harrist	Chicago	R	A	1	6	9–3
269	5	05/20/48	Grove	Chicago	R	A	2	1	13–2
270	6	05/20/48	Grove	Chicago	R	A	0	5	13–2
271	7	05/22/48	Pearson	Chicago	R	A	1	9	10–2
272	8	05/23/48a	Feller	Cleveland	R	A	1	4	6–5
273	9	05/23/48a	Feller	Cleveland	R	A	2	6	6–5
274	10	05/23/48a	Muncrief	Cleveland	R	A	0	8	6–5
275	11	06/11/48	Klieman	Cleveland	R	H	0	9	8–10
276	12	06/20/48a	Widmar	St. Louis	R	A	0	8	4–2
277	13	06/20/48b	Stephens	St. Louis	R	A	0	8	6–2
278	14	06/20/48b	Biscan	St. Louis	L	A	2	9	6–2
279	15	06/21/48	Bearden	Cleveland	L	A	0	4	13–2
280	16	06/22/48	Zoldak	Cleveland	L	A	0	8	2–5
281	17	06/24/48	Feller	Cleveland	R	A	0	9	4–0
282	18	06/25/48	Newhouser	Detroit	L	A	0	9	2–4
283	19	07/09/48	Hudson	Washington	R	A	1	3	9–0
284	20	07/21/48a	Muncrief	Cleveland	R	H	1	3	7–3
285	21	07/22/48	Feller	Cleveland	R	H	3	5	6–5
286	22	07/25/48b	Gillespie	Chicago	R	H	1	1	7–3
287	23	07/25/48b	Grove	Chicago	R	H	0	5	7–3
288	24	08/01/48a	Wight	Chicago	L	A	0	6	8–2
289	25	08/14/48	Harris	Philadelphia	R	H	0	5	14–3
290	26	08/15/48a	Marchildon	Philadelphia	R	H	1	9	3–5
291	27	08/21/48	J. Coleman	Philadelphia	R	A	1	7	6–0
292	28	08/23/48	Moulder	Chicago	R	H	2	8	11–1
293	29	08/27/48b	Gromek	Cleveland	R	H	0	4	7–2
294	30	09/03/48a	Thompson	Washington	L	H	2	1	6–2
295	31	09/03/48a	Thompson	Washington	L	H	0	3	6–2

296	32	09/03/48b	Wynn	Washington	R	H	2		5–2
297	33	09/05/48	Hudson	Washington	R	H	0	2	5–3
298	34	09/10/48	Caldwell	Boston	R	A	3	10	11–6
299	35	09/11/48	Thompson	Washington	L	A	0	5	6–3
300	36	09/16/48a	Hutchinson	Detroit	R	A	0	4	1–2
301	37	09/19/48b	Ostrowski	St. Louis	L	A	1	1	9–6
302	38	09/19/48b	Ostrowski	St. Louis	L	A	1	1	9–6
303	39	09/20/48	Kennedy	St. Louis	L	A	0	4	8–7
304	1	06/28/49	McDermott	Boston	L	A	1	3	5–4
305	2	06/29/49	Kinder	Boston	R	A	2	5	9–7
306	3	06/29/49	Johnson	Boston	L	A	0	8	9–7
307	4	06/30/49	Parnell	Boston	L	A	2	7	6–3
308	5	07/04/49b	Parnell	Boston	L	H	0	5	6–4
309	6	07/17/49a	Gumpert	Chicago	R	A	0	7	3–7
310	7	07/20/49	Zoldak	Cleveland	L	A	0	5	7–3
311	8	08/05/49a	Drews	St. Louis	R	H	0	4	10–2
312	9	08/06/49	Embree	St. Louis	R	H	0	5	20–2
313	10	08/06/49	Fannin	St. Louis	R	H	0	9	20–2
314	11	08/11/49	Kramer	Boston	R	A	2	4	6–7
315	12	08/28/49a	Haefner	Chicago	L	A	1	9	8–7
316	13	09/05/49a	Brissie	Philadelphia	L	A	3	3	13–4
317	14	09/10/49b	Harris	Washington	L	H	1	4	3–4
318	1	04/21/50	Harris	Washington	L	H	1	7	14–7
319	2	04/28/50	Nagy	Washington	L	A	0	2	4–5
320	3	05/17/50	Overmire	St. Louis	L	A	0	5	11–9
321	4	05/21/50a	Wynn	Cleveland	R	A	3	2	14–5
322	5	05/21/50a	Bearden	Cleveland	L	A	0	5	14–5
323	6	06/02/50	Scarborough	Chicago	R	H	1	8	6–5
324	7	06/03/50b	Wight	Chicago	L	H	2	7	6–3
325	8	06/05/50	Feller	Cleveland	R	H	0	9	2–3
326	9	06/06/50	Garcia	Cleveland	R	H	0	4	2–16
327	10	06/07/50	Newhouser	Detroit	L	H	0	4	5–4
328	11	06/18/50a	Kretlow	St. Louis	R	A		8	15–5
329	12	06/18/50b	Dorish	St. Louis	R	A	1	3	9–0
330	13	06/22/50	Feller	Cleveland	R	A	0	2	2–6

331	14	06/23/50	Trout	Detroit	R	A	0	7	9–10
332	15	06/25/50a	Newhouser	Detroit	L	A	1	1	8–2
333	16	06/30/50b	Masterson	Boston	R	A	0	8	2–10
334	17	07/02/50	Papai	Boston	R	A	1	5	15–9
335	18	07/23/50	Rogovin	Detroit	R	H	0	6	5–6
336	19	07/26/50	Graver	St. Louis	R	A	1	6	6–3
337	20	07/30/50a	Gumpert	Chicago	R	A	1	7	15–7
338	21	07/30/50b	Holcombe	Chicago	R	A	0	2	4–3
339	22	08/18/50	Brissie	Philadelphia	L	A	0	9	3–2
340	23	08/20/50a	Keliner	Philadelphia	L	A	2	1	6–4
341	24	09/02/50	Haynes	Washington	R	H	0	2	9–2
342	25	09/10/50	Hudson	Washington	R	A	0	2	8–1
343	26	09/10/50	Hudson	Washington	R	A	0	6	8–1
344	27	09/10/50	Harris	Washington	L	A	1	9	8–1
345	28	09/12/50	Wynn	Cleveland	R	A	2	1	7–8
346	29	09/14/50	Newhouser	Detroit	L	A	0	2	7–5
347	30	09/16/50	Trout	Detroit	R	A	0	6	8–1
348	31	09/19/50	Cain	Chicago	L	A	0	4	3–4
349	32	09/23/50	Parnell	Boston	L	H	1	1	8–0
350	1	04/27/51	Parnell	Boston	L	A	0	6	3–4
351	2	04/28/51	Sima	Washington	L	H	1	1	6–4
352	3	05/20/51	Starr	St. Louis	R	H	1	5	7–3
353	4	05/24/51	Cain	Detroit	L	H	1	6	11–1
354	5	05/30/51b		Boston		A	2	6	4–9
355	6	06/07/51	Widmar	St. Louis	R	A	0	8	7–5
356	7	07/27/51	Pierce	Chicago	L	H	0	8	3–1
357	8	07/29/51a	Kretlow	Chicago	R	H	1	1	8–3
358	9	07/29/51a	Kretlow	Chicago	R	H	2	6	8–3
359	10	08/09/51	Moreno	Washington	R	H	0	6	6–4
360	11	08/26/51a	Rogovin	Chicago	R	A	0	2	2–3
361	12	09/28/51b	Stobbs	Boston	L	H	2	6	11–3

WORLD SERIES HOME RUNS:

#	Date	Pitcher	Team	R/L	H/A	#oB	Inn	Final
1	10/10/37	Melton	New York	L	A	0	3	4–2

2	10/06/38	Dean	Chicago	R	A	1	9	6–3
3	10/07/39	Thompson	Cincinnati	R	A	1	3	7–3
4	10/02/47	Hatten	Brooklyn	L	A	1	5	8–9
5	10/05/47	Barney	Brooklyn	R	A	0	5	2–1
6	10/09/49	Banta	Brooklyn	R	A	0	4	10–6
7	10/05/50	Roberts	Philadelphia	R	A	0	10	2–1
8	10/08/51	Maglie	New York	R	A	1	5	6–2

All-Star Homer:
7/11/39 at Yankee Stadium, off Detroit's Bridges in the fifth inning, none on. Bridges was a rightie and the final was Americans over Nationals 3–1

Note: a/b after date indicates first or second game of a double-header
All scores are given Yankees First

Gone Fishing with Joe DiMaggio

DAN STONEKING

A PUZZLED EXPRESSION crossed the face of Joe Di-Maggio.

"You want to interview me where?"

"Down on the docks at the bay while we're fishing," I said. "Would that be alright?"

It was more than twenty-five years ago. We were sitting in the Yankee Clipper's restaurant in San Francisco that's located only a Mark McGwire blast from the bay. DiMaggio had agreed to a thirty-minute interview about the baseball events of those days, the possibility that somebody would break his fifty-six-game hitting streak, the chances of Hank Aaron catching Babe Ruth for the all-time home-run lead, the Yankees of the early seventies compared to the Yankees of DiMaggio's day. That sort of stuff. But I hadn't mentioned the fishing.

"Fishing?" he asked.

"Let me explain, Mr. DiMaggio." I paused. "In Hemingway's *The Old Man and the Sea,* one of my favorite books—

have you ever read it? No matter—in this book, Hemingway writes about this old fisherman, Santiago. Santiago is talking to a young boy about fishing and sometimes about baseball. At one point, the old man tells the boy that he would like to go fishing with the great DiMaggio because he knows that DiMaggio's father was a fisherman. So for some weird reason that I'm not sure I fully understand myself, I'd like to do what Santiago wanted to do in the book, and interview you while we are fishing. Does that make any sense?''

''Fishing?'' he asked again while deciding how to answer my unusual request.

There was a long silence.

I thought, this is what it must have been like being a pitcher going against DiMaggio. Wait him out. Patience. Patience. Patience. DiMaggio excused himself and went to talk with a man who was the manager or maître d' at his restaurant-bar. ''I am going fishing,'' he said. ''I'll be back in an hour or so.''

We were gone for most of the afternoon, sitting on the wharf with lines in the water The day was sunny; only Alcatraz was shrouded in fog. In those few hours I got an understanding of the grace and graciousness, the charm and charisma and some of the mystic character of this man who played center field for the New York Yankees. We talked mostly about baseball and about DiMaggio and his contemporaries and some of the players of the early seventies such as Rose, Killebrew, Clemente, Carew, Oliva, Bench, and the Robinsons, Brooks, and Frank. As expected, DiMaggio said some polite things about all of them.

We talked about other things, too, Americana stuff: DiMaggio's childhood, growing up with a father who was indeed a fisherman in San Francisco, what his baseball success meant for the image of Italian-Americans. Colleagues had warned me not to ask him anything about his late ex-wife, Marilyn Monroe. ''Ask him anything about Marilyn and your time is up,'' they said. ''He is a pretty private guy. When it comes to Marilyn Monroe, he just turns off.'' Thus, the only time MM came up in the conversation was when we talked about Mickey Mantle, the man who succeeded Joe D in center field for the Yankees.

Early in the interview, DiMaggio endeared himself to me forever. He said he thought the greatest player he ever saw was Willie Mays. Since Mays was also my childhood idol, I was impressed with his good judgment. But what about Ted Williams, one of his contemporaries?

"Ted is probably No. 2 on my list," said DiMaggio. "He played for Boston of course, and the Red Sox were a big rival of ours. The best left-handed hitter ever. We both had pretty good seasons in '41. In those days I think there was more respect among the players than there is today. I had a tremendous amount of respect for Williams. Still do. We became friends later. In those days you just didn't fraternize with players on other teams."

DiMaggio and Williams, I learned later, were a mutual admiration society. In an interview a few years later with Teddy Ballgame, Williams said that DiMaggio "was the greatest player I ever saw. What DiMaggio did in that streak of fifty-six games ...I know how hard, almost impossible, that is to do. And it wasn't just his hitting and that classic, smooth swing. He made everything look so easy out there, so fluid."

America will remember Joe DiMaggio for a lot of things. Nine World Series championships with the Yankees in his fifteen years in New York. Three American League MVPs. The Hall of Fame. Selling us on his favorite coffeemaker, his favorite bank. And of course that he was once married to Marilyn Monroe.

But can there be any baseball fan—fanatic or casual—from New York to Los Angeles, Miami to Seattle, San Antonio to Minneapolis-St. Paul who doesn't know something about DiMaggio's fifty-six-game hitting streak in the summer of 1941?

It happened a year before I was born. But I grew up with it, along with baseball's other magic numbers: Ruth's 60 home runs (broken by Maris and last summer by McGwire and Sammy

Sosa), Ruth's career home-run record (rewritten by Aaron), Hack- Wilson's 195 RBI mark (still intact), and of course, DiMaggio's incredible hitting streak, challenged only once—by Rose—in the last fifty years.

"There is nothing more difficult than hitting a baseball," the Thumper, Williams, always said. "Just consider that the best who ever played the game failed six times in ten. To go up there and succeed for fifty-six consecutive games is absolutely amazing."

As great a hitter as Williams was, his longest consecutive-games streak was twenty-three in a row. That was also accomplished in the summer of 1941 when the Splendid Splinter finished with a .406 batting average but still lost the American League's most valuable player award to Joe D. On the day of fishing and talking, Joe DiMaggio spoke freely about his streak. He recalled being "in a slump" when the streak started in mid-May. He remembered the Yankee record before his streak was twenty-six straight games by Ruth. He recalled that shortly after the streak began, a teammate, Lou Gehrig, made his "luckiest man in the world" speech knowing he was dying.

"I couldn't have done what Lou did that day," said DiMaggio. "I am not that kind of person. Lou was reserved, private in many ways. I think a lot of us were in those days. I know I was lot like him. I learned a lot about how to conduct myself from Gehrig. I marveled at his consecutive games played record. That to me is an amazing record. But like my record, it might be replaced one day. But if someone ever does it, I will tip my cap. But that will never replace Gehrig. It took great courage for him to do what he did and I will never forget his words. I always felt like I was the luckiest man in the world. That day he made us all feel how lucky we were."

DiMaggio vividly remembered the day the streak stopped in Cleveland when Indians' third baseman Ken Keltner robbed him twice with backhanded stabs down the line. "Got me by half a step twice," DiMaggio said. "It had rained that morning in Cleveland. The base path was little soft. I think if it hadn't rained, I would have had beaten out one of those."

DiMaggio started a sixteen-game hitting streak after the fifty-six-gamer ended on July 17. Without the rain, without Keltner's snazzy glove and strong arm, the record might well be 73 games—nearly half a season in those days of the 154-game schedule. DiMaggio remembered the times in the streak when he surpassed Ruth's club record and then Willie Keeler's mark of forty-four straight games. "Those were like mileposts," said DiMaggio. "In a way, they kept you going. I wasn't going after any record. Hits meant I was helping my team win. You didn't think about record, not until later. I was asked when the streak was stopped if I didn't feel better," said DiMaggio. "I said, 'Of course not.' I wanted to keep getting hits every game for the rest of the season."

The Yankee Clipper hit .357 that season, more than 50 points behind the Thumper's .406. But it was DiMaggio who led the Yankees to the American League pennant 15 games better than Williams' second-place Red Sox, who was named the MVP, one of three such seasons Joltin' Joe was so honored. They wrote a song about him that season of 1941 that people like the Andrews Sisters used to sing. More than twenty-five years later they were still singing songs about Joe DiMaggio—only this time it was Simon & Garfunkel asking where he had gone and along with him certain values in America.

I saw DiMaggio play only on a fuzzy television screen and in newsreel clips. But memories of those visions portrayed the ease and grace with which he played the game. His hitting, his uncanny way of patrolling center field, his six-foot-two, two-hundred-pound perfect-for-baseball body running the bases so effortlessly.

What must it have been like to be a baseball fan in the summer of 1941?

There was war in Europe but America was not fighting there

yet. Pearl Harbor was still just an anonymous naval base in the Pacific. Few could imagine that DiMaggio, Williams, and other baseball greats would soon depart the green fields of America's ballparks for years of military service abroad. Joe DiMaggio was in center field for a Yankees team which, then as now, some people loved and some despised. But everybody loved Di-Maggio.

Though there are some parallels, it probably wasn't quite the same in the season of 1941 as in the magical summer of 1998 when McGwire and Sosa went head-to-head, mano a mano for Maris' place in history. Almost half a century earlier DiMaggio was this graceful machine, consistently delivering day after day, game after game, while Williams was perhaps not given his due until September arrived and his average was still above the .400 mark.

Like a truly great star, DiMaggio knew to exit the baseball stage at the top of his game. You never saw his skills in decline. Even my hero, Willie Mays, didn't do that. The legacy that he left the game—a dignified reserve, a peerless grace and class to his movements and public statements—will resonate forever.

It wasn't that DiMaggio was not aggressive as a ballplayer. One of his most impressive stats was his home-run to strike-out ratio. Although not necessarily a power hitter, he hit 361 career homers. He struck out only 369 times. DiMaggio wasn't as selective as Williams, who just wouldn't swing at a pitch out of the strike zone and would glare at an umpire who judged a pitch otherwise. The most walks DiMaggio ever received in a season was eighty, a low number for such a dominating batsman.

"I never went to the plate thinking to get a walk," he said that day on the wharf. "The fans didn't come to the park to see me or any player walk. They came to see us hit, field, and run the bases. Gehrig had taught me that. He said that without the fans, there is no game, or at least no game as we know. I tried to never forget that."

It was an attitude that other great players brought to their sports: Michael Jordan, Bob Cousy, and Bill Russell, Jean Beliveau, Wayne Gretzky, Dick Butkus, Joe Montana, and Roger Staubach.

"You just never wanted to go out there and have a bad day," said DiMaggio.

We did, however, have a bad day fishing. Not one bite. Not one nibble. But had Hemingway's Santiago been there, he would have forgiven us our poor angling skills. He'd have known that there was nothing quite like wetting a line with the great DiMaggio.

Dan Stoneking is the past president of the Twin Cities chapter of the Baseball Writers of America. During his twenty-years of work at the Minneapolis Star, *he was several times named Minnesota Sportswriter of the Year. Among Dan's most memorable baseball experiences—as a nine-year-old child he was at the Polo Grounds in 1951 to witness Bobby Thomson's home run off Ralph Branca. He currently lives in Orziba, Mexico, where he teaches English, journalism, and political science. This article was first published in the July 1999 issue of* Elysian Fields.

DiMaggio Fan Became Lawyer, Friend

MARV SCHNEIDER

THE ONE-STORY BUILDING where Morris Engelberg has a law office is identified by a large sign as the Yankee Clipper Center.

Among the dozen or so parking spaces in front of the building in Hollywood, Florida, was one reserved for the Yankee Clipper himself, Joe DiMaggio. It was space No. 5, the number he wore.

Engelberg's spot is right next to it—that's how close the lawyer had become to the Hall of Fame center fielder.

He was DiMaggio's lawyer, his next-door neighbor, the executor of his will, and the buffer between the baseball great and anyone who wanted to get near him—fans, media, and businessmen.

"He was very protective of DiMaggio. He kept Joe in a cocoon, which is exactly what DiMaggio wanted," said Marty Appel, a former Yankees public relations director.

"DiMaggio always had someone like that in his life. Morris

Engelberg was the last one. But Joe always made the decisions, especially when it came to the business of memorabilia.''

To Engelberg, however, the relationship went beyond business deals.

When DiMaggio died Monday shortly after midnight, Engelberg was at his bedside. And on Thursday, he was a pallbearer at the funeral.

"An Orthodox Jew a pallbearer at a Catholic funeral. What do you think of that?'' Engelberg said.

It was not the first time their religions had crossed.

DiMaggio held Engelberg's grandson, Harrison, when the baby had his ritual circumcision, an honor usually reserved for a religious, righteous man.

"The rabbi asked me, 'He's not Jewish?' I said, 'No, but he is righteous,' '' Engelberg said.

Just how close they were became apparent in December, when DiMaggio was fighting the lung infection that eventually killed him.

"He was in bad shape, in and out of a coma, he was bleeding from the nose, he couldn't breathe. I figured this was it,'' Engelberg said. "That's when I realized the date, December 11.

"I squeezed his hand and said, 'Joe, you can't die the same day as my father.' ''

His dad had died three months before Engelberg was born, and some might say DiMaggio was the father he never knew.

"I grew up in Brooklyn, where everyone was a Dodgers fan, but I was a Joe DiMaggio fan,'' Engelberg said. "I had pictures of him, I memorized his statistics. When I was ten years old I combed my hair in a pompadour like DiMaggio did.''

Engelberg turned fifty-nine the day before his hero died, and it was the first time in sixteen years that DiMaggio was unable to give him an autographed baseball bat as a birthday present. Engelberg's favorite was the one he got when he turned fifty-six. DiMaggio wrote: "Keep the streak alive.''

Engelberg never lost his adoration of the Yankee Clipper,

even as an adult. At six-foot-five and with the trim build of an athlete, Engelberg even resembled DiMaggio from behind.

Engelberg prefers dark-colored, well-tailored suits, white shirts, and conservative ties, carefully knotted—just the way Joe D used to dress.

Engelberg, who played basketball at Brooklyn College, emulated DiMaggio's batting stance and smooth gait in the outfield when he played sandlot baseball.

"I ran in a couple of New York marathons, and when I finally completed one, my uncle said, 'Well, now you've accomplished your goal,' and I told him, 'All I have to do now is meet Joe DiMaggio,' " Engelberg said.

When he got that opportunity, he was stunned.

A client with an interest in a Florida golf resort had hired DiMaggio as a public relations spokesman and asked him to call the lawyer at his home.

"My wife answered the phone, and said it was Joe DiMaggio. I couldn't speak," Engelberg said. "I had to compose myself, and told her, 'Tell him I'll call him back.' "

The next day, they met at the resort for breakfast.

By then Engelberg was a successful business lawyer and DiMaggio confided that he was concerned about losing his job as a spokesman for the Bowery Savings Bank in New York. He appeared in television commercials and newspaper ads.

"He told me he needed the income," Engelberg said. "He was getting well under six figures a year."

The two went to New York to negotiate a new contract, and Engelberg said he got a three-year deal that put another digit in front of what DiMaggio had been making.

"I called Joe and told him to meet me at the Stage Deli," Engelberg said. "I told him what the deal was. He reached into his inside jacket pocket, took out a checkbook, and wrote a check for $20,000.

"There was no way I was going to take money from the man

I had worshipped. I tore up the check, dropped the pieces on the table, and told him his fee was the tab for the corned beef sandwiches.''

But there also were deals that never came off, like the one Simon & Schuster thought it had wrapped up for a DiMaggio book. Engelberg thought so, too, but DiMaggio skimmed the outline and vetoed the idea.

''There were about nine pages dealing with DiMaggio's marriages to Dorothy Arnold and Marilyn Monroe, and the rest had to do with his baseball career,'' Engelberg said.

''But Joe said, 'I'll be going on all those TV shows for interviews and all they'll want to talk about is Marilyn.'

''He turned down a lot of money because of that, but Joe was not impressed with wealth. He would say, 'How much do I need?' ''

Engelberg said DiMaggio never forgot his background.

''Joe came from a poor family. He slept in the same bed with his brothers when they were growing up,'' he said. ''They didn't have much.''

For a good deal of his adult life DiMaggio lived in hotels. But, finally, he found himself in an elegant resort community in Florida that was not near restaurants where he could get pasta, pizza, or kosher-style deli food, and he grew unhappy.

That's when Engelberg persuaded him to move to a home built right next to his in a gated community They spent a great deal of time in each other's den, watching baseball and football, and playing with Engelberg's grandchildren and DiMaggio's great-grandchildren.

''The houses are almost duplicates,'' Engelberg said. ''The only thing different are the keys.''

Dedication Day: The DiMaggio Monument at Yankee Stadium

PHIL MINTZ

THREE HOURS BEFORE game time on Joe DiMaggio Day at Yankee Stadium, below the still-empty left-field bleacher seats, Ricky Ledee, a twenty-five-year-old Yankee outfielder from Salinas, Puerto Rico, stands alone in Monument Park in his warm-up uniform, looking to the ghosts of departed Yankee greats to help him.

Ledee, a highly touted prospect in his second season with the team, is struggling. The previous October, Ledee had been the first rookie outfielder since Tom Tresh in 1962 to start for the Yankees in the World Series. And the left-handed hitter produced, going 6-for-10, with three doubles and four RBIs, in the Yankees' four-game sweep of the San Diego Padres.

But now, on April 25, just three weeks into the 1999 season, Ledee is slumping. Scheduled to start left field today he's batting just .136. And he's struck out about half the time he's walked to the plate. So while the rest of the Yankees are out on the field stretching, taking batting practice, and shagging flies, Ledee has slipped through the bull-pen gate at the 399-foot sign and into the small, parklike area set aside to memorialize stars from the Yankee past.

At the base of the stadium's flagpole are the three pink granite monuments with bronze plaques that once stood in fair territory in Yankee Stadium's deep center field, before the ballpark was closed for renovations during the 1974 and 1975 seasons.

There is the one for former Yankee manager Miller Huggins, which the team put up in 1932. Another—"a tribute from the Yankee players to their beloved captain and teammate"—was erected shortly after Lou Gehrig's death in 1941. The third, for George Herman "Babe" Ruth, was set in place in 1949.

To the left of the flagpole is a fourth granite marker, erected by the Yankees in 1996 in memory of Mickey Mantle, "a magnificent Yankee." And this morning, to the right of the pole, there is a fifth monument, still cloaked with a white, red, and blue Yankee banner. It is for DiMaggio, who died on March 8 of complications following lung surgery. He was eighty-four years old.

This isn't Ledee's first visit to Monument Park. He's been here a few times, including just before last year's World Series. It brought him luck. Now he's back. "I'm struggling a little bit, and I'm looking for inspiration," he explains. "It's impressive," he says, looking back at the monuments, "the way the team recognizes the big players."

Above the bleacher seats, the lighted numbers on the clock on the scoreboard loom large. Ledee, holding his black Rawlings glove, suddenly looks a little sheepish, like a high school student who has stayed too long in the hallway on the way to his next class. He nods his head toward the field where his teammates are taking batting practice. "I gotta go," he says. He slips back through the gate and onto the field.

The power of memory is strong here in Yankee Stadium, where, since 1923, many of baseball's greatest glories and most spectacular achievements have unfolded, including twenty-four

World championships. And to many baseball fans, it is Di-Maggio, who played in the Bronx for thirteen seasons between 1936 and 1951, including nine of those championship years, who stands as the best all-around player who ever put on a uniform.

Outside the outfield fence, the elevated subway train rumbles by. Scalpers stand on the sidewalk, offering tickets to the crowd heading for the gates. It's clear that the majority of the 51,903 customers who will fill the stadium today, packing all but the upper reaches of the outfield grandstand, have never seen DiMaggio play. A few carry banners and signs honoring the Yankee Clipper. Some wear shirts with DiMaggio's number, 5. But there are plenty of fans wearing T-shirts honoring the current crop of Yankee favorites, including Derek Jeter, Tino Martinez, and Bernie Williams.

But even these new Yankee fans have heard about DiMaggio, many from their parents or grandparents. Mimi Borowich and Zalman Berger, teenage high school students from New Rochelle, New York, talk about DiMaggio as they wait on line to buy hot dogs. They say they each come to a few games a year, and they certainly didn't want to miss this one.

"I know that he was one of the greatest players of all time," Borowich says, a battered Yankee cap perched on her head. She's skipped studying for her college entrance tests to come here today. "He was a good man. I know that he thanked God for making him a Yankee."

"Very honorable," agrees Berger, who's wearing a 1998 World Championship cap and T-shirt.

Nearby, Don DeVito, seventy-three, who grew up a Yankee fan in Brooklyn, puffed on a cigarette and remembered the very first game he saw at Yankee Stadium. It was in 1939, Lou Gehrig Day. "My uncle took me. Mayor La Guardia was there. And the fellow from the post office, Jim Farley. Lots of bigwigs. There wasn't a dry eye in the house."

As a teenager, DeVito played third base for St. Athanasius in the Catholic Youth Organization league in Brooklyn, and Di-

Maggio would drop by for some clinics. "He'd come down to the Prospect Park ball fields to help the kids. I was fourteen, fifteen years old. He would teach the kids how to field, throw, and bat. And he'd sign autographs. We wouldn't have to pay thirty-five dollars for an autograph like we do today."

DeVito, a retired trumpet player, says that he admired DiMaggio's "class" most of all. "When he'd hit a home run, he'd run around the bases with his head down. He didn't want to show up the pitcher. He was a ballplayer's ballplayer. That's what I remember."

Down on the basement level of Yankee Stadium is the locker room. It is named the Pete Sheehy Clubhouse, for the longtime clubhouse attendant who began as Babe Ruth's batboy and was still there more than fifty years later. It was Sheehy who assigned DiMaggio number 5—following in the steps of Ruth's number 3 and Gehrig's number 4—and brought the demanding star a cup of coffee each day, and tea when DiMaggio switched to that for a while.

In the late 1940s and 1950s Hank Bauer suited up in this room. And now, decades later, the former right fielder stands with a crowd of reporters and points out the spot where DiMaggio's locker had stood, near where first baseman Martinez now puts on his work clothes. As part of the DiMaggio Day ceremonies, the Yankees have brought together six teammates from 1951, DiMaggio's final season: Bauer, Phil Rizzuto, Yogi Berra, Jerry Coleman, Whitey Ford, and Gil McDougald. Now old men, they are sharing, possibly for the last time, memories of a teammate they describe as prideful, aloof, and able to intimidate teammates with a single glance.

"I thought he was God. He was the greatest ballplayer, to me, that I ever saw in Yankee Stadium," says Bauer, at seventy-seven still sporting a variation of the Marine-issue crew cut he favored as a ballplayer. "I never saw Ruth or Gehrig, but I saw

Joe. If you made a mental mistake he'd just look at you and you got the message. We respected him very highly."

Bauer came up in 1948, when DiMaggio's reputation as a demanding loner had already been firmly established. "I remember my first game here. A ball was hit to right center, I called for it and I caught it. Joe just glared at me. After the game, we lit up some cigarettes. I said to him, 'Joe, did I do something wrong?' He said, 'No, you didn't do something wrong. But you're the first SOB who ever invaded my territory.' "

Ever see DiMaggio make a mental mistake? someone asks. "Never," Bauer says. But Bauer recalls the day in August 1951, when DiMaggio turned to him in batting practice and complained that he was hitting too many balls to right field. DiMaggio asked Bauer what he was doing wrong. "I said, 'You're asking *me* Joe? Well Joe, you're getting old and your bat's starting to slow up.' He said, 'Horseshit.' But it was his last year."

Across the room, Nick Testa is putting away some batting-practice balls. Testa, a onetime Yankee's batting-practice pitcher, had a brief minor league career as a catcher in the 1950s and early 1960s, and appeared in one major league game in 1958 with the San Francisco Giants. As a minor leaguer, Testa would groove pitches to the retired DiMaggio when he would pass through towns such as Omaha, Nebraska, and Sioux Falls, South Dakota on exhibition tours.

"They'd always ask the catcher, because he could throw the straightest," Testa says. "I would just lay it right in there, right in the middle of the plate, about that high. He hit maybe two out of four out of the park. It was like pitching to a god."

Most of the current Yankee stars had just a passing acquaintance with DiMaggio, during one of his infrequent visits to Yankee Stadium. David Cone recalls that DiMaggio had once discussed his pitching with him. Cone says he was flattered that DiMaggio even knew who he was.

Bernie Williams, who plays DiMaggio's old position, says that he never had a discussion with DiMaggio. "He always seemed very busy, very preoccupied, a lot of people coming up to him. I wish that I had a conversation with him. I regret it now."

Cone and Williams were both members of the 1998 team that won 125 games, the most ever. Most of those players are back for another season with the Yankees. Two players from that record-setting team, however, are in another part of the stadium. Pitchers David Wells and Graeme Lloyd are down the corridor in the Toronto Blue Jays locker room. They had been traded, along with second-string infielder Homer Bush, prior to the 1999 season. The Yankees got pitching ace Roger Clemens in return.

Wells and Lloyd are setting a table in the center of the Blue Jays locker room. Wells, the beefy Metallica-loving pitcher, had pitched for the Yankees for two and a half years, and had pitched a perfect game on May 17, 1998. The trade hurt him. Wells is an avid admirer of Yankee tradition who once pitched a game in a thirty-five-thousand-dollar souvenir Babe Ruth cap. He says he was glad to be in the stadium for Joe DiMaggio Day, even if he was wearing the visitors' royal blue jersey for the occasion.

"I think it's great the way the Yankees do these things," Wells says, flipping idly through a *Parade* magazine. "Monument Park is something to see. To be a part of that . . . you're immortal."

Wells says he met DiMaggio a few times. "I got to talk with Joe," says Wells, whose loose-cannon clubhouse demeanor resembles the rough edges of players such as Lefty Gomez and Billy Martin, among the few DiMaggio teammates able to pal around with him. "I know he was a dick to other guys, but he was nice to me."

Why? Wells, his T-shirt revealing his large arms and tattoos, laughs. "I don't think he wanted to challenge me."

Then he gets serious. "When I first came in here, people would say things like 'He won't sign autographs' and 'He's really mean.' But I went over with four baseballs and he signed them. I've got a nice picture, sixteen by twenty, of him signed. One time, I was buying a Babe Ruth bat. The guy who was selling it sent it to me. I went up to Joe and said, 'You know a lot about Babe Ruth. Take a look at this bat.' He was looking at it and said, 'It's not even close to Babe Ruth's bat.' I sent it back. I told the guy he had a bad bat.''

Fifteen folding chairs are set out on the field behind home plate, near where a white interlocking NY is painted on the grass. Down the first and third baselines, the Yankees have painted large baseballs with a ''5'' at the center. The flags above the outfield bleachers are fluttering at half staff, not for DiMaggio, but in memory of twelve Colorado high school students and a teacher gunned down days earlier by two students at the school.

Yankee players, who are wearing a ''5'' on their uniform sleeve all season, sit on the steps of the dugout. On the third-base side, Blue Jays players do the same. Before the game, Jim Fregosi, the Toronto manager, advised his players not to linger in the locker room and be on the field for the ceremony. He told them it's an important day, and that years from now, people are going to ask them about it.

The pregame ceremony, which starts a bit late to make sure the stands are filled, opens with Bob Sheppard, the Yankee public address announcer since 1951, re-creating the lineup for October 10, 1951, the sixth game of the World Series and DiMaggio's last game. As the fans focus on an empty ''field of dreams,'' Sheppard's elegant voice introduces the New York Giants starting lineup—Eddie Stanky, Alvin Dark, Whitey Lockman, Monte Irvin, Bobby Thomson, Hank Thompson, Wes Westrum, Willie Mays, Dave Koslo.

Then he begins with the Yankees: Rizzuto. Coleman. Berra. DiMaggio's name is fourth on the list. ''Number 5. Joe DiMaggio. Number 5.'' McDougald, Johnny Mize, Hank Bauer, Gene Woodling, and Vic Raschi complete the lineup.

Returning to the present, the six returning 1951 Yankees are brought out from the dugout, the strongest cheers going to Berra, who only this year has returned to Yankee Stadium after patching up a longtime feud with Yankee owner George Steinbrenner. The crowd quiets as Cardinal John O'Connor offers the invocation. A year before, O'Connor had criticized the Yankees and major league baseball for playing early-season games on Good Friday. The tiff appears forgotten.

"Almighty God, Joe DiMaggio always thanked you for making him a Yankee," says O'Connor, who two days earlier presided over a memorial service for DiMaggio in Manhattan's St. Patrick's Cathedral. "Today, we thank Joe DiMaggio for becoming a Yankee."

Manhattan District Attorney Robert Morgenthau, talks about DiMaggio's charitable work. Phil Rizzuto praises his teammate's play. "Never made a tough play. Never had to dive for a ball or lose his hat. He was uncanny the way he'd get a jump on the ball. Then the best thing was to see him hit a triple. To get those long legs of his running, going from first to third. It was a thing of beauty."

Then, in a theatrical touch that captivates the crowd, singer Paul Simon, wearing a Yankee cap and holding his acoustic guitar, strides to a spot in short-center field, about the same place that DiMaggio would stand in his playing days. For thirty years, Simon and DiMaggio have been linked by a song that Simon wrote for the movie *The Graduate,* "Mrs. Robinson."

The crowd hushes. Simon picks the opening notes, sings one verse, a second, and comes around to the refrain that in one image tried to sum up the angst of the 1960s:

Where have you gone, Joe DiMaggio?
A nation turns its lonely eyes to you
Boo-hoo-hoo.
What's that you say, Mrs. Robinson?

Joltin' Joe has left and gone away
Hey-hey-hey

DiMaggio once said that he didn't understand what that song was about.

A four-minute video of DiMaggio's baseball career is shown on the stadium screen as the old-timers head out to Monument Park. There, DiMaggio's granddaughters, Kathie DiMaggio Stein and Paula DiMaggio Hamra, lift the Yankee banner off the monument.

"Joseph Paul DiMaggio, the Yankee Clipper, 1914–1999" it reads. "Recognized as baseball's greatest living player . . . Led the Yankees to an incredible nine championships in his thirteen-year career. A baseball legend and an American icon. He has passed, but he will never leave us."

The field is cleared and the Yankees, who are just a few percentage points ahead of the second-place Blue Jays in the standings, take the field. For Ledee's first two at bats, the visit to Monument Park doesn't appear to be helping much. He strikes out the first two times up. In the sixth inning, with runners on first and second and the Yankees up 2–1, he knocks a single between the shortstop and the third baseman, allowing Martinez to score and giving the Yankees a two-run lead. But the Yankees squander the advantage, allowing the Blue Jays to tie the game in the top of the ninth. Ledee strikes out again, and draws an intentional walk. It's up to Bernie Williams—DiMaggio's heir—to knock in Chuck Knoblauch with the winning run in the bottom of the eleventh. After sliding across home plate, Knoblauch jumps to his feet. Among the players giving Knoblauch the high-five is Ledee.

After the game, Ledee dresses quietly in front of his locker, across the room from where DiMaggio once sat. Reporters leave him alone, and head for the stars of the game. Knoblauch shows a mark on his hip to prove that he really was hit by a pitch in the eleventh inning. David Cone says he had to stop his warm-up routine to watch Paul Simon sing. Someone suggests to Derek Jeter that someday there might a monument to him in the stadium outfield. Jeter shakes his head. "I played three years," he says. "You've got to play a lot of years to get out there."

Bernie Williams, meanwhile, is at the center of it all. Everyone wants to know the significance of the current Yankee center fielder becoming the hero of Joe DiMaggio Day.

Right now, he says, he's just happy the team got the win that pushed them more firmly into first place. But he adds, "I know years from now, I'll sit back and remember. It will be a special moment."

Literature About Joe DiMaggio, 1936–1986

JACK B. MOORE

S O FAR I have discussed many of the print sources of Joe DiMaggio's story when they had some contribution to make in establishing the details of his life or myth. I will now examine selected books and articles along with a few other miscellaneous popular print items that played a part in determining or reflecting what the public knew about DiMaggio as his image as a popular hero and cultural symbol evolved. My purpose is to indicate the contributions these works made to the establishment of his narrative, his story, rather than to focus on his life as I have done up to this point.

One of the first writers to set DiMaggio before a national audience, even before he entered the major leagues, was Quentin Reynolds, one of the country's best known journalists. In the mid-1930s he was a feature writer for *Collier's*, then one of the country's top magazines in terms of distribution and almost as popular as its chief competition, *The Saturday Evening Post*. Reynolds only occasionally wrote sports articles for *Collier's*.

During World War II he became a leading war correspondent and wrote a best-selling account of England's fight for survival. He was respected by his readership and by other journalists for his smooth writing and for his knowledge of current events. He was an experienced journalist with a wide readership extending far beyond the sports pages.

He wrote for the September 7, 1935, issue of *Collier's* an article about minor leaguers who were potential major league stars. The first player discussed and the player whose picture dominated the article's two-page spread was the Seals' Joe DiMaggio, who was according to his manager and Reynolds' friend Lefty O'Doul, "About to Shine." O'Doul bet Reynolds "that within two years every baseball fan in the country will have heard of DiMaggio," whom Reynolds admits had been previously unknown to him. Emphasizing DiMaggio's throwing ability ("the best arm" O'Doul had ever seen) and his 1933 record-breaking hitting streak, the article does not mention that he was destined for the Yankees. DiMaggio's Italian ancestry and identification with San Francisco are stressed: Reynolds claims that "ever since Ping Bodie of Telegraph Hill hit the big leagues it has been the ambition of all San Francisco Italian youngsters to be ballplayers." However, Joe's Americanization is also suggested: he "started playing ball as soon as he heard of the game and he heard of it before he heard of marbles or boccie, which is a great pastime among Italians in that section."

The size of DiMaggio's family is not alluded to, but his "crab fisherman" father and ballplaying brother Vince, who first "brought his kid brother to [the Seals'] camp," are mentioned. He is characterized as "Dead Pan Joe," though the accompanying photograph shows him smiling while spearing what looks suspiciously like a planted baseball in his upthrust mitt, and is compared to the Yankees' Bob Meusel, who also had "ice water in his veins." Reynolds refers to DiMaggio's injured leg but only to insist that he is now "sound again and . . . [b]etter . . . than all right," and reports that the Yankee scout Joe Devine considers him the West Coast's best prospect. Ty Cobb thinks "he's going to be a bigleague sensation someday." Beyond predicting greatness for DiMaggio, then, the article introduces a number of future elements of his story, including his San Francisco and Italian background, his impassivity or coolness of character, and his triumph over injury, to audiences who had not yet seen DiMaggio play.

Reynolds alludes sarcastically to Mussolini in the article, though he does not directly compare DiMaggio with him. Lefty O'Doul had bet Reynolds that DiMaggio would shortly be a star. The sportswriter Sid Mercer tells Reynolds if he gives O'Doul good enough odds he will "bet you that Germany won the war" and "that Mussolini discovered the North Pole." Thus the unassuming DiMaggio is by faint implication compared to the braggartly Mussolini.

The article might have been cause for bestowing the title of baseball prophet of the century upon Reynolds, for picking this "pearl out of the minor league oyster bed." Unfortunately, the other mollusks his article dredges up are Ted Duay, Harvey Green, Steve Messner, Albert Milnar, Ward Cross, Manuel Onis, Howard Mills, John Hassett, Frankie Hawkins, Gene Lillard, Joe Holden, Hal Kelleher, and Lyn Watkins, a generally lustreless string of artificial pearls more suggestive of bargain jewelry counters than Van Cleef and Arpels. Milnar's lifetime batting average over a decade in the big leagues was .203. Lillard pitched two years in the majors and emerged with a 1–2 record, Kelleher pitched four years and achieved the same percentage with a 2–4 record. Hassett hit a more than respectable .292 after seven years with three big league teams including New York, for whom he hit .333 in the 1942 World Series. Manuel Onis' record was best of all. He hit 1.000, in his only major league at bat, with the Brooklyn Dodgers in 1935. Concerning the others, *The Baseball Encyclopedia* maintains a clamlike silence.

Reynolds followed up his first *Collier's* article with another on June 13, 1936, "The Frisco Kid," focusing on DiMaggio alone. With a light, half-comic touch that his readers enjoyed, Reynolds (who had by this time met his subject) developed more fully several of the salient elements of DiMaggio's life first mentioned the year before, and added a few new details, some of which were wrong or misleading but which did not disturb DiMaggio's basic image. Again Reynolds identifies him as a popular Italian-American and once more alludes to Mussolini satirically. Depicting DiMaggio as a member of a large and not wealthy Italian family, Reynolds names all Joe's brothers and sisters for whom his poor father had to provide food, confirmation suits, and (for the girls) "hair ribbons and pretties," and then asks "and how's that for a family, Signor Mussolini?" Characterizing DiMaggio in more detail than in his first article, Reynolds portrays him as a simple, "nice-looking twenty-two-year-old youngster" whose seeming flaws turn out to conceal virtues. That he cuts out clippings of himself at night is not conceit, Reynolds declares, just thoughtfulness in providing his "kid sister back home in San Francisco" with reports that give her "a big kick" when she pastes them in the scrapbook she keeps. Still a "Deadpan Joe," he is merely following the orders of his former mentor Lefty O'Doul, who warned him never to clown around. He'll talk baseball "all day" but prefers listening, and reminds Reynolds of another 1930s athlete just beginning to become an American hero, "another Deadpan Joe—Joe Louis." That the New Deal Democrat Reynolds would link these two ethnic stars is particularly revealing, since both sport stars would become symbols of America during the Depression and war years.

Thus, early in DiMaggio's career he was already being written about nationally as a pleasant, quiet, reserved young man of exceptional baseball skills, who came from a poor, large Italian-American family. Adding depth to this all-Italian-American image Reynolds again notes that DiMaggio overcame the damage to his leg in 1934 and that though "the victim of a rather odd but painful accident" during spring training he later collected three hits his first day of major league play. Reynolds was one of the first national writers to tell what would become the legendary story about DiMaggio's joining the Seals, setting down for *Collier's* readers the star-is-born monologue delivered by Spike Hennessy to DiMaggio as the eighteen-year-old kid peered at his brother Vince through that knothole at Seals' field: "Listen kid . . . I'll get you into the ballpark. . . . in fact, I'll fix it so you can work out mornings with the team." In similar style Reynolds prints manager Ike Caveney's momentous line of 1933, "Go up there, DiMaggio."

One statement by Reynolds that misdirected a few writers was that DiMaggio "didn't know whether he wanted to play baseball or be a fisherman." He claims that "Brother Tom . . . strictly the Head Man in the family now . . ." settled that dilemma by ordering his younger brother to stay in school. This would accord with both the American work ethic and democratic educational ideal; in reality, however, DiMaggio of course neither wanted to fish as his father had, nor did he remain in school. Reynolds informed his readership that DiMaggio was "more concerned about getting out there in the bay with his father's fishing boat" than with playing baseball. When his school coach Ed White told him if he put his mind to it he "might be good enough to play for the Seals sometime," DiMaggio murmured (according to Reynolds) *"Sei mutto da leggare,"* or in Reynolds' translation, "You should be put in a straitjacket, you're that crazy." Now, Reynolds states, "there are those who insist that he will eventually develop into the greatest right-hand hitter since Rogers Hornsby." He had played his first major league game little over a month before on May 3.

Just one month after Reynolds' article, *Time* published on July 13 an unsigned piece on DiMaggio and featured him on its cover. The article reiterated that DiMaggio was a player of exceptionally high skills from a big Italian-American family in San Francisco, a humble and responsible lad who was "the American League's most sensational recruit since Ty Cobb." The ballyhoo surrounding DiMaggio's appearance with the Yankees according to *Time* set him up for a quick downfall, but "far from achieving the collapse which his billing led sophisticated baseball addicts to expect, Rookie DiMaggio proceeded to make the notices seem inadequate," for example by batting .400 his first month and being named the Associated Press "hero of the day" seven times.

Time also reprinted the story about DiMaggio's discovery by Spike Hennessy at the famous knothole, correctly adding that he received his big chance at the start of the 1933 season, when the Seals were short an experienced outfielder because brother Vince had badly hurt his shoulder and was unavailable for duty. *Time* also noted his tendency to injure himself, citing both the bad leg and burned ankle he had to overcome. His principal virtue according to the article was "his ability to make timely hits." DiMaggio was considered already perhaps the finest clutch hitter on his team. Although Lou Gehrig was hitting .398, according to the article "rival pitchers consider DiMaggio more likely to break up a game."*Time* did not reckon that DiMaggio was equal to Babe Ruth in power but claimed he was "already almost as much a hero as Ruth used to be. The clubhouse boy who sorts the Yankees' fan mail estimates DiMaggio's to be as large as Ruth's. Most of it comes from Italian well-wishers," the boy said, although how he knew this is unstated.

Time also reported DiMaggio's seeming behavior flaws only to turn them into popularly endearing characteristics. "When New York sportswriters first encountered DiMaggio, they mistook for exaggerated evidences of self-assurances his promises to make good which, it became apparent even before he had time to fulfill them were actually the entirely defensive protestations of a naturally diffident youth [twenty-two years old, actually] who had never before been more than 200 miles from home." *Time* further noted to DiMaggio's advantage that "like many young brothers in large Italian families, young DiMaggio is characterized by a solemn, almost embarrassing humility which is exceedingly useful because it causes his elders and superiors to take paternal interest in him.''

Even more pointedly than Reynolds' article, the *Time* cover story roots nice-boy DiMaggio in his Italian-American family, stating that he used to help support it by selling newspapers (his life imagined already as a typical poor boy makes a good movie scenario) and that he sends almost his entire salary home so his folks can live in comfort. Though a star Yankee in New York, DiMaggio still has close ties to parents and siblings. Marie gave him a signet ring when he left for training in faraway Florida, and maintains his scrapbooks. Older brother Tom almost got him put back on the fishing boats when he advised Joe to hold out for a piece of the purchase price the Seals received for him. That family story ended happily however; Joe received his extra money and did not have to return to the boats. The anecdote underscored the article's unstated theme, which was that DiMaggio was a great success in all ways, on the field and off. He had become a star, he was still a good boy, and with the extra money he got from the Seals, according to *Time*, he bought his brother Mike a fishing boat. After he was sold to the Yankees, at a celebration in his honor he was too frightened to say a word of the prepared speech of thanks the team's trainer had written for him and drilled him on. Now, *Time* remarked ''he has since become an accomplished radio speaker.'' Ben Franklin's rise had been faltering compared to DiMaggio's.

Before his second season in the majors, DiMaggio was written about in books intended for children and for readers primarily looking for entertaining, light stories about various sports stars of the day. In *Famous American Athletes of Today* (Fifth Series) his virtues were extolled by Harold Kaese alongside those of baseball's Dizzy Dean and Gabby Hartnett, track's Jesse Owens, and boxing's Jimmy Braddock. All the articles in the popular volume are adulatory, and often treat their subjects as exemplary heroes whose lives provided inspiration and guidance to young-sters. This follows a familiar pattern in American sportswriting which has tended to separate an athlete's game exploits from his basic character, praising the one while often ignoring the other, or modifying the athlete's real behavior to conform to his playing identity. The article on Braddock, for example, without going into his nature very deeply at all, presents him simply as a Depression hero who after a promising start and precipitous decline "started" in 1934 "the most remarkable comeback in pugilism" culminating with his heavyweight title defeat of Max Baer, a vastly more glamorous opponent, characterized usually by later writers as a fighter of great skills which he misused by behaving like a "madcap" or "playboy." Reduced to stevedoring as a result of his early, botched fight career, Braddock eventually "left the dull, drab, sheep-run life of the slums and dock walloping and went forward to the golden, glittering life of a world champion." The moral-political lesson his achievement as a plucky, hardworking Irish-American lad triumphing over Baer, who "disported himself during 1934 in a giddy whirl of nightlife," must have been obvious even to readers untrained in allegory. Unfortunately the Cinderella Man, as writers termed him, was defeated in his first defense of the title against Joe Louis on June 23, 1937, the same year *Famous American Athletes* lauded him, and Louis would inherit most of his Depression fame (though Braddock was reputed to have a contract guaranteeing him a percentage of Louis's profits for about ten years).

In Kaese's article, DiMaggio is depicted as an all-around star of the greatest magnitude who in his first major league year "batted so powerfully, fielded so steadily, threw so accurately, and ran the bases so speedily, that the New York Yankees won the American League pennant." The "fuzzy-cheeked youngster" was "the key man, the spark plug." Kaese at the time was a sportswriter for the *Boston Evening Transcript* so he could not be accused of puffing a local hero. He supplies quotations from Joe Cronin and Joe McCarthy to corroborate his claim that DiMaggio was the Yankees' winning difference, reporting Cronin's words that "any one of four other teams in the league" would have won with him, and McCarthy's pre-season remark that "we are depending on DiMaggio to take up the slack and win the pennant for us." Like several later sources, Kaese repeated *Time*'s opinion that DiMaggio's entrance into major league play "was the most brilliant since the debut of Tyrus Raymond Cobb in 1905" without checking to see that Cobb hit only .240 that year, the very lowest in his career.

DiMaggio's Italian-American and San Franciscan background are mentioned along with his large family. Kaese gets closer to the truth about DiMaggio as a prospective fisherman than Reynolds had, stating that while Joe worked on his father's boat from time to time, he was never part of its fishing crew. Against the grain of tradition that hard work coupled with education brought success, DiMaggio is described as having been bored by school and worked only one day in his life. "I joined an orange juice company, but after peeling oranges—and the skin of my fingers—for eight hours, I resigned." It was not DiMaggio's adherence to the work ethic for which he was held up to readers. Instead, the key to his success is determined by Kaese to be his behavior. "How Joe DiMaggio came through with flying colors so gloriously . . . is probably answered in one word, disposition." DiMaggio was "one of the least emotional athletes ever to play in the American League." His "nerves carry ice water." His "even temperament was DiMaggio's greatest asset as he met adversity." He is a "deadpan" with no nerves and "about as much" color as "a bucket full of whitewash." Though he lacks Cobb's "explosive brilliancy" and Babe Ruth's "boyish bent for trouble," DiMaggio possessed "a complete mastery of baseball" that Kaese says may enable him to surpass either player. While "many athletes become famous because of their personalities as well as their abilities" DiMaggio should become famous by virtue of ability alone. This would make him an "extraordinary" player indeed.

Kaese's account was one of the most detailed to appear in popular nationally distributed print so far. It contains statistics from DiMaggio's semi-professional days, and supplies a story that, though not as picturesque as Reynolds' knothole tale, generally coincides with one that Vince DiMaggio related, that Vince suggested Joe play the final few days of the 1932 season for the Seals. Kaese adds that in 1933 Joe edged Vince from his job, a story that frequently was accepted by later writers and by some of DiMaggio's first-year teammates. Vince stated that Joe took his job only as any acceptable outfielder might have, for his arm was so sore he could not play, and he was ripe for replacement; there was no struggle or competition between the two, as traditionally there is in fairy tales between younger and older brothers. For its time, Kaese's article was highly informative and relatively accurate. The only truly bad mistake Kaese makes in his narrative is to call his subject "Joseph Thomas DiMaggio." Worse, the layout of the book was designed so that at the top of alternate pages the name of the hero of that section was printed in large letters easily seen by readers while flipping through the book. So on page after page the name "Joseph Thomas DiMaggio" is printed like a mocking echo that must have infuriated Kaese, who clearly took pains of his own in compiling the narrative.

By the start of the 1939 season, the predictions of writers such as Reynolds and Kaese seemed to have come true. In its first issue (May 1) after the opening week of play, *Life*, perhaps the most read or most looked at magazine in the country, called DiMaggio in its lengthy cover story about him "baseball's No. 1 contemporary player." The article by Noel F. Busch accompanying the picture story provides a sometimes curiously written commentary on the eight-page picture spread *Life* presented on the young but already dominating player, mainly furthering the image of DiMaggio as a performer of almost unparalleled skills who exemplified—but with a bizarre twist Busch provided—the American success story. He is once more strongly characterized as the cherished idol of fellow Italian-Americans (in the same issue Mussolini's son-in-law Count Ciano is depicted assuring Albanian citizens that the Italian takeover of their tiny country was only "to bring order and progress") who brought huge flags to unfurl during Yankee games. But, DiMaggio is almost but not quite mocked by Busch as a lazy guy who just happened to possess great athletic abilities enabling him to play supremely well and thus profitably employ that "muscular lethargy" of "good athletes . . . which enables them, when called upon for reflex action, to furnish it with an explosive violence garnered from doing nothing at most other times."

Though the article contains praise of DiMaggio's game-winning talents, offering many examples of his hitting and fielding skills, Busch consistently patronizes his subjects and comes close to depicting him as an antihero. Though several of the pictures surrounding the article show DiMaggio in less than heroic poses, they are more traditionally complimentary of him. It is as though for one audience (the kind that looks only at photographs) *Life* decided to offer standard, worshipful fare; for more literate readers they provided intellectually snappier and presumably wittier matter. The article's first sentence confronts the reader with a verbal picture of DiMaggio entirely at odds with the handsome, smiling, pleasant hero shown in a full head shot on *Life*'s cover. Busch describes contrarily enough, DiMaggio as he appeared opening day three years previously: "a tall, thin, Italian youth equipped with slick black hair, shoe-button eyes, squirrel teeth, and a receding chin." The cover photo shows a very changed person with naturally damp-looking hair brushed back neatly but not slickly underneath his baseball cap, bright eyes, a smiling mouth with good, strong, fairly even teeth, and almost a square jaw—a friendly, well-fed but far from fat face. Busch's depiction of the rookie DiMaggio coupled with the cover photo represents an aspect of DiMaggio's success: his physical appearance seemed modified, and over the years he would become more and more handsome as he aged gracefully and succeeded as a person even more. At the same time, it introduces an element of satire in Busch's portrait that he maintains to his conclusion.

Following the curiously derogatory opening paragraph, Busch praises DiMaggio for more than justifying the high price paid for him (given incorrectly as $50,000) and proving he was an even better player than early expectations—so often misleading—promised. Because of his powerful bat, clutch hitting, and all-around ability, "experts are agreed that DiMaggio is entitled to more of the credit" for the Yankees' predominance "than any other single member of the club." Thus he is declared the key component of a winning team, a position of eminence Busch emphasizes he has achieved while laboring "under severe handicaps," a series of injuries and his 1938 holdout for more money, which Busch calls a "strike . . . not due entirely to avarice. Another factor was his brother Tom, vice president of San Francisco's energetic Fisherman's Union." Tom had to learn that baseball was run along "Fascist" and not democratic lines, and that his brother was not entitled to a greater percentage "of the money he brought to the box office."

Busch's clownish tone describing the holdout cynically accepts the rightness of baseball's monopolistic grip on its players and suggests the futility of attempts to change the system in a capitalistic society. The "strike was a failure." Players are rivals and there is no chance for solidarity among them, therefore when they act individually, as DiMaggio did, and apparently as they are trained to act, they will always be defeated. DiMaggio learned that fans favor management in most cases, especially those like his, for "a young man in his third term of a major league competition should be satisfied with $25,000 a year."

The knothole story of Joe's discovery is once more related, but Busch uses his ethnic background as another excuse to satirize the work ethic and success myth elements so frequently stressed in DiMaggio narratives. DiMaggio, Busch states with a verbal straight face, was lucky he was born to his Italian family and was in character diffident. "Italians, bad at war, are well-suited for milder competitions, and the number of top-notch Italian . . . baseball players is out of all proportion to the population." Doubly fortunate, DiMaggio was "lazy, rebellious, and endowed with a weak stomach" while his other brothers and sisters were "docile" and obedient. Joe refused to fish because it made him sick and "driven to idleness," so he began to play baseball with the other kids around the block. "Joe DiMaggio's rise in baseball is a testimonial to the value of general shiftlessness." His Americanization is also viewed comically and in terms of blatant ethnic stereotyping. "Although he learned Italian first, Joe, now 24, speaks English without an accent and is otherwise well adapted to most U.S. mores. Instead of olive oil or smelly bear grease he keeps his hair slick with water. He never reeks of garlic and prefers chicken chow mein to spaghetti."

While the article treats DiMaggio as an authentic baseball star, perhaps the best contemporary player of all, it makes fun of him as a person. His "sudden transformation from a penniless newsboy to a national celebrity" is shown based on solid athletic achievement, but Busch is constantly smug and patronizing about DiMaggio off the field, a young man who "has never worried his employers by an unbecoming interest in literature or the arts, nor does he wear himself down by unreasonable asceticism. In laziness, DiMaggio is still a paragon." Busch says he is happy only on the field or at home and the article concludes late in the morning in the house DiMaggio bought his parents, as Rosalie DiMaggio upon a signal from Joe—the raising of the Venetian blinds in his bedroom across the courtyard from her kitchen—starts making his favorite breakfast, an "omelet flavored with onions and potatoes. . . . He sits down in the kitchen comfortably and eats it."

The article is exceptional in the literature about DiMaggio. While not precisely debunking him, it presents him comically and unheroically. The piece is rarely quoted by other writers except to deride it. Why Busch took the stance he did—why *Life* printed the piece as it stands—is difficult to fathom. The photographs which the text accompanied, probably the focal point for most *Life* browsers, present a far more traditional view of the Yankee hero. The first picture is a portrait of the DiMaggio clan, a large, happy brood at home, flanked by proud parents and packed with sons, daughters, and grandchildren. Subsequent photographs depict him as a child, and then as a conquering hero paraded through the streets of San Francisco following the 1936 World Series victory. One five-picture sequence shows the family's first small, drab house in San Francisco, the "handsome house" DiMaggio bought his parents "when he grew rich and famous," his mother and father (a bit forlorn) at the new home, and two shots of his famous restaurant which cost, *Life*, materialistically points out, $100,000. Twelve smaller pictures of a batting sequence are ribboned across the top of two consecutive pages, while twelve showing his skill in center field stretch across the bottom. He is shown listening to a cash register, tasting spaghetti, surrounded by starlets while being groomed for a movie scene, pretending to play a ukulele poolside with more young women, hauling up a dead fish, handling (gingerly) a crab with his father—all standard "casual" celebrity shots very mildly parodying such pictures and at the same time providing interested fans with informal views of their star at play. One photograph shows him with fellow champ Joe Louis. The caption says, like Louis, "DiMaggio is lazy, shy, and inarticulate." Another depicts him at training camp in St. Peterburg signing autographs for kids: "Like other celebrities, DiMaggio sometimes cynically signs a pseudonym." One odd view shows a trouserless DiMaggio from the back, his shoulders slumped, and reveals that "Sliding Pads Are Worn Under DiMaggio's Pants."

Together, the article and photographs present a star of "sensational" exploits on the field, but an ordinary person off. Slanted to maintain the interest of sophisticated readers, the article, while not iconoclastic exactly, offers a distinctly tongue-in-cheek portrait of the young star whose achievements sportswriters sometimes treated as though they were the labors of Hercules. It is easy to develop an exaggerated view of sports heroes if you see them only within the boundaries of their own insulated and hysteria-filled activity. Busch's article is in some ways refreshing, nearly a put-on, except that sometimes its humor (with allusions to Italians as bad fighters and smelling of garlic) seems, today anyway, questionable. At any rate, his view of DiMaggio has not lingered long among other later writers, and is not even mentioned in the standard *Reader's Guide to Periodical Literature.*

In 1941 DiMaggio's reputation, which had since 1939 leveled out at a very high point, soared higher as he pursued and overcame the consecutive hitting record. This achievement placed him on a special plateau and forever established him as a baseball star of unique achievements. *Time*'s story for July 13 in now typical fashion rehearsed his poor and Italian immigrant background to contrast him with what he had become. As the son of a fisherman he was perhaps "shy and inarticulate. He may have been once, but he had plenty of poise this day. He is a good-looking chap, with black curly hair, sparkling eyes, and a rather long nose which gives him a sort of Cyrano de Bergerac profile." Though at bat he still had his old "dead pan" he had loosened up in private, particularly when he roomed with Lefty "Goofy" Gomez. *Time* reported the pair once would "drop paper bags full of water out of hotel windows, but this doesn't happen anymore." Another anecdote demonstrating his fondness for the comic book *Superman*, implied his continuing non-intellectualism as did his stated preference for pulp westerns. But he did not read much anyway, since it hurt his eyes, *Time* related. His coolness as a hero is exemplified by the story told of his meeting with Ed Barrow when still a rookie and Barrow warned him about the attention he was about to receive. DiMaggio responded, "Don't worry, Mr. Barrow . . . I never get excited." DiMaggio is clearly presented in the article as he would be frequently throughout his career, a spectacularly gifted but unas-

suming player not given to trumpeting his achievements. He is
quoted saying he did not think much about breaking Willie Keeler's record until he got "within three games of it," and concerning the adulation he received he said "I like to be popular,
who doesn't? But I don't pay much attention to the fans. While
I give them all I have, and *I* hope I can make good for them,
primarily I am out there playing ball for the club—and for myself," for "this is the way I make my living."

Clarke Robinson's article in *World Digest* for October 1941
has already been discussed because of its strong presentation of
DiMaggio as a symbol of America on the eve of World War II.
One of a series of "Silhouettes of Celebrities," the piece ironically preceded the December issue's "Silhouette" of Admiral
Harold R. Stark, who would be removed soon from his position
as Chief of Naval Operations of the Navy in the aftermath of
the American disaster at Pearl Harbor. With the excitement
caused by DiMaggio's streak still dominating the description of
DiMaggio, he is introduced to readers as "the biggest thing in
baseball today," a player liked by all who freely gives his autograph to "urchins" and is "idolized by his fellow Italian-
Americans." Very brief mention is given to his wife Dorothy,
who was pregnant at the time the article was written. This fact,
along with the unimportant information that his favorite foods
were shrimp cocktail and steak, seems to be included because it
humanizes DiMaggio, because all these details make him even
more of a typical "Joe." Like other Americans transformed into
a national symbol during times of crisis, he was portrayed as
both common and extraordinary, one of the people and yet exceptional, therefore fit to represent the American spirit: "Since
boyhood he's always been an open air young man doing the
manly things that youngsters like." Though Robinson does not
refer to that year's popular song, it is clear he views DiMaggio
as someone all Americans would like "on our side."

The 1941 *Current Biography* entry for him was also written
following his batting streak. Since the publication regarded itself

as a research guide, its depiction of DiMaggio is particularly interesting. The article's first two paragraphs focus on the slump he was in prior to his hit streak, whose achievement is then noted. Thus the article emphasizes his ability to come back after experiencing bad times. Then his life is outlined with occasional errors in fact: he was born in Martinez the youngest of nine children. His Italian father was a fisherman and so were two older brothers. Joe DiMaggio sold newspapers "to help support his family" (something which may have been true in desire but not in fact) which was poor: "his father, with nine children to support, couldn't afford any extras." Lefty O'Doul, it is claimed, first let him practice with the Seals in 1932. In 1933 as soon as he was switched from shortstop to the outfield "from the very first day . . . he covered . . . [it] like a tent." The article portrays him as a naturaly gifted player and not one who had to work hard to achieve his considerable greatness. He was the "greatest player the Coast League had ever produced," and (quoting but not attributing *Time*) "the American League's most sensational recruit since Ty Cobb."

DiMaggio's knee and foot injuries are described, and his hold-out in 1938 (in the article mistakenly stated to be 1937) is called his only mistake so far. What seemed at first his brashness, resulted from his youth, for he is "essentially" a "modest fellow with a sense of family responsibility typical of his Sicilian-American upbringing." His popularity among Italian-Americans is tremendous: "30,000 San Francisans tried to crowd into the Cathedral of St. Peter and Paul on the occasion of his marriage to lovely Dorothy Arnold, an actress." Thus fact and fancy are mixed in this standard biographical source which leaves mainly the impression of DiMaggio's natural skill, and how far he had come from his early days as a poor Italian lad. After all, "Joe has been praised by Taub (haberdasher to America's famous athletes) as a smooth dresser."

The 1951 *Current Biography* entry on DiMaggio was written after his retirement. It refines the 1941 picture, and adds details

to portray an athlete who has fulfilled his early promise as a
performer but also as a human being. The famous streak is mentioned of course but new space is given his comeback against
bone spurs and Boston in 1949 and specifically notes his history
of "playing when in pain from illness or injuries." The account
is more sober, emphasizing his solid achievements but placing
these in a new context: "known for years for his powerful hitting, graceful fielding, and silent, deadpan proficiency," he was
also famous "for having overcome a series of physical mis-
haps."

The review of his life and career as a player is more free from
error. His newspaper route is alluded to but no claims are made
that he helped support his family by it. Lefty O'Doul is called
his guide but not his discoverer. A few more details are supplied
suggesting how he also grew up while playing baseball: "the
shy youth began to imitate the better-dressed, more sociable
teammates" and also "received the guidance of Seals' manager
Lefty O'Doul." The ugly duckling turns into a swan partly
through his own powers of observation, then, and partly through
his apprenticeship to wise mentors. The article implies that while
still primarily a "natural" baseball player, DiMaggio worked at
becoming socially skilled and capable of writing, with the help
of Tom Meany and Marion Simon, the instructional book, *Baseball for Everyone* (1948). When he was booed for holding out
he said, "It got so I couldn't sleep at night." Aloof in the locker
room, mild-spoken, "never speaking ill about other players,"
the DiMaggio presented in *Current Biography*'s 1951 review of
his life is a person of considerable growth, one who had not
merely lived through a greater number of experiences since the
1941 biography, but whose character had been enriched by the
life he led. Now he was divorced but had his own son. He is "a
theatergoer and . . . there are flecks of gray in Joe DiMaggio's
curly black hair." He describes himself as "shy, sensitive, and
restless." He has changed and not just aged.

Lucky to Be a Yankee (1946) was the first book devoted entirely to telling the highlights of DiMaggio's life and career. Although nothing in its introductory material indicates that it is anything but an autobiography written by DiMaggio himself and thus possessing the authority and insight of a firsthand revelation, it was actually composed by Tom Meany. Much of the information Meany relates could have come only from DiMaggio, who oversaw the book's writing and collaborated with Meany on its constitution. Though in a specific sense DiMaggio did not create the book word by word, he ultimately controlled its general outlines and thus shaped it both by the information he provided and the themes whose expression he permitted (or prohibited). Therefore I shall examine the book as though DiMaggio wrote it, although technically speaking he did not, though much of the book's content results from Meany's craft and not DiMaggio's.

Lucky to Be a Yankee stands in a long tradition of autobiographical works written in America by famous men or women intended to supply basic factual information about their subjects, to satisfy public curiosity about an interesting life, but also to explain to audiences how the well-known persons became the important people they are. Benjamin Franklin's so-called *Autobiography* is a well-known book in this genre. Such books typically not only deal with certain critical events in the lives of their heroes that are thought particularly significant and revealing, but also omit other events which do not correspond with the image of self that the subject wishes to present to his or her audience. Often, the autobiographical writers are aware that they are offering themselves as models of achievement and character to their readers. Also the autobiographies must frequently create ways to defend themselves from the appearance of excessive egotism in writing so much about the self, even while parading before the reader a series of experiences establishing the subject's importance. American autobiographies also often contain some unconscious or explicit awareness of the subject's identity as an American, which until very recently, since America was a country largely made up of people from other countries or whose parents were from other countries, was not an element of identity that could be taken for granted. This last concern may be primary and overt or it may be submerged as in DiMaggio's book, whose very title, relating as it does to the national pastime and employing a national nickname, could easily be interpreted in light of his parents' immigrant status as *Lucky to Be an American*.

Even before the book's autobiographical narrative commences, its preliminary text places DiMaggio in a context that affects his forthcoming presentation of self. In the fullest version, James A. Farley introduces the reader to the book. Farley was himself a well-known power in New York and Democratic political circles, and from 1933 until 1940 he was Postmaster General of the United States. A sport enthusiast and part of the very traditional male world of Broadway celebrities DiMaggio often socialized with, Farley represents the outside, great world beyond sports that has recognized DiMaggio's exploits. DiMaggio's story, Farley emphasizes, "could have happened only in America, the story of Joe, the son of immigrant parents, of a boyhood which was far from luxurious, and his rise to national eminence on the strength of his baseball ability." Through baseball "the DiMaggios were able to forge ahead." DiMaggio presents a classic American success tale.

In a foreword, Grantland Rice, perhaps the best known sportswriter of his time, treats DiMaggio more narrowly as a player, one of a special breed demonstrating "perfection." DiMaggio has often been termed a perfect player and sometimes, particularly during his early years, a model of mechanical perfection (Harold Kaese in 1937 referred to him as "a mechanically perfect batting machine"). In a literal sense, no human performer is perfect: Babe Ruth strikes out, Jack Johnson misses a jab. What Rice refers to is a skill raised to such a degree that at times it presents the illusion of perfection: "Joe DiMaggio possesses that magic gift of perfection in his swing at the plate." Rice further distinguishes DiMaggio's greatness as an athlete (Farley focused upon his social significance) by noting his "effortless ease" that no other athlete quite possesses, underscoring one of the autobiography's recurring themes, the naturalness of Di-Maggio's skill. "If ever an athlete was meant for a sport, DiMaggio was meant for baseball." Rice's attitude here helps explain why DiMaggio's story can safely be used as a model for American youth despite his early refusal to work hard as young Americans should: he was special, he was only naturally following a higher destiny that did not want him to follow the standard path to success. In drifting into baseball, he was obeying some force that had singled him out for his special fate, one that brought him great fame but also great pain and many days of toil. So in the end, he worked hard anyway.

Finally the full version of the book contains "Acknowledgments" presumably by its autobiographic author, dedicating the book to "Baseball, the great American game," to the fans, to the "sportswriters who have always given me a 'break,'" and to all the ballplayers in both leagues, "a clean bunch of fellows and all grand sports." Here can be seen the world the book will illustrate and the audience for whom it is intended. Clearly this is to be a nice book about a clean sport written about and performed by decent people. It will give offense to few if any, and will present an innocent, sanitized view of the game either for children, or for adults who view baseball and sports as embodying the best in American life. Like Franklin's far more cynical and yet equally manipulative work, it offers the public a scrubbed and idealized version of reality. The book presents a pastoral version of baseball and DiMaggio's life, which is perhaps appropriate because baseball more than any other American sport is seen as re-creating a pastoral mode of life with its big grassy spaces and slow pace. It is the most old-fashioned of our team sports.

The basically prewar (dealing with events prior to DiMaggio's return to play in 1946) version of the book begins with a story of failure, though at a high level, in the All-Star game of 1936 when DiMaggio flopped. In this fashion DiMaggio indicates both the skill he exhibited even as a rookie, and his modesty, for he presents himself in a failing performance. He can afford to do this because for him failing was atypical, but still he demonstrates the humility that is one of the chief character traits he displays in *Lucky to Be a Yankee*. As a good moralist, he draws lessons from his poor play: "that anything can happen in any one ball game," and "that things are hardest, just when they look easiest." He learns the dangers of "overconfidence." He often tempers tales of triumph with cautionary reminders of his flawed skill. After he hits a triple his very first time at bat with San Francisco, he plays shortstop and either heaves the ball "over his first baseman's head or into the dirt." Cheered for throwing out a runner to win a game against Detroit his first season with the Yankees, he admits his toss was not good because it traveled to Bill Dickey on the fly rather than on one bounce as it should have, so it could be handled more easily or cut off if desired. At other times his lack of egotism is demonstrated by the humble interpretation he gives events. He admits that after four weeks with the Yankees he needed a police escort to get into the stadium but claims this was partly because "the fans knew all about the others and I was virtually a newcomer." In most instances the modesty or humility seems real and not assumed.

Chapter 1 (in the prewar version) is titled self-derisively "The Old Horse Laugh" and Chapter 2 is "The Old Horse Lot." Here he returns briefly to his childhood. The book is not long and the individual chapters are never extensive—there are seventeen of them totaling 180 pages of narrative. The book's language is unpretentious and natural, almost in the vernacular, with few metaphors and nothing young boys might call flowery. It is quite effective in conveying DiMaggio's seemingly uncomplicated, even-tempered nature. In Chapter 2, the language is particularly appropriate for conveying the story of DiMaggio's earliest years when he was just another boy growing up in a big, poor Italian

Joseph Paul DiMaggio, The Yankee Clipper

Joe, in 1941, after tying Wee Willie Keeler's record 44 consecutive game hitting streak. He would extend the streak to 56 games before being stopped.

Joe homers to help win the fifth and final game of the 1949 World Series.

**In an era before television, photos like this one helped
newspapers shape the image of the young superstar.**

Joe, sitting at a typewriter, ostensibly writing one of the several books and articles attributed to him.

**Santa Joe celebrates Christmas with wife,
Dorothy Arnold, and son, Joe, Jr.**

**Joe having breakfast at the Hotel Elysee along with his
brother Tom, son Joe, Jr., and mother Rosalie.
It was said of Joe that he led the league in room service.**

During his career Joe often signed baseball cards for his fans, particularly the younger ones. In later years, commercial autographings became a significant source of his income.

NATIONAL BASEBALL HALL OF FAME LIBRARY
COOPERSTOWN, N.Y.

Joe with Yankee owner Jacob Ruppert, Jr. Born in Ohio to a family of modest means, Ruppert made his fortune in Cuba following the Spanish-American War.

Joe with pitching hero Allie Reynolds following the fourth game of the 1951 World Series. Behind in the series two games to one, Joe's homer helped the Yankees to a 6-2 win over the New York Giants. The Yankees would go on to win the series four games to two.

**Joe, now retired, interviewing Yankee manager
Casey Stengel early in the 1952 season.**

Joe standing next to his plaque following his 1955 induction into the Baseball Hall of Fame.

Joe signing autographs at a 1958 Old-Timers Game.

**Joe giving batting tips to Yogi Berra (left)
and Mickey Mantle (center)**

Joe and his recently divorced wife, actress Marilyn Monroe, are shown arriving at New York's State Theater to attend a preview showing of Marilyn's latest film, *The Seven Year Itch*.

The casket of Joe DiMaggio is carried down the steps of Saint Peter and Paul Parish by friends and family members, including his son Joe, Jr., San Francisco's North Beach district, 11 March 1999. DiMaggio died 8 March 1999 at age 84.

family. Baseball was his only game because since he did not like to work fishing, he had to occupy his time somehow, playing on no "fancy cut out diamonds, with green grass and all the trimmings." He and his chums commandeered in time-honored boys' fashion an old lot used to park milk wagons (when they were still drawn by horses, thus plunging the reader back to a much earlier, seemingly simpler world), with rocks for bases, an oar for a bat, and a ball held together by tape. Most of the boys played without gloves because they were too poor to buy one. In this world a young boy might very well be discovered while peering through a knothole.

Fans and fiction readers alike enjoy stories about lowly beginnings, but what most want more is the march toward success together with demonstrations of greatness. DiMaggio begins satisfying this craving in Chapter 3, "With the Seals." But his story of success here and elsewhere in the book is never an unalloyed tale of triumph, for success (what kids often desire from narratives of heroes is a pornography of pure success they would probably soon be surfeited with) extended and unabated is traditionally a prelude to disaster: it is suspect. DiMaggio uses success to introduce three themes. First, he insists that his skill at least in "hitting is a God-given gift," not an ability that can be acquired by diligent practice. He respects techniques that can add to a player's ability, and offers a few toward the conclusion of his story, but he states flatly that he knows he is a professional "because at the age of eighteen I had a natural gift for hitting and for no other reason whatsoever." Thus at once he advances his greatness, and disclaims credit for it.

An example of his great hitting—the 61-game streak for the Seals—presents another lesson that success taught him, "the tremendous factor team spirit is in baseball." Throughout the book the teams he played for are seen as families to which he belonged, peopled with parental figures (coaches) and siblings (fellow players). The Yankees were so good in 1938 because they "were happy about playing together. Everybody was interested in the welfare of everybody else.'' What pleased him most his rookie years ''was the rapidity with which I had been accepted as one of the family.'' For DiMaggio ''the Yankee were more than just a bunch of stars. They were a team in all that the term implies.'' The celebration the team gives him for hitting 56 straight was ''the greatest thrill I've ever had in baseball. . . . It's nice to know that the guys you work for think you're a regular guy, too.'' Though outside reports indicate that friction existed on Yankee teams from time to time throughout DiMaggio's career, and that sometimes he was less than a popular figure with all his teammates (when he held out in 1938, for example, and again when he retreated into himself during slumps in the 1950s), this cozy, boy's view of familial camaraderie remains constant in the autobiography.

Finally, in Chapter 3, the reader learns DiMaggio's successes are often attended by bad luck, particularly in the form of painful injuries. Though much of DiMaggio's life and career is omitted from the book, the major injuries are detailed in expressive language. The pain of the knee injury he received in 1934 ''was terrific, like a whole set of aching teeth in my knee.'' It sounded like ''four sharp cracks'' and made him fall ''as though I had been shot.'' In supplying information about his injuries DiMaggio was recording part of his history but also adhering to the image of the wounded hero he possessed even prior to his comebacks from injury in the late 1940s. He conformed to the model of the victorious comeback hero that people have traditionally admired, but also supplied a special attractiveness to young American boys growing up the years he played, who themselves often found masochistic delight in their play portraying soldiers, cowboys, or Indians who were invariably and often spectacularly wounded in play. Rare was the boy who did not possess a repertoire of dying gestures or who did not relish staggering crazily from a bullet slug in the gut that did not quite prevent him from performing some disabled act of valor. Socialized to learn to accept and even appreciate pain, boys were later expected to wage games or fight wars wounded, and DiMaggio was the sort of maimed star who would appeal to their sense that men played with pain.

DiMaggio, however, is no warrior manqué in *Lucky to Be a Yankee*. Clearly he likes to win and plays hard to achieve that goal, but in no way does he foreshadow the winning-is-everything, viciously competitive spirit of Vince Lombardi. There is rather something courtly in his attitude toward competing—the good player does his best, but performs with a gracious and even noble spirit. He reports that in the last days of the 1935 season with the Seals, when he is fighting for the batting leadership with Ox Eckhardt, the official scorer gave him a hit on a ball that fell before a stumbling center fielder who otherwise would have caught it. "I didn't want any base hits of that type," he says, and went to the official scorer after the game "to demand that he change the hit to an error." Later, with the Yankees, he states his admiration for Joe McCarthy emphasizing that "he stresses dignity." Describing Ernie Lombardi's "snooze" in the 1939 World Series, he courteously explains: "In justice to Lombardi . . . I believe he was momentarily stunned when Keller ran into him." His behavior as he describes it is nearly always gentlemanly. He describes his confrontation with Whitlow Wyatt in the 1941 World Series as the result of communications garbled in "the heat and tension of the game." Wyatt and he "never got within twenty paces of each other" during the incident, and afterward he says "there were, of course, no hard feelings. Wyatt came over to our dressing room after the game to congratulate us" and even wished the Yankees a pleasant winter. He is one of the "clean bunch of fellows and all grand sports" with which DiMaggio peoples his major leagues.

Launched into the great world of the "Big Apple" in Chapter 4, DiMaggio continues his growth as he is able to see "America for the first time." He finds happy camaraderie among the Yankees and is even "treated . . . swell" by his "friends" the sportswriters. There is in fact no one in the entire book who is sharply criticized, no antagonisms that are rehashed. He gives the impression that baseball is inhabited by exceptionally pleasant and helpful people, all of whom respect each other. "That First Season" described in Chapter 5 becomes after his burned foot heals a season of triumph culminating in a World Series victory, only the first of many for one of the game's great winners. He concludes this episode of victory over adversity with the happy recollection that his mother watched him and the Yankees win and became "hysterical with joy." Her own social progress (in part advanced by his) is symbolized by the thrilling surprise she felt seeing the Statue of Liberty for the second time in thirty-four years—the first being when she had entered the country a poor immigrant from Palermo. The episode of 1936 ends with Di-Maggio heading on the train back to his home in San Francisco, a trip he will almost invariably make in the following years after riotous New York wins. He "had had a good season, a group of wonderful fellows as teammates," and lots of stories to tell the old gang. Like a good fabulist, he does not have to underscore his point here: the big city star was still one of the boys back at his old home, where he still belonged. Winning had not gone to his head.

Nor would it in 1937 with the "happy" Yankees, a team with great players but "no big shots in the disparaging sense of the term." The "whammie" on him brings a sore arm and tonsillitis and once more prevents him from playing opening day, but once he breaks into the lineup all is well again. With new stars such as Tommy Henrich and old reliables like Lefty Gomez and Red Ruffing, the Yankees win their league by thirteen games and DiMaggio for a brief time challenged Babe Ruth's home-run record. The Giants fall again, in five games, in the World Series and after "a great season" all DiMaggio "wanted was to get home and rest." He had again experienced all a kid could hope for: some adversity and pain to triumph over, the friendship of a good and happy crew, enough stardom and victory to satisfy the most gluttonous success seeker, and at the end of the long delightful tiring day, sweet home to return to from the great world beyond.

Home meant family and in *Lucky to Be a Yankee* DiMaggio often recollects with pleasure his mother, father, sisters, and particularly his brothers, while recounting his progress toward greatness. Rosalie and Giuseppe are not portrayed in full detail, but they are always mentioned warmly throughout the text. Joe's desire not to fish, and his decision to quit school are not dramatized with nearly the schmaltzy intensity that other authors, such as Gene Schoor, employ to dramatize these events. A paragraph in the prewar version stating that though his father finally believed that fishing made him sick he concluded his son "was a kid who never would amount to anything, anyway," was dropped from the later 1949 and 1951 editions. In another paragraph Joe says he was not "particularly happy during my two years at Galileo High, through no fault of the school" (this is a no-blame book) but that if he could live the years over again (are you listening, boys and girls?) he'd have stuck with school longer, thus proving his "mother's judgment on the subject of education was correct"—she wanted him to continue—"as it was in most all other matters." When, late in the book DiMaggio travels "Along Memory Lane," over a page is devoted to his pop, a "Santa Claus" who proudly prepared meals for special vistors to the DiMaggio restaurant in San Francisco, and avidly scanned the newspaper box scores each morning during baseball season to see how his three sons performed.

DiMaggio's brothers Vincent and Dominic complete the picture of close family unity the book very comfortingly provides. Vince's role in preparing the way for Joe's decision to make baseball his career is suggested though not fully developed. DiMaggio recalls thinking as a teenager that since "Vince was making good in a big way" and could "get dough for playing ball," he could, too. And it is while trying to see Vince through the knothole in the Seals' fence that Joe is so magically plucked from sandlot ball by Spike Hennessy. In DiMaggio's version, incidentally, no sign of strong parental resistance to his decision to become a professional appears. As DiMaggio relates his own story, from time to time he will note the added pleasure he received knowing his brothers were also doing well in baseball, and is open in his continuing admiration for the skills of both; Dom, he thinks, is the "best defensive outfielder I've ever seen." Joe seems totally without jealousy when he writes that "Pop's pride and joy was Dom, the smallest and youngest of us." So the book very definitely locates DiMaggio in his parents' family even years after he had established for a time his own family of wife and child. The book is dedicated "to little Joe" and he tells one anecdote about his wife Dorothy helping him break a slump. The 1951 version however cuts a reference to "Dorothy . . . the best catch I ever made in my life" which first appeared in the original text and was retained in 1949. DiMaggio's marriage is referred to only fleetingly and his mother and father occupy his thoughts and his life more than his wife, which seems appropriate for the boy's world the book presents. In this almost shadowless world there is no room for DiMaggio's divorce or his father's death, which are both unmentioned though teammate Lou Gehrig's passing is mourned.

Rich in anecdotes about the background to great events in DiMaggio's playing career and very earnest in the traditional morality it urges implicitly or explicitly throughout its narrative, but thin in developing any of the personal or professional conflicts that might have vexed him, much of *Lucky to Be a Yankee* is devoted to stories about other players. Many of the photographs show not DiMaggio but star performers such as Tris Speaker, Babe Ruth, and Ty Cobb, older greats in whose company their pictures here suggest DiMaggio belongs. Dom DiMaggio is also depicted, as is the 1937 Yankee team and Red Ruffing. Another photograph recaptures thirteen members of the DiMaggio clan when Joe played for San Francisco and Vince for Hollywood in 1933. As a group, the pictures demonstrate DiMaggio's skills, link him to the tradition of older stars, root him in his family, and closely identify him with all the good fellows he played with, particularly with the Yankees he contributed so much to as a team player.

One chapter tells about the noble Lou Gehrig, and another concerns "The Gay Cabellero" Lefty Gomez. These sequences balance each other and provide human perspectives generally lacking in DiMaggio's self-related narrative. The passage on Gehrig is somber in portraying his gradual physical deterioration and death in what should have been his prime. Gomez is Gehrig's and DiMaggio's antithesis, "El Goofo," possessing all the comic sense and color DiMaggio lacked. The chapter "All Stars Aren't Yankees" tells pleasant anecdotes about fine fellows like Bob Feller, Ted Williams, and Jimmie Foxx. Career shadows such as Foxx's drinking problem are naturally not mentioned.

The sections of *Lucky to Be a Yankee* written after its original publication continue the themes of the earlier version. DiMaggio is still a team player for whom "hits can't mean much to a ballplayer unless they mean a lot to his ball club." He is still proud about his family (including son Joe) and after a victorious season heads for his San Francisco home again. The pain of playing increases but his comebacks (including the famous one in 1949) are more triumphant. There are still no bad guys in the game, and what in reality was his barely stifled rage at being taken from the lineup by Casey Stengel is laundered into "Stengel asked me to take a little rest." The fans are still swell and not just the Yankee fans; at the end of the season when he plays in Boston not feeling his best, the Boston fans cheer him with an affection that particularly delights him. The book becomes more reflective, has less to say about spectacular exploits and more to tell about enduring wounds. A major controversy described in the prewar edition was his holdout in 1938, an episode that clearly bothered him, for he discussed it twice. In the later edition he mentions his 1949 flap with the press who had been hounding him to learn the extent of his injury. Both disputes are offered in highly sanitized versions that ignore the bitterness

DiMaggio originally felt for management and the press. Both pre- and post-war editions of his autobiography smooth some rough edges from DiMaggio's career. The chapters added concerning the 1949–50 seasons contain their moments of joyful triumph, particularly the new Chapter 2 called "Good to the Last Drop," which tells of 1949; but more than the previous segments they speak of an aging hero of diminished abilities who knows he "would be foolish not to admit that I was just about stepping off the hill and going down the incline," who "was a young fellow once upon a time" that "somebody had to move over on the bench to make room for." None of the new material is placed at the end of the book however. It is all added to its first half, so that a kid or fan wanting immersion in a kid's world could read *after* he had learned about Joe in the 1950 season about his "hitting in 56 straight" in 1941 and about all the other good guys like Gehrig and Gomez. The reader of later editions would find out that Joe McCarthy's career with the Yankees ended in 1946. The reader would not be told that McCarthy was apparently drinking too much and that his departure was accompanied by behind-the-scenes turbulence among Yankee management that continued several seasons and found its public expression in the swirl of managers the team experienced before management settled on Casey Stengel. The reader would learn no more about DiMaggio's own war years in the later editions than the scant few references provided originally. They were for DiMaggio drab years apparently of unheroic events. Along with bad things like divorces and his father's death, such news was banished or hidden in DiMaggio's public recollections.

In *Lucky to Be a Yankee*, DiMaggio, like Huckleberry Finn's Mark Twain, told the truth mainly, but of an entirely different kind of world from the rapacious and egocentric land Twain described. DiMaggio's world is one of great personal achievement won through natural and inimitable gifts, a world of good parents and children, of families who stay together, where nice guys finish first—and second and third and fourth. DiMaggio describes himself in as low-key fashion as possible, considering the nature of his career. He stresses that he is a decent fellow who behaves decently among other decent fellows, who loves his mother and father, who does not give up even when hurt, who plays for team and not for self. He is very convincing in his autobiography, and seems a likable fellow worthy of emulation. He understates his greatness while in the act of portraying it, and manifests a likable humility that becomes ingrained as one of his major characteristics as a victorious hero.

In his fine book *The American Dream and the National Game*, Leverett Smith estimates that DiMaggio's autobiography was intended for an audience of fourteen-year-olds. In fact there is little in the book that identifies it particularly as written for juveniles when one takes into account that its information and delivery are similar to what had been written about DiMaggio on sports pages and in national magazines for a decade previous to its publication. Its tunnel vision focusing upon certain of DiMaggio's baseball exploits and highly selected aspects of his private life presents nothing strikingly different though the book is far more detailed than any prior single item had been. Its persistently moral tone also found its counterpart in earlier newspaper and periodical literature. DiMaggio's (or Meany's) language and his attitudes toward baseball and his life in it would not have made adult readers of sports literature feel they were intruding upon a child's book. DiMaggio's autobiography may have presaged later texts intended and marketed strictly for juveniles, but it was not one of them.

A few comic book versions of DiMaggio's life offer better models for stories intended strictly for young audiences. A brief sequence about DiMaggio written at the peak of the first half of his career, before he entered military service, appeared as part of a longer "authorized story of the UNBEATABLE YANKS" appearing in the July 1942 issue of *Trail Blazers* comic. This issue also featured stories on three other successful entertainment figures, the nineteenth-century magician Robert Houdin, announcer (then for the Brooklyn Dodgers) Red Barber, and radio star Fred Allen. The portion featuring DiMaggio is only five panels long and the drawings of him do not in the least resemble him: most of the players drawn in the article look alike. In one panel a scout (so labeled) looks interested in DiMaggio but his sight line leads directly to DiMaggio's knee and the scout thinks "Great hitter but I'm afraid of his leg." In the next panel a large, seated figure with "Yankees" written across his chest picks up a toy-sized doll marked "DiMaggio" and grins broadly at it. Captions note that the Yankees took a chance and bought DiMaggio for five players and $25,000, which they did not pay until the end of his last minor league season, which the comic states is 1936, and adds that the Yankees won their gamble. The third panel shows DiMaggio jumping up and down like a spoiled brat, yelling for $25,000. A caption adds he "is quieter now." The fourth panel shows his restaurant, very crudely drawn, and says he operates it in San Francisco though he "remained in New York the past winter." The largest panel shows DiMaggio completing his swing and dominates half the one-page sequence. DiMaggio is but one of several Yankee players depicted in what is essentially a story in praise of the tightly organized, ostensibly well-paying and eminently successful Yankee organization. Lou Gehrig receives more space and is depicted more positively and more nobly. The most distinctive characteristics of the section on DiMaggio are the poorness of its drawing and the lack of unity in its unheroic presentation of him.

A later story about DiMaggio appearing in the May 1948 issue of *True Comics* is far longer and incorporates more aspects of the DiMaggio myth as it existed at that time. "The Story of Joe DiMaggio, America's Greatest Baseball Player" is the comic book's lead item. Its cover depicts a recognizable Jolter blasting a home run, to judge from the facial expressions of the catcher, umpire, and fans who form the illustration's background. The story draws its information about "The Yankee Clipper" from some of the earlier magazine articles but mainly from *Lucky to*

Be a Yankee. It begins incorrectly, however, in Martinez, California, where Joe's father bawls out his callow son for playing baseball, for "wearing out shoes and pants when you should be helping me fish," and accuses him of being "lazy." "A few months later" when Joe announces at the family dinner table that he has a job selling newspapers, his father derisively says that is just the job for him: "All you've got to do is stand and yell." Vince suggests he try out with the Seals, but Joe—eating spaghetti—claims he is "not good enough." Found outside the knothole looking in at the Seals, he is hired by them and "learned there was more to baseball than just hitting the ball": a picture shows him throwing far beyond the first baseman's reach. The ensuing pages essentially follow DiMaggio's story as he presented it in his autobiography, depicting his 61-game Seals streak (including the praise Tom Sheehan gave him for hitting his best pitch); his knee injury and subsequent purchase by the Yankees; the friendly welcome given him by his new teammates; his 1936 pre-season ankle injury; his unpopular 1938 holdout; his batting streak when brother Dom supposedly robbed him of a hit; and the party his teammates gave him for hitting in 56 consecutive games. An error in the story whose source was not DiMaggio's book is the statement that he played his first major league game in May 1935. *True* adds a patriotic panel not based upon DiMaggio's autobiography showing DiMaggio saluting Joe McCarthy and saying "I've come to say good-bye. Uncle Sam needs me," to which McCarthy stoutly replies, "Fight to win like you always did on the diamond, Joe." DiMaggio spared his readers such false heroics. The caption to a final picture of Joe catching a fly, running out a hit, and gripping a bat, briefly relates his career since the war, his return "to even greater heights" in 1947 (it does not mention the relatively unsuccessful 1946 season) and his third most valuable player award.

Even more than *Lucky to Be a Yankee* had, *True Comics* presents DiMaggio in a magical, self-enclosed world in which his rise to success seems even more like a fairy tale. The story's first words misrepresent fact but place DiMaggio in a simple, ethical context young readers could identify with. He is "the boy who wanted to sell newspapers," and thus a right-minded young lad. The very next panel however shows him not on the street corner holding a newspaper but standing at bat while his father clenches his fist and shouts at him that he should be helping him fish. In the next panel the father is dangerously close to DiMaggio with both fists upraised almost as though he were going to pound his skinny son on the chest. The father's body is drawn in an aggressive posture to emphasize his anger, while DiMaggio stands slack and slump-shouldered as few good batters but many a teenage boy did. Unlike his picture on the magazine's cover he does not look like DiMaggio as he ages through the succeeding panels. This results from poor artwork more than conscious editorial design, but also perhaps enabled the story's readers to more easily place themselves in his position.

"A few months later" DiMaggio is shown in his family's dining room together with Vince, Dom, and Papa DiMaggio. Joe's mother is absent, and in the drastically restricted comic book depiction of his life only one woman from his personal life appears, the sister he visits when he injures his leg ligaments. Joe enters (to his left a large crucifix hangs on the wall: his household is religious, a point made and then not underscored further) and announces he has a job selling papers. His father uses this as an opportunity to insult him for his uselessness. Brother Vince rescues him by saying "Stop teasing him, Pop," and suggests that since he has a job with the Seals, Joe should try out too. The story is only four panels long at this point, and while the first two panels showed Joe playing baseball, the game was among kids and highly informal, so in terms of the sequence of events the magazine has offered, Vince's suggestion is highly unrealistic. If the story is viewed as a fantasy children would enjoy placing themselves in (the mean, unbelieving father, the good, indolent son who really does have special talents), the

narrative's omission of background makes sense; like the artwork itself, only the few salient surface details are illustrated.
Event is uncontaminated by preparation just as panel drawings
contain only essential details. Caught looking through the Seals'
knothole, Joe is whisked to an office, told by an unnamed man
that his play had been observed, and marched toward the dugout
saying "what a break!"

Almost five pages of panels illustrate Joe's childhood life and
his play with the Seals. On the team he is drawn still as a spindly
youth, bodiless under his unattractive uniform. Slightly over
three pages show him performing with the Yankees at which
time his body becomes bigger and stronger. Many an adolescent
fan could have dreamed of achieving similar progress, of dis-
proving ominous parental predictions, of overcoming awkward-
ness and the occasional bad luck that finally seemed the only
force capable of hindering DiMaggio from becoming a star.

The comic books offered a greatly compressed and simplified
view of DiMaggio and his life, by design a two-dimensional
reduction of his story. In the *Trial Blazers* narrative he is shown
as a one-time crybaby who somehow learns not to complain and
thereby to fit in better with his team and win even greater financial rewards. The penultimate panel shows him yelping for more
money, but then explains that he no longer behaves in this fashion, while the final panel depicts his restaurant. The implication
is that not complaining is profitable. In his autobiography,
DiMaggio takes almost five pages to discuss the holdout issue
and finally, grudgingly, concludes that since "the fan pays the
freight . . . he has just as much right to boo as he has to cheer.
. . . I took it, but I didn't like it." The point is not that the comic
books lack space to discuss nuances of interpretation but that the
nuances are not desired in their formula. In the *True Comics*
story, DiMaggio's apprenticeship years on the San Francisco
sandlots are not illustrated because while his discovery is significant his preparation is not, because young readers are inter-

ested in becoming stars but not really in the training stardom
usually demands, and because, after all, how does one prepare
to become Joe DiMaggio? The hero's life is miraculous.

Even more stripped down in iconographic content are the
baseball cards on which DiMaggio has appeared. Some of these
are valuable to collectors not so much because of DiMaggio's
talent or popularity, but because of their relative rarity. The 1939
"Play Ball" card is fairly expensive, bringing a price of about
$125 in the early 1980s. Issued by GUM, Inc., the series origi-
nally included about 250 "leading baseball players." Di-
Maggio's photograph is not complimentary, showing a
thin-faced, buck-toothed star whom the text nonetheless calls
"the greatest outfielder in baseball today." Among DiMaggio's
listed accomplishments are his .398 batting average for San Francisco in 1935, his American League home-run championship in
1937, and the fact that he was the leading vote-getter in the 1938
All-Star game. His hitting is emphasized. His present-day and
very inexpensive "SUPERSTAR" card reveals him as an older
player, fuller faced, studying the hitter at bat while kneeling on
deck. The card's point of view identifies him as a past hero,
"The Yankee Clipper . . . one of the greatest outfielders of all
time. Voted the Greatest Living Ballplayer in 1969." Seen as a
giant among stars, "he held baseball's vastest turf, Yankee Stadium's center field, in the palm of his hand during his years with
the Yankees." His .398 and .346 rookie year batting averages
are supplied, and the card adds that "his lifetime average .325
was despite injuries and time out for the service during the war."
Here DiMaggio is seen from a distance as larger than life and
yet, though the card's inscription is considerably shorter than the
"Play Ball" printed message, more human: reference to his injuries and service years adds some depth to his portrayal which
in the "Play Ball" card was primarily a statistical outline. The
"SUPERSTAR" card also shows how time smooths out un-
wanted edges in the picture of heroes, claiming "he was an automatic Hall of Famer in 1955" while glossing over his failure

to achieve appointment in 1953 and 1954, the first two years he was eligible. Cards and comic books, while offering interesting partial portraits of DiMaggio at different stages of his career, and circulated widely, could present only highly selected angles of his image. After the war years, lengthier recitals of his accomplishments proliferated in articles and books.

Baseball for Everyone (1948) was intended for children and teenage boys (the book shows no awareness that girls might like to play baseball, too), and was supposedly written by DiMaggio, though he acknowledges in the book's introduction the "cooperation" of Tom Meany and Marion Simon. Some of the information the book contains seems to stem directly from DiMaggio's experiences, though again, the shaping and some of the detail was doubtless provided by Meany and Simon and some data possibly originated with the "many authorities" the book's dust jacket blurb claims that "DiMaggio consulted." Some of the writing is rather clinical and surely was not articulated by DiMaggio: "A National Recreation Association survey shows that in 1946, the most recent year for which figures are available, 1,153 cities reported the operation of 4,323 municipal baseball diamonds." Yet even stray advertisements today still maintain the pretense that the book is DiMaggio's.

The book offers sound enough but not startling advice: "The leg on which the slide is made must be relaxed"; "Hold the bat loosely and as the pitcher delivers get the bat parallel to the ground." Sometimes the advice is not so much technical as admonitory. "If a boy sincerely believes that he has a chance to become a professional ballplayer, he should not haggle too much about a bonus." Though DiMaggio admits he had been a holdout, he exculpates himself by declaring his case is different because he was a professional and already a regular, and the youngster would just be trying to get his foot in the door (ignoring that he haggled with the Seals over a percentage of his sale price to the Yankees that he felt entitled to). Generally he shows good sense in his attitudes toward children's sports. He feels that the regular diamond, for example, is too big for kids to play on, straining their small, undeveloped arms and teaching them bad habits. The catcher might learn (like Harry Dunning of the 1938 and 1939 New York Giants against whom he played in the World Series) to take an extra step throwing to second base.

Some of the book's charm resides in the stray information DiMaggio provides his young audience about his own early years when, he admits ruefully, he was called a "Dead Pan." He was about ten when he first started playing, he says, and when he was a boy he and his friends would "buy spikes in a sporting goods store and have the neighborhood cobbler attach them to a pair of ordinary street shoes." Emphasizing neither his Italian nor his large family background, he uses his own experience sometimes in a way that would have been reassuring to young boys hungry for encouraging words in their dreams of greatness. He quotes Joe McCarthy, who said if a player has the skill plus the determination, "he'll make the majors, no matter what the odds may be." Sweet music to boys who bounced balls off stoops, shagged flies with their friends, took endless turns at bat and swung hard and never missed by much, really. Generally, the book is as low key as DiMaggio himself seemed, at worst harmless and at best offering some sound instruction emphasizing playing well rather than winning at any cost. Today, it seems old-fashioned. Several years after its American publication it was translated into Italian as *Baseball* (undated but probably 1952) even though as its preface states (in Italian) that "to speak of baseball to an Italian is like speaking of soccer to an American."[1] DiMaggio is called "one of the greatest baseball players (he has just retired from 'active service') and still retains his popularity—is probably the most popular player in the United States."

Jack Sher's lengthy article in the September 1949 *Sport* is clearly an adult view of DiMaggio as a great but aging player whose surface image is misleading. "DiMag: The Man Behind the Poker Face'' is not so much an exposé as it is an attempt to look hard at the reality of DiMaggio's life. The essay concludes not by debunking DiMaggio's heroic attainments but by placing them in the context of a very human existence containing real shadows that do not disappear as easily as the setbacks in comic book drawings.

Sher knew DiMaggio and many of his Broadway friends directly, but his view of him seems relatively objective and not the standard, glorified view of many of the early articles presented. Either Sher wrote naturally with greater sophistication than the earlier journalists who had told DiMaggio's story or he was simply participating in a newer kind of sports journalism that practiced greater realism in its portrayals of sports heroes. Much of his information seems to come directly from DiMaggio's autobiography which he says he has read, especially details relating to DiMaggio's childhood and first years as a professional. So he once more relates that Joe came from a poor but good immigrant family, that he was discovered looking through the knothole, that Tom Sheehan stopped in the game he was pitching against the Seals to congratulate DiMaggio on hitting his best pitch. Sometimes Sher personalizes his, by then, generally available information by adding that he reported it as it was presented in DiMaggio's autobiography and ''as he told it to me.'' Sometimes he adds interesting details to the known account, noting that DiMaggio remembered his family's poverty in particular terms of not having enough money to see the film *All Quiet on the Western Front*. Sher is openly DiMaggio's advocate but he is aware also that the best of DiMaggio's career was over and that DiMaggio was entering a new stage in life for him, that he was making what pop sociologists would later term a ''passage.''

Sher's picture of DiMaggio in 1949 is a portrait of a hero— but. . . . There is an undercurrent of uneasiness about DiMaggio's stardom in the article. Sher calls him ''the most beautiful performer of our era,'' yet seems bothered that ''he has never been glorified to the degree of other diamond greats,'' a remark that seems strange in retrospect. For Sher, DiMaggio's problem is that he is no longer the almost constantly gifted player he once seemed. He is aging. The injuries that he endured and came back from were coming back upon him. He was at that moment in his career when an athlete ''realizes that he is no longer able to do, wholly and completely, the things that have set him apart and above all other competitors.'' He sees DiMaggio as a success story, relating that when he was a Seals rookie and asked for a quote by a newspaperman, he did not know what a quote was: now, in Toots Shor's words, everyone knew ''the kid *attained* class.'' But when Sher ranks DiMaggio with the very greatest players such as Ty Cobb, he justifies his rating by claiming ''no ballplayer can be completely judged by what is found in the record books,'' a rationale supporters of DiMaggio tended to offer after his postwar career but not often advanced during his first seven years in the majors. Sher offers DiMaggio's injuries and wartime hiatus as reasons for the statistical decline.

Sher recognizes that DiMaggio has mellowed since his rookie days. He ''has a gentle, warm quality that men who are wholly masculine always have.'' He no longer is characterized as a comic book reader, for Sher says he reads authors such as C. S. Forester and according to DiMaggio himself ''books that make a comment on our times, such as *The Naked and the Dead*'' and Roger Butterfield's *The American Past*, a good pictorial history of the United States. But beneath his poker face DiMaggio the great team player was ''an incredibly lonely man.'' This is a new way of viewing DiMaggio who, while perceived as a loner previously, was not usually depicted as lonely. ''When he's not playing baseball'' Sher says, ''the roof seems to have fallen in.'' Sher adds to the image of DiMaggio the idea that outside his now waning life in baseball, there existed an emptiness in his life. This is a commonplace in hero's narratives (Tennyson's ''Ulysses'' languishing at home after wondrous wandering, or Grant without a Civil War, even when President). Echoes of this theme would be heard later, particularly in the accounts of DiMaggio's after life by Gene Schoor, Maury Allen, and Gay Talese. Sher wrote toward the end of DiMaggio's career but while he was still active, so he had fresh in his mind pictures of the star's sensational 1949 achievements even while observing how his body was giving out. He concludes that DiMaggio was still "the guy who made the hard ones look easy," but his article proves he knew soon the easy ones would be hard—and that would be difficult for DiMaggio's fans, harder still for Di-Maggio, now a hero with limited horizons.

Dan Daniel's very long article—monograph really—prefacing the 1950 *Sporting News* baseball annual is a much breezier but still very good journalistic introduction to DiMaggio's life, lacking Sher's thoughtfulness but still providing one of the most sensible overviews of DiMaggio's career by a writer who knew and admired him but did not view him with awe or sentimentality. Daniel was a prototype pre-World War II sportswriter, a much respected working journalist at his best writing for the sports pages with enough wit and accuracy to make his daily reports enjoyable as well as informative. He had no pretensions to greatness as a writer, and his style is not as facile as Meany's, but neither is it intrusive. Once his jaunty sportswriter's idiom is accepted (sportswriters are "aces," DiMaggio is "The Jolter," "Giuseppe," "Josephus," home runs are round trippers and four baggers that are belted, swatted, and crashed) he can be read with a simple pleasure if not delight. Where he is wrong, he is clearly in the wrong, and usually because his good heart would not permit him to be accurate, for example when he links Ruth, Gehrig, and DiMaggio together as "humble." Ruth certainly was not. Daniel had the advantage of knowing DiMaggio over the years, of having DiMaggio's confidence in him as a fair man and one of the sportsmen along Broadway whose company Joe so greatly enjoyed. He was a good newsman who seems to have checked what facts he could without performing like a professional researcher.

Daniel's greatest success in "Joe DiMaggio" (subtitled "My Friend—The Yankee Clipper)" is to present a sensible view of DiMaggio, his family, early years, and status with the Yankees. For example, he is the first journalist, certainly in a book or periodical, to write of Giuseppe DiMaggio Sr.'s war record with the Italian Army in Abyssinia. He is reasonable about home conflicts, saying that Joe's father feared the boy would be lazy (common among parents) and that Joe's seeming diffidence hid his wait to find something he really wanted to do. Concerning Joe's start in professional baseball, Daniel is similarly sensible. He says, "Spike Hennessy, who scouted the sandlots for Owner Charley Graham's San Francisco Seals of the Coast League, had known and helped Vince DiMaggio. After seeing Joe in a few sandlot games, Spike took him to the boss and eventually wangled him into a workout with the Seals." This may not make great myth, but it possess authenticity. He is however aware of the mythic dimensions of DiMaggio's story, pointedly remarking that he embodied "The Great American Success Story," but his awareness is without pomp or pretense. Though more articulate than DiMaggio, he probably perceived the world in much the same way, without heroic vision but with the eyes of somebody real in ordinary society. He does not make DiMaggio into something he is not, nor present baseball as a sacred game. He reports on the squabbles preceding Joe McCarthy's departure in 1946. His appraisal of DiMaggio is unsentimental. His language lacks aesthetic grace, but it does not bloat DiMaggio's image through straining for higher effects. His statement explaining what the American dream represented in DiMaggio's life in 1936 is in its way perfect: "he was to get aboard the gravy train at last, to taste the glory and acclaim that America lavishes so bountifully on its sports heroes." Beyond providing fresh, firsthand information about DiMaggio's family background and his professional life, Daniel's greatest accomplishment is to present DiMaggio as a great player and good person but not as a national legend, nor as a tragic hero. It is a limited view by a limited writer, one of the last of DiMaggio's older contemporaries to write at length about him from the vantage point of having seen him closely and off the pedestal. It is a refreshing, informative, if circumscribed view.

The pictures accompanying Daniel's article are also well chosen, and show DiMaggio in a variety of situations; swinging for big hits; joking with fellow servicemen; his "cool, steady gaze, which puts fear into the hearts of opposing moundsmen"; with Colonel Ruppert; with his family in San Francisco (the old *Life* photo); jubilantly showing his chest muscles in 1936; eating his wedding cake; signing autographs; dancing with a barely dressed "nightclub" performer in Mexico City. Even his famous bad heel is presented in X ray and under bandages. The photographs, like the text, make DiMaggio real, like snapshots from a family album.

In the same year that Daniel's piece appeared (1950), Gene Schoor published the first of his books on DiMaggio, an account that traverses much of the familiar territory Daniel also recorded, but written in a more excited style and with a greater sense of inspirational glee than Daniel was able or cared to project. The work is based partly upon the essential facts of DiMaggio's life as they were recorded in his autobiography, and upon research in older articles that is difficult to follow precisely, because like Daniel, Schoor credits no secondary sources. Sometimes Schoor's unquestioning acceptance of DiMaggio's book perpetuates errors while seeming to corroborate fact. He tells how Dom DiMaggio robbed Joe of a hit just before he broke Keeler's consecutive hit record, repeating Joe's (or writer Tom Meany's) mistake. Sometimes Schoor's attributions are slightly misleading. When in Schoor's book DiMaggio relates the story of the celebration the Yankee players threw for him after his 56-game streak was over, Schoor introduces the narrative with "As Joe tells it," and then places most of DiMaggio's phrases in quotation marks. In Schoor's text it looks as though DiMaggio had related this to Schoor, but what Schoor appears to have done is modify simply and silently DiMaggio's story as it appeared in the autobiography. The practice, which Schoor apparently employed in later books on DiMaggio, would not have bothered his readers though it provides some problems for the historian.

Schoor's talent, not yet fully developed here, was his conscious sensitivity to the fact that in writing about DiMaggio he was dealing with a legend, so that even in this basic and brief study (not much more than an introduction to a collection of photographs) he begins to register the dimensions of DiMaggio's myth. Schoor begins a process he will develop more fully in his subsequent treatments of DiMaggio's life: he takes the various elements and episodes in DiMaggio's life that proved most popularly appealing to his public, and focuses consistently and in increasingly dramatic detail upon them. In Schoor's works, DiMaggio comes more and more to resemble the image that large numbers of his fans thought him or wanted him to be. And—not so much here but in his two other longer books on DiMaggio—he dramatizes that image, recording scenes showing that image in action. The more Schoor writes about DiMaggio, the more his life resembles a motion picture about an archetypal popular hero, what used to be called a "biopic."

Schoor accurately spots nearly all the themes running through DiMaggio's life story as it has become generally (if sometimes unrealistically) known. In his retelling he may sentimentalize and sensationalize the themes somewhat—fairly enough the title *The Thrilling Story of Joe DiMaggio* announces that his is not to be a subtle, academic analysis—and writes with an appropriately campy flair. Others might state that boys in America dreamed of playing baseball, but Schoor says, "There's something about the horsehide-covered ball that holds the promise of glory for every American kid, and it is men like Joe DiMaggio who keep that promise alive." On DiMaggio's ability to play with pain he writes, "It was that same fighting spirit which pulled him out of the hospital, following a siege of that debilitating virus pneumonia, [and] get out on the field for the last eleven games of a torrid season to beat out the Red Sox for the League flag. The flesh was weak and the legs were wobbly, but that will to win which spells Joe DiMaggio sent the Yankees" to the World Series. DiMaggio's reaction to these events? " 'I'm lucky to be a Yankee,' says the Clipper in his humble manner."

The interesting photographs which Schoor's text introduces document the portrayal of DiMaggio as a star performer who is also an extremely nice and almost saintly person: Joe's mom "fondly looks at a picture of her son as she tunes in the ball game"; "The kids of the National Children's Cardiac Home in Miami present Joe with a scroll"; "Little Joe sits on the bat rack and takes in the scene at Yankee batting practice"; Joe with his family leaving for the Yankee camp in 1936; with Ty Cobb after a World Series; in the batting cage—"Ask a big leaguer how he does it and the Clipper will tell you it's work, work, and more work"; with Jim Braddock and Joe Louis; "S/Sgt. DiMaggio is the typical G. I. Joe, as he disembarks from a Navy transport at Hawaii"; "America's top star always lends a hand in the typical American way. DiMag takes time out to chat with a polio victim in Jersey City's Medical Center after launching the Sister Kenny Polio Fund Drive"; giving batting tips to a one-armed boy; with Joe Louis and Gene Schoor on the radio.

Schoor invents nothing new in his verbal and visual picture of DiMaggio, but he assembled most of the features of DiMaggio's image that were popular with the American audience, and refines the shape of the image to project DiMaggio's heroic dimensions more clearly. A few of his details may be wrong or misleading—for example he states DiMaggio was born November 29, 1914 (not November 25)—but there is no doubt that beginning with this *Thrilling Story*, he was presenting a clear and compelling reflection of what DiMaggio had come to mean to America. Most writers portrayed DiMaggio as a nice guy, but like a combination public relations director and cheerleader, Schoor provided touching documentation.

"He's Hero No. 1 to all kids in New York, from Pelham Bay

to the Bowery. He's Hero No. 1 for kids all over the country. They elected him Honorary Mayor of Mending Heart, Florida, the National Children's Cardiac Home. . . . If anyone deserves a place in the hearts of the kids of the country, it's Joe.'' Schoor's account is an enthusiastic hagiography. His DiMaggio sells papers to help the family, endures paternal resistance to play baseball, overcomes frequent injuries, plays always for the good of the team, practices hard, performs with "flawless precision" like "a highly calibrated machine" but unlike a machine helps his fellow players like Charlie Keller and Joe Page with good advice. He even gets "visibly angry" when asked what he thought of "Negroes" like Jackie Robinson playing in the big leagues. "What difference does a man's color make?" he broadmindedly replies. "All that matters is—can the guy play ball.''

What does not conform to DiMaggio's lovely image is generally omitted from Schoor's story. His parents and siblings and child are mentioned but not his ex-wife, as though his son were born through parthenogenesis. His sulks are ignored. His holdout in 1938 is noted but miraculously no one emerges badly in the paragraph discussing it, neither DiMaggio, management, nor the fans. When Schoor takes DiMaggio down from one pedestal, the "Horatio Alger hero comes to life," who has "won his way to fortune and into the hearts of the American people," is placed on another pedestal. He "doesn't shove his weight around" and hires no publicists. "In his personal life, Joe is the average American citizen. He likes to fish and hunt" and "talk with the old gang" back at the San Francisco docks. He's Mr. Wonderful.

Schoor ballooned his version of DiMaggio's story into two additional books, *The Yankee Clipper* (1956) and *Joe DiMaggio, a Biography* (1980), which seem like two editions of the same work, the latter narrative expanding and updating the earlier but retaining much of its content. The overall picture of DiMaggio that emerges from all three works does not change radically. Particularized dialogues between many of the individuals whose names are often mentioned throughout the literature on Di-

Maggio constitute a major feature of the longer book(s). Many of the interludes in DiMaggio's life are turned into dramatically conceived scenes reminiscent of Hollywood biographies about poor kids growing up in teeming cities and making their way to stardom (or ultimate disaster as criminals): *Rhapsody in Blue, Pride of the Yankees*, and seemingly numberless Jimmy Cagney and John Garfield films provide analogs for the presentation of DiMaggio's early years. Many of Schoor's scenes, such as the squabbles over Joe's alleged laziness between his mother (kind and understanding) and father (angry and frustrated) invite casting games. Sarah Allgood would be too Irish for Joe's mother. Maybe Rosemary DeCamp? Beulah Bondi? Morris Carnovsky, though Jewish, could handle Giuseppe's role, or even better Lee J. Cobb, who anticipated Schoor's Giuseppe in his portrayal of Joe Bonaparte's papa in *Golden Boy*.

The game is not pointless, for it demonstrates how devotedly Schoor has packaged the DiMaggio story into an immediately recognizable picture portraying not exactly real life, but the reflection of real life many Americans are familiar with, through popular media formulation. The seeming ease with which he accomplishes this trick, sticking mainly to the actual outlines of DiMaggio's life while embellishing some of the details, demonstrates how perfect a candidate for popular mythologizing DiMaggio was.

The book is highly successful in dramatizing the DiMaggio myth. A case could be made (but probably should not be) that its frequently bad writing is appropriate since it is the verbal equivalent of the vulgarized form of the myth that Schoor presents, just as *Rhapsody in Blue* and *Pride of the Yankees* vulgarized their subjects. The book contains clichés ("A hush fell over the giant stadium. You could hear a pin drop in the stands") and turgidly lush descriptions ("The fog rolled in silently off the bay, wet and cool, a dirty gray blanket that settled swiftly in thick folds over the city, dimming the streetlamps to a feeble flow") that seem like products of an automatic writing machine programmed to communicate in the idiom of bad movies, bad sports columns, and parodies of Dashiell Hammett.

As history, the work has clear deficiencies. Its dramatizations and descriptions made it in 1956 the most substantial third-person picture of DiMaggio's life, and even its 1980 version which had to compete with other biographies of similar length seems in extensive detail a definitive if gushy account. However, readers who compare the two editions (or books) might question the authenticity of both presentations in certain particulars.

Some of Schoor's revisions correct his old mistakes. In 1956 he wrote that DiMaggio was born November 29, 1914, but in 1980 he corrects this to November 25. In 1980 he also no longer describes as he did in 1956 Dom DiMaggio's phantom catch of the ball Joe never hit him during his streak. Twice in 1980, Schoor corrects errors he made in 1956 about Dom's age. Sometimes he adds details perhaps because greater research had provided him with information, or perhaps simply to add verisimilitude. In 1956 he wrote that DiMaggio was reading a comic book the day he started his 56-game streak, in 1980 Schoor writes he was reading *Superman*, possibly as a presage of what DiMaggio was shortly to prove himself. Sometimes he adds humanizing details, for example in 1980 pointing out that DiMaggio's wife was pregnant during the hitting streak. In 1980 he also adds Sher's 1949 story about DiMaggio not knowing what a "quote" was. Some trivial changes are difficult to evaluate since no sources are supplied. In 1956 the crowd at DiMaggio's first minor league game is reported singing to a record of the national anthem; in 1980 they are described as silent. The "Army chow" that disagreed with DiMaggio's stomach in the 1956 version becomes "Army food" in 1980. Some modifications detract from the 1980 version's historical value since they remove factual material. In the 1956 version Schoor related that while DiMaggio waited in 1949 for his heel to grow less painful his father died, and DiMaggio traveled back to San Francisco for the funeral. In 1980 this detail is omitted, though why is unclear, unless Schoor thought it would jar his readers. But this is doubtful since he mentions that at the end of the 1949 season, Rosalie DiMaggio herself had cancer, and Giuseppe's death is alluded to once, when Rosalie is praying.

Some textual changes are particularly perplexing. Much of the book is dialogue and it is not always possible to tell what Schoor has reconstructed from reports the principals involved have told him (especially since he gives no sources, primary or secondary); what he wrote figuring that this was what it must have sounded like; and what he invented for his own literary purposes. Spike Hennessy's summation to Charley Graham about DiMaggio's prospects appears in two separate versions in 1956 and 1980 which match each other generally, but are verbally quite different. Either one seems plausible. Were he writing a novel this rewriting would be acceptable, but both the 1956 and 1980 texts are presumably biographies.

He also changes descriptions of actions for seemingly no reason at all—at least he provides no biographer's reasons—and this practice lends an arbitrariness to much of his incidental information. In 1956 he describes DiMaggio sitting on the edge of a pier overlooking San Francisco Bay by writing, "He just sat without thinking." In 1980 Schoor says, "He just sat thinking." Either DiMaggio was thinking as he sat or he wasn't. Is the reader to assume that between the writing of the 1956 volume and the 1980, Schoor somehow discovered that DiMaggio was in fact thinking as he sat? In the 1956 book at the conclusion to Chapter 5, prior to Joe's tryout, Vince and Joe discuss Joe's sandlot career and Vince's pleasure at being paid to play. Joe wonders out loud if that kind of career offers a good deal or not, "but in his heart" he knows "for the first time in his life, what he wanted." Then he falls exhausted asleep and later Papa DiMaggio passes his room and mutters as he watches his son, "That's a funny boy. . . . I don't know what's gonna be with him." It is a touching scene appearing in print nowhere else and one wonders how Schoor knew about it since Joe's father had been dead many years before Schoor's book appeared. In 1980 the sequence is shifted from its original location. Instead, at the end of the following chapter, and now after the tryout, Vince says Joe is going to play shortstop tomorrow, and Joe becomes very excited. In bed later that night Joe fantasizes being the hero and the goat next day. Then he falls "into an exhausted sleep," the same sleep Schoor had him in 1956 falling into months before. And Papa DiMaggio in his quaint accent wonders again, what's gonna be with his funny boy? Who told Schoor he had been wrong in 1956—or is the entire scene spurious?

In 1956 Schoor printed what was supposedly a newspaperman's report during DiMaggio's first spring training with the Seals. It says he is "tall, gawky, inclined to be rather surly," but also "he's the best-looking hitter seen this spring." In 1980 the report says, "He's tall, stringy, sullen, and tough to interview. . . . He is the most sullen player I've ever seen." The story's tone has become much harsher. What did the reporter really write? In 1956 Schoor wrote that when DiMaggio heard the fans' jeers in 1938 after his holdout, a Philadelphia Athletics third baseman turned to him and said, "They're sure on you, DiMag. . . . What's eating 'em?" In 1980 Schoor writes that the player said, "They're sure on you, DiMag. . . . I guess it's because you're holding out for more money?" Why did it take the player twenty-four years to become more knowledgeable? In 1956 Schoor writes that Bill Essick, the Yankee scout, called Charley Graham to discuss DiMaggio's future. In 1980 he writes that Essick called Ed Barrow, though Essick gives the same report he had given Graham in the 1956 version. Ed Barrow is assigned words in 1980 mainly spoken by Essick in a conversation with Graham related in 1956. Finally in the 1980 version Essick calls Barrow to tell him to buy DiMaggio, and Barrow calls Graham to stipulate the conditions of the deal. But then when Graham calls DiMaggio to tell him the good news, he asks Essick—last heard from in the sequence calling Barrow—how soon DiMaggio is to report for his physical. The grinning Essick says tell DiMaggio to start packing. But how did Essick get to Graham's office after speaking to Barrow on the telephone? The lines of the story, telephone and narrative, seem tangled. The deal was less confusing in 1956.

Whatever may be the factual validity of Schoor's treatment of individual episodes in DiMaggio's life, whether or not the revisions he made in his biography reveal capriciousness or care toward reproducing the life faithfully, he seems on target in presenting the mythic image DiMaggio has achieved. The individual parts of the story, most of which in their general outlines conform to the known facts of DiMaggio's life, collectively add up to the figure of Joe DiMaggio depicted most frequently in the mass media. Schoor is complete in proceeding scene by scene through DiMaggio's known career, showing the early years with his big, affectionate family; the momentous discovery ("Someday, Charley, that kid's going to break a few records around this league. Or my name's not Ike Caveney") of DiMaggio's skill after the knothole incident; stardom in San Francisco; the silent trip with Lazzeri and Crosetti to the Yankee training camp; the injury jinx; all the big and little stories told to fit precisely into the myth. DiMaggio's comebacks are epic, his achievements as a human being and a player heroic.

Some parts of the story are related in much greater detail than others that in a rounded historical account would seem just as significant. It is appropriate that Schoor reproduces a picture of Joe's family life in as lengthy a fashion as he does, though DiMaggio's parents seem stereotypes, particularly DiMaggio's father who is at first the story's misguided heavy, like a dense father, in teenage films: "I'm telling you, Rosa. That boy's never gonna be no good. Never." According to Vince DiMaggio, Giuseppe was not opposed to the idea of Joe's playing professional baseball, as Schoor here depicts him. Before Joe ever signed a contract, Vince had shown his father the money baseball could bring. The chapter on Marilyn Monroe is curiously bland. Schoor writes about the rich relationship Monroe and DiMaggio intermittently maintained after their marriage in one brief two-sentence paragraph that euphemistically buries Monroe's suicide in the phrase "tragic death."

Occasionally, as when he portrays Rosalie DiMaggio praying beside her bed in San Francisco for her Joe, who walks fitfully through a New York apartment agonizing over the wounded heel he feels may end his career, the book appears to manipulate events to produce cloying sentimentality. Sometimes details seem contrived to fit the demands of storytelling. Before Joe plays his first Seals game, Schoor portrays a scene where Ike Caveney comically, dramatically, and anxiously asks Vince DiMaggio if his brother can really play. "Is he any good? Don't kid me, Vince" he shouts. But the Seals had full scouting reports on Joe at the time, and Caveney may even have seen him play. The scene would probably be funny and effective in a film, but seems contrived. Still, there is perhaps no clearer full-length picture of the DiMaggio image than Schoor's. It represents nearly all the component elements of DiMaggio's legend, and offers a generally accurate overview of his career. As a popular biography its craft is better than that of the wretched filmed *Babe Ruth Story* with William Bendix, but not as powerful as *Pride of the Yankees*, the Lou Gehrig story in which Gary Cooper so successfully combined his quiet, rock-stable rightness with Gehrig's tale of a second-class hero and first-class victim.

There is a tendency to treat sports heroes ultimately as somehow victims, perhaps because that is so often their fate. Both Babe Ruth and Lou Gehrig are strongly remembered in their final incarnations saying good-bye, the playful, greedy, priapic Ruth hoarse with cancer, and Gehrig's dying voice echoing hollowly around Yankee Stadium repeating how fortunate he had been. Schoor is one of the first writers to identify the element of sadness in DiMaggio's once bright rookie's story. Though Schoor's book thoroughly details the full news and excitement of DiMaggio's life as a baseball star, he concludes both his 1956 and 1980 versions of DiMaggio's story with the same chapter showing Joe in 1955 sitting around at Toots Shor's (actually long gone in 1980) talking to writers and agents the day he was elected to the Hall of Fame. One of the agents suggests to Joe that he make some profitable personal appearances but DiMaggio scornfully replies, "I'm a former ballplayer, not a circus freak." After Joe leaves—early—one of the writers says, "There . . . goes one of the greatest players in the history of baseball." Another writer comments, "And one of the greatest guys." Schoor himself adds the last words in the book, the final image of DiMaggio, "And one of the loneliest men in the world." It is as though DiMaggio had left the spotlight to walk into darkness offstage: no matter how great the adulation of him remains, how friendly and fulfilled he seems in public appearances, there is in his image now an area of inviolate sadness, a part of himself he will not let others touch. Schoor shows that DiMaggio also embodies a counter-myth, that the American dream when achieved may bring success but not necessarily happiness.

Schoor was not the only writer to present multiple studies of DiMaggio around the time of his retirement in 1951, when books and articles increasingly portrayed DiMaggio as a fully developed part of the American scene, and as a star whose active career had run its course. The DiMaggio story had been developing exploit by exploit, article by article, story by story over the years. Now was the time for his image to be transmitted back in a full if not final form to the public who had participated as spectators in its development and to others for whom DiMaggio was a legend from the past.

Tom Meany, who had already collaborated on DiMaggio's autobiography, wrote a pamphlet titled *Joseph Paul DiMaggio, the Yankee Clipper* as part of an "All-Star" series of short monographs about sports figures in 1950–51. Though rambling and impressionistic, the work profits from Meany's extended, first-hand relationship with DiMaggio. Noting the success DiMaggio has achieved in his "rags-to-riches" career, Meany illustrates DiMaggio's progress by reporting that even while DiMaggio sat in his hotel room relating experiences to him, a bellhop knocked to announce that the Broadway and film actress Tallulah Bankhead was returning DiMaggio's automatic record player: truly he had traveled a long way from North Beach. Meany emphasizes Joe's comebacks rather than his bright promise and triumphs although these are documented. His DiMaggio is a player of proven if not unparalleled greatness, whose popularity he says "ironically enough . . . stems from his injuries, or rather from the spectacular comebacks he has made after them. Every time Joe has been floored by the jinx he has come up fighting." Meany also remarks that "Joe's personal life has been as tangled as his baseball playing has been smooth," a side of DiMaggio unrevealed in his autobiography.

Meany also referred to DiMaggio's "entangled marital status" in an exceptionally frank magazine article written for *Collier's* in 1952 titled "Joe DiMaggio As I Knew Him." This short piece perhaps more than any other of similar length presents DiMaggio as a real person. Meany contends that DiMaggio is "one of the most misunderstood" ballplayers of all time. "He leaves active baseball almost as much an enigma to the fans as he was in 1936." DiMaggio's recollections delivered to Meany range over some of the high points of his life and legend. Andy High's notorious scouting report ultimately published in *Life*, that so devastatingly spotlighted DiMaggio's weakness, played no role in his retirement, DiMaggio says, claiming "scouting reports don't bother me." DiMaggio states he knew in Phoenix during spring training for 1951 that the season might be his last. He was surprised only that the year turned out so badly. "I really thought I could make my last year a good one. I had a bad one instead. I guess the reflexes just weren't there anymore." Concerning the famous story of the sinister taxicab driver's prediction that his hit streak was going to be snapped, DiMaggio says "I paid no attention" to it. When after the game Lefty Gomez cursed the "dirty so-and-so" who had "jinxed him," DiMaggio thought he meant Ken Keltner or one of the Cleveland pitchers.

Contrary to the image that Schoor and others would in a few years popularize, DiMaggio felt he was generally not a loner, and lists Frank Crosetti, Gomez, Joe Page, and Billy Martin among his particular friends. He also disagrees with the stories about him eating alone and sulking his last years with the Yankees, and shows he is upset over tales of his alleged feud with Casey Stengel. He tells Meany that his famous salary dispute with Ruppert in 1938 was not nearly as acrimonious as the confrontation with Barrow in 1942, when according to DiMaggio he was first offered a $2,500 cut in salary, and Barrow insinuated he was "lucky to be playing ball" at all considering the war. "I don't think anything ever burned me up as much as that did." Meany himself reveals that he helped Joe write his autobiography and instructional book, aided with the former by Joe's ex-wife with whom he was attempting in 1946 to reconcile. By 1947 Dorothy had remarried and Joe was "pretty lonely then."

Meany also comments on Joe's 1952 anxieties about being a baseball announcer and suggests DiMaggio's perfectionism was part of the difficulties, noting that Joe preferred "filmed programs" where directors could "edit out mistakes." The illustration accompanying the article places handsome and smiling DiMaggio in the center of other drawings of him hitting, running, fielding, and running bases. The article's final sequence represents DiMaggio's social success: Joe adjusts his suspenders "so that his trouser cuffs hang evenly. Adolphe Menjou," the dapper actor whose mode of correct dress made him fabled as a paragon of high class conservative fashion, "couldn't have been more meticulous."

Meany also stressed DiMaggio's attainment of "class" while rehearsing once again his famous baseball exploits in one section of *The Yankee Story* (1960), contrasting the difficulties DiMaggio experienced privately while publicly becoming a quick sensation. "While baseball came easily to DiMaggio, the ability to handle the responsibilities of stardom did not. . . . He had a horror of autograph seekers which approached claustrophobia" and his "tangled marital affairs contributed greatly to his moodiness." For a long while according to Meany he seemed comfortable only with a small band of friends and as late as 1957 when Meany visited him was still somewhat shy and reticent, though greatly improved in social skills. "Fame came too quickly for DiMaggio," Meany concludes, "and he was a long time developing a personality to cope with it." Meany's assessment, coming as it did from one who had worked closely and in a friendly fashion with DiMaggio over the years, seems particularly honest in showing DiMaggio as he really was and not as fashioned for hero-worship. The magnitude of DiMaggio's off-the-field growth, uneven as it was, is enhanced by the frank view Meany offers of him. As Meany's writings show, the man whose cuffs hung so neatly was built upon the boy who never finished high school. Being able to dress himself as handsomely as Menjou perhaps made DiMaggio better able to act surely, but possibly also disguised his social insecurity. DiMaggio's style revealed and concealed the man within.

Yankee announcer Mel Allen avoided penetrating DiMaggio's public image in his chapter on DiMaggio in *It Takes Heart* (1959). He limited himself to demonstrating DiMaggio's skill, thoughtfulness, and courage. In one anecdote Allen relates, DiMaggio displays his gentlemanly professionalism in the 1950 World Series, when New York beat Philadelphia in four straight games. After Granny Hanner booted an easy grounder in the third game, DiMaggio, on second base, consoles him. "Don't worry about it, Granny,' he said gently . . . it happens to the best of them." Allen concludes, "As one of nine men, DiMaggio is the best player that ever lived."

Even though the post-DiMaggio Yankee years were among the team's most successful, and new great players like Mickey Mantle and Whitey Ford performed in the tradition of the all-time superstars—which meant extraordinary media focus followed their winning exploits—DiMaggio continued to be written about often in the daily and periodical press and in books. Some of these items more concerned his role in Marilyn Monroe's life than his baseball prowess, but still kept his name before the public in a positive fashion, enriching his story as a baseball player.

Some of the best writing about him was still evoked by his hit streak. Like his sensational 1949 comeback this was an intensely dramatic fact about which ample and very specific documentation existed. His career statistics while impressive were not as towering as those of the very greatest of players, such as Cobb, Ruth, and Speaker, to whom he was compared in ability, but no player could match the excellence he displayed in the streak. Writers could tout DiMaggio's mastery of intangibles, but more and more they were addressing audiences whose memories of his play were dim or nonexistent. The streak was verifiable. It possessed an undeniable authority in the constant battle between the ancients and the moderns (any current generation of stars against previous generations) that is waged throughout sports literature.

Dave Anderson's "The Longest Hitting Streak in History" appeared July 17, 1961, in *Sports Illustrated* and was later revised as part of "The DiMaggio Years" section of *The Yankees* (1980). Anderson stressed that the streak was an unparalleled sports achievement for DiMaggio and a unique experience for baseball fans mainly because of "the relentless day-by-day pressure of the last few weeks of the streak." Anderson also recognized that when DiMaggio ultimately became a symbol of heroism whose significance extended beyond sports, it had been in large part "the hitting streak" that "shaped that symbol." Many of the components of the streak's narrative recited in later retellings like episodes in an epic are mentioned in Anderson's swiftly paced and compressed account. The slump the streak broke for both DiMaggio and the Yankees; the time it was first noticed and the subsequent buildup of national excitement around it (with DiMaggio relatively solid and without much noticeable nervousness); vignettes such as Bob Muncrief's refusal to walk him or the loss of his favored bat; the great smash he hit between Yankee-killer Johnny Babich's legs; the streak's famous termination presaged by the prophetic cabbie—all are presented as details each adding its own spice to the story. Moreover, Anderson recognizes that the event was "a sociological phenomenon" and places it in the historic context of the worldwide drama building during that "strangely smoldering summer," when President Roosevelt spoke to national audiences of the coming "national emergency" and William L. Shirer's *Berlin Diary* was a bestseller.

One of the silly details Anderson includes to add quirky verisimilitude to his picture of what 1941 was like in America is the popularity of the novelty tune "Hut-Sut Rawlson on the Rillerah." Al Silverman also features the song, perhaps as a symbol of something that like the streak is ultimately unexplainable, in *Joe DiMaggio, the Golden Year, 1941* (1969), one of the best books on DiMaggio.

Silverman presents information not just about the streak, but about DiMaggio's life and career. Though exasperatingly enough to the historian he provides no listing of his sources, he clearly performed considerable research preparing for the book, checking contemporary newspapers and magazines for fresh and accurate information, and undertaking interviews with a range of DiMaggio's teammates and opposing players. Far less sentimental and portentously dramatic than Schoor, Silverman presents the star as a performer of triumphant physical skills, a good man, and a great athlete but no demigod. One way Silverman achieves this tempered portrait is by including the comments of many of DiMaggio's contemporaries, both players and sportswriters, who viewed him as a player of exceptional abilities but also as a real-life fellow mortal and not some fabulous image projected on the national movie screen. The book's major structural flaw is perhaps forced upon it by the "Golden Year" series of which it was a part, for its development is not chronological. Instead, chapters on segments of the streak are alternated with chapters about DiMaggio's childhood and years of play, so that it is some-what difficult to follow his evolution. Otherwise, Silverman's book is one of the best portraying DiMaggio realistically with freshness and insight.

A foreword by Murray Olderman indicates the complexity of DiMaggio's image, positing two popular views of him, the glam-orous superstar and the noble recluse, and suggests that counter-images lay beneath the surfaces of each of these pictures, the "sullen, aloof man" whose personality came alive only on the field and its opposite, an "amazingly effusive" and often genial "source of news for writers." Silverman's text focuses on what is best and most likable about DiMaggio mainly by presenting details of his playing career with just enough personal back-ground to suggest that he emerged a good and successful man from his immigrant family. There is some talk of his "fall from epic grace" at the end of his streak, and early in the book he is called "the once and future king of" a Yankee dynasty. The book's final sentence terms him a "noble American folk hero" whose actions "will be remembered and talked about and passed on from father to son for as long as they play this game of ours called baseball." But generally the narrative supplies a straight-forward exposition of details and anecdotes.

Silverman sees the streak as the adventure that enabled DiMaggio to enter "the hearts of his countrymen" at an espe-cially tense and uncertainty-filled time. Demanding skill, luck, an iron will, and the capacity to endure pressure, the streak cap-tivated a nation hungry for escape as had few other athletic achievements in the country's history, because it evolved slowly but very steadily, containing no breathing spaces during which attention upon it could relax or falter. Day after day greater at-tention was given it, and the nature of the attention became more intense. Occasionally Silverman's details are questionable or call for some corroboration, such as the claim that it was common for radio programs to be interrupted to relate the ongoing pro-gress of the streak, or that during 1936 after Yankee games were over police radios in San Francisco broadcast a summary of DiMaggio's activities that day. Far more frequently Silverman's facts are accurate and arrived at not through memory or hearsay but by slogging through contemporary newspaper accounts or checking and cross-checking with participants in the events of the streak or DiMaggio's career. Thus he corrects the story that Dom robbed Joe of a hit the day he broke Willie Keeler's record, though curiously does not note that DiMaggio himself remembered the event this way.

Not only is Silverman the fullest source for information about the streak, but his alternate chapters provide good and often new information about other aspects of DiMaggio's life and playing days. The section on DiMaggio's youth was perhaps the most lively and plausible retelling to that time. Nearly always in narrating the familiar outlines of DiMaggio's first, spectacular years of ascendency as a baseball star, Silverman is able to insert revealing new data, or an interesting slant that vitalizes the perspective on his famous subject. He refers to a column DiMaggio or more likely his ghostwriter conducted in 1936 in *The New York World-Telegram and Sun*, that ended when the season finished, with DiMaggio's charming claim that the Yankees in their entire history since 1903 had "never before had a young ballplayer who was so determined to make good as your friend Joe DiMaggio." While other writers often noted how carefully DiMaggio considered the picture of him given to young children—claiming he refused to pose with a cigarette for example—Silverman recalls an advertisement that claimed "Win or Lose—Joe DiMaggio, Kirby Higbe & Millions of Fans Agree—'There's Nothing Like a Camel.' " The cigarette company announced that "more than a symbol of American League power at bat . . . DiMaggio is power itself. Game after game, for 56 consecutive games, he came through with at least one hit. And day after day, he chooses Camel cigarettes—because, in his own words, 'They're milder.' " Silverman lets DiMaggio himself voice his outrage at what he considered the "insult" of Ed Barrow's proposal to cut his 1942 salary. To underscore the theme of DiMaggio's rise in American life, he repeats relief pitcher Johnny Murphy's simple remark, "When I see Joe now . . . I tell him what great strides he made in his personal life . . . He's an interesting man to be around now." Silverman's own language is unpretentious and effective, though without art. He does not strain after effect but usually employs a relatively simple and clear prose style. Only occasionally does he err badly, as when he writes that in 1938 when DiMaggio sought significantly more money "Barrow literally blew him out of the office."

Silverman uses what he terms "Stop-Action, 1941" sections to report what was happening in the world beyond DiMaggio's streak in 1941, to suggest the context in which DiMaggio's greatly popular act was occurring. Thus the streak is studied both in isolation, and as part of the history of its day. The "Stop-Action" sequences are similar to John Dos Passos' "Newsreel" chapters in his trilogy *U.S.A.*, employing songs, newspaper headlines, and news briefs to communicate impressionistically the spirit of the day. One subject the items often return to is the developing world war, which Silverman directly relates to the baseball story his book tells, for example by mentioning player insecurity over the continued fate of the game, when draft registration was a fact of their lives. Some historic analogs seem strictly coincidental: DiMaggio's feat took place the same year James Joyce died, Virginia Woolf committed suicide, and Ava Gardner and Mickey Rooney wed. Others are more relevant. The special ceremonies commemorating "I Am an American" day, May 18, are viewed as rituals of national declaration and resolve at a time of growing crisis, into which DiMaggio's concurrent exploits fit with particular appropriateness. In Central Park that day, Mayor La Guardia decreed a celebration at which Eddie Cantor (a Jew), Bill "Bojangles" Robinson (a black), and Kate Smith (a quintessential WASP) starred. At Yankee Stadium, the Italian-American DiMaggio made three hits and knocked in one run.

Silverman calls DiMaggio rightly enough a "symbol of the time." He adds that "life was uncomplicated and understandable in 1941, and that was the way Joe DiMaggio played baseball." In this he seems correct only in the last half of his statement. DiMaggio was one of those rare athletes who for a time provided a sustained, simple, gloriously enjoyable event to contemplate. For a briefer time the American 1980 Olympic hockey team achieved the same burningly intense escape of national joy. But the era in which DiMaggio added flavor and relief was neither uncomplicated nor particularly understandable, except in the broadest historic terms. At the end of an economic depression and the beginning of a war, America in 1941 was as complex and mysterious a country as it ever had been or would be. What Silverman shows is that DiMaggio provided an excitement, a spark that brightened the lives of many who were then beleaguered with their own ordinary fearsome pressures, as people are when any hero sends up a flare signaling greatness, making them wonder what the equivalent to a 56-consecutive-game hitting streak would be in their lives.

In the last few pages of his book Silverman briefly describes the agonies and triumphs of DiMaggio's last seasons in baseball. While he deals with the off-the-field youth of DiMaggio, he includes very little information about his life after retirement. Similarly, he devotes an entire brief chapter to recollections of what was occurring in America on December 7, 1941, when the Japanese attacked Pearl Harbor, focusing mainly on DiMaggio and several of his teammates, while he compresses Joe's war service into one quotation that expresses quite clearly the impact of the war on him. "I thought it would never end," DiMaggio says. "Those years never seemed to move at all." Though he seems interested in the childhood out of which the legendary hero developed, Silverman seems unconcerned with the course of DiMaggio's life after his playing days, beyond simply noting he was "a hero in an Ernest Hemingway novel and a hero in a best-selling song, 'Mrs. Robinson,' that grooves for a new and different generation.'' He avoids discussion of Marilyn Monroe completely, almost as though that episode would muddle the clear image of the hero he presents throughout most of his book.

Though the picture of DiMaggio that emerges from Silverman's book is a strong and real one of him as a player, it is a partial portrait of him as a man. Even more partial a view is presented in Ann Finlayson's *Three Power Hitters* (1970), a book typical of those on DiMaggio clearly intended for children. Sometimes recycling comments from earlier sources (once again DiMaggio is claimed to have been the ''greatest rookie since Ty Cobb'') her dramatic technique often resembles Schoor's. In one early scene DiMaggio while still a Seals player is telephoned late at night by his ''boss'' and is told that since ''Babe Ruth is too old to play another season'' the Yankees ''need a new young hitter to step into his shoes.'' The shocked rookie replies ''the Yankees have bought me?'' as though his sale were a total surprise. Mama and Papa DiMaggio quarrel over whether or not son Joe is a lazy baseball bum, and Rosalie waves her finger at Giuseppe and scolds him as though participating in a situation comedy. DiMaggio amply demonstrates his mother's faith in him by performing all the familiar exploits, and Finlayson notes for her young readers that ''often the highest praise showered on'' her exemplary hero ''has been for his workmanship. He did not make scenes or cause trouble or demand the spotlight.'' One of his great rewards was that ''nobody admired him more than his own teammates.'' Clearly he was a model youth, quite worthy of emulation.

Presenting his life in greater detail and for a broader audience, Bob Broeg similarly portrayed him as a classic American success story in *Super Stars of Baseball* (1971). Broeg emphasizes the hard conditions of DiMaggio family life where ''the family lived in close quarters'' with the boys and girls in two separate rooms but ''spilling out into the living room and dining room'' when Papa DiMaggio left for work at four A.M. Yet ''the poor foreign-born fisherman's son'' grew up into ''the game's No. 1 living player," a man "who seemed aloof, yet one who married the most glamorous motion picture actress of the generation," and who reigned as "the living symbol of the game's first century." Broeg accentuates DiMaggio's triumphs in baseball and in life. The DiMaggio he depicts has grown in wisdom through suffering. His great comeback over pain made the 1949 three-game Series with Boston for him "the most satisfying of my life and . . . taught me about faith and people." He is an American who has arrived at great heights splendidly through his skills, certainly not a lonely, bitter man.

DiMaggio's injuries are stressed in nearly all the accounts written about him after his retirement, not to depict him as a victim, a player cut off in his prime like Lou Gehrig, but to underscore his indominability and fortitude. The injuries thus became a positive part of his image, distinguishing him from some of the athletes with whom he was often compared at the start of his career, such as Cobb or Ruth. Thus in the 1949 edition of Robert Shoemaker's *The Best in Baseball* his story was included in a chapter titled "After the Babe: Gehrig and DiMaggio" while in the 1974 edition of the same book Gehrig remains "After the Babe" but DiMaggio is placed in his own chapter, "Yankee Clipper." Both editions note that he was a "cool, efficient operator" who "appeared to be somewhat aloof from fans and players alike" and "machine-like in his perfection," but the 1974 text adds that "injuries plagued DiMaggio in his later years. At one time his throwing arm was so sore that he could make only one good peg a day from the outfield." The injuries humanized him and proved finally that he was not a machine: machines break down and get fixed, but they don't feel pain or come back.

In the years following his retirement, the testimony of other ballplayers also became increasingly important in establishing DiMaggio's abilities, because fewer observers had seen him perform and perhaps because his statistics did not quite match those of the highest rank of all-time stars, such as Ruth, Gehrig,

Speaker, Wagner, and Cobb. Throughout the 1960s and 1970s
fellow baseball players continued to be reported among his
greatest admirers. Though from time to time newspaper accounts
during his career alleged that some of his teammates were grum-
bling about him, for example during his 1938 holdout, specific
players were customarily not named voicing alleged criticisms.
The great Yankee pitcher Spud Chandler's reminiscences told to
Donald Honig in his nostalgic *Baseball When the Grass Was
Real* (1976) several decades after Chandler retired are as much
a panegyric as anything written by his literary image makers.
"Of course we had Joe DiMaggio," Chandler says, explaining
the Yankees' success, "and that was a ball club in itself. For
all-around ability and everyday play, DiMaggio was the greatest
player I ever saw. . . . The most complete ballplayer I ever saw.
And he was a great team man, very loyal to the ball club; he
gave his best, he never caused any trouble, he never got into any
arguments." For Chandler as for so many writers, DiMaggio was
an exemplary hero.

For Robin Moore and Gene Schoor, co-authors of *Marilyn &
Joe DiMaggio* (1976), DiMaggio was a romantic (almost an
epic) lover. All the other books about DiMaggio had virtually
omitted Marilyn Monroe from his life. Moore and Schoor rec-
tified this lack with a vengeance. Their hot-breathed approach
was well illustrated by the picture of Marilyn and Joe kissing on
the book's paperback edition cover and in the blurb accompanying the picture: "It was an impossible love story. They were
married for less than a year, but they were in love 'til the day
she died." Partly a biography of Marilyn Monroe, partly a review of DiMaggio's life and athletic greatness (following the
story line of Schoor's 1956 treatment) the book achieved heights
of enraptured prose unfound elsewhere in the literature about
DiMaggio, though the inventiveness displayed in describing several scenes would be familiar to readers of Schoor's earlier work
on the famous athlete, here metamorphosed into "baseball's
great lover," sadly playing now in an "American tragedy."

Certainly the Monroe episode was an important part of DiMaggio's life, and their unhappy marriage has become an event filled with cultural implications for many writers. Moore and Schoor perform the helpful service of trivializing aspects of the relationship, though this may not have been their goal. That Monroe was not particularly impressed by DiMaggio on their first (prearranged) date until Mickey Rooney came to their table and began fawning over him restores a salutary banality to their romance. When they depict the New York City crowd screaming "Higher! Higher!" as hot air blew up between Marilyn's legs during the famous filming of *The Seven Year Itch* revealing Marilyn's "ruffled white nylon panties" and bare legs, the level of their prose nicely parallels the level of unromantic, unpleasant sexuality the mob's shouts revealed. The disgust they show DiMaggio feeling upon observing this scene doubtless recaptures his feelings about what he considered Monroe's shameless public eroticism. There is some doubt that he was actually in attendance, however, as they describe him. Since they give no sources for their depiction, it is difficult to conclude how accurate that part of their re-creation is. While their account may be perfectly factual, their language seems more appropriate to a lurid detective novel or romance, for example when it describes an evening in San Francisco when Joe was absent and "Marilyn had a great urge to move into the mysterious shroud which covered the waterfront. The fog comes frequently to San Francisco"—true enough!—"and Marilyn had been sensuously drawn to it before. This particular night, she could not resist its siren call." That Moore and Schoor wallow so often in this kind of musky verbiage does not improve the idea of their reliability.

Moore and Schoor are in the tradition of many books mainly about Marilyn Monroe written during the 1960s and 1970s that include sections on DiMaggio. It is difficult and here unnecessary to trace the tangled lines of descent of these books particularly since most contain essentially the same view of him as a great baseball star and a man of honor; a successful man with a sure sense of himself; a man who has experienced suffering. They display DiMaggio in action however not as a baseball player but as a man in an exciting and ultimately destructive and failed sexual relationship, and this of course was foreign territory to the books viewing him as an athlete. Some of the Monroe books seem calculated to satisfy if not glut the voyeuristic readers' appetite for signs of DiMaggio's lust and thus to demonstrate his defectiveness. But his continuing affair with Monroe was part of his record and therefore something absolutely necessary to write about when he is being dealt with as a culturally or historically significant person. Scenes such as the one Moore and Schoor refer to after *The Seven Year Itch* incident, when "people in the adjacent rooms at the Hotel Regis reported that they heard shouting in the DiMaggio suite, scuffling, then hysterical weeping," if they can be authenticated, probably must be included in detailed accounts of the DiMaggio story. Perhaps it is even necessary to repeat Monroe's leering innuendoes about DiMaggio's great sexual prowess (he and Frank Sinatra, she said, had something in common, and it was not that they were Italian) reported in Lena Pepitone's 1979 dresser's-eye view of the actress, for the insight they provide on Monroe if not on DiMaggio.

Norman Mailer's flights of speculation first published in 1973 concerning what the couple's life together—so romanticized and trivialized and glossily distorted in newspapers and magazines— was like in all its sad postcoital boredom, may illuminate a cranny of the American scene untraversed by romantic fiction or standard situation comedy views of American love. For observers interested mainly in DiMaggio's figure on the national scene, what is perhaps most interesting about how the matter of Marilyn Monroe has been processed and assimilated into the DiMaggio story is that mainly what does not conform to the accepted image of DiMaggio has been rejected for inclusion in his myth. What resides in the DiMaggio myth after the stories of his years with Monroe have been told and retold, is not that he was a great lover who bedded America's creamy and luscious sex queen, but that he experienced pain in his relationship with a doomed and lovely woman whom he gallantly tried to save, and that he behaved nobly at her funeral. For him it was another comeback triumph (after the dismally failed marriage) that demonstrated his heroic integrity and selflessness.

The literature about his experience with Monroe demonstrates the scars the affair left on his image. That these would be viewed as scars of honor and not of folly or human frailty (for Monroe was seen as the frail one, not DiMaggio) shows the power his image possessed. Gay Talese's July 1966 *Esquire* article is a mournful account of the twilight of this scarred god now forced to live as an aging human. The illustration introducing Talese's story is a dreadful, nightmare companion to other cover representations of the hero that appeared when he was living times of triumph: in it, an unidentifiable black-suited man swings his bat in empty Yankee Stadium. Titled " 'Joe' said Marilyn Monroe, just back from Korea, 'you never heard such cheering.' 'Yes I have,' Joe DiMaggio answered," and subtitled "The Silent Season of a Hero," the eligiac piece begins with a quotation from *The Old Man and the Sea* stating that Santiago would like to take the great DiMaggio fishing because he "would understand." In the context of Hemingway's novella DiMaggio's understanding is related to his having once been poor, but in the article it is clear his understanding stems from having mastered the pain of his experience with Monroe. The pain brings knowledge but not, as Talese describes his life, happiness. Vince, the article suggests, may be happier. DiMaggio's San Francisco upbringing and years of baseball glory are described, as are parts of his life with Monroe and his present daily occupations. His baseball past is viewed as a glorious time, his life with Monroe dreary. Marilyn is shown "running hysterically, crying as she ran, along the road away from the pier" in San Francisco. Billy Wilder is reported saying "I shall never forget the look of death on Joe's face" when he saw the crowd surrounding Monroe's leggy exhibition over the subway grating in New York City. In

Japan when DiMaggio saw Monroe after her success with the screaming troops in Korea and she told him he had never heard such cheering, he said (glum and angry) yes he had. The lost love embittered him. He snubbed Robert Kennedy at a Yankee celebration in New York because he thought he was part of the beautiful crowd responsible for her death.

Now in San Francisco as Talese describes him, he seems restless, prowling about with nothing really important or satisfying for him to do. He plays golf, attends with Lefty O'Doul a farmer-filled banquet where the local candidate for sheriff distributes campaign leaflets at the door: "How did we get sucked into this?" DiMaggio asks O'Doul out of the side of his mouth. He coldly isolates himself from an interviewer waiting for him in Tom's restaurant but from somewhere in or near the premises telephones him and shouts "You are invading my rights. . . . get your lawyer." He ogles a pretty lady filing her nails at a gas station, and later in a bar apparently picks up another woman. The crowds still love him, but who or what does he love? What is there for him to do? What is there in his life to replace the illusion of love with Monroe or the real cheering of the old crowds when he was being praised for what he did and not for what fans had been told he had done? Certainly Talese does not show that the great DiMaggio would understand all this.

Peter Golenbeck in *Dynasty, the New York Yankees 1949–1964* (1975), also wrote about a scarred DiMaggio and included in his section "The Early Years" the same anecdote about Monroe and DiMaggio in Japan that Talese told. Similarly, his picture of DiMaggio is really several pictures, the phenomenal baseball star (particularly in the prewar years) and the moody, reclusive celebrity; the once-shy rookie who did not know what a quote was, and a sulky player always who bore "a self-imposed cross" of perfectionism and responsibility for the team, so that "every game he played became an intense, bitter personal struggle." Golenbeck's DiMaggio is a man surrounded by "mystery and mystique." Not only will DiMaggio apparently give him no interview (and the book's strength is the almost one hundred other interviews Golenbeck gathered for it) but when he asks Joe's brother Tom for a few words concerning Joe's childhood Tom looks at him "disdainfully" and leaves the room in which Golenbeck remained "mouth open."

But this new realism about DiMaggio did not destroy the older, less disquieting image so often portrayed in the popular media. There is no sullen dissatisfaction in James Stewart-Gordon's August 1976, *Reader's Digest* "Most Unforgettable Character" article which talks briefly of the dignity given Monroe's funeral by DiMaggio's control over it, while ignoring all the grittier aspects of their marriage. Retelling many of the old stories of DiMaggio's childhood and brilliant career ("radio news reporters interrupted the war news of Hitler's invasion of Russia to announce that Joe DiMaggio had broken the world's record by batting safely in 42 [*sic*] consecutive games") Stewart-Gordon concludes with an appraisal whose tone if not literary style reflects the view of DiMaggio presented so dramatically by Gene Schoor. "But what has set him apart," he asserts, "are his personal characteristics of graciousness, the bearing of a Venetian Doge and a genuine modesty. No one knows how many sick kids, hospitals, and old-time ballplayers Joe has visited and helped—because he refuses to talk about it." This is essentially the same DiMaggio Michael Gorkin presents in his March 1979 article in *50 Plus* (the 50 stands for years). Written for older readers, the story's prose and pictures emphasize DiMaggio's contentment and success as a sixty-four year old American. On the magazine's cover and in the pictures inside he looks absolutely great. Other photographs from his past show him with his big Italian-American family, at bat, with Joe, Jr., and in a San Francisco motorcade after his first year in the majors. His growing up is briefly retold; that his father once called him "lagnuso (lazy)" but ultimately "became a fan like everyone else" is pointed out. "He's never forgotten," Gorkin adds, "that he was a fisherman's son—and he's remained proud, but humble, all his

life.'' Now DiMaggio exemplifies the idea that ''not all old athletes fade away.'' His work with the Bowery Savings Bank has
brought him increased fame among the kids who never got to
see him play, and money, too. Both the bank and the Mr. Coffee
people ''acknowledge that profits have jumped considerably in
the six years since Joe DiMaggio has been working for them.''
No longer bothered by attention, according to Gorkin, DiMaggio
had a fine past (one picture shows him pleasantly with Marilyn
Monroe) and an equally good present. His outward appearance
reaffirms and symbolizes his success and inner fulfillment. He
looks ''as athletic as ever, but with a sad smile playing across
his tanned face. He had just been asked what it had been like to
be an American hero at the age of thirty-six and then have to
retire.'' Now he is a representative senior citizen, who was once
a rookie. ''Speaking frankly,'' DiMaggio answers, ''for a guy
whose only real talent was on the ball field, I've made out fine.''
And as a senior citizen, he appears as successful as he had been
a rookie. ''I've now become an expert on retirement.'' The picture is not all glowing. He admits that while he never thought
of himself after retiring as a ''fallen hero,'' as some others did,
''all he felt at the time was simply like an old ballplayer out of
a job. I didn't know what to do with my life.'' While still deeply
disappointed that his marriage to Marilyn Monroe did not work
out, he clearly is depicted as having made the successful adjust-
ments his new second life after baseball stardom demanded. So
he is twice a success story. His new life is far from perfect—
women constitute ''one area where there has been relatively little
fun'' Gorkin clinically observes, and though DiMaggio considers
himself lucky to have achieved a second career in the business
world, he says he still wouldn't mind managing if the right deal
came along. Still he has shown continued emotional growth as
he has aged gracefully. Now he is a ''warm, even outgoing,
public personality,'' Gorkin claims. He still embodies the old
integrity, however: he works only for products he believes in.
Though he admits because of baseball his back is a wreck, his

life is obviously, as revealed in the article, not. He is described at the article's conclusion as smiling. It might not be a smile of joy but it suggests at least satisfaction with his life.

It should be obvious that while a great deal of scattered information about DiMaggio has been published, he has never been portrayed in the depth and complexity a fully dimensional biography of him would demand. Further, there has been little serious attempt to resolve the sometimes conflicting testimony in reports about him: he is reticent, he is expansive; he is a team player, he is sulky; he is gracious, he is petty; he praises Casey Stengel, he abominated him; he is bitter, he is satisfied. One could conclude: of course—he is human. But his intricate humanity has never throughout his career been subject to the kind of scouting that a well-known writer or a leading politician might have received. His public image as it has evolved has controlled the literature about him. He has grown and changed over the years, matured in the public's eye as Babe Ruth never did, but then, from the first years of his stardom a strong element of his image has been that he was developing, from a rookie standout to a team leader, from a gawky kid to a classy dresser. He was becoming increasingly a figure of responsibility demanding respect.

The best book incorporating DiMaggio's many sides, accommodating both his myth and many details of his reality, is Maury Allen's *Where Have You Gone, Joe DiMaggio? The Story of America's Last Hero (1975).* Allen is an admitted fan of DiMaggio's, and at times the people he interviews on DiMaggio sound more as though they were talking about a monument than a man, but the portrait assembled includes so many comments about the "last hero" that he emerges as a highly detailed figure of many moods and attitudes and not just heroic temperament and behavior.

One of the book's greatest strengths is that it is based mainly on oral history interviews with a spectrum of men (and one woman) who knew DiMaggio from various vantage points throughout his life, in addition to some secondary print sources which Allen at least acknowledges at the start of his text even if he does not cite them throughout his narrative. By using the words of DiMaggio's teammates, employers, opponents, associates, and friends, Allen is able to endow nearly all the standard claims about DiMaggio with what seems documented substantiation. His completeness and naturalness as a ballplayer is confirmed by his manager Joe McCarthy, teammate Bobby Brown, and Cleveland Indians catcher Jim Hegan. His perfectionism is underscored by Eddie Lopat and Billy Martin, the "thousand percent" he gave that placed so much pressure on him is noted by Allie Reynolds. All the praise given DiMaggio over the years seems verified in seemingly authoritative fashion here, not merely by claims but by illustrative stories. Even the most extreme adulation is made to appear valid. Joe McCarthy declares, "He never made a mental mistake. He never missed a sign; he never threw the ball to the wrong base." Hank Greenberg, his rival and along with McCarthy a respected member of the Hall of Fame, recounts a time he was surprised to see DiMaggio make a mistake, but the accompanying story he tells suggests the error could have been committed only by an athlete whose skill enabled him to enter higher realms of play: DiMaggio shocks Greenberg by catching an extremely long ball hit by him, and then forgets to pick off a runner who has strayed far from first because he never dreamed the catch could be made. Other familiar themes declaring DiMaggio's special value—that he played while in great pain, that he was actually often underrated because he did things so easily, that he was a team leader who made the difference between victory and defeat for so many Yankee teams, that he never realized how great a star he was, are all advanced and accompanied usually by stories told by people who were there watching him play, who seemingly know what they are talking about.

The book is organized in roughly chronological fashion. Though some of the interviews contain reflections about a variety of periods in DiMaggio's life, generally the vignettes are arranged stretching in order from his early years to his most recent. Often Allen is able to illuminate or bring freshly to life familiar sequences in DiMaggio's story, by presenting information through an apparently authentic voice. Thus DiMaggio's family background is discussed by Tom DiMaggio, who points out that tales of his father's resistance to baseball overstate the issue, but that Giuseppe DiMaggio did fear Joe would not receive an education that would enable him to advance in life. A boyhood chum of DiMaggio's, Frank Venezia, tells of growing up with Joe, whose parents he recollects as "hermits" into whose house no one ever got invited. He further states that Joe and he were shocked when they went to high school and saw kids there so much better dressed than they.

Lefty Gomez talks about Joe as a rookie with the open warmth and affection his stories suggest Joe also felt for him, and relates the improbable sight of DiMaggio playing on his nose as though it were a banjo—surely a rare glimpse of the apprentice hero. Ken Keltner explains how it felt to participate in Joe's streak, and the Yankee team doctor Sidney Gaynor produces an insider's clinical explanation of Joe's fabled wounds, the heel, knee, and shoulder injuries that limited his career while providing it with a special grandeur. On a more gossipy level, Phil Rizzuto presents information on "The Trouble with Stengel," as one of the chapters containing Rizzuto's revelations is termed. Rizzuto is openly critical of Stengel and claims that DiMaggio shared his feelings. Jerry Coleman says "I really think Casey hated him." An especially well constructed section, "The Last Season" includes pictures of DiMaggio's frustrations and anxieties from the perspectives of Rizzuto, Coleman, Gene Woodling, Gil McDougald, Hank Bauer, and Eddie Lopat. The story their combined words tell is sad but not sentimental. As a perfectionist who hated to see himself in situations where he might seem inadequate, the final years posed a problem for DiMaggio solvable only by retirement. Coleman tells of a particularly poignant episode in "The Trouble with Stengel" when DiMaggio was robbed of a hit with men on bases. Terribly disappointed, he returned to the dugout and kicked a bag he thought was empty, that was actually filled with baseballs that went rolling over the field. "His face got red but we all turned away and nobody moved. . . . I bet if you ask a dozen guys on the bench if they remember that day today they'd say they never heard of it. Nobody would want to remember anything that embarrassed DiMaggio."

But a problem with the book is the same problem with much oral history. To what extent are the words of Allen's informants reliable? To what extent have they been guided even unconsciously by the nature of Allen's questions and his stated mission? One must also ask if Allen received information he decided not to include in his picture, that another writer might find important. How were the interviews edited? Sometimes it would seem a relief to read that somewhere in the major leagues, even on DiMaggio's team, existed a player who thought DiMaggio a mean bastard, and had a verifying story to back up his opinions, not because it is thrilling to see popular heroes disparaged, but because so sharp an opposing view would provide needed contrast to the nearly always reverent (though sometimes briefly critical) attitudes toward DiMaggio.

Ballplayers who are asked to publicly comment on their colleagues are often very guarded in their responses. Even when people reveal what they think, their information may reflect only their attitude and not reality. Tom DiMaggio claimed that his father was disturbed about Joe's education, but apparently none of the older DiMaggio boys completed high school, and Tom and Mike directly entered the fishing business with their father's approval. Education presumably was a way of getting clear from poverty, but according to Vince DiMaggio, by the time Joe was ready to play, Giuseppe, Sr., had been shown that baseball was a way to advance and make money. The point is not that Allen prints erroneous information in retelling Tom's opinions, but that other opinions on the same sequence might reveal other versions of the truth. One firsthand account is better than none at all, but cannot always be relied upon, and there is always the problem that not only do informants frequently tell interviewers what they think they want to hear, they often are not certain of the facts of their utterances themselves. Uncorroborated oral history places the interviewer at the mercy of his or her respondents unless their remarks can in some way be checked. In *Where Have You Gone, Joe DiMaggio?*, Phil Rizzuto tells about his first major league tryout, when he was sixteen. He says he was hit on the back by a pitch, causing Casey Stengel to tell him to leave and "go get a shoebox, kid, you're too small anyway." The same story also appeared in Allen's book on Casey Stengel. In *The Scooter, The Phil Rizzuto Story* by Gene Schoor (1982), it is Giants' coach Frank Snyder who tells Rizzuto "What makes you think you can play ball? Go home and get yourself a shoe-shine box." Which firsthand Rizzuto version is correct? Finally, sometimes remarks that might appear factual to the casual reader are only inauthoritative opinions. Allen provides no guidance here: all opinions seem equal. For example, what is the ultimate import of Toots Shor's evaluation of DiMaggio as "very decent, very strong, good morals, good family instincts"? What qualifies Shor as a judge of "family instincts"? Or is the remark just more show-biz gush like "Zsa-Zsa's truly a very beautiful person"? At least when "Old Reliable" Tommy Henrich says DiMaggio "was the most moral man I ever knew. He couldn't do anything cheap; he wouldn't do anything that would hurt his name or hurt the Yankees," the reader can appreciate Henrich's sporting frame of reference and judge his comment's significance accordingly.

Though the book mainly validates DiMaggio's status as a hero, some commentary squarely if briefly indicates shortcomings and limitations in his character. Various witnesses (most of them his friends or teammates) refer to him as cold, moody, and given to harboring grudges for slight reasons. As a boy, for example, he snubbed one of his best friends because he failed to leave a game he was playing to accompany DiMaggio downtown to pick up newspapers. As a man he snubbed the loyal Toots Shor because Shor passed a remark about Marilyn Monroe that DiMaggio didn't like. In his private life he is shown mostly as a good person whose flaws and misbehaviors are quite ordinary and unheroic. That is an angle on DiMaggio the purely adulatory and worshipful books and articles do not reveal, just as he did not supply that sort of insight about himself in his autobiography. Phil Rizzuto's comments about Joe and his wife Dorothy support a conjecture easily gained but rarely documented from reading much of the literature about DiMaggio, that he was most comfortable with men and that he did not really understand how to deal or live in any full way with the women he was romantically interested in. Rizzuto remarks that after the 1942 World Series the Rizzutos and DiMaggios dined and had drinks at Rizzuto's apartment. Rizzuto was to leave for Norfolk and the Navy the next day. "Cora and Dorothy got along real good, but Joe would get a little moody and leave for a few minutes every so often. He didn't like the idea of sitting and talking all night with the women." DiMaggio was so disgusted seeing Marilyn pose for still photographs in New York streets before the crowd howling for her to let her skirt blow high again, he "went to Shor's and drank heavily." These signs of frailty or incompleteness surely constitute no evidence of secret deviousness or viciousness in him, but only suggest that he behaved like an ordinary person, though one whom few ever thought of as ordinary.

Allen supplies relatively little information concerning DiMaggio's marriage to Dorothy Arnold though he provides more about their lives together than do most book-length sources. Surprisingly he prints no interviews with Arnold or anyone who might know how she felt about her life with DiMaggio. Similarly, he pays scant attention to DiMaggio's war years.

The book's last quarter is downbeat because there Allen writes or presents interviews mainly about DiMaggio's declining skills and the bitter frustrations he tried unsuccessfully to keep to himself, and his involvement with Marilyn Monroe. Though it is clear that DiMaggio never permitted himself to sink into the retirement swamp that drags down so many star and average professional athletes after their playing days are finished, his remorse over Monroe pervades the stories Allen chose to fill the last pages of his book. This DiMaggio is a man who has coped fairly successfully with life after stardom, but he is not a happy man. To what extent this reveals the true DiMaggio and to what extent Allen is here portraying the standard melodrama of the unhappy aged hero is difficult to determine. Certainly the evidence Allen provides to bring out the shadows in DiMaggio's last years is effective. The picture is relieved sometimes by such testimony as that of Robert Spero, then a vice president of the advertising agency Ogilvy and Mather, who tells how adaptive DiMaggio became to the demands of the Bowery Savings Bank commercials, how he loosened up gradually on the film sets and even began "making suggestions" to the director. His friend the lawyer and sportsman Edward Bennett Williams seems to speak for many when he calls DiMaggio "a very lonely man at times." DiMaggio told Williams he "burned in" his "belly to be the best there was." Williams remarked that this "put pressures on DiMaggio as a player that were beyond belief. He wanted to be the greatest ever, and there was no settling for anything else." With that kind of greatness as his goal he would inevitably be unhappy, for in sports absolute greatness is evanescent even if amazingly enough it is achieved.

Many of the details Allen relates about DiMaggio's life with Monroe are in other books, but some are new and revealing. Again, Allen shows DiMaggio more fallible, and perhaps because of that more real and human, than most sources where he is the primary subject. Monroe's press agent Lois Weber Smith, even though as she admits she never met him, provides an astute view of DiMaggio that seems consonant with his passionate attachment to the woman he clearly could not possess for very long. Smith's comments are conjectural, but they seem worth pondering and even if uncomplimentary to him, also show better than the weekly gift of flowers on her grave the bitter depth of emotions Monroe apparently compelled in him. "I am sure Marilyn was afraid of him, physically afraid. She said Joe had a bad temper. He was obviously rigid in his beliefs. There must have been a great ambivalence in his feelings toward her."

DiMaggio has been presented like a comic book hero, in books such as Gene Schoor's he is like the hero of a film, and sometimes in Allen's book he has touches of a self-lacerating character from a Dostoevski novel. Allen saves his interview with DiMaggio for last. Here he is presented—or presents himself in a guarded fashion—as a successful but not satisfied man. Allen either asked him no questions about Monroe, or deleted them from his print account of their talk together while DiMaggio relaxed during a golf tournament in Florida. He looks good, but clearly nothing ever replaced baseball for him. "It was all I knew," he says, "it was all I ever wanted to know." The golf is fun, the commercials are all right, "but it's not like playing ball." To Allen there is "a brief sadness in DiMaggio's eyes" when he mentions playing the game.

When Allen questions him about Casey Stengel, DiMaggio's "face twisted in a strange smile. 'The old man had his ways and I had mine. I don't want to say any more about it,' " and he doesn't. (Earlier, Allen quotes Stengel for three pages mostly in praise of DiMaggio, including the ambiguous remark "What do you mean did I get along with him? I played him, didn't I?") DiMaggio also discusses at length his dissatisfaction that he never achieved his ambition to own at least part of a club. He adds that he had a "wonderful career" with "pleasant memories," but the interview does not report many of them. It ends with a fat bald man yelling to DiMaggio that he was there that night in Cleveland when Keltner robbed him. He says, "I remember it, Joe, I really do." DiMaggio says "softly" that he does too, and that concludes the book. The ending seems to suggest that the young DiMaggio has vanished from himself, just as he disappeared from Mrs. Robinson and the rest of us.

Hank Greenberg says of DiMaggio early in the first half of the book that after forty years "I guess I really don't know him. I don't know him. I don't know if anybody knows Joe Di-Maggio." That seems to sum up Allen's point of view, the message about the last American hero that he wants to deliver to his audience. In some ways the message is substantiated by the technique Allen employs, mostly permitting a variety of respondents to set forth their observations and opinions about DiMaggio with a minimum of author's comment. In this way it appears that not just one but many Joe DiMaggios are described. But of course Allen had guided the interviews into their final form, selected and arranged them, and thereby shaped the pictures they presented. If he is saying how can anyone understand Joe DiMaggio one reply could be of course, how can anyone be understood? How can one understand one's parents, children, husband, wife, self? Not to understand people in any final, clear, simple fashion is a characteristic of the modern intellectual world. Post-modern art abjures understanding, frequently replacing it with pure presentation, which is what Allen has almost done. It seems appropriate that the modern hero is a person not to be understood.

Another sense in which Allen's last hero is difficult to understand is that he represents a time now gone. Throughout the text there is an undercurrent of the old against the new: in the old days you didn't have to play night games. In the old days you could travel more slowly on the train and live in a community of fellow athletes. Today the players carry briefcases and separate in each city away from home to see their brokers. How could a totally dedicated individual like DiMaggio, who as Phil Rizzuto remembered would talk volubly with his teammates only about baseball, be understood in the company of today's incorporated performers (though in an older incarnation he has become a handsome businessman himself: that is a different DiMaggio).

Yet there is much that Allen shows that is understandable about DiMaggio. He was a star and even though he has remained a bright star perhaps longer than any of his sports contemporaries (Ted Williams is still splendid but not nearly as often before the public; Joe Louis stayed around in the hearts of his countrymen but his real presence was an embarrassment when first his fortunes then part of his mind eroded), nothing will replace his active days of greatness. He aged gracefully and overcame the trauma of his experience with Marilyn Monroe, a woman he loved deeply and whose suicide shocked him. He has a grown son and a more than comfortable income and the respect of his country, but he was playing on top once and never will again, and certainly that must bring him sorrow sometimes. People who are not stars or celebrities who have successfully developed in their own lives, ordinary people also often grieve for their youth or early maturity. It is part of the romantic tradition that seems ingrained in what was once called human nature. So to an extent, the idea that DiMaggio is not understandable or that he is discontent sometimes or in a mild fashion much of the time (if that is so) constitutes a very human part of his story. If the hero does not die young and at his or her peak, the trail of decline after greatness becomes inevitably part of their narrative, and it is a part Allen firmly fixes onto DiMaggio's myth. He shows convincingly that DiMaggio experienced a falling away from physical ability but not a sharp and disastrous fall. That there was eventually a parallel decline of the spirit may be a valid observation and an important comment on the real life of a hero in America. But it could also be a conventional literary attitude imposed upon the story of a successful athlete and person.

George DeGregorio's *Joe DiMaggio* (1981) is not nearly so mythic or melancholy a figure as Maury Allen's last hero, though according to the opinion of a close friend in a section of the book describing DiMaggio's retirement "he is definitely a lonely guy. . . . A lot of it stems from not being really close to baseball. And . . . he still misses Marilyn Monroe.'' Nor is he the heroic film version of himself that Gene Schoor presents, a sportswriter's dream of almost seamless perfection. Neither is De-Gregorio as powerful as Allen in depicting the narrative of his grand rise to fame not just as as baseball player but as a culture hero. Yet this unpretentious book is a fresh and relatively accurate recitation of the details of DiMaggio's life, and arguably the most realistic of DiMaggio's full portraits. In this book people talk like people and not as though they were being recorded for a movie sound track or Smithsonian Institution archive, and DeGregorio provides details on many of the important events in DiMaggio's off-the-field history most other writers do not. One of the book's deficiencies as a story is one of its strong points as factual narrative: it lacks a clear point of view toward its material, and thereby seems more objective than the other biographies.

DeGregorio seems to have relied more on research into other books and particularly into newspaper files, including at least one San Francisco paper, than his predecessors. Though newspapers, even the ubiquitous *New York Times* can be notoriously inaccurate, especially concerning historical background, they are a rich source of detail on day-to-day matters. The book also gains from some oral interviews; Ernie Sisto, a *New York Times* photographer who knew DiMaggio from his earliest years with the Yankees, is the outside voice DeGregorio most often weaves into the description of events to provide helpful explanations. Sisto seems like an average fellow with good sense, and so he and a few others supply a sort of chorus of normative commentary.

DeGregorio presents new details or expands greatly on the old information concerning a number of events in DiMaggio's life or the life of his family. He is presented less completely as a star performer and more as a person who has to deal with everyday life like everyone else. A fuller version than any other of his 1938 holdout offers a realistic view of contractual confrontations; details about DiMaggio's armed service career reveal the dreary landscape of that episode and show how absolutely different it was for DiMaggio from his baseball years, suggesting why he might have changed so greatly as a performer when he finally returned to playing games. DeGregorio constructs a solidly three-dimensional view of DiMaggio's life. All the triumphs on the baseball field are shown, the wounds observed and comebacks retold, but these events occur surrounded by a fuller range than usual of private or unsensational activities that were also part of DiMaggio's life. Rosalie DiMaggio's trip back to New York in 1936 to see Joe star in the World Series is described in considerable detail for the first time in a book; his life with Dorothy Arnold is presented at far greater length than usual. One photograph in the picture section shows Dorothy nibbling a pencil at one of Joe's games, bored but glamorously dolled-up, her sharply drawn eyebrows perfectly arched. Information about Toots Shor and George Solotaire clarifies their male, Broadway world DiMaggio found so comfortable. The problems Giuseppe DiMaggio faced early in World War II as an Italian who had never become an American citizen has little effect on the public's view of his son but everything to say about the real difficulties the old man had to face in his lifetime, and further demonstrates how distant in his way of life Joe DiMaggio had grown from his father. Equally unheroic but revealing as an insight into the problems even great stars must confront is the explanation of DiMaggio's meeting with Judge Landis in 1940 about possible outside meddling in Joe's contract negotiations. Usually DeGregorio simply narrates these stories. Sometimes he draws conclusions from them and these are ordinarily sensible, as when he comments on DiMaggio's failure to accompany his mother one night during her 1936 visit, because he had to go out with the boys. Mrs. DiMaggio accepted his decision without question. DeGregorio observes that the pampering shown Joe here by his mother, ''the female acceptance of male preference,'' could be a reason for the failure of his two marriages.

DeGregorio does not sharply differ from most of the previous writers who presented versions of DiMaggio's life, and helped construct his image even while they were reflecting it, but he presents him in a more comprehensive fashion operating in more fully described surroundings. DiMaggio is shown as a player whose special "talents were gifts," who could perform great tasks "instinctively," a man of extraordinary achievements who lived in the ordinary world of haggling for salaries, failed marriages, submission to military routine, and was subject to the physical decline brought by age and injury. While not a completely balanced biography—far more is written about a two-month trip DiMaggio took late in 1951 to play ball in the Orient than about his life with Marilyn Monroe—it is an unusually substantial portrait. The virtual elimination of Monroe from the text constitutes a defect but not one that undermines DeGregorio's accomplishment in depicting a believable, real hero.

The book begins with DiMaggio's hitting streak occurring during a time of war preparations and Andy Hardy films. The streak is described again in added detail about a third of the way through the book. It is a central symbol of DiMaggio's greatness as a player and the event that according to DeGregorio more than any other made him "a symbol of cosmic masculinity; a creature of animal magnetism desired by women, approved by men." At the conclusion of the book DiMaggio has long since played his last game. He is reported still lamenting for Marilyn Monroe, lonely if not a loner, but also as a successful spokesman for commercial firms because he is a greatly known and respected man. On the book's last page his friend Ernie Sisto, a newspaper photographer and therefore in theory anyway a man who deals in accurate pictures, tells how bitter DiMaggio was that no good place was ever found for him in the Yankee organization. This hurt DiMaggio, Sisto says, though he never admitted it. DiMaggio said, "Ah, fuck them," according to Sisto, "Ah, fuck them," about the owners. The remark if made tells that DiMaggio still was not the kind to give up. The words are unheroic, but seem real enough. They are not found in any other account of DiMaggio and it is nice to think that even though he figured he was *Lucky to Be a Yankee*, he could say "Ah, fuck them" too.

DeGregorio concludes his book with the detail that "in January of 1980, Joe DiMaggio became a member of the Board of Directors of the Baltimore Orioles." Maybe this was just another business deal, or a symbolic gesture rather than a meaningful appointment. Still, it was a sign of success in the real world where men like Joe DiMaggio live for only a short time.

It is strange and intriguing that after so many years of often intense public attention, Joe DiMaggio still retains an elusive quality, a part of himself that seems always obscured from the view of his fans, fellow performers, and friends. He has not become the kind of person or hero whose character one feels can be encompassed. There remains a teasing incompleteness about his figure, as though one perhaps small but key piece to our understanding of him were absent, or beyond the camera's range. Possibly he has kept the piece hidden or perhaps it never existed, as though he were somehow in himself unfinished. Although the literature about him is filled with the reminiscences of those who knew him, no one seems to have been his intimate friend, to have felt they possessed deep understanding of him.

The reasons that he has achieved such great fame within and far beyond the world of sports seem relatively clear. There was his talent, which for a time focused attention on him as a dominating player, and which after he had passed the period when he could perform almost daily with superior skills still enabled him to play usually at a level higher than most of his fellow performers, and even occasionally allowed him to hit peaks only few could attain. There were for much of his career his day-to-day skills at bat, in the field, and on the bases. There were his unparalleled major league batting streak and his comeback against Boston in 1949. There was his leadership ability, hard to quantify but easy to register in the responses of his teammates.

Furthermore, he possessed personal attributes of birth and personality that made him particularly attractive to Americans at first in the 1930s and continuing until the present time. He fit snugly into the mold of the poor boy who makes good, the immigrant's child who reaps success in the new world. As an Italian-American he benefitted from the adulation of an emerging ethnic group particularly ready to create and reward heroes who could in turn symbolize the group's successful arrival on the American scene. He played for two teams based in cities with large Italian populations ready to offer him strong support, places able to provide him with unmatched opportunities for disseminating his exploits throughout the country. When he arrived at the training camp of his only major league team, he was heralded as the man who would take the place of the greatest star his team had ever known, and he fulfilled the expectations of those who had announced and were awaiting his appearance.

As he matured from a rookie to a greatly respected team leader, from a veritable young man of the provinces (his North Beach Italian-American community) to a gentleman with at least a veneer of suavity and sophistication, as he progressed from the sandlots of San Francisco to the seemingly glamorous and tricky streets of Manhattan and Hollywood, he displayed admirable traits that always eclipsed the less attractive characteristics that were equally a part of his temperament, but that were—typically in the instance of heroes—often excused as the prerogatives of a great man under pressure. That he played with pain, came back again and again after he was hurt, helped make him a symbol of human courage. That he practiced his sport with the devotion of a craftsman and the sometimes inspired dedication of an artist, that he felt he should play both ends of a doubleheader with complete involvement even in sultry heat because some kid might be in the stands who had never before seen him perform, helped make him a symbol of almost priestly purity in a secularized and corrupt, highly commercial world. And that he was so often a winner made him even more attractive as a symbolic American: even when he lost, for example in his relationship with the doomed Marilyn Monroe, he seemed to emerge a winner, even more fixed as a hero who had to endure and could finally surmount a real and messy problem.

He seemed destined to play baseball the way Keats appeared to have written his odes, with easy grace (after much painstaking revision) and beauty. One writer viewed him as lazy and many as sullen, but these were also traditional characteristics of the hero, petulant, driven to excel, single-minded in purpose, smoldering inside to perform nobly, and either uncaring when he was not at his ordained task or bitterly angry when not succeeding at it: Grant rocking on his front porch waiting for the Civil War, or Gary Cooper brooding before the showdown in *High Noon*.

When his playing days were over DiMaggio, unlike most sports figures, maintained an afterlife as a cultural symbol mentioned through song and story. The bright light these works have cast upon him has been augmented by the mellower afterglow he has projected as a commercial spokesman. Always it has been his dignity, his integrity, his success that have been emphasized as he evolved from a raw high school dropout with few apparent skills, to an internationally known hero.

Still, he seems more comprehensible as a symbol or hero than as a real person. Perhaps that is because from the start of his major league career—almost from the beginning of his minor league play—the audience of onlookers around him, fans and reporters, have not seen him as an ordinary person. After his 61-game Seals streak, and through his introduction as Babe Ruth's successor, he has been viewed in the heroic mold, as a special breed of competitor. But all along inside that hero was at first just another not highly educated young man from a good, loving, stable immigrant family. Numbers of writers knew that about him and passed the information along to the public, like scenes from the childhood of a legend. He was neither viewed nor treated as the ordinary young man he was without his rare gifts as a performer. Despite the glaring attention he received, he managed to grow up inside the hero's covering in which his talents and the praise sung about him had encased him, like the armor of a knight—that like a knight's armor made him seem bigger than life-size and less human looking, too.

So what is perhaps most truly amazing about him is that cloaked in his legend he has retained his ordinary measure of basic decency and responsibility, mixed with ordinary measures of human frailties—his occasional ill temper, his sulkiness, his residual, inviolate coldness. Were he the fellow down the street, he would doubtless be a likable if withdrawn person, not one you could ever get very close to. He had his ways: probably his first and second wives found that out. He liked to be with the Broadway boys, he was not good at small talk (or deep talk either), he was uncomfortable when not living in his own style. But then, he was loyal, reliable, and in his own way caring. It is not a part of his record that he ever exploited any relationship though he may have monitored his relations with the press more than anyone realized. He was great enough to meet presidents and be written about by important, idolizing writers who thought him a symbol of greatness, but inside he appears to have always remained an ordinarily good, humanly imperfect person. He grew a little lopsidedly like most people do, but he grew up. The faults he kept do not seem to have resulted from the adulation he received, from the successes he attained. He seems unwarped by fame though his image was fabricated mainly from adulation, and blemished only as probably all are who grow up in the bruising real world.

Immersed in the hyperbole, bloat, and falseness that admiration on a grand scale seems inevitably to accumulate, he has remained an ordinary man. That is often glibly written of celebrities, stars, and heroes, but it seems true of DiMaggio. He seems at heart the same person he would have been had he followed his father's wishes and become a fisherman getting up every day to work hard, hanging out in his spare time with the other fishermen. This is to his credit, but also suggests his limitations. Perhaps the piece that seems missing in him is actually an illusion based upon incessant misperception. Perhaps we simply do not want to see that he has remained his own real, bounded, essentially good but unglorious person. Or perhaps that view reflects only another shard, another fragment of his image: his mystery, that we do not wish to admit we have helped manufacture.

NOTES

1. I am indebted to Professor Gary Mormino of the history department, University of South Florida, for his translations from the Italian here.

Jack B. Moore specializes in American cultural studies at the University of South Florida. He has twice been a Fulbright professor, at Fourah Bay College in Sierra Leone and at Stuttgart University in Germany. With Rex Burbank, he edited a three-volume anthology of American literature, and has published books on subjects as diverse as author Maxwell Bodenheim, civil rights activist W. E. B. Du Bois, American skinheads, and Joe DiMaggio, the last of which was a nominee for the Casey Award as the best baseball book of 1986. Among his many other credits, he has written prizewinning short fiction, which has been published in such well-regarded places as Esquire, Kansas Quarterly, *and* The Long Story.

Literature About Joe DiMaggio, 1987–Present

JACK B. MOORE

Y THE MIDDLE of the 1980s, it was clear that anyone writing about Joe DiMaggio was dealing with a legendary hero exceptional in the world of sporting heroes in his magnitude outside the world of sport. Not only was his status as a very special athlete firm, but the afterglow of his growing cultural significance cast a light back upon his exploits as a player, so that in time he would become to many who had never seen him perform or for whom baseball was just another American game, thought of not simply as a great player but as the game's greatest star since Babe Ruth, a reputation his statistics (except for his amazing hitting streak) would not clearly support. Statistics are one reality, but in the real world, so is perception, however derived.

My own *Joe DiMaggio: A Bio-Bibliography* (in paperback *Joe DiMaggio, The Yankee Clipper*, 1986) attempted to set the reality of DiMaggio's life straight, to establish at least an outline of the facts of his life (some of which like his early annual holdouts ran counter to cherished views of him) from the mis-information that had evolved naturally enough through years of often excellent but sometimes incorrect reportage. I also examined the literature about DiMaggio that presented him to the American public, whether baseball fans or not, that contributed to his public image and helped produce the important American hero that he had undeniably become. And I attempted to tease out and analyze the reasons he had achieved the very high, almost unique position he had reached in the American culture: how and why he had become a particular variety of culture hero, one who came to embody the noble ideals presumably most valued in American life—a person our culture would like to think represents us at our best.

Among the elements that contributed most to his evolution as a hero of mythic proportions, I focused (beyond his undeniably high if not supreme athletic skills) upon his role at a particularly critical time as a model for Italian-American integration into and success in American life; his fortunate and stable location as a Yankee in New York City—a member of the sport's most enduringly successful enterprise, in America's cultural center; his ability to embody shifting public needs in the three decades of his playing career (for example, a quiet, unassuming, take-charge team player during the Depression); his remarkable appearances in culturally important texts such as *The Old Man and the Sea*; his marriage to Marilyn Monroe and his apparently noble contribution to her myth, which came to burn perhaps even brighter than his, yet intensifying, not dimming it.

By the time my book about DiMaggio appeared, writing about sports had changed significantly from what it had been during the years when DiMaggio was starting to develop as a star and his story beginning to evolve. More and more, sports and sports figures were being investigated by a variety of professionals whose interest in their subjects was heavily intellectual, academics for example, writers intrigued by sports' highly illuminating cultural dimensions. And sportswriters themselves were increas-

ingly college-trained along with their pragmatic education as reporters. So that they were subjecting their play territory, once
thought of as the kindergarten of reporting, to a different kind
of cultural scrutiny. DiMaggio was one of the first of the great,
living legends (Muhammad Ali would be another) to receive
extensive treatment in this changed cultural environment. The
image of DiMaggio that emerged was of a more human and
flawed figure, and at the same time a more symbolically heroic
icon.

Christopher Lehmann-Haupt's *Me and DiMaggio* (1986) is a
post-modernist view, a kind of *Waiting for DiMaggio,* more informative about its writer than his ostensible subject. The order
of interest suggested by the book's title is reinforced by its sub-
title, *A Baseball Fan Goes in Search of His Gods.* Lehmann-
Haupt's father was a "transplanted German intellectual," a
"curator of rare books at Columbia University" who had only
disdain for baseball. His son would discover the splendors of the
game at a critical stage of his growing up as an American, when
he was entering his teen years and heard Mel Allen's "bronze
gong of a voice" announcing Yankee games, mostly triumphs.
During the first broadcast Lehmann-Haupt heard, Joe DiMaggio
hit three home runs off Bobby Feller. The boy Christopher becomes hooked on baseball, though in a form that seems more
fantasy than reality, filled with echoes of Allen's voice that
"turned professional baseball into a figment of my imagination."

Who better for a young boy who liked "images better than
reality" to fixate upon and ultimately brood over than Joe
DiMaggio, an athlete more and more written about as possessing
"mystery"?

When a grown-up, Lehmann-Haupt, a book editor and re-
viewer for *The New York Times,* decides he will write a book
about baseball. Like an intellectual on the loose in a fantasy
camp, he wanders around spring training in Florida to the amuse-
ment and bemusement of players and professional sportswriters

alike. Reggie Jackson, whom an anonymous but perceptive fan calls a "hot dog" not all the "mustard in the whole world" could "cover," makes him by contrast think of "Joe DiMaggio and his quiet grace."

Lehmann-Haupt plods like a rookie tanglefoot through spring training and the 1979 season, increasingly dispirited by his ineptitude as a reporter, baseball's inability—real baseball's inability—to compel his interest, Thurmon Munson's death (a signal to Lehmann-Haupt the Yankees will lose the pennant), and finally, his failure to connect meaningfully with Joe DiMaggio. Lobbing to Rod Carew (then first baseman for the California Angels) a softball question about his possible fantasies of baseball stardom, Carew glumly responds, "I never had any heroes." When he finally corners DiMaggio at an Old-Timer's Day celebration in Portland, Oregon, and tells him his plan to write "one of those books in which the author is the hero, or antihero. Sort of like Norman Mailer writes," the Living Legend vacuously says, "I haven't met Norman Mailer." Actually, Lehmann-Haupt could have more accurately said he was writing a less dark version of a book like Frederick Exley's *A Fan's Notes,* though it is also doubtful DiMaggio had met Exley (who not so incidentally would provide a quote for Lehmann-Haupt's eventual work: the book review editor is better connected to writers than athletes).

The author's search for his baseball god increasingly centers upon the game where DiMaggio hit three home runs, which becomes more eventful for Lehmann-Haupt than for DiMaggio. More precisely the search focuses on what happened the evening *before* that game. About the game itself, DiMaggio possesses a fairly clear recollection: he remembers individual pitches thrown to him, and that Bob Muncrief was on the mound. But Lehmann-Haupt also hears from an informant that DiMaggio was taken to dinner by a Cleveland mobster and spent all night drinking and gambling the evening before his big day and got to bed around 5:30 A.M. or 6:00 A.M. DiMaggio is understandably vague about the pregame ritual. Homer would have gloried in this carousing of a divinity, but Lehmann-Haupt, with his apparently childhood dream of godly behavior, is disturbed. DiMaggio sometimes broke training! He fraternized with gangsters! Lehmann-Haupt calls Baseball Commissioner Bowie Kuhn and asks him to speculate about the tale and Kuhn replies he won't give the story ''credibility by commenting on it.''

But Lehmann-Haupt doggedly pursues what happened—or he is pursued by a desire to discover what happened—and readers interested in what happened may be intrigued by both pursuits as bits and pieces of new evidence are rearranged into shifting pictures of reality. However DiMaggio felt about Lehmann-Haupt's incessant probing would be his story if he cared to tell it, which is highly improbable. He is presented as increasingly bothered, possessing a ''look of injured wariness'' when Lehmann-Haupt questions him, regarding the writer ''with injured calm.'' Finally Lehmann-Haupt admits, ''I was beginning to feel like a bully. It was as if I'd cornered a magnificent animal that I'd been searching for all my life—a mountain ram perhaps, or an eagle—except that instead of holding a camera in my hands I seemed to be aiming a high-powered rifle.''

Lehmann-Haupt's rifle may not have been as high-powered as he imagined—as he tells readers he imagined—it to be. But in his sights we can see a double image of DiMaggio, the dream, magical DiMaggio of the author's fabrication (the hero), and the human DiMaggio, ex-baseball star, ex-salesman for the Bowery Savings Bank.

More than any other sport in America, baseball is the popular game of nostalgia—the feeling that generates Lehmann-Haupt's fool's errand. Prizefighting is older but too cruel and dirty and ill-adapted to mass participation; football a latecomer to mass audiences and mass participation, and for various reasons not a game millions of kids—boys *and* girls—remember Dad (or Mom) took them to or played with them after work in the backyard. So perhaps baseball is more fertile soil for sentimental recollection of heroes. One day when genetic engineering will guarantee that everyone will be tall, and society can ensure equal motivation to all, baseball may be challenged by basketball.

Nostalgia is a form of being haunted by the past, a condition naturally attractive to historians. David Halberstam is a popular historian, as opposed to an academic historian: a distinction of style and technique, not a hierarchical differentiation. He has been quite successful in tapping his own and the general public's interest in big events of American history, including his prize-winning and widely distributed books about the Vietnam War (*The Best and the Brightest*) and powerful American figures (*The Unfinished Odyssey of Robert Kennedy, The Powers That Be*). Thus he is an author of considerable authority about the American scene. Halberstam is also like Lehmann-Haupt a fan, and he has written about baseball midway between focusing on the sport as a sportswriter would, and centering on himself as fan, on his reaction to the sport (for example in *The Breaks of the Game*), almost as a writer of fiction, as Lehmann-Haupt did. His two books dealing with DiMaggio thus combine history and nostalgia in a weighty yet subjective fashion, and reveal DiMaggio as both human (sometimes grand, sometimes flawed) and a culture hero embodying the valued qualities by which a culture would like to think it is best represented.

Summer of '49 (1989) in fact begins with an epigraph from Joseph Campbell's *The Hero with a Thousand Faces* (Lehmann-Haupt selected for his more bounded view, an epigraph from Marianne Moore's *Baseball and Writing*): "A hero ventures forth from the world of common day into a region of supernatural wonder: fabulous forces are there encountered and a decisive victory is won: the hero comes back from this mysterious adventure with the power to bestow boons on his fellow man." Heavy stuff, hopefully not referring to Halberstam himself! But saturated with sentiment, too, since the title obviously reflects the title of the hauntingly sentimental coming-of-age film (with a hauntingly beautiful star Jennifer O'Neill and a hauntingly lovely Michel Legrand sound track), *Summer of '42.*

The often written about long season of 1949 was one of DiMaggio's most painful years, and one of his most triumphant: his last time of intense performing greatness, achieved against sharp adversity. Following an operation on his injured heel in November 1948, DiMaggio limped through spring training and would not play until the critical Series at Boston beginning June 28, 1949, when his heel miraculously cleared up. As nearly every book written about DiMaggio since then relates, he hit .455 in the Series, with four home runs. He wrecked the Red Sox. He would continue to play well but gradually wound down eroded by painful ailments until with a dozen games left, he was too sick to perform. The Yankees also this year suffered a greatly publicized number of injuries but limped along, slowly losing their lead, until with two games to play they were one game out, and playing the league leading Boston in Yankee Stadium. Still weak, DiMaggio returned to the lineup, providing inspiration and three hits, including a double and triple, before pulling himself out for the team's benefit. The Yankee's two victories were a stunning achievement. That is the season Halberstam writes about.

DiMaggio is the central figure for Halberstam, but he is one among many, surrounded by other heroes and satellites on both the Boston and Yankee teams, notably Tommy Henrich, who became the "symbol of the Yankees" with DiMaggio out; pitchers Allie Reynolds, Vic Raschi, and Joe Page; Boston pitcher Ellis Kinder; second baseman Bobby Doerr; and of course Ted Williams. Describing a broad canvas of players and the assorted characters—the owners, managers, sportswriters, and minor celebrities clustered around them—and dramatizing an entire season of play, Halberstam works at reconstructing a chunk of American life on which he makes it seem worth expending so much loving remembrance and presenting so much intricate detail. It is as though Halberstam is saying, my memory of this time, what I have discovered about it, is important to understanding American life, to explicating a nation's sense of self-identity: big tasks.

He provides a number of side trips into the off-field life of his heroes to show how the players were a part of their real time. Henrich for example, who "throughout his career . . . could be counted on to get the game-winning hit," also "epitomized the ballplayers born and raised in the America that preceded the New Deal." Unlike young white men maturing after World War II, they would not assume relatively easy access to college. "Henrich's generation had come from an America where a few people were rich, a few more were middle class, and a vast number were poor" and stayed poor. But baseball could lift poor white Americans into the middle class they could probably otherwise never enter. DiMaggio himself represented "the embodiment of the melting-pot theory, or at least the white melting-pot theory . . . the son of a humble immigrant fisherman."

Little new information about DiMaggio is revealed in the book beyond the nature and extent of Halberstam's feelings about him. A by-now-eponymous writer is quoted during a debate about whether marrying Marilyn Monroe was good for DiMaggio, saying that "it's got to be better than rooming with Joe Page." Some versions of this story credit DiMaggio with its display of wit. In the grand tradition of sportswriting and some popular but not academic histories, Halberstam almost never supplies specific sources for his details, so where he lifted the anecdote from would be hard to track. He does supply a bibliography that seems to be incomplete. His retelling of DiMaggio's wondrous three-day return to the lineup in Boston is curiously undistinguished particularly since this would seem a fine opportunity for Halberstam's penchant for pumping portent into his narratives. He is more dramatic describing the World Series between the all-white Yankees and Brooklyn with Jackie Robinson, Roy Campanella, and Don Newcombe, particularly good at the epic fastball pitchers' duel between Newcombe and Allie Reynolds resulting in a two-team total of twenty-four strikeouts and only seven hits.

Generally, Halberstam's book is richer when he describes the scene around DiMaggio, with good characterizations and brief histories of people like Toots Shor ("sensitive and abrasive . . . straight out of Damon Runyon"), Ellis Kinder ("an old-fashioned, unreconstructed carouser"), and the perennially enshadowed (except in Boston, where he was "Better than his brother Joe") Dominic DiMaggio. Like Lehmann-Haupt and others, Halberstam also credits Mel Allen as the voice of Yankee glory during their greatest years, perfectly nicknaming Tommy Henrich "Old Reliable," and over radio literally "amplify[ing]" DiMaggio's "deeds" with his "voice."

In what has become the traditionally somber coda to many a paean to the glories of a previous season, Halberstam writes of Ellis Kinder's death at fifty-four; Red Sox owner Tom Yawkey's ill treatment of a black player, Piper Davis, he had signed for the 1950 season; the decline of Boston pitcher Mickey McDermott; the cold trading away of 1949 Yankee star pitcher Vic Raschi; the debilitation of Yankee great Charlie "King Kong" Keller; the ruthless maneuvering by general manager George Weiss leading to Tommy Henrich's retirement.

Joe DiMaggio becomes another example of the athlete in decline, a story of human frailty, but a special case. After a good year personally (1950) and a humiliatingly bad one (1951) he retires and flops as a postgame sports show host, "stiff and awkward" reading his printed lines on so-called idiot cards. "The rest of his life," Halberstam quotes an unnamed "friend" saying, "has been devoted to being Joe DiMaggio," becoming "something of an icon," but an "eternally wary" one, unable "to balance the scales between fame and privacy." When friends or teammates telephone him he often "pretends that he is not Joe DiMaggio."

Interestingly, after he writes in his cathartic *Epilogue* of the sad demigod DiMaggio has become, Halberstam returns to chronicling the lives after 1949 of the people he had mentioned in his bittersweet telling of that summer. He describes a pleasant Old-Timers' Day reunion of Reynolds, Raschi, Keller, and Boston's appropriately named infielder Johnny Pesky; another happy get-together between Henrich and Doerr; Boston fan and erstwhile big leaguer Bart Giamatti's ascendence to Yale University's presidency and then that of the National League; Yankee fan and erstwhile big league right fielder Joe Lelyveld's work as a Pulitzer Prize–winning reporter for *The New York Times*; Ted Williams' splendid play for another eleven seasons interrupted once for a dangerous stint as pilot during the Korean War, his last home run at his last at bat in Boston, written about beautifully in John Updike's "Hub Fans Bid Kid Adieu," his increasing adulation and neo-mellowing. Halberstam tells of other *Summer of '49* players' times after baseball, some good times, some inevitably bad times. None of the players achieves DiMaggio's iconic stature, none seems so isolated in terms of image.

DiMaggio was not among the many players Halberstam interviewed for his book that is crammed with oral history, thus providing Halberstam with "the only bad moment in my book." Except for a solitary and brief telephone conversation during which DiMaggio was "wary" but acquiesced to another meeting that never took place, the two never conversed. Halberstam ruefully records this piece of information suggestive of a mild (if that is possible) paranoia on DiMaggio's part (or of Halberstam's mild arrogance) and concludes DiMaggio certainly has "a right not to be interviewed" and genially—or is it gruffly—adds "he still remains the most graceful athlete I saw in those impressionable years."

In Halberstam's celebratory lament for an underappreciated epoch, *The Fifties* (1993), DiMaggio returns now as "the greatest baseball player of his era," the "greatest athlete-hero of the nation" mating with the nation's "greatest sex symbol, Mar-

ilyn Monroe'' in what a picture caption in the book hyperboli-
cally but perhaps correctly announces ''was the tabloid's dream
wedding—the nation's greatest baseball player marrying its sex-
iest actress.'' Halberstam presents no evidence to back up his
claims, more problematic about DiMaggio than Monroe. Ted
Williams and Stan Musial are mentioned a few times—Musial
as a ''great baseball player,'' but Halberstam provides no extended analyses to substantiate what he and the audience he
imagined must have come to think was a self-evident evaluation.

Instead, he focuses upon DiMaggio encrypted in Monroe's sad
legend, exhuming standard stories of the couple's brief romance
and more sensational uncoupling, including DiMaggio's glum
response that yes, he had, to Monroe's ecstatic boast about her
reception in South Korea, that he had never heard such cheering,
a rejoinder most famously repeated by Gay Talese. The
exchange, whether fact or factoid, has taken on an unchallenged
life of its own so that it is now quoted as gospel, not apocrypha.
Like so much celebrity history, how such an intimate exchange
was overheard or who leaked it later remain generally unasked
and therefore unanswered questions, another of which is who
tabulated the number of 100,000 soldiers Halberstam reports observed Monroe's sexy girl-next-door performance ''in an outdoor
instant amphitheater'' not far from Korean battlefields.

In rehearsing the famous scene in DiMaggio's life narrative
where the angry ex-player watches air blow up his wife's skirt
between her legs before gawking New York sidewalk passers-
by, Halberstam pinpoints another quality the aging DiMaggio
would increasingly be attributed with after his performing days
with their display of consummate grace were over. He refers to
him, watching from the crowd's corner ''stone-faced and silent,''
as ''a man who perhaps more than any athlete of his generation
valued his *dignity*.'' It is revealing of Halberstam's attitude toward the ''greatest baseball player'' that he does not substitute
the word *reputation* for *dignity* here.

Many writers, whether or not they were conscious contributors to the myth of DiMaggio's pre-eminent greatness among the stars of his day, recognized that his all-around skills—as hitter, clutch hitter, fielder with a powerful and accurate arm, base runner, team leader, winner, rare strikeout victim, for example—distanced him from many athletes who bettered him in one or two areas of performance: Williams and Musial could hit better, but neither was known for fielding well, nor did base runners ever declare they feared their throws to cut down runners. DiMaggio's major statistical achievement (beyond the number of times his teams won pennants or World Series) was of course his hitting streak, whose magnitude as a record became greater the longer it was not broken. Babe Ruth's home-run records for season and lifetime fell, Gehrig's consecutive games played fell, but to this day DiMaggio's fifty-six-game hitting streak still stands as a record of paramount greatness.

Michael Seidel's *Streak: Joe DiMaggio and the Summer of '41* (1988), written three or more decades after Dave Anderson's and Al Silverman's excellent magazine and book-length accounts, provides even greater awareness of DiMaggio's mythic status and his streak's almost fabulous nature than those fine works. Like Silverman especially, Seidel weaves weighty and trivial history into the pattern of DiMaggio's dramatic sporting accomplishment (Hitler's Germany on the march, Rudolf Hess flying crazily to England to broker peace, Stetson Stratoliner hats selling for $6.50), a technique Seidel employs to magnify rather than minify the event's importance. Seidel never pumps up the wartime references to produce the false crescendos occasionally sounding in some writing on The Streak. Steven Goldman's "Remembering Joe DiMaggio" in *The New York Yankees* (1999), an official Yankee yearbook, somehow links DiMaggio's batting 1-for-5 "against Eldon Auker of the St. Louis Browns" with the sinking of the American merchant ship *Robin Moor,* an event occurring the same day that President Franklin Delano Roosevelt called "an act of intimidation" to which America did "not propose to yield." According to Goldman, however, as "a consequence of [DiMaggio's] still unsurpassed achievement . . . the nation" was given "hope when there was none." Most historians would classify this comment as a dubious or at least very problematic, difficult to substantiate assertion.

Seidel is a college professor and so his retelling possesses a heavier tone than that of most sportswriters, the difference between an organ's resonance and a piano's. But his cultural historian's stance is typical of the kind of attention DiMaggio was increasingly receiving. Typical also is the conflation of personal nostalgia and cultural import distinguishing Seidel's version of the player as hero of a not-quite-vanished era. He dedicates his book "to the memory of Jack Seidel, for whom Joe DiMaggio was a great a source of admiration and wonder as he has always been for me," and quotes Lefty Gomez on the hold DiMaggio has on fans "who didn't know him, but they know him just as well as their fathers did," perhaps since (though neither Gomez nor Seidel says this) DiMaggio the star lives now far more vitally in memory of his exploits than he can in acting them out.

Seidel does state that his intention is "to inscribe DiMaggio's great streak in a context worthy of the memory it invokes," and in doing so writes a sort of *DiMaggiad,* which he says is not a biography but a book capturing "the rhythms of a legendary sequence, perhaps the most admired sequence in sports history." Understandably, though Seidel supplies clearly and dramatically a panorama of details involved in and surrounding DiMaggio's "sustained performance" that he considers unparalleled, his language also produces a view of the event possessing appropriate *gravitas,* substantially, generally unfound in sports reporting. He is after all writing about a great streak, which he finds fulfills the achievements embodied in the classic Greek term "*aristeia,* whereby great energies are gathered for a day, dispensed, and then regenerated for yet another day in an epic wonder of consistency."

The occasionally weighty portentousness of Seidel's narrative (which is often just good, solid, rich, intelligent reporting), turning at least this phase of DiMaggio's story sometimes into an epic, was hardly isolated as DiMaggio's image transcended the sports page. One of the more cerebral of syndicated columnists (admittedly the competition is not tough), George Will, in a print debate with Donald Kagan, Hillhouse professor of history and classics at Yale and author of a multivolume history of the Peloponnesian War, stated that while he "share[d] Kagan's awe for [DiMaggio's] fifty-six-game hitting streak," he would not have admired DiMaggio less had a rougher official scorer ended it by calling a questionable hit an error. Will, a conservative who refers to Kagan as "too much of a liberal individualist," offers DiMaggio's wise restraint as a sign of his greatness. "Baseball people will tell you that what made DiMaggio into DiMaggio was judgment of the sort that enabled him to pass through an entire career without ever getting thrown out going from first to third." In good neoclassic fashion, Will's DiMaggio knew his limits. Kagan prefers Seidel's heroic voyager on the seas of his streak. Stephen Jay Gould, Harvard paleontologist and neo-Darwinian, a frequent popular commentator on evolution and other scientific matters, seems a romantic in his attitude, expressed in the essay "The Streak of Streaks" printed in *DiMaggio: An Illustrated Life* (1999). He asserts that DiMaggio achieved "a unique assault upon the otherwise unblemished record of Dame Probability." He accomplished "the finest of legitimate legends because it embodies the essence of the battle that truly defines out lives. . . . He cheated death at least for a while." Who could ask for anything more?

Former great pitcher Tom Seaver's overview of *Great Moments in Baseball* (with Marty Appel, 1992) and Paul Joseph's team-centered *The Yankees* (1997) simply praised The Streak's day-by-day qualities, and Seaver even suggested Wade Boggs might be the one to duplicate or surpass it in 1993.

Sportswriter Joseph Durso supplied an equally conventional and prosaic view of the living legend in *DiMaggio, the Last American Knight* (1995). According to Durso the book began as an autobiography he would ghostwrite or collaborate on with DiMaggio. But although DiMaggio apparently let Durso know "he didn't like any" of the books written about him so far, DiMaggio finally "decided he would rather have his privacy than two million dollars," what publishers would have paid him to tell his tale to somebody. Apparently he refused to talk about Marilyn Monroe with his friend Durso (who appears as a minor character in Christopher Lehmann-Haupt's book about *his* quest to get DiMaggio to unseal his lips) and that was a publisher's sine qua non.

At first, Durso describes with unintentioned but informative comedy DiMaggio's life after baseball and the high state of his image. The Bowery Savings Bank wanted a spokesman "who conveyed something of the good old-fashioned values," someone like John Wayne. The key word here is probably *conveyed*, which should not be confused with *possessed,* since another candidate was Gary Cooper, in real life notorious for his womanizing and for his less-than-heroic compliance with the House Committee on UnAmerican Activities during his *High Noon* meeting in 1947 with them as a representative of the Motion Picture Alliance for the Preservation of American Ideals. DiMaggio was suggested, though he was "old" and "obviously and unrelentingly Italian." An interview with him at the Stage Delicatessen was arranged, a favorite haunt of DiMaggio's, other celebrities, and celebrity-gazers, where he was always assured he could sit "privately," and though Durso does not note this, be both a center of care and attention and alone. Clearly alone. DiMaggio "*projected* [my italics] humility, dignity, integrity"— what the Bowery wanted to emphasize about itself in its advertisements, so he was finally selected as spokesman, a role he performed well and that suited his self-image (Durso reminds readers he turned down offers from Grecian Formula hair preparation as well as Polident false-teeth gum).

Durso makes a few attempts at rooting DiMaggio's story in American life at large, relating anecdotes about John Barrymore at the San Francisco earthquake for example, and then retells most of the old stories of DiMaggio's immigrant background and ascendancy as a great player. Some very familiar episodes reappear in familiar language: when DiMaggio injures himself in San Francisco, his "left knee popped like a pistol shot"; DiMaggio admits he can't drive as he travels silently to St. Petersburg and his first big league training camp with Tony Lazzeri and Frank Crosetti; and when he gets there Dan Daniel writes "Here is the replacement for Babe Ruth." Durso interrupts his brisk, straightforward if routine narration here for a twelve-page chapter about the Ruth years, and then back at the training camp Red Ruffing remarks again, "So you're the great DiMaggio."

Sources for Durso's details are not supplied, perhaps because so much material was by then in some sportswriters' heavenly public domain, but occasionally he cites details from specific accounts without any attribution at all, for example in discounting the once famous knothole story of DiMaggio's discovery by Spike Hennessy. But Durso was on the New York scene at least after World War II, and his opinions on the pre–Rat Pack (Bat Pack?) hangers-on about DiMaggio are informative if subjective: dead Toots Shor, who is described in Durso's Broadway columnist's lingo as owning a "watering hole," is described more caustically than of old, "a fat abrasive man—who put conversation at a low level where he could deal with things on his own terms." He supplies a New York reporter's insider's explanation about how the embarrassing scouting report on DiMaggio was released in *Life* following the 1951 World Series, but it would be good to know why he thinks Walter Winchell was with DiMaggio when Marilyn Monroe posed for the famous, incendiary *Seven Year Itch* photograph, since sources vary on whether even DiMaggio himself was watching. He shrinks—or his unsupplied source reduces—the crowd of howling GIs watching Monroe in South Korea from Halberstam's 100,000 to a more reasonable but still undocumented 50,000.

Roger Kahn's first book about DiMaggio, the somewhat soppily titled *Joe and Marilyn: A Memory of Love* (1986), was a sharper look at the famous romance and breakup than Moore and Schoor's *Marilyn & Joe DiMaggio*, though like the earlier work many of its anecdotes seemed as much fanciful as factual, so that the book is ultimately confusing as a true story. Kahn's version of DiMaggio in his *The Era 1947–1957* (1993) could be described as sourly nostalgic. In a book about a "magnificent" time that had achieved legendary proportions in Kahn's memory of it—subtitled *When the Yankees, the Giants, and the Dodgers Ruled the World* (or at least Kahn's circumscribed world of sporting exploits), DiMaggio is definitely a flawed hero. The book typifies the new sportswriting: still heavily sighing "oh boy, gee whiz," and awed as Gulliver in relating action in an out-of-proportion world of Brobdingnagian giants; sometimes selectively mean, easily disappointed, cynically muttering "baloney."

Kahn, for example, reviews DiMaggio's war record as few writers (the New York *Daily News*' Jimmy Powers was one) had done before in print anyway. "His tours of duty took him no closer to the battlefield than the New Jersey pine flats." Further, the athletically ever-graceful DiMaggio was "graceless . . . to complain about the relative rigors of service" in a way that combatant Hank Greenberg, who fought in South China and rose "from private to captain" never did. Sportswriters and gossip columnists had long noted DiMaggio's visits to nightclubs with attractive young women whom he would be said to be "squiring." But Kahn sees this unexpectional activity in a moralistic fashion. He notes (squeals? finks?) that George Weiss "wasn't happy with Joe DiMaggio running after showgirls" and himself views him during *The Era* as "something of a roué," defined in the *American Heritage Dictionary* as a "lecherous and dissipated man; a profligate." It is almost as though the greatly gifted star were also greatly wicked. And Kahn darkens the standard description of DiMaggio as often a solitary person, to declare that "like a very few," Charles Lindbergh for example, "Joe Di-Maggio is a neurotically private public man."

The male world originally promoting and sustaining Di-Maggio is similarly presented in a less pleasant manner than ordinary. Dan Daniel it seems, like other earlier New York City sportswriters, wrote "promotional copy" for the New York baseball clubs. In a manner resembling the way literary sons (younger writers, if not genetically connected lads) often devour their literary fathers, Kahn nibbles at the Toots Shor gang—Jimmy Cannon, Bill Corum, Red Smith—when he remarks "if any of them ever wrote a critical sentence about [DiMaggio], it has escaped my research."

So during the time Kahn calls "the most exciting years in the history of the sport" and "New York was the capital of the world," DiMaggio is an ambivalently presented figure. A pitcher says "Every job has its drawbacks . . . the drawbacks of my job is that I gotta pitch to Joe DiMaggio," and Ty Cobb is quoted claiming DiMaggio "was perhaps the greatest natural ballplayer who ever lived"—but one who "hated exertion" and engaged in not a "lick of exercise" during the off season. Casey Stengel says, "I got this fella who sucks up all the glory and plays only when he feels like playing. I never had one like that before." A publicist accompanying DiMaggio on a trip to Vietnam says, "I had to pack and unpack for DiMaggio every day. He said he didn't know how to pack a suitcase. All his life he'd gotten somebody to pack and unpack for him."

Kahn is of course focusing on years when DiMaggio's skills were impaired by injuries and "just overwhelming pressure." And though he reprints statistics ranking DiMaggio in only the "second echelon of the top offensive players of all time," he disagrees with David Halberstam's suggestion that Jimmy Cannon created the legend of DiMaggio the Hemingway hero, "as elegant off the field as on it." DiMaggio according to Kahn created his own legend, "Cannon was merely the scribe." Great exploits by DiMaggio (the "Emperor" as Kahn sometimes calls him) such as his 1949 triumph in Boston that Kahn refers to, contributed to that legend. But his final year would be one of "small glory," his batting average "sixty-six points below his lifetime standard." And there is a suggestion that he was responsible for Mickey Mantle's knee injury that year, at least as Kahn has Mantle relating the story about DiMaggio waving him away from a fly ball because "DiMaggio always wanted to look good out there." The result: "Mantle's knee would not be all right ever again." All in all, Joe DiMaggio's theme is not one of the happier melodies sounding throughout what Kahn terms in his last chapter his "Recessional" about a grand time.

A few years later, in *Memories of Summer When Baseball Was an Art, and Writing About It Was a Game* (1997) Kahn again included DiMaggio in a trip whose nostalgic compulsion is suggested in its dedication "to a pair of aces, Gordon Kahn, my father, and Gordon Kahn, my son." His recollections now are a bit mellower though still far from worshipful. DiMaggio tells a kind of joke: fooled by a cooked-up trick pulled by pitcher Fred Hutchinson and coach Charlie Dressen into believing Dressen could clue him about the pitch Hutchinson would throw, so that he is almost beaned, DiMaggio tells Dressen he wants "no more help. I intend to stay alive." Another time he is "a proud old Roman senator" performing "an act of tribute" to another great player. Though Willie Mays never saw DiMaggio play when Mays was growing up and DiMaggio was at his greatest, Kahn reports he was still Mays' idol and so gains glory through reflection.

Kahn rehearses Donald Honig's comparison of Mickey Mantle and DiMaggio, that Mantle for all his skills on the field "did not have the cool dignity of Joe DiMaggio . . . Where DiMaggio had been [perceived as] noble in his quiet modesty, Mantle seemed dull," then adds his own commentary: "But during his thirteen seasons as a Yankee, DiMaggio sustained a carefully fashioned image: humble perfection . . . He drank with power columnists Jimmy Cannon, Bob Considine, and Red Smith. He even picked up his share of tabs.'' Yes he ''played ball with a special, stately grace.'' Still, the press attention he received in New York constituted ''a long love letter.'' Kahn seems both awed by Mickey Mantle's accomplishments and dismayed at his unruliness, his disorderly life, his abuse of his superb talents. In classic terms Kahn does not use, Mantle was ecstatically eruptive, a Dionysian, DiMaggio offers cool and restrained, Apollonian. Kahn himself offers a more earthbound comparison. Mays made 429 putouts as a center fielder in 1962. In DiMaggio's best year, 1941, he made 385. But he also notes DiMaggio struck out amazingly rarely, a quite Apollonian feat.

Life after baseball for DiMaggio in Kahn's memory was the life of a god in decline. Though DiMaggio told *New York Times* columnist Arthur Daley ''I want to be forgotten,'' he never was. He would have dinner at President Reagan's White House honoring Mikhail Gorbachev along with Joyce Carol Oates and Van Cliburn (and distinguished others). He would be uncomfortable receiving an honorary Ph.D. from Columbia University. He would coach briefly for the Oakland A's. He would make millions of dollars as a commercial spokesman, and from signing memorabilia like baseball bats. He would be ''stalked by one of the country's cerebral giants, Christopher Lehmann-Haupt'' (either sycophancy or sarcasm: possibly an in joke). He would perform some (publicized) charity work.

Kahn finally asks a question frequently asked of heroes who are or were also real people. ''Which was the 'real' DiMaggio? The one that people perceived or the one that played the part that people perceived?'' He supplies an answer typical in a cynical age reluctant to rely on absolutes: ''In the long run, what difference did it make?''

Incidental or peripheral commentary on DiMaggio in baseball books not focusing so centrally on him these years ordinarily was far more adulatory than Kahn's often dyspeptic view. Donald Honig, quoted though greatly and negatively revised by Kahn, offered a near idolatrous portrait of the hero in *Baseball America* (1985). For Honig, DiMaggio was a "touchstone for elegant perfection for a half-century . . . moving without blemish or misstep through the decades, solid and polished and reliable, with an impenetrable mystique." Honig tells of DiMaggio's standard exploits to support his contention that the player was "riveting and perfect . . . the man . . . stoic and aloof and private," though apparently not neurotically so as Kahn speculates. In fact the complementarity of his sporting and behavioral qualities is "for a legend, an ideal blend" according to Honig. DiMaggio is "a canvas by Rembrandt, a sculpture by Rodin, a score by Mozart." Obviously, he's the tops. Moreover, though Honig repeats the problematic story of DiMaggio's disdainful reply to Monroe after she entertained the troops in South Korea, he says DiMaggio's "myth" is one "that has had little apocrypha take shape around it."

To list all the complimentary remarks made randomly about DiMaggio in books dealing mainly with other baseball subjects would be redundant, but Bobby Thomson's remembrance in Seth Swirsky's *Baseball Letters: A Fan's Correspondence with His Heroes* (1996, another book similar to Kahn's "dedicated to my father and to my sons") is typical: "I admired Joe DiMaggio because he played the game with dignity and grace." In Ron Smith's discussion of *Baseball's Greatest Players* (1998), DiMaggio is eleventh (Babe Ruth is first, Ted Williams eighth, Stan Musial tenth) and termed "aloof, mysterious, graceful, and dignified."

Of course cliometricians offering statistical analyses fortified with slide rule (and then computers) and often arcane theories quantifying variables (size of home ballpark, wind-chill factor, late career decline, quality of bat timber, absence or presence of black ballplayers) fed or nibbled at the reputations of the great performers. Evaluating hitters (not considering other abilities such as fielding or clutch hitting or leadership) Michael Schell, an associate professor of biostatistics at Princeton, listed Di-

Maggio as number nineteen in his book *Baseball's All-Time Best Hitters* (1991). His "adjusted average" is .311, Ted Williams' is .327 (Stan Musial's is .325, Hank Aaron's, .308. Tony Gwynn is top of the list at .342). For an unequaled and more earthbound résumé of New York Yankee data before, during, and after DiMaggio's tenure with them, Walter Le Conte's *The Ultimate New York Yankees Record Book* (1984) is still indispensable. It includes, for example, "every score of all 12, 545 Yankee games from 1903 through 1983."

Comparing DiMaggio on and off the field with his contemporary Ted Williams remained a major topic in books featuring either of the two. Halberstam noted in his *Summer of '49* Williams' comment that "it is probably my misfortune that I have been and will inevitably be compared with Joe DiMaggio," and that Williams said in *My Turn at Bat* he was the better hitter, but DiMaggio "was the greatest baseball player of our time." Halberstam comments on how different Williams' childhood was from DiMaggio's warm family upbringing. Williams seemed ashamed of his Salvation Army mother, "The Angel of Tijuana," and chagrined that she seemed to care more for her Army clientele than himself. His father was no companion for him. His house was filthy and the lack of care he felt his parents showed toward him seemed symbolized by the single graduation present he received, "a fountain pen from a friend." Growing up in this environment was humiliating for him, in Halberstam's eyes.

Michael Seidel in his *Ted Williams, a Baseball Life* (1991) more greatly contrasts the two men as players, though how they participated in the game was of course reflected (or helped form) the kind of men they were. He repeated Dominic DiMaggio's often quoted (for example in George Will's *Bunts*, 1998), brotherly evaluation, focusing as much on a matter of behavior or character as game performance, that DiMaggio "would swing at a bad pitch" if it might help the team (for example if a teammate was attempting to steal or a hit and run was being attempted) but Williams would not. Catcher Jim Hegan agreed: Seidel quotes him saying DiMaggio "was more dangerous than Williams with men on base. Williams will take a ball or balls with men on even if the pitch is just a fraction of an inch off the plate." Seidel also found meaning as I had in the two players' contrasting pseudo-autobiographic book titles—DiMaggio's effacing *Lucky to Be a Yankee* and Williams' egocentric *My Turn at Bat*. But the Columbia professor—as he says Williams himself "pointed out"—was aware of the role New York and the Yankees played in their mutual enterprise to support their star and emblazon his image throughout the sports world and the country at large. And he also recognized DiMaggio's less than charitable estimate of Williams in an interview with Cliff Keane. Asked for an appraisal of hitters he had seen, DiMaggio replied that Williams was the "greatest left-handed hitter I ever saw." Then asked about his Boston rival's general, overall ballplaying abilities, DiMaggio simply repeated he was . . . still "the greatest left-handed I ever saw."

Ed Linn in *The Life and Times of Ted Williams* (1993) asserted that early in their overlapping careers Williams "was always generous in his public statements about other players," including DiMaggio, concerning whose most valuable player award in 1941 when Williams himself hit .406 he was reported stating "they picked a good man for it." Then as time passed and Williams "found himself being consistently rated below DiMaggio, he began to resent it." When DiMaggio retired in 1951 after hitting .263, Linn alleges "Ted could not resist saying, with a touch of malice, 'when I hit .260 I'll retire too.' "

Sometimes Linn's own evaluation of the two centers on differences in what they offered as players and people more than on which was the better player. "Joe was multidimensional as a player and one-dimensional as a person. Ted was one-dimensional as a player and multidimensional as a person. . . . Joe DiMaggio was grace and Ted Williams was spirit." But finally Linn calls "Joe DiMaggio . . . the greatest ballplayer of his time," and even relates an incident at Fenway Park when

Williams was complaining about being booed for loafing by taking a double against the Yankees that fans thought could have been a triple. Linn writes that through the thin wall separating the two teams "came the unmistakable voice of Joe DiMaggio" remarking "Ted . . . you're a crybaby." Typical of Linn (and like so many other writers of baseball books) he does not authenticate this exchange. It may have occurred and it may not have. But its placement in a book about Williams, also termed by Linn "a sulky and indifferent fielder," throws into highlight the strength of DiMaggio's popular reputation. Linn does describe Williams at an Old-Timers' Day celebration the day before Ted Williams Day in 1991 (the fiftieth anniversary of the two players' fabulous season) hugging the "churlish . . . remote, frail" DiMaggio, but the affectionate act could be interpreted as Williams paying obeisance to the greater hero, just as it could be seen demonstrating his more courteous behavior.

DiMaggio's final days, stretching from his hospital admission October 12, 1998, through the false report of his death January 25, 1999, and to his demise March 8, seems a mordant, bizarre version of his day-to-day streak, generating great and increasingly adulatory publicity about his past, his life stature, and his life's meaning, and implicitly questioning how long his life, like his streak, would last. It is already fixed as part of his legend. Though it contains grotesque elements, for example he supposedly saw the premature newsbreak that he had died, ultimately the deathwatch told of a dignified man controlling his privacy, manipulating the media as he had with Marilyn Monroe's funeral to preserve in this instance his self-respect that reflected the respect with which he desired others to regard him. And as with Monroe's funeral, he did not want the outside world to leak in with its impurities to stain him. At least, that is what seemed to be happening as he was dying.

His death was a national event of great magnitude, and worldwide news of significance, a big day whose meaning needed

analysis and interpretation in the history of the world's sole superpower. Several New York dailies, including the *Daily News,*
The Times, and *Newsday,* published special sections filled with
photographs and slices of the star's history, chronicling the
DiMaggio years. The "special souvenir section" of the *Daily*
News, for example, featured a poster-size photograph of young
DiMaggio posing with, rather than swinging his bat, with a war-
news- or scare-size caption overhead, bidding FAREWELL YAN
KEE CLIPPER. Inside were time capsules and articles such as
STARCROSSED: JOE NEVER WED TO FAME about his marriage to
Monroe; SCOOTER [PHIL RIZZUTO] LAMENTS LOSS OF MENTOR;
FANS SAY A PART OF US DIES WITH JOE (including comments
from fans President Bill Clinton, Senator Daniel Moynihan, Muhammad Ali, and Donald Trump); YANKEES—HIS DEATH MEANS
THE END OF AN ERA; YANKEE GREAT A HERO FOR THE AGES;
and predictably FEAT TO TOP 'EM ALL, "THE STREAK."

Mostly the newspapers presented familiar and totally elegiac
history, though some stories took an offbeat slant. An article by
Stuart Miller in the New York *Daily News* on March 13, 1999,
listed many of the negatives about DiMaggio, his relatively unimpressive statistics, his sulkiness, the repeated assertion that he
insisted upon being introduced at Yankee Stadium as "the
greatest living ballplayer," not, according to Miller, to denigrate
DiMaggio's greatness, but to attack "the media's penchant for
hyperbole and mythmaking [that] shortchanges the historical record." Another article in the *Daily News* on April 27, 1999, questioned whether DiMaggio's friend Morris Engelberg was simply
carrying out DiMaggio's wishes during his fatal illness or
whether he was "just a greedy profiteer." Part "gonzo" journalism, partly in the sad tradition of *Mommie Dearest,* was a
hiply written, depressing article by Robert Huber in June's *Es*
quire variously titled "I Live This Way Because I Want To. The
Whole Sad Story of Joe DiMaggio, Jr." (on the cover), and "Joe
DiMaggio [Jr.] Would Appreciate It Very Much If You'd Leave
Him the Hell Alone" (inside). As Joe, Jr.'s life heads downward

after his time of reflected glory growing up, DiMaggio appears as a character in a now-familiar type of child-of-the-star's film, an increasingly distant, emotionally peripheral figure in his son's life. His most positive gesture is for a time loving his two young granddaughters. Otherwise he is occupied with his stardom, occasional women, his male friends, and himself. Joe, Jr., at one time a Yale student, is depicted essentially as "a bum" disconnected from his father during DiMaggio's last years.

Roger Angell's "Talk of the Town" essay in *The New Yorker* March 22, 1999, was more typical of the worshipful tone set in periodical magazines, but is also tempered by Angell's keenly realistic, often restrained perception of the man DiMaggio, his strengths and frailties. Beautifully written, Angell's brief piece begins by noting DiMaggio "managed a suave departure— hardly glancing in our direction before ducking into the dugout," and praising how he handled dying: "He was always a tough out." Angell perfectly describes the essence of perhaps the most iconic image of DiMaggio at work, the artist at bat, "his legs spread wide, his shoulders and upper frame violently torquing," and reflects on what makes DiMaggio so special compared to today's sports celebrities, that there will be "no post-swing lurching or staggering . . . no fist-pumpings or pauses for self-congratulation if the hit should turn out to be something special." DiMaggio is certainly a grand hero for all those spectators who like Angell, value restraint. He is "the classic player of our century."

Angell also nicely remembers Prince Philip pausing before shaking hands with DiMaggio and asking "*The* Joe DiMaggio?" Angell couples this anecdote that is revealing whether true or not—like so many parts of DiMaggio's story—with an authoritative, first person remembrance of talking small talk with "Joe D" a couple of times, not getting much from this "guy—the first star player I knew all about even before his arrival," and not minding that since "I didn't want any more from him than what I had," a view of his seemingly effortless but actually often tortured performance, a man "at the end . . . still shy, dignified in dark suits and a silk tie—an American noble." After his death, the newspapers and magazines were also filled with letters from ordinary people, typically noting that "the sports aura in which DiMaggio flourished is apparently gone forever" or recollecting some gracious act like the time in his restaurant in the middle 1960s DiMaggio "sat down with a ten-year-old ballplayer [the letter writer] to talk baseball and gave me his autograph" (both from *Time*, April 12, 1999).

Late in DiMaggio's life, *The DiMaggio Albums* (1998) advertised itself as presenting "Selections from Public and Private Collections Celebrating the Baseball Career of DiMaggio." Complied and edited by Richard Whittingham, this two-volume work contains an extensive and interesting selection of newspaper clippings, magazine articles, photos, and other DiMaggio-related memorabilia. What it does not contain is good documentation or useful commentary. Where later DiMaggio examinations such as Christopher Lehmann-Haupt's or David Halberstam's would frequently concentrate more on the journey than on the destination, this is a voyage that consists entirely of destinations—sequential destinations to be sure—but end points nonetheless, much as if one were walking through a museum of raw materials devoid of explanatory signs and tour guides.

Such commentary the book contains is attributed ostensibly to DiMaggio, though it is highly questionable that he wrote it, nor is the information included more than tangential to what appears in the book. Perhaps the strongest argument that DiMaggio himself authored the work is that the writing is both terse and unrevealing. Certainly, the claim that this is DiMaggio's writing is hurt by the editor's attempt to perpetuate the myth that DiMaggio's long-known-to-be-ghostwritten *Lucky to be a Yankee* was also written by DiMaggio himself.

Nonetheless, for the volume and rarity of material it contains, *The DiMaggio Albums* is a superlative source of information, lavishly produced and unparalleled in its own variety of comprehensiveness.

Among the commemorative books spurred by DiMaggio's last illness and his death, two were noteworthy for presenting either unfamiliar material about his life and legend, or reexamining the contours of his remarkable career in a particularly cogent fashion.

Joe DiMaggio: An American Icon, edited by Susan M. Mc-Kinney (1999), reprinted selected articles that originally appeared in the New York *Daily News*, together with an impressive number of pictures from the ample files of "New York's Picture Newspaper." Some of the articles are prescient, such as one appearing November 21, 1934, declaring that "Babe Ruth's successor in box-office and fan appeal was purchased by the Yanks today." Some, like the item originally printed November 23, 1934, asserting "DiMag might be a $75,000 pig in a poke" are now comically misleading: " 'Wrenched knee failing to respond to treatment. Eyes affected by strong floodlights in Seals Park San Francisco.' This was the cryptic report sent to headquarters by the scout of a rival corporation interested in the purchase of DiMaggio." Most of the articles by various *News* reporters are of course greatly complimentary of the Yankees' great star, describing many of the major exploits that are part of his fabled story. But some are more cool toward him, certainly not reverential, reflecting the reality of how attitudes can shift from day to day in the life of any public hero, while his iconic status is developing or decaying. While "Italian Fans Applaud DiMag's Pay Demands" on January 31, 1937, apparently later in the year, on October 1, other fans were not so supportive, for Jimmy Powers chastised DiMaggio for being "shortsighted" and "not being better" to them, the way Powers said Bill Terry of the Giants was. Powers was one of New York City's most important sportswriters, particularly so during television's early years, when he doubled as a TV announcer and personality. Other articles show he was often critical of DiMaggio, once accusing him of having joined the armed forces for less than heroic reasons, and another time contending that Jackie Robinson was grossly underpaid compared to DiMaggio, who was frequently injured and therefore often out of the lineup. The *Daily News* also turned DiMaggio's wedding to Marilyn Monroe into something less than a serious affair, reporting January 16, 1954, that the pair spent their wedding night in a four-dollar-a-day motel room, and that DiMaggio replied to proprietor Ernest Sharpe's rhetorical query "I don't suppose you want twin beds," with a snappy, lusty "Oh, boy, I'll say not." DiMaggio did, however, apparently ask for a TV in the room.

DiMaggio: An Illustrated Life (1999), edited by Dick Johnson, with text by Glen Stout is several books in one. Its numerous photographs well illustrated the major events in DiMaggio's life and his progress as an American hero. Stout's narrative chapters present an accurate résumé of DiMaggio' life and baseball career, both well researched and sensibly interpreted. Unusual in books about DiMaggio, sources are often properly attributed, and a good bibliography is appended. Stout clearly admires his subject, but does not permit his feelings—appropriate for a celebrative, elegiac book—to blind him from noting some of the shadows in DiMaggio's image as a hero. He notes, for example, that DiMaggio may have received the benefit of the doubt from some official scorer during his fifty-six-game streak, but rightly recognizes the record's magnitude despite—or including—this possibility. Stout is similarly open about DiMaggio's war record, which was not the crowning glory of his career but hardly a disgrace. Stout responds to arguments that DiMaggio's statistics were often not as impressive as those of other players in certain specific areas by noting that he was famous for producing under the pressure of being the team leader of a squad that was always expected to win, and that his all-around skills were difficult to match.

DiMaggio: An Illustrated Life also contains inter-chapter essays by different writers on individual aspects of DiMaggio's greatness, the essay "The Streak of Streaks" by Stephen Jay Gould and "God of our Fathers" by Luke Salisbury, for example. Ted Williams contributes a brief (now), typically gracious foreword calling DiMaggio "my greatest rival but . . . also . . . a good friend."

In 1999, the "staff of Beckett Publications" also published *Joe DiMaggio*, revisiting familiar, solid work by writers such as George DeGregorio, Michael Seidel, and Maury Allen. A distinctive feature of the illustrated book is a section on the growing industry of DiMaggio memorabilia such as signed baseball cards and bats and a variety of kitschy items salvaged from DiMaggio's restaurant, which closed in 1986. These include matchbook covers, ashtrays, and even swizzle sticks, that like saints' relics will doubtlessly increase in monetary value in the years ahead as long as DiMaggio's legend prospers.

The richness of DiMaggio's legend will increasingly depend on what is written about him. That legend originated in his bright 9 1111talent but flourished because of the light he cast— or writers cast on his behalf—over our culture far beyond the world of sport. His fabled, unrepeatable greatness seems destined to remain long in our nation's memory. As a real performer, he will continue to be written about and wondered at. As a hero of myth, his magnificent swing by itself deserves to be a constellation.

Sunday, 1941

PHIL MINTZ

In those days I'd skip St. Joe's,
And stand for hours at 14th Street,
Peddling pencils for three cents apiece
Until I had enough in my pocket to hop
The turnstile, scamper onto the D train,
And head uptown to watch him play.

In the first car, by the front window,
Men in suits and broad-brimmed hats
Studied the racing charts and bet on
Joe's team as the train rocked up through
Harlem where black men in soiled clothes
Boarded with worn copies of the *Daily News*.

At 161st Street I'd climb into the sunlight,
Where boys hurried fathers toward the ticket booths,
And young men dawdled with their dates,
Sneaking a kiss against the stadium walls
While smiling cops urged keep moving, keep moving,
And, somewhere inside, he sat shirtless,

Drinking coffee, taking that extra base.

In Boise

RICK WILBER

THE WHEEL RUTS are still there, aimed west toward Oregon.

Drive to the south side of Boise, like I did the other day, and cross over the Americana Boulevard bridge and then go left into Ann Morrison Park. Park it there in that lot with the cottonwoods all around it, then walk down that bluff and into the green grass at the north edge of the park and you'll see them for yourself: two shallow ruts, maybe six feet apart, running alongside the Boise River. A century and a half ago, Conestogas—a line of them that must have seemed to stretch all the way back to Missouri—filled those ruts all summer long, settlers heading to Oregon, looking for land and a good life in the Golden West. They knew where they were headed, and Boise wasn't anything more than a day or two's stopover on their way there. It was just a place to rest the oxen and buy some provisions before the final four-hundred-mile push along the Oregon Trail.

I thought I knew where I was headed, too, back in 1941. I figured Boise for a place where I'd spend a few months before moving up to Columbus, Ohio, and then to St. Louis and the big time, joining the likes of Johnny Mize and Enos Slaughter and Terry Moore and those other Cardinals of the early 1940s.

I had a fastball with a lot of movement on it, you see, and I knew that was all I needed. Rare back and let 'er rip, just blow it right by them, that was my philosophy.

I came west from Decatur, Illinois, riding the old Union Pacific through Missouri and Nebraska and Wyoming and on into Idaho. Took me two days, what with changing trains in Denver and spending one miserable night sitting upright in the Pullman coach as we rattled through the Rockies. But I didn't mind the sleepless travel, I was eighteen years old and was going to be the next Bob Feller, and some bumpy tracks weren't about to get in my way.

Boise felt cool to me for the first day of June, coming from Illinois, where it'd been hot as blazes and limp-rag humid. I was met at the station by Jack McDevitt, the backup catcher and player-manager for the Boise Pilots in the newly reformed Pioneer League. McDevitt was about five-foot-ten, wiry, with thinning brown hair under that fedora he wore. He was dressed in a suit, single-breasted with a belt in the back the way they wore them then. Under his left arm he carried, of all things, a catcher's mitt, a new Rawlings Ernie Lombardi model. He didn't say why.

He seemed a nice enough guy at first, and normal as he could be. He was on the downside of a career that saw him playing for the Phillies and then the Redlegs for a few years. A good defensive catcher and decent hitter who never quite got a chance to be a starter, he'd had more than a cup of coffee but that was about all. Now he was making the shift to managing and Boise was his first stop on the road back to the bigs. We shared that,

I remember thinking that first day. Both of us out in the Wild West to get started on our new careers. Both of us thinking we knew where we were headed.

McDevitt got me to my boardinghouse, introduced me around to Mrs. O'Connor—Mother Mary, she said she liked to be called—and the other players who lived there. Andy Harrington, Gordie Williamson, Bob King, Marvin Rickert, and Eijii Sawamura. Sawamura had been a pitcher for the old Boise Rising Suns, a popular team there for a while in the mid-1930s. Sawamura was gone a couple of weeks after I showed up, called home by his family in Nagasaki. He was the first Japanese I ever met and I liked him a lot, he had a heck of a sense of humor. A couple of years later, less pleasantly, I met a lot more of them.

We were all in the front room, going through the handshaking routine, when McDevitt stopped right in the middle of talking to a little group of us, held out his hand to tell us to be quiet, and then took that glove out from under his arm and put it up to his ear, the mitt opened wide.

I wasn't paying too much attention at first, too busy smiling and listening to Harrington warn me about Haydn Walker, the owner, who was, he said "a nice enough guy when he's sober. But that ain't often."

I laughed at that, thinking he was joking, and then I saw McDevitt raise that hand again, listen to that mitt for a few seconds, then put the mitt in front of his mouth and start talking. "Joe," he said, "listen, kiddo, I know what they're saying, but that's not the way it is. You're hitting the ball fine. Hell, you got a ten-game streak going, d'you know that?"

He paused, put it back to his ear to listen again, then back to his mouth, saying "There you go. Yeah, that's what I figured. You're coming around nicely, Joe, just keep swinging, OK? And don't worry about that stiff neck. You had the same thing last year, too, and it loosened up in the heat, right?" He listened, nodded. "Well, it'll be hot in St. Louis, Joey, always is. I think you'll go on a tear. Just keep those feet apart in your stance, right? And bring those wrists through first, got it?"

McDevitt listened, nodded again. "Yeah, Joe, no problem. I'm here when you need me. Yeah, sure. OK. Talk to you later, kiddo." And he closed the mitt and shoved it back under his left arm.

I looked at Harrington, the question on my face.

Harrington just smiled, shook his head, whirled his finger around his ear, and whispered "He's crazy as a loon, kid. Thinks he's talking to DiMaggio."

"Joe DiMaggio? *The* Joe DiMaggio?"

He laughed. "The very one, kid." He put his arm over my shoulder. "Look, kid, Jack McDevitt's a hell of a swell guy, but he's got some strange habits, OK? He reads all the damn time for one thing—newspapers, magazines, history books. You'd think he was a damn professor.

"And now there's this thing with DiMaggio that's been going on for the past week or so. Hell, Jack never hit better than .268 in six years in the bigs, but he thinks DiMaggio needs his advice—not to mention they're talking to each other through a catcher's mitt." He laughed, shrugged his shoulders. "I don't think Jack even knows Joe D, to tell you the truth. Jack spent all his time in the National League."

Then Harrington turned away from me, smiled, and walked over to McDevitt to put his arm around his shoulders and start chatting about the Pilots and how much the kid—that'd be me— could help the pitching rotation.

And I did help the rotation there at first. I was eighteen, with a rising fastball and a ton of confidence. I'd been mowing them down back home, after all—star of my high school team at Decatur Central High, and then getting great ink playing for the Central Illinois All-Stars in a tournament at St. Louis' Heinie Meinie Field after I graduated. Heck, I threw a no-hitter there in late May, and a one-hitter a couple of days later. That's when

Freddie Hawn, a scout for the Cardinals, came calling and now, full of myself, here I was a professional in the Cardinal organization, on loan to the Boise Pilots.

A week later I got my first chance to pitch, in the final game of three against the first-place Twin Falls Cowboys. I was darnnear perfect, throwing a two-hit shutout, with ten strikeouts and just one walk. Hell, I even had a stand-up double in the fourth to drive in one of our four runs.

Do you know what it's like to be in control of a game like that? There's no feeling like it in the world. I knew, absolutely *knew*, I could get every batter out. My fastball was hopping, with Cowboys waving at it as it went by. I even got two strikeouts with my curve. Been eating my Wheaties, you know what I mean?

The win tied us with Twin Falls for first place and I pretty much figured I was pretty damn swell. An hour later, when we climbed into our broken-down old Ford team bus after the game and headed toward Ogden for a pair of rain-out doubleheaders, I was sure I was on my way to great things. I figured the fans in St. Louis would be screaming my name by August or September.

I couldn't sleep for thinking about the game. The bus rattled and groaned as McDevitt, doing the driving, ground it through what gears it had left, up toward Sawtooth Pass and then down the other side on Route 83 into Ogden. There was great scenery out there somewhere, I remember thinking, but between the dirt on the inside of my window and the rain on the outside I couldn't see any of it.

I was in the second row, behind Harrington, who had the knack for sleeping soundly even in that bus. Dizzy with my own success, and maybe a little homesick, I sat back and tried to drift off, tried not to think too much about how glorious and wonderful my future in the game was certainly going to be if only I could make a few friends and not be quite so lonely.

Eyes closed, thinking about home, I heard someone softly

talking. I looked up and it was McDevitt, holding his glove to his ear with his left hand while he drove that narrow mountain road in the rain with his right. He was talking to the pocket of that old Rawlings mitt.

"Well, ain't it just like I told ya, Joe?" he was saying. "You just stay with it and it'll come. That's great, kid, just great."

He put the glove to his ear for a moment, listened, then put it back in front of his mouth to speak again. "Three hits? That's great. You got those Yanks going now, Joey. I'm telling you right now, you fellows are gonna have a great season."

He listened some more, nodded. "Yeah, that's just swell, Joe. Doubleheader tomorrow? Yeah, for us, too, down in Ogden. Yeah, we won tonight, the kid pitcher did a heckuva job, I think maybe he's a prospect."

He listened again, then moved the glove back and ended with "Yeah, you, too, Joey. Knock 'em dead. Yeah, and keep that stance wide, right? Yeah, OK. Yeah, you, too."

And McDevitt set the glove down to the side of his seat and put both hands back on the wheel before leaning forward to peer through the windshield wipers as they pushed the water around on the windshield. We were through the pass now and heading steeply downhill on that slick, narrow mountain road. I wanted to ask McDevitt about what was going on. I wanted to find out if he was mad as a hatter, crazy for talking to Joe DiMaggio through his glove in the middle of the Utah rain. But I didn't ask, he was concentrating hard on keeping us on the road and I didn't want my curiosity to kill us all. And then the moment passed and Harrington woke up and started talking to me about developing a change-up and then, finally, as we drove along the edge of the Great Salt Lake and on into Ogden, I managed to catch a couple of hours sleep.

When we got to our hotel in Ogden I bought a copy of the *Post Register* to read over breakfast and there it was, top headline on the back sports page: DIMAGGIO'S THREE HITS BEAT BROWNS.

I didn't know what to make of that.

After breakfast, I got a couple more hours sleep in the Golden Spike Hotel and then it was time to get to the ballpark for our doubleheader. I got there early, that's the only way for a kid pitcher to get any cuts at all in batting practice. In the clubhouse—a new place, but bare, with a concrete slab floor and some wooden benches and an open wooden locker for each of us, nails tapped into the sides and backs—I sat there and pulled on my sanitaries and then my red Pilots socks with the three white stripes, rolling the socks and the bottom of my pants and the sanitaries all together up near the top of the calf. I was still at the stage of my career then when just putting on the uniform was a thrill.

McDevitt came by as I finished. He smiled at me. "C'mon, kid, I want to watch you take a few swings," he said, and then he walked me through the tunnel and into the dugout and that bright Utah sunshine. It was hot, with the wind blowing in from the desert and the salt lake, the air so humid and salty you could feel the stuff on your skin and taste it in the air.

I stepped into the cage to hit a few and McDevitt talked for a minute or two about my swing, about how I needed to level it off and tighten it up some, that I wasn't ever going to be hitting home runs and I should worry about singles.

I'd hit that double off the wall the night before, but I wasn't going to say anything to him. He was the skipper and I was the rookie and if there was anything I'd learned in just two weeks of being a professional, it was to keep my mouth shut.

And then, as I swung level and flat, slapping line drives out over short, he said this to me: "Kid, I know you was awake last night when I was talking to Joe."

I didn't say anything.

"Joe and I was roommates back in '33, with the San Francisco Seals," he said. "Joe was having some trouble at the plate and asked me to take a look at his swing. Well, I thought he had a hitch in there, and then was trying to catch up with it, punching at the ball instead of swinging through. We worked on it some, and . . .''

"And he went on that streak," I said, backing up from the plate for a second or two. I turned to look at McDevitt. "Everyone knows about that, when he hit in sixty-one straight. That's the professional record."

"You got it, kid," McDevitt said, and turned to spit out a big hunk of tobacco. "He's trusted me ever since, that's all. You see me talking to him, well, that's all it is, just a little free advice. I keep up with how he's doing and I give him some advice here and there."

"Sure," I said, thinking about how all that good advice was being sent through the deep pocket of a Rawlings catcher's mitt. I didn't know what else to say, so I just stepped back into the box and waited for the next pitch from Harrington to come into me, straight down the middle, perfectly understandable. See the ball. Hit the ball. It's a simple game, really.

That evening I spent the first game in the bullpen, waiting for the weather to cool down some and watching us lose the opener, 3–1, on a long home run off a sweet swing by Swish Nicholson, a guy who earned his nickname a couple of years later with the Cubs when he hit twenty-nine of them.

The nightcap I spent in the dugout, right next to McDevitt. He wanted me to watch the Ogden hitters and tell him what I saw, the strengths and weaknesses. That was harmless enough, and even got to be interesting as Howie Petersen pitched a pretty good game at them, keeping a shutout going through the first five. Then the catcher's mitt rang in McDevitt's head and it all got strange.

We were watching Petersen get behind in the count in the first two hitters he faced that inning before getting them both to fly out to left. When he went 2–0 on the third guy with a couple of breaking balls, one outside and one in the dirt, I figured it was time for serious worry; but McDevitt sat up like he'd heard something the rest of us couldn't find on any radio dial and then he picked up that mitt and gave it a listen.

He nodded. "Sure, Joe," he said, "yeah, he's got that sloppy curve and then he'll try to run it in on you with the fastball. He never throws that curve over the plate, so wait on him and then go for the pump, OK?"

Petersen came in with a fastball and the guy drilled it, foul, to left. At least it was a strike.

"Sure, Joe," McDevitt was saying, "but you got to go down and get that fastball and knock it right out of there, OK?"

He paused, listened. Petersen, working fast, came in with another curve in the dirt. Ball three. "Joey," McDevitt was saying into his glove, "you got to trust me. He'll come in with that fastball down and in, you just be ready."

He listened again, nodding. Petersen came in one more time with the curve, in the dirt and outside for a walk.

"Joe," McDevitt said, "I got to get out there and talk to my pitcher. Stay on the line. I'll be right back." He handed me the catcher's mitt. "Here, kid. Talk to Joe while I get out there and settle Howie down, all right?"

I stared at him.

"Just say hi, kid. He won't bite," he said, and walked up the dugout steps and out onto the field.

I held the mitt to my ear. There was nothing. "Hi," I said, figuring it couldn't hurt. Still nothing.

"Mr. DiMaggio?" I tried. Silence, but then McDevitt, halfway out to the mound, turned back to look at me, put his hands out, palms up as if to ask me how the conversation was going. I shrugged, shook my head slightly.

He frowned. "Keep him on the line, kid," he yelled, and then turned back to stride out to where Petersen stood, the ball in his hand, waiting for him.

So I tried again. "Um, Mr. DiMaggio, this is Delbert Potter. I'm a pitcher here with the Boise Pilots? Jack McDevitt—he's our manager here—he says I should say hi and keep you on the line for a couple of minutes. He's out talking to our pitcher right now and he handed me this, um, glove . . .''

The dugout was awfully quiet. I stopped talking into the mitt and looked down the bench. They were all looking at me, some of them grinning. I looked out toward the mound and McDevitt was walking back. He was giving Petersen one more hitter to get things straightened out.

"How's it going, kid?" he asked me as he reached the top of the dugout steps.

I put up my hand to shush him, listened intently to the mitt for a second, then put the pocket of the mitt close to my mouth, said "Yes, sir, Mr. DiMaggio. Absolutely. I'll tell him you said so. Yes, sir. And good luck today. That's right, fastball, low and inside, sir. Yes, sir, that's what he says." I gave it a listen again, then "And thank you, Mr. DiMaggio. OK, then. Thank you, Joe."

And I pulled the mitt away from my face, folded it together, and tossed it up to McDevitt. "It's going fine, Skip," I said. "Mr. DiMaggio—Joe—says thanks for the tip. He'll be watching for that fastball."

"That's great, kid. Thanks," said McDevitt, catching the mitt as he came down the steps before plopping down on the bench. "Now let's see what old Howie can do here with the bottom of their lineup."

Howie, it turned out, couldn't do much. We lost the first game, and then the second, too, to fall out of that tie for first.

DiMaggio, in St. Louis, had three home runs and a double off the Browns.

It went on like that for the next few weeks, McDevitt talking to DiMaggio through that catcher's mitt with me acting like some sort of receptionist when McDevitt couldn't talk, chatting away with the glove like it all was for real, then listening while McDevitt gave Joe D plenty of advice on how to handle things

as the whole nation started paying attention—a lot of attention—
to The Streak.

There was a war going on in Europe, we knew, and the Japanese were marching all around China. War fever had even
reached into Boise, with B-25 bombers practicing their bombing
runs from Gowen Field, the big new airbase just half a mile past
the ballpark's left-field fence.

But baseball is what mattered, from our struggles to hang on
to first place in the Pioneer League to Jack McDevitt holding
that big, floppy Rawlings mitt up to chat with DiMaggio about
how to keep that streak going.

When Joe broke the Yankee record of twenty-nine games on
a bad-hop single that ate up Luke Appling at short for the White
Sox, it was McDevitt on the mitt congratulating him before
handing the glove over to me so I, too, could tell Joe way to go.

When Bob Muncrief, a rookie right-hander for the Brownies,
had Joe stymied the whole game, it was McDevitt who told Joe
not to worry, he figured the kid wouldn't walk Joe in the eighth
but would pitch to him out of pride, and he was right. Joe singled
to save The Streak. In the next day's *Boise Statesman* I read
where Muncrief said, ''I wasn't going to walk him. That
wouldn't have been fair—to him or to me.''

When the Yankees were finally in first place a couple of
days later and playing at home, McDevitt was on the mitt with
Joe as Tommy Henrich came up in the eight with a man on
and one out. McDevitt told Joe not to worry about a double
play, Henrich would bunt the man over to help out and sure
enough that's what happened. Henrich asked Joe McCarthy if
he could bunt and McCarthy said yes. The sacrifice moved the
runner over and gave Joe one more at bat. He doubled and
kept The Streak going.

It went on like that for weeks, the guys finding it pretty funny
there for awhile. Eventually, though, the sportswriters in Boise
found out about it—from Harrington, I think—and it all got
pretty sour. The guys thought the joke had gone on way too

long, and it was taking attention away from the field, where we were playing pretty good and in a race for the Pioneer League pennant.

McDevitt never let on the whole time whether he even knew we all thought it was just a prank. As far as he seemed to be concerned, it was very simple, Joe DiMaggio needed his advice and he was happy to help.

We stood out in left during batting practice one afternoon and he explained it to me as those bombers roared behind us.

"That's what my job is now, kid," he told me. "I'm supposed to be a coach, to help kids like you learn to play this game a little," he said. And then he'd grinned suspiciously. "Plus, I'm supposed to win some, too, and damned if we're not doing that, right, kid?"

He turned around and watched a bomber coming in for a landing. "You ever think about history?"

"I can tell you who led the National League in hitting every year this century," I said, "just try me."

He smiled. "I bet you can, kid. But what I was wondering about was this war we're heading into. Going to be some history made. Might not be too long before them pilots find themselves dropping the real thing instead of sacks of flour, you know what I mean?"

"You really think it'll come to that?" I asked. The way McDevitt read every newspaper he could get his hands on I figured he knew what he was talking about. Me, I hadn't read anything but the sports page in maybe my whole life.

"Yeah, kid, I do. I ain't got much of an education, but it looks like to me we're going to be in this thing one way or another, and soon. And I'll tell you what, kid, we won't be out here playing ball if the whole country goes to war, you can count on that. There'll be more important things than baseball."

"What'll we do then?"

"Ballplayers?" He shrugged. "Go fight, I guess. Wouldn't that be a mess?"

"Sure would," I agreed, thinking mostly of myself.

He turned his back on the bombers and looked back into the field. "Hell, kid, we all make our own history one way or another, you know? Joe's going to get his made with this streak. Me and you, who knows? How you going to make the history books, kid?"

A month before I'd have answered with something about being in the Hall of Fame. But now I wasn't so sure. The Pilots were winning, sure, fighting it out for first all the way with Twin Falls and then, later, with Ogden, too. But my pitching had gone south as the hitters caught up with my fastball and learned to sit on my curve. After a couple of more real disasters as a starter, by early July I was in the bullpen in middle relief, trying to get my confidence back and get the ball over the plate.

Somewhere along the line I realized I was in a terrible rut—like those tracks out past the left-field fence in Airway Park in Boise.

The field was new, then, and a gem—I realized how lucky I was to play there once I'd seen the other parks in the league. But just beyond the fence ran those wheel ruts of the Oregon Trail. I walked in them all the time, they were on my way to the park from Mrs. O'Connor's boardinghouse. Walking along, knee-deep in ruts that began in Missouri and kept on going all the way to the Williamette Valley in Oregon, I could picture those Conestogas moving along slowly, steadily to whatever waited for them, following that trail like there were no options to go anywhere else, do it any other way. They must have been hell to get out of, those ruts. I know mine were—the fastball getting ripped, my curve not fooling anyone, my new change-up a disaster. I wanted to just pack it up, leave go of it all, and head home to Decatur.

Through it all I kept helping McDevitt talk to Joe, listening in as McDevitt said Joe D should swing on that 3–0 count like he did to get the hit in the fortieth game, then hearing McDevitt

relay Joe's description of how he'd slapped a double of Dutch
Leonard to tie Sisler's record.

And I anguished with them both when DiMaggio's favorite
bat was stolen between games of that crucial doubleheader in
Washington.

I was out on the mound, struggling to get through the fifth
inning at home against Lewiston, the last-place team, when
McDevitt got that call. I'd walked the first two men I faced, then
dropped down a gear to get it over the plate and given up a triple
off the wall, before walking the next guy. Finally, the guy after
that hit a scorcher to short, but Tommy Seals at second turned
it into a slick double-play that got me some outs but cost me a
run. I looked into the dugout to see how McDevitt was taking it
all, and he was talking to that catcher's mitt.

I was a wreck, all the craziness of that long, hot Boise summer
running around in my head so fast I was dizzy with it. I stood
there, looking at McDevitt, willing him to notice me out there,
have some pity on me, take me out, send me home, end all this
misery. Instead, when I needed him most to be my manager, he
was talking to that glove.

I glared at him until Harrington, sitting next to him, noticed
me and elbowed him. He looked up, frowned, then stood up,
climbed those dugout steps and waved at the ump for a time-out
as he walked toward me, that catcher's mitt tucked away like
always under his left arm.

"What's up, kid?" he asked.

"I don't have it, Skip. I think maybe, well, you know . . . "
I said lamely, handing him the ball.

"You know what, kid," he said. "Somebody stole Joe's bat
between games of that doubleheader."

"Oh, Christ Almighty." I was a religious man, even back
then, and I never used the Lord's name in vain, but I couldn't
believe it. Here I was in the middle of a real mess and all
McDevitt could talk about was DiMaggio and that damn streak.

He could see how mad I was at him, but it didn't faze him.

Instead, he just smiled, said, "Hey, kid, hang on a second. I got to tell Joe something." And he put the catcher's mitt up to his face to talk.

"Tell Joe something!" I yelled at him, reaching out to pull the glove away, all the worries and the anxieties and the fear boiling up out of me at last. "Why don't you tell *me* something, McDevitt? For Christ's sake, man, I'm trying to pitch to these guys and all you want to do is talk into that damn mitt!"

He just smiled. "That's good. Nice to see some fire in those eyes." He tossed me back the ball. "Now let's see if it works, kid," he said, and put the glove back up to his face, mumbling into the pocket as he turned around to walk back to the dugout.

I turned around to stare at my teammates, all of them looking at me, slapping their fists into their gloves, shouting encouragement like this was all just an ordinary part of the game.

All right, then. I stood three for a moment, my career in a shambles before it ever got started, my manager talking to Joe DiMaggio through his mitt while I watched my dreams blow away in that hot summer breeze.

And then I started to pitch, angry as hell, buzzing the first one high and tight, giving the Idaho Falls batter a nice, clean shave for ball three. Then a curveball for strike two, and then another fastball, right down the middle, my best against his, and he swung and ripped it to left, a line drive right at Mel Nelson, who caught it without taking a step.

From the mound, I could hear McDevitt in the dugout, saying "I'm telling you, Joe, the bat's in Newark. And I got friends in Newark. I'll call 'em and you'll have the bat back tomorrow, Joe, swear to God."

And the bat, I read in the sports page later, really was in Newark, and Joe did get it back and keep The Streak going. And darned if I didn't win that game, too, 7–5, for my third—and last—professional win.

It all ended a couple of weeks later, on July 17 in Pocatello. I was on the mound in relief again. Jake Coates, our catcher, was sitting it out, so McDevitt was behind the plate, trying to teach me a few things while he could.

I was still mad as a hornet at him, and while he'd kept on with the conversations with Joe D, I hadn't played any of those stupid tricks with the DiMaggio mitt since that night back in Boise. But he ignored all that and treated me like everything was copacetic, smiling and grinning and telling me how great my stuff was. That just made me madder, and I reared back harder, putting about everything I had into that fastball and shaking off the sign every time he called for a curve or a change-up. Hell, I figured I'd just fire away at him. And it felt good, to tell you the truth, though the Pocatello hitters were hammering me pretty good and I was having a hard time protecting a six-run lead we'd built up in the first four innings.

In the sixth it started getting obvious. Pocatello's number-three hitter slapped a sharp liner to left that landed in front of Nelson. Then the next guy took a couple of strikes before he swung on my best fastball and ripped it right back into McDevitt's glove. It would have gotten us out of the inning, but McDevitt couldn't hold on to it, and on the next pitch the guy went to the pump with a towering home run that's still up there somewhere, sailing through the Idaho night sky looking for some mountain peak to plow into.

McDevitt came out to talk to me, clanking up to me in that beat-up catcher's gear, his mask up on top of his head, his glove on his left hand.

"Got that one up some," he said, and I nodded. I figured he'd be talking to DiMaggio any second now, The Streak was up to fifty-six and going strong.

I was feeling mean. "You should've hung on to that third strike. We had that guy."

McDevitt smiled thinly, held up the Rawlings mitt. The web was torn from between the thumb and first finger, the leather lacing dangling there. "Didn't realize it until just now, kid. That foul tip ripped right through my mitt."

"I'm sorry."

"Yeah, me, too, kid." He held the glove up to his ear. "It ain't working so I can talk to Joe, either." He shook his head. "Too bad. I got a bad feeling about Joe today."

"Sure," I said, "a bad feeling."

"And I got a bad feeling about your stuff, too, kid. I think they got you figured out. I'm gonna bring in Townie. We got to protect this lead and win this one."

I nodded. I knew I was done. Hell, I'd known I was done for the past month. If I couldn't get anybody out in the Pioneer League, I sure as hell wasn't going to be striking them out for the Cardinals any day soon.

And so I went to the bench, and then into the showers, and, just a few weeks later, back home to Decatur.

In Cleveland that night, DiMaggio was up against Al Smith, a veteran leftie. Bob Feller would face him the next night, and most people figured Feller could stop The Streak if anyone could.

But Smith got the job done: a nice play at third by Ken Keltner, a walk, another nice play at third by Keltner, and then a groundball into a double play and that was it.

In Boise, McDevitt worked on fixing that mitt between innings and got it done in five minutes, but he said it didn't work anymore. Not that it mattered. By the time our game was in the fifth, the Yankee game—and DiMaggio's streak—was over.

By September I was back on the farm in Illinois, worrying about soybeans and corn instead of Joe D and Jack McDevitt's catcher's mitt. While I was out standing knee-deep in corn furrows, the Yankees won the pennant, seventeen games in front of the Red Sox.

Later, I heard from Andy Harrington that Jack McDevitt died at Okinawa. He was top turret gunner and flight engineer on a B-25 and they were attacking Japanese gun emplacements on the beach, flying in so low that they left a wake in the lagoon. When they pulled up to drop their bombs, some enemy sharpshooter—who knows, maybe Eijii Sawamura—got at them with antiaircraft fire and that was that.

McDevitt and the others couldn't get out in time, and so they all made it into the history books as part of the price the country paid. I bet McDevitt wished, right there at the end, that he had that catcher's mitt with him, that it worked again and he could talk to Joe one last time before they went into the water.

I can see that in my mind, see him talking to Joe, saying goodbye as the plane's right wing caught the water, sending the plane careening in and breaking up over the reef line.

As for me, I wound up fighting the war with a typewriter, writing about the real heroes as they waded ashore at Guadalcanal and Ie Shima. I met a lot of ballplayers along the way, guys ripping out the heart of their careers to do the right thing for themselves, for their country, guys making history. I never ran into DiMaggio in all those years or anytime after, even though he was doing his duty, too.

I know—I always knew—that Jack McDevitt was crazy as a loon and none of that happened the way it seemed to be happening. Joe could have cleared all that up for me just by looking at what I could show him, by putting the mitt on his left hand and chuckling a little and telling me it hadn't happened that way.

But I didn't really want to know, not that way. What I wanted, what I've kept alive, is the thought that maybe it really *did* happen that way, that my season in Boise was part of something important, something that mattered.

And that catcher's mitt? McDevitt gave it to me when I got on the train heading home, said he thought I'd earned that much, at least.

Now it sits right here, looking comfortable in my bookcase, right next to the bowling trophy the wife and I won in 1974, Airway Lanes, Top Couple, 176 average. She died a couple of years ago, so I'm lonely again the way I was in 1941; but we had a good, long run while she was here—four kids, a pack of grandkids, even a great-grandson now who looks to me like a natural hitter.

Every now and then, just for fun, I pick the mitt up, fiddle with the laces some, pound my fist into the pocket a few times, and then start talking, chatting with Jack McDevitt and Joe, pretending that they can hear me, pretending that they care about what I have to say.

I put it to my ear for a quick listen sometimes, but the old mitt has nothing much to say to me. Except for this one re-markable thing: fifty-six games, from May 15 to July 17, from a single off White Sox pitcher Edgar Smith to a double-play against the Indians, Boudreau flipping the ball to Mack to get it started. A .357 average that year, with thirty home runs, forty-three doubles, eleven triples.

You can look all that up. It's in the history books, where it belongs, where it will probably be forever.

Rick Wilber is the author of a new collection, Where Sar-agioln Waits and Other Baseball Stories *(University of Tampa Press), as well as the forthcoming novel* Bone Cold *(Tor Books). Wilber's short stories, essays, and feature articles appear regularly in a wide range of magazines and newspapers, including* Fantasy & Science Fiction, Sport, *and* Elysian Fields. *He is also the author of several college textbooks on writing fiction and nonfiction for publishers including Wadsworth, Allyn & Bacon, NTC, and St. Mar-tin's Press. Dr. Wilber is a journalism professor at the University of South Florida.*

Fifty-six

RANDY MILLER

THE HOTEL PHONE rings at 3:38 A.M. Out of reflex, nothing more, my hand grabs the receiver and I hear a creative torrent of swear words delivered in a Queens accent. I pull the phone from the wall, knowing the desk clerk deliberately let the call through. The calls will keep coming. This I know.

Outside, a faint singsong of derision rises from a knot of Yankee fans clustered on the sidewalk below:

Cuuuuth-bert! Cuuuuuth-bert! You suck!

That's dedication.

I pad into the rest room and take my seat. I am silent. My eyes are drawn to the portable coffee machine. A Mister Coffee.

He is here. Even in this hotel bathroom it becomes clear that I will never escape Joe DiMaggio. Never.

Until this May 1, you almost certainly didn't know me, Scott Cuthbert, backup third baseman at large. Running out of time at age thirty-three. I'd had the proverbial cup of coffee for five teams over nine seasons and until recently was spending time with the Durham Bulls, the Triple-A farm club for the Tampa Bay Devil Rays. On April 29, the Rays sent me a summons after their starting third baseman tore his rotator cuff. When I arrived in St. Pete the next day, the equipment manager handed me jersey number 56, a number that designates you as a temp worker in the world of baseball. After all, it had taken me six years to get my ugly mug on one major league baseball card.

That evening, the Rays' second-string third baseman plowed his Range Rover into a light pole and fractured his collarbone. Until the Rays could cut a deal for a true starter, the coaches told me, I'd start. And then I went 4-for-9 in my first two games, enough to stay on the roster once the brass made a deal. This was my last opportunity, I figured. Might as well have some fun.

And then the Elias Sports Bureau stepped in and noticed that Scott Cuthbert had a thirty-one-game hitting streak. I hadn't noticed. There'd been lots of days I'd gone 0-for-4 in Pawtucket and Birmingham and other towns where you travel by bus rather than by chartered jet. But Elias was counting only major league games. Going back eight years, in fact, to the last game of that season. The Giants put me in as a pinch-hitter and I blooped one of those windblown doubles in Candlestick. It was my first major league hit.

I didn't get another major league at bat for two years.

Then, as the papers and the statisticians have repeated, I spent seventeen days on the Chicago Cubs roster and went 6-for-28 in six games, with exactly one hit in each. Next season, back up for September, where I added three more to a streak I didn't know I had. And, later, as my travels continued to Minnesota, Pittsburgh, and Kansas City—more sips of coffee.

As far as I was concerned, there was no hitting streak. After the last sip of coffee, the organization would return me to the minors and typically I'd have my share of 0-for-4 days. Some pencil-necked, bean-counting, number-crunching statistician noticed that in my last thirty-one major league games, I'd hit safely in all thirty-one of them. Then came expansion. And the Rays' bad luck with third basemen. And some pencil-necked, bean-counting, number-crunching statistician noticed my name on a major league roster. One of the Devil Rays' publicists, Mike Flanagan, thought the chase would help attendance. He prepared a press release that made my life an unexpected nightmare. The attendance went up, but it seemed like every new fan at Tropi-cana Field was a New York retiree who worshipped Joe D.

In my next start at the Trop, I smacked a gapper to right center to score a run but was thrown out stretching it into a double. After the inning, a voice rose with anger from the crowd above our dugout.

"Who do you think you are, Cuthbert? You ain't no Di-Maggio, you bush-leaguer! You ain't even Dom DiMaggio! Or Vince!"

When your name is Cuthbert, you get used to people chewing on you. But I sneaked a glance anyhow. The voice belonged to a scrawny guy with a Randy Johnson face wearing a Yankees cap and one of those "Baseball Is Life" T-shirts. And there she was, behind him, about three rows back on the aisle, applauding my hit.

Her platinum-blond hair shimmered under the artificial light. You could see a childlike magic in her gleaming blue eyes and her smile was bright and alive. Her slacks were tan and her blouse a tangerine shade that almost glowed. And she was gone the next time I looked. It was her, I'd swear it. You know who I mean.

I saw her somewhere in the stands every game after that. I tried sending batboys with notes to get her phone number. They couldn't find any gorgeous blonde in a robin's-egg-blue dress or the bright salmon T-shirt or the emerald golf shirt. And the hits, most of them dribblers and bleeders, kept falling in.

Two weeks later, the pressure increased. Eighth inning, Oak-land, bases loaded, tie game, 0-for-3. The skipper left me in to face the A's All-Star closer. He blew a couple of heaters past me that I hardly saw. I began my next swing early and somehow his slider bent right onto the bat and the ball arced just inside the right-field line for a game-winning single. I swore I could see her in a purple sweater right next to the ugly yellow foul pole, waving her arms to the left like an umpire's signal.

The win put us over .500, but the reporters, aside from a couple of local cheerleaders, cared only that I had tied Pete Rose at forty-four games in a row.

Waiting ahead lay the very much sainted Joe DiMaggio and his record fifty-six-game hitting streak. The media and public decided quickly. Scott Cuthbert, career minor leaguer, had no business being mentioned in the same sentence as Joltin' Joe. The public at large hadn't appreciated Roger Maris when he surpassed Babe Ruth's home-run record either—and Maris had been an excellent major league ballplayer. I was just a borderline player trying to earn a regular job.

The cheap shots poured in like it was happy hour at the Thunderbird Tavern: one New York writer placed Cuthbert on a Top 10 list of the most hated people of all time—behind Hitler and Oswald, but ahead of Castro (Fidel's arm never threatened Koufax's records, he explained). Another suggested that some scorer from some game in my past issue an affidavit stating that a previously scored hit should be changed into an error. For the good of the game, he wrote sanctimoniously.

Berman and Olbermann and some of the other horsehide-loving announcers agreed. What the heck, Olbermann had been opposed to Cal Ripken, Jr., breaking Lou Gehrig's consecutive-game record. It might have been David Letterman, or maybe it was Imus or sportswriter Mike Lupica, who summarized what almost everyone was thinking: "Here's a cup-of-coffee lifer who has a career batting average of .235, zero home runs, nine career RBIs, and twice as many strikeouts as hits. For the love of God and the love of baseball, will somebody stop this man before it's too late?"

Several chided me for wearing number 56—how dare I display such arrogance? It seemed like the only people rooting for me were Flanagan and the Rays' front office. Well, there was one guy on the team who adopted me as a friend. Naturally, that would be the bull-pen catcher, Bret Carroll.

These days, the bull-pen catcher doesn't have a spot on the twenty-five-man roster. Every team has someone like Bret, some minor leaguer who crouches cheap. The backup catcher can't be bothered to do all of that work for his million-dollar salary. The bull-pen catchers not only catch relievers but also warm up outfielders between innings and handle other menial tasks beneath the big leaguers.

During batting practice, we talked.

"You ought to tell them to give you a different number so the vultures will stay off you," Bret said.

"I didn't ask for fifty-six. I wanted something below forty like a regular player."

"Hey, look at me, I'm wearing seventy-seven for Pete's sake."

"I keep trying to tell them I don't think it's a legitimate record. I don't remember ever hitting two weeks straight. Not even in high school."

"Well, buddy, you get one tonight and you've hit two weeks straight."

"Sure. At least these are all in one season." I lowered my voice. "Would you do me a favor tonight, Bret?"

"Not if I have to face one of those reporters," he said, chuckling.

My face fell a half-inch; Bret was the only one I could trust on something like this.

My reaction game me away. "I'm pulling your chain, man," Bret said, and laughed some more. "What do you need?"

"If I get a hit . . ."

"When you get a hit."

"If I get a hit," I corrected. "I'd like you to look in the stands toward the direction of the hit. You'll spot a gorgeous blonde.

At least I think you will. She'll be wearing the brightest outfit up there.''

"You got something going on?''

"I don't know. I keep seeing her during the games, but nobody can find her. I'd just like to meet her, that's all.''

"Scotty, you can't let the pressure get to you, kid,'' Bret said in that tone of voice that indicates only a half-joke.

"Just look, okay, Bret?''

"I'm just saying you can get some paranoid tendencies when you bounce up and down from the minors like a yo-yo.''

The rest of my teammates didn't exactly rush forth with support because like everyone, down deep, they didn't really believe some busher like me ought to have this kind of success. I didn't blame them; I was still the temp in the locker room. So the congratulations weren't exactly overflowing.

In game forty-five, the skipper signaled for a sacrifice bunt in the ninth inning. I don't know whether he always bunted this late with the game tied or whether he just wanted to end The Streak so his team could shoo away the media hordes. I laid one down and the thing died two inches from the chalk with the third baseman, the pitcher, and, to be truthful, everybody else in the ballpark willing it foul. Everyone except the blonde behind the on-deck circle who waved it fair in her electric-blue suit with orange scarf.

Bret said he was too busy warming up the relief pitcher to see her.

After that, the skipper told me that he had phoned each of the opposing managers left between now and Memorial Day to discuss the situation. Joe Torre, the Yankees' manager, hoped somebody would stop Cuthbert, but, he said The Streak had to be stopped honestly. Put Cuthbert in the lineup. No pinch-hit sacrifices. No intentional walks unless the game situation dictated. It would taint DiMaggio's record to stop Cuthbert's streak with an unfair contrivance.

When the Orioles came to town, they tried a shift by placing three infielders right of second base and instructing their pitchers to throw nothing but outside breaking stuff. After two strikes in my first time up, I swung and splintered the bat sending a soft liner through the spot where the shortstop normally waited. The ball rolled to the wall, toward a flash of green cotton and blond hair in the first row of the bleachers. For game fifty, the first sellout at the Trop all year since opening day, I came up in the eighth inning with a teammate at first and no one out. My perfect double-play grounder bounced off the runner's ankle. The rules state when that happens, the runner is called out and the batter records an automatic single. I swear she sat cheering just over the dugout box seats wearing scarlet and I thought I could make out her famous beauty mark. Bret apologized for missing her and said he was in the can.

In Cleveland, for game fifty-one, the sellout crowd almost lynched the umpire when he called my twisting Texas Leaguer fair. But the replays showed that it had kicked up chalk dust when it landed on the line. Guess who looked to be sitting just past the line, seven rows up? I could see her clearly on the replay screen.

The next day, their ace threw one at my head and got a standing ovation. He was pitching a day out of rotation, but I'd seen every ace on every staff we'd faced for three weeks now. His next pitch was just hittable enough to dribble past second for the sort of cheap single that had marked my career.

Over the weekend in Toronto, another seeing-eye single pushed me to fifty-three, a Baltimore chopper gave me fifty-four, and, with two nations watching, I skied a homer into the second row just inside the left-field foul pole for hit fifty-five. Nobody ran out to congratulate me like Aaron or demanded a victory lap like Ripken. My teammates did come out to meet me at the plate as polite Canadian applause rippled down. There was more excitement over which fan would grab the ball and cut his deal for profit. It landed just a few rows short of a cheering blonde in a lavender sundress.

The press conference after the game seemed to last fifty-six days. The questions, for the most part, all seemed to reflect the basic theme of "what's a schlub like you doing here?" They didn't listen that all I wanted to do was to stay up in the majors and that even I thought my streak was bogus. They already had their knives sharpened and were hoping I'd say something to justify their anger.

After that cross-examination, I thought about all of the day-dreams of my youth—winning the World Series with a grand slam, riding in the ticker-tape parade, winning the game and the girl in the final reel. Those fantasies had vanished somewhere on those long bus rides down in the minors; there the dream was simply to get off the bus and into a steady job in the bigs. It looked like that dream had come true, but now the record of all baseball records sat one base hit away.

Then came the flight to LaGuardia. The minor league wonder would get my shot to pull even with Joe D in Yankee Stadium. On Memorial Day.

So that gets us to now. I know that sleep is no option—not that there had been much before the phone call from the guy with the Queens accent. So I study the scouting report and sip the bitter fruits of Mister Coffee. And I try not to want this record so very badly.

It's six hours before game time and Bret's plan begins. I slip down the freight elevator and sneak down a corridor to the kitchen exit, where a Yellow Cab waits. Bret made sure that the taxi company sent a recent immigrant from the Middle East rather than some diehard baseball nut who might spirit me away to the bottom of the Hudson River. Send me Latka, he'd specified, not DiPalma or Alex or even Nardo.

I lie flat on the seat as the cabbie turns out of the alley to a street where a smallish crowd is ready to harass that poor Cuthbert fellow. They barely notice us. When we're five blocks away, I know the plan has worked. It's time to confront my buddy.

"I have the feeling you've been ducking me, Bret. Just give

me a straight answer: Have you seen this gorgeous blonde or not?''

His eyes turn narrow and when he finally speaks, it bubbles out in a hoarse half-choke.

"If I tell you I haven't seen her, you'll think you're going crazy. If I tell you I've seen her, then I'm going crazy. Look, Scotty, I don't always get to watch, but I seen a girl up there two or three times. Maybe four.''

He pauses and the voice is suddenly clear.

"But not like you described.''

"What are you talking about?''

"I don't know what you're seeing in her, Scotty. She's not, uh, unattractive, kind of cute, in fact, but she's not drop-dead gorgeous either. And maybe I don't know my fashion, but I'm not seeing any bright colors there, either, pal. Lot of earth tones.''

I just stare somberly. "That's not her. She looks just like—''

"So you tell me. The only one I keep seeing . . . well, Scotty, I'll look again. Every time you're at the plate. If she's there, I'll send somebody to get her.''

"I'd appreciate it, Bret." We sit quietly and in a way, separately.

Minutes later, I walk through the Yankee Stadium players' entrance and head into the locker room. The clubhouse boy finds a couple of candy bars for breakfast—no sense trusting the hotel's food staff—and a Styrofoam container of coffee and I wander out to the field.

It's my first trip to the House that Ruth Built and DiMaggio Added To. None of my previous American League stops included a road trip to New York City. With no one around, I can't resist a walk out to the center-field monuments.

Especially one of the monuments.

The DiMaggio shrine seems to shimmer in the early-morning sun, but that could be attributed to my bleary eyes or my coffee jones. I read the plaque aloud, my voice soft against the silence of an empty ballpark. And then I look into the eyes of his lean, handsome face and say what I haven't told the writers or my teammates or anyone.

"I'm sorry, Joe. I don't want any part of this dream, but I'm just doing my job."

And in the silence, for a magical moment DiMaggio speaks to me in his clear voice that I'd been privileged to hear only on commercials.

"Remember Gionfriddo," it says. And then the grounds crew turns on the sprinklers, drowning out the silence.

I'm enough of a baseball historian to remember the film of Gionfriddo's catch of DiMaggio's shot in the '47 Series. But I ask the clubhouse boy if he could round up a baseball encyclopedia and, like the miracle workers that they are, he comes back with the newest edition. I turn to Albert Francis Gionfriddo, who spent virtually all of his career with the anemic Pirates before going to Brooklyn. His catch was his biggest highlight of the Series and his career; he'd never played another major league game after that big moment.

Albert Francis Gionfriddo, born Dysart, Pennsylvania. I turn the pages.

Francis Scott Cuthbert, born Point of Rocks, Maryland.

I think I know what DiMaggio's ethereal voice, or call it my own subconscious, was trying to tell me there amid the giants. Some are destined for greatness that lasts and some, like Gionfriddo, get one piece of it.

It's finally game time and the fans are chewing on me already. Interestingly, on Memorial Day, the Yankees are throwing a Cuban pitcher who knows how to paint the black of the plate. I strike out looking in the third inning to a cheer that could move a skyscraper. Two hitless at bats later, I'm kneeling in the on-deck circle, scanning for the blonde. The batter singles and my walk begins to the plate amid 50,000 boos.

I dig my spikes into the dirt of the batter's box. It isn't my style to crowd the plate, which is why I get so many scratch hits. The first pitch is inside and my reflex jump out of the box draws cheers. A chant of "hit him" goes up from the crowd. The second pitch nicks the corner for a strike.

I step from the box and look past the picture toward the center-field monuments. There's no voice, no sign from above. No sign of the glamorous blonde, either. But somewhere inside, I realize that whatever happens will be OK.

I step back into the box. His big overhand motion tips me off that he's coming with his heat and as I swing I know I've caught it on the bat's sweet spot. The ball takes off for the left-field corner. I hurry my way around first. I look and some rookie left fielder barely up from Columbus scurries into the corner and, just like Gionfriddo, makes a desperate running backhand catch.

As the cheer erupts, I slow down. Without conscious thought, I exaggeratedly kick at the dirt just as DiMaggio did all those years before and that Yankee crowd, baseball-wise, understands the tribute.

Some backslaps in the dugout follow and I ask the skipper to pull me from the game—no more at bats today. I don the black warm-up jacket and perch alone on the bench. Bret comes from behind.

"Quick, come into the tunnel. I've got someone you want to meet."

The spikes clatter against the concrete floor and there, by the locker-room door, is a blond woman. Her dishwater hair isn't shimmering platinum and the total package won't ever make the cheesecake magazines and the Hollywood scene. She's wearing a black skirt and hose, white blouse, black vest.

But I see vibrancy in her eyes and in her smile. It's a nice smile, an honest smile. It's real.

"Scott Cuthbert, meet Christine Manson. Christine, I think you've seen Scott. I don't know if he's seen you. But he'd like to," Bret says, turning toward the door.

She smiles and our eyes meet for a minute. Hers are not the perfect blue I had imagined, but a dependable brown, like coffee with a splash of cream. I blurt out, "So, Christine, I understand that you were about the only one out there rooting for me."

"It hasn't been easy cheering for you. I've taken some abuse for it. And I had to pay scalpers' prices for the ticket today. But I wanted to be here in case . . . I'm sorry you didn't get your hit."

"That's OK, Christine. The truth is, I'm really glad it's over."

A muffled roar goes up from the stadium. The PA begins playing "New York, New York." The game is complete and the Yankees win.

"Would you join me at the hotel tonight for a cup of coffee?" I ask.

"That would be delightful. I think you're something special."

"Well, Christine, anybody who roots for me is something special. Especially one as pretty as you."

"Thanks," she said, smiling. "But I'm no Marilyn, you know."

The press conference lasts for a while and the team bus heads back without me to the hotel while I'm changing. First one in, last one out. I'm thinking about Christine and her eyes. And thinking about the other one who didn't show up today.

Baseball isn't fantasy. It's real and fifty-five straight games of hits are exactly that—even if they're spread over eight years. I earned it, no matter what the critics say. For most of us, baseball isn't Technicolor fantasies of perfection. I think I'll be happier as the guy who almost broke a record, not the mythical wanna-be who would forever bear the albatross of fifty-six.

The cab is waiting, but I want one more look. I know the meter is running as I walk back into the dugout. I climb those steps onto the hallowed field of Ruth, Gehrig, and Joe. I look toward the monuments and there she is, standing next to Di-Maggio's shrine. She turns toward me and waves as the wind gusts through the stadium. I think I see her white skirt billowing high. Even as she fades from sight, that billowing image lingers.

I can almost hear her laughing across the breeze. There is a kindness that glistens in the afterglow. And I know that Joe was right.

DiMaggio's Bat

George R. Lausch

*M*Y GRANDFATHER SUMMONED *me to his bedside the week before he died.*

"Sit, Tony, sit. I need to talk to you."

I pulled up a rickety cane chair and sat facing him. At eighty-six, he still looked sturdy and alert, seemingly invulnerable. There were no visible signs of the cancer that had wormed its way into his liver and kidneys.

"How you feeling, Gramps?"

"Bad enough to tell you my secret. I've kept it too long now. The story of Joe DiMaggio's bat."

If Gramps had a religion, it was baseball. And if his religion had a deity, it was Joe DiMaggio. I had heard about "The Yankee Clipper" most of my twenty-one years, though I had seen him play only in the newsreels. To me, DiMaggio was a venerable old phantom who sold coffeemakers on television. But Gramps exploded in anger when I joked about Mr. Coffee.

It never occurred to me that Gramps had any secrets, and I didn't know why he wanted to reveal this one to me. He stared off in the distance, assembling pieces of a scattered memory. Then he began his story:

Before your grandmother and I moved to New York City to open the restaurant, I worked in a place called Bennie's Cafe. Washington, D.C., 1941. I helped Bennie with the cooking and the bookkeeping, trying to learn enough and save enough to open my own place.

Bennie knew I loved baseball and some days he'd let me go to Griffith Stadium to watch the Senators. When the Yankees came to town, I always had one ear to the radio. "Go, go, Louie," Bennie would squawk. "Go watch your Yankees so you can come back and give me an honest day's work!"

I loved the Yanks because I loved Joe DiMaggio. Lean and swift and graceful, I held my breath when he shagged a fly or stroked a hit. Such control! Such power! In 1941, no one could stop him. Fifty-six games in a row he hit safely. No one will ever match it. And no one will ever go through what I went through that summer.

Our nephew Phillip was visiting then. Your great-aunt Carla sent him from Newark. She prayed we could do something with him. Nineteen, cocky, and defiant, always checking himself in the mirror, Phillip worshipped the ground he walked on.

He hated the Yankees and loved the Red Sox. I should say, he hated DiMaggio and loved Ted Williams, the Boston out-fielder who hit .406 that year.

"DiMaggio's nothin' next to Williams," Phillip said at dinner one night. "He's prone to injuries. He has no range in the field. And if his hits didn't have eyes he'd be batting .200. Williams could do better with a broomstick."

"No!" I shouted. I knew he was baiting me, but I couldn't stomach the lies. "You are wrong, Phillip. You have never seen DiMaggio play. He dominates center field like no one else. He has hit in forty consecutive games this season. Tomorrow against the Senators he will break George Sisler's record!''

''I read the papers, Uncle Louie. He has been very lucky. And tomorrow, who knows? Maybe his luck will change.''

''I tell you what. Tomorrow you and I will go to the doubleheader at Griffith. You will watch DiMaggio play. You will see why I call him great.''

So the next day, June 29, we went to the stadium. Thirty thousand people, 100 degrees. DiMaggio made us forget the heat. After making out three times in the first game, he doubled in the sixth inning. One more game and the record was his.

Phillip was not impressed. He looked everywhere but at the field. I had wasted the ticket on him. After the first game he said he was going to the toilet. I got a beer, then came back and settled in for the next game. DiMaggio smashed a single in the seventh to break the record. Our cheers shook the stadium as he tipped his hat. If only Phillip had come back to witness this historic event. He was nowhere to be seen.

When I returned home, Maria—your grandmother—told me that Phillip had caught a train back to New Jersey. He packed his belongings and left in a hurry. ''I do not understand that boy,'' I told her. ''He leaves in the middle of a doubleheader and now this. Poor Carla!''

I turned on the radio. The sports report was all DiMaggio. But the news was not all good. A reporter had learned that a player named Willie Keeler had a *forty-four-game* hitting streak in 1897. Three more games DiMaggio needed to surpass him.

That was not all. Between games someone had snuck onto the field and stolen DiMaggio's favorite bat from the dugout. The radio said it was a model D-29, sanded and boned and oiled to perfection. DiMaggio, like other ballplayers, was superstitious. It was bad luck to change bats during a streak. He was very upset. He said he would not press charges if the bat was returned. Tommy Henrich, the third baseman, had lent him a bat for the second game. But he was still shooting for Keeler's record.

"Why would someone steal his bat?" I asked Maria. "What is it about this world that corrupts people? War in Europe and thieves at home!"

The next day I telephoned Carla to see if Phillip had arrived. I wanted to talk to him. She said he was home, but would not come to the phone. "He told me to give you a message," Carla said. "He says, 'It is not over yet. We will see how great he is without his rabbit's foot.' "

I took the next train to Newark. An ominous feeling had come over me. I knew Phillip hated DiMaggio. He had tricked me into taking him to the doubleheader. He had acted nervous and left after the first game. He was a mixed-up boy, but would he really do something so vile? I had to find out.

I arrived late at night. The Yanks had the day off. They were playing a doubleheader against the Red Sox in New York the next day. Carla was surprised to see me. She told me Phillip was out with his friends. I waited for him in the darkened living room.

Phillip came home after 1:00 o'clock. I had hoped that I was wrong, but when he turned on the lights and saw me, I knew. He ran. I chased him down streets and across yards. He stumbled and I finally caught him. I pinned him against a fence and he confessed. He said he had taken the bat on a dare, and he had bet money that the Red Sox would stop DiMaggio. He thought stealing the bat would help his odds.

I wanted some remorse from him. I wanted him to see the wrong he had done. All I got was arrogance. "I would do it again," he said with a smile.

My anger exploded. I hit him, again and again. "You bring such shame to our family!" I yelled. "You have interfered with this great man!" I stopped when I heard him whimper like a child.

"Where is the bat?"

"I sold it for gambling money," he answered.

"To whom? Where can I find him? I must get it back to DiMaggio."

"I do not know his name. I met him in a tavern. I just took his money and gave him the bat."

I searched and searched for this man. Three days later I found him. I told him I wanted the bat, but he would not give it to me. I had to buy it. Maria wired the money. It took nearly all our savings, but I did what I had to do.

The bat was in my hands on the Fourth of July. I wrapped it and sent it to Yankee Stadium, with a note to DiMaggio. It said how sorry and how ashamed I was that someone in my family was responsible. I asked only that he never reveal my name or Phillip's to anyone. My shame would keep me quiet.

DiMaggio's streak had continued. Three days earlier, he had hit safely in both games of the Red Sox doubleheader. He broke Keeler's record during the next day's game against Boston. As you know, he went on to hit in eleven more games before Cleveland finally stopped him.

The story does not end there. Once he got his favorite bat back, DiMaggio donated the one he used to break Keeler's record to the USO. It was raffled off to raise money for the war effort. And the bat Phillip stole? It broke in two a couple days later when DiMaggio hit a pop-up. The bat he used to complete the streak now rests in the Hall of Fame.

So why do I tell you this story, Tony? Two reasons. The secret has weighed heavy on me long enough. I never saw Phillip again. He got involved with gamblers, spent time in jail, and later disappeared.

As time went on, I knew I had done wrong by him. Stealing the bat was a terrible thing, yes, but I spoke with my fists instead of my head. I might have shown him the error of his ways. But I lost my chance when I lost my temper.

Phillip's plan backfired because it proved what I always believed about Joe DiMaggio. By taking his bat, he had given

DiMaggio more adversity to overcome. And he rose to the challenge. It was not his bat that made him great. It was the man himself.

The second reason? You, Tony. Sometimes when I see anger in your eyes or hear you sass your mother, I think of Phillip. I thought maybe his story would help you. You are a good boy, Tony. Stay loyal to your family. Remember that what you do, good or bad, affects many people. Choose the good.

I am tired now. I must rest. Come see me later.

The next time I saw Gramps was when they lowered him into the ground. It wasn't until the clods of earth struck his coffin that I realized the depth of my sorrow. In his way, he had been good to me, oftentimes better than I deserved.

His story stuck with me. Was it true or was it fabricated to teach me a lesson? I went to the library and pored over countless books about DiMaggio, but I found nothing to substantiate what he said. I found nothing to refute it, either. For some reason, the details of the theft of DiMaggio's bat have been lost to history. I concluded that the story had sprouted from Gramps' fertile imagination.

The package arrived two weeks later. An accompanying note from my father said that he had found it among Gramps' effects and it was addressed to me. I unwrapped it slowly, trembling with anticipation. It was an old Louisville Slugger, marked with a D-29 on the knob. The two pieces of the barrel, split lengthwise, were tied together with black shoelaces. A faded inscription near the label read, simply, "To Louis, with gratitude. Joe DiMaggio."

In a blur I recalled all of Gramps' stories about DiMaggio, the man he worshipped above all others. Until that moment I never fully understood why. There have been many great players, but it took a great man to return the bat in forgiveness to the thief's family.

I hefted the Louisville Slugger. Regardless of the truth or fic-

tion of the story, the bat was as real as the love I felt for my grandfather.

I pictured myself at the plate in Yankee Stadium, facing a snarling pitcher who tried to heave a fastball past me. I stepped into the pitch, swung from the hips, and felt the bat meet the ball. The sting, like electricity, moved up my arms and settled in my heart.

George Lausch owes his love for baseball to his grandfather, who taught him to appreciate its history and traditions, and the 1987 Minnesota Twins, who taught him the joys of the modern game. Currently a trade magazine editor, he has worked as a high school teacher, science writer, library information specialist, and newspaper editor. George and his wife Susan live in Mt. Prospect, Illinois His short story "DiMaggio's Bat" first appeared in the 1992 World Series issue of Elysian Fields.

Epilogue

MICHAEL SEIDEL

*7*HE BRILLIANCE OF DiMaggio's record streak in 1941 is attested to by the intensity of interest and the sheer thrill attending any serious pursuit of it. Players approaching the streak, like Pete Rose in 1978 or Paul Molitor in 1987, with the concentration, the nerves, and the stamina to take the measure of its excellence, are nonetheless haunted by the fabled number 56 hovering somewhere in the middle distance. DiMaggio's great streak is not only a hitting marvel but a formidable obstacle, a record that by its very achievement adds pressure to those mounting a challenge to it.

Famous numbers are part of baseball's mythology, and they seem to stand guard at the larger statistical treasure trove so essential to those who follow and love the sport. Statistics are at once the stuff of baseball's memorial infrastructure and the provenance of the idiot savant; they mark the connections from at bat to at bat, game to game, season to season, decade to decade, and at the same time soothe the baseball insomniac. Here are

some stats. From May 15, 1941, to July 17, 1941, DiMaggio
fared as follows against the rest of the American League.

	G	AB	R	H	2B	3B	HR	AVG
Philadelphia Athletics	5	21	6	11	2	1	2	.524
St. Louis Browns	12	48	14	22	5	0	5	.458
Chicago White Sox	12	45	11	19	1	1	3	.422
Cleveland Indians	7	26	7	10	4	0	1	.385
Washington Senators	5	21	7	8	1	1	1	.381
Detroit Tigers	7	32	6	12	2	1	2	.375
Boston Red Sox	8	30	5	9	1	0	1	.300
Totals	56	223	56	91	16	4	15	.408

These are the nuts and bolts. For good measure, DiMaggio
scored as many runs, 56, as he had streak games, just as he
scored as many runs, 41, as he had streak games at the time he
tied Sisler's modern-day record. He struck out only five times
during the whole of the streak, walked 21 times, and was hit by
two pitched balls. The pitching staffs of the Philadelphia A's and
St. Louis Browns provided the most wholesome food for Di-
Maggio's feasts. Only head to head against the Boston Red Sox
and Ted Williams did DiMaggio falter slightly, hitting .300 to
Williams' robust .520 in those eight games. Williams outhit
DiMaggio .412 to .408 for the games included in the streak,
though DiMaggio had 36 more official at bats (he rarely walked
and Williams rarely didn't), 14 more hits, 3 more home runs, 1
more double, 4 more triples, 5 more runs batted in, and a better
slugging percentage, .717 to .684.

Chicago White Sox lefties Thornton Lee and Edgar Smith
tossed DiMaggio the most balls that began as pitches and ended
up as hits, six apiece. During the course of the streak DiMaggio
faced three pitchers named Harris (Mickey for the Red Sox, Lum
for the A's, and Bob for the Browns) who allowed him what
seemed like a modest seven hits combined. But poor right-hander

Bob Harris of St. Louis gave up five of those hits. He faced DiMaggio six times during the streak, and DiMaggio hit .833 off him, making Harris the sweepstakes winner for the 56 games. He would get his revenge later in the season. As for DiMaggio's performance against the best pitcher in the league, he faced Bobby Feller in two games and stroked three hits off him in six at bats for an even .500 average.

For the entire 1941 season DiMaggio hit in 114 of the 139 games in which he played, impressive but not as impressive as the major league record held by Al Simmons while playing for the Philadelphia Athletics in 1925. Simmons hit in 133 of his 153 games that year, amassing 253 hits and a .384 average. The city of Philadelphia has a lock on this sort of consistency. Chuck Klein of the Phillies holds the National League record by hitting in 135 of his 156 games in 1930, with 250 hits and a .386 average.

During DiMaggio's streak the Yankee record was 41–13, but aside from DiMaggio only three Yankees averaged above .300 from May 15 to July 17: Phil Rizzuto at .368 (aided by his own 16-game hitting streak), Red Ruffing (including his phenomenal pinch hitting) at .351, and Red Rolfe at .305. Ted Williams still led the American League when DiMaggio's streak ended, hitting .395, though DiMaggio had snuck in behind him at .371, with Travis following at .370, Heath at .369, and Cullenbine at .362. Yankee pitching was superb all streak long, with the two staff veterans, Hall of Famers Lefty Gomez and Red Ruffing, winning six and seven games respectively, while losing none. Johnny Sturm said that DiMaggio put out a little extra for the vets on the Yankee staff; it seemed as though they, too, put out a little extra for him during the days of his streak.

Hard upon losing his streak on July 17, DiMaggio gained a second wind. He hit in 16 straight games, beginning July 18 in Cleveland with a single and a double against Bobby Feller, who beat the Yankees 2–1 for his nineteenth win of the season en route to 25 for the year. On July 23, the next time DiMaggio faced Al Smith of Cleveland, he smashed a home run, just a reminder that though Smith might have gotten him twice on July 17, he hadn't put him in his hip pocket. On this same July 23, the rookie phenom who had received so much publicity during DiMaggio's streak, Dick Wakefield, fanned three times in his first game for the Winston-Salem Twins of the Piedmont League.

DiMaggio continued his new streak until an August 3 doubleheader against St. Louis. He came to the plate four times in each game without a hit. John Niggeling collared him in the opener, and Bob Harris, whom DiMaggio had slapped around unmercifully during the streak, hung him out in the nightcap. From August 3 on, DiMaggio never hit in more than 7 straight games. On August 29, with DiMaggio out of the lineup recovering from a sprained ankle, the Yankee team planned an evening at the Shoreham Hotel in Washington in his honor. Lefty Gomez told DiMaggio that they were going to dinner that night where he, Gomez, wanted and then to a movie. Lefty was tired of all the glad-handed DiMaggio hangers-on at the usual American League watering holes. DiMaggio said fine but told Gomez to hurry; he was famished. Then he paced in annoyance as Gomez went through a complicated dressing ritual until Selkirk phoned him that all was ready. "Shake a leg, I'm hungry," said DiMaggio. Gomez complied, but on the way down the hallway he veered off toward Selkirk's room, and DiMaggio followed, rolling his eyes at yet another delay.

The door opened to the entire Yankee team. Pitcher Johnny Murphy and his wife had coaxed a craftsman at Tiffany's in New York to hurry a hand-tooled, elegant silver cigarette humidor with a detailed image on its lid of DiMaggio swinging a bat. Beneath a simple "56" the inscription ran "Presented to Joe DiMaggio by his fellow players on the New York Yankees to express their admiration for his consecutive-game hitting streak, 1941." Everything about this gesture pleased DiMaggio. The streak was in its way as handcrafted as the gift honoring it; the Yankees were eager even before the season ended to give

DiMaggio a token of the excitement he had given them. Di-
Maggio could not say enough in thanks at the time or say it
exactly right since, but he was deeply gratified.

After DiMaggio's streak ended in July, *Newsweek* magazine
ran back-to-back profiles, the first honoring the Yankee center
fielder and the second bemoaning the fact that the national attention paid to the progress of the hitting streak had all but obscured another legend in embryo, Ted Williams' mission to crack
the .400 barrier for the season. With the streak now over, Williams made the last months of the season his own. He returned
to the Red Sox lineup on a regular basis on July 22, after being
consigned by a recurring foot injury to pinch-hitting service from
July 11. His slightly sagging average rose to exactly .400 against
Cleveland on July 25; more important, Williams' bat helped
Lefty Grove win his 300th major league game that afternoon.
The score was a rather free 10–6, but Ted hit a two-run homer
and Jimmy Foxx a two-run triple to break a late-inning tie for
Grove's long-awaited milestone victory.

Williams turned on what gas was left in his tank in early
August (from August 7 through August 21 he hit .466), and that
gave him the points he needed when he flagged toward the end
of the year and precious decimals began dropping from his average. Before a final-day doubleheader against the Philadelphia
A's, Williams was at .39955 (officially rounded off to .400), but
he insisted on taking his cuts. He remembers umpire Bill
McGowan dusting off home plate on his first at bat and telling
him that a player has to be loose to hit .400. Loose he was. In
the first game he chalked up four hits, including a single and a
home run off Dick Fowler and singles off Porter Vaughan and
Tex Shirley. Connie Mack, who usually stuck it out with his
pitchers, gave Williams enough variety to spice up his life and
average to .404. In the second game Mack gave Williams a gift
of Fred Caliguiri, a rookie whose major league career was sensibly brief. Williams singled and slammed a gigantic shot off
the speaker horn in right field for a double.

His six hits on this remarkable day buoyed Williams' average to .406 for the year. In addition, he had cranked up for 11 home-runs in the last month of the season to take the major league lead that year at 37. No one but Williams in the American League ever hit over .400 and over 20 home runs in the same season, though Rogers Hornsby for the Cardinals in the National League took the home-run crown with 42 during his .401 year of 1922. Hornsby's performance that year and the years surrounding it remains extraordinary. From 1921 through 1925 his five composite years averaged out to .402, and his home runs totaled 140. Even Ty Cobb paled before this feat.

While Williams slugged his way to the last .400 season by a major league ballplayer, the Yankees were making a travesty of the American League pennant race. On September 4 they clinched the pennant 20 games up over the then second place White Sox. This was the earliest ever in the majors, surpassing the 1904 Giants in the National League and the 1910 Philadelphia A's in the American, both of whom had clinched after 137 games, with the Giants playing a total of 153 games and the A's 150. The previous 154-game record was held by the 1936 Yankees, who clinched on September 9 after 137 games. At season's end the 1941 Yankees had won a total of 101 games, played .656 ball for the year, and held a 17-game lead over the Red Sox, who had sneaked past the White Sox for second. Chicago ended up in third, with Cleveland, having faded badly since the crucial July series with the Yankees, dropping to fourth.

The pennant race in the National League was an entirely different story, with the Dodgers scrapping and clawing to clinch a couple of days before the end of the season after a sequence of nail-biting extra-inning ball games that had the whole borough of Brooklyn in a cold sweat. In their own last-ditch efforts, the Cards brought up a minor leaguer on the roster expansion date, September 17. The young slugger, Stan Musial, had already moved to Rochester from Springfield late in July. He played in the first few Cardinal games after his elevation and hit .545 (12-for-22) until he cooled down later in September to a mere .426.

DiMaggio finished the year hitting .357, behind the league-leading .406 of Williams and the runner-up .359 of Cecil Travis, but he led the majors in runs batted in at 125 and registered 30 home runs. Later he won over Williams as American League MVP and as Associated Press Athlete of the Year for 1941. In the National League, Pete Reiser, at the age of twenty-two, led the circuit in hitting with a .343 average, displacing Arky Vaughan as the youngest ever to do so. Vaughan had been twenty-three when he won the National League crown in 1935, hitting .385. Reiser was a superb ballplayer, and though he was hotter for most of the year than the proverbial pistol that gave him his nickname, he would just lose out to his teammate Dolf Camilli for the National League MVP in 1941. He won rookie of the year honors hands down, both hands in that he could hit from either side of the plate and throw with either arm; in the majors he threw with his right arm and hit from the left side. In center, he could catch anything that didn't have a rocket attached to it.

Reiser and Camilli, plus a tough pitching staff headed by Kirby Higbe and Whit Wyatt, led Brooklyn into their first World Series ever against the Yankees. The Dodgers had won only two previous pennants, in 1916 and 1920, and had lost to the Red Sox and the Indians on those occasions. This year they had been bankrolled for another shot. Late in September the *Saturday Evening Post* ran a fascinating story about the tactics of Larry MacPhail during his time running the club, "Yes, You Can Buy a Pennant." The article pointed out what a crafty executive could do with $833,110, starting with as little as the $100 he shelled out for the near rookie Pete Reiser. MacPhail's major deals included, among others, $80,000 in 1938 to the Phillies for Dolf Camilli; $25,000 for Whit Wyatt from Cleveland in 1939; $132,000 spent for Joe Medwick from the Cards in 1940;

$25,000 for Roy Cullenbine, whom he got from Detroit in 1940 and unloaded the same year to the St. Louis Browns; $100,000 for Kirby Higbe from the Phillies in 1941; and $50,000 to the Cards for Mickey Owen in 1941.

The 1941 World Series had its glories and legendary moments, but it also picked up one piece of unfinished business from DiMaggio's streak. Back at game 40 on June 28, Johnny Babich of the Philadelphia A's had said he intended to give DiMaggio slim pickin's to swing at that day. Dodger pitcher Whit Wyatt, when interviewed by reporters, thought Babich was overly charitable. He said that in the National League DiMaggio's strike zone would start at his Adam's apple. Apparently both DiMaggio and Wyatt remembered those gentle words in the second game of the Series when Wyatt took the mound. DiMaggio flied out in the fifth inning after two rare strikeouts and two earlier pitches under his chin. As he passed the mound returning to the dugout, he shouted out, "This Series isn't over yet." Wyatt responded, "If you can't take it, why don't you get out of the game?" DiMaggio's version of Wyatt's question had a racier second clause. Uncharacteristically, DiMaggio went after the Brooklyn pitcher, but no damage or even contact took place as both benches emptied, the players milled about, and the umpires settled things, which is what everyone seemed to want. Wyatt proved he was a man of his word, perverse as that word might have been, and DiMaggio proved he had read the local sports pages back in June.

In the Series, the Yankees won the opener behind Red Ruffing, who defeated reliever Hugh Casey 3–2. Joe Gordon hit a two-run homer and a game-winning single. Whit Wyatt, while irritating DiMaggio, also stopped a 10-game Yankee consecutive-win streak in the World Series by turning the previous day's score around in favor of the Dodgers. When the teams moved to Ebbets Field for the third game, the Yankee left-hander Marius Russo, suffering a miserable cold, held off the Dodgers 2–1 as Charlie

Keller, not expected to play because of a badly sprained ankle, drove in DiMaggio with the game-winning run. Earlier in the day DiMaggio got his first hit of the Series, a single.

Game 4 was perhaps the most famous in World Series history. Kirby Higbe of the Dodgers started against Ately Donald. A two-run homer by Pete Reiser had given the Dodgers a 4–3 lead into the top of the fabled Yankee ninth inning. With Hugh Casey working in relief, Johnny Sturm died on a full-count ground-out. Red Rolfe then tapped to Casey for an easy out number two. It looked like a wrap. But Tommy Henrich forced the count to 3–2 before taking an awkward cut at a slithering—some witnesses might have guessed slobbering—Casey pitch heading for the inside corner. Henrich was completely fooled, and his bat made no contact with Casey's savage and mysterious delivery. Mickey Owen's catcher's glove, to his utter dismay, made only slightly better contact with the pitch. Henrich flew to first base as the errant third strike rolled far behind the plate; half the Yankee team had to be summoned from an overly hasty retreat down the dugout runway toward the clubhouse. Poor Owen's surprise was greater than anyone's. The man was no slouch in back of the plate. From September 22, 1940, while with the Cards, to August 29, 1941, after his trade to the Dodgers, he had played flawlessly at catcher, amassing 508 putouts and assists without a single error. This play was a fluke, and the reputation earned by it was sadly unmerited.

Nevertheless, there stood a crestfallen Owen in foul territory, and there at first stood the ghost of Tommy Henrich's strikeout. All Dodger history passed before the Brooklynites' stunned eyes. DiMaggio followed with a line single to left. Keller, with the count 2–0, doubled high off the right-field wall to drive in both Henrich and DiMaggio and put the Yankees a run ahead. Bill Dickey walked; Gordon doubled over Wasdell's head against the left-field wall, driving in two more runs; Rizzuto walked; and finally, Johnny Murphy, Yankee relief pitcher, put Hugh Casey and the Dodgers out of their misery with a roller back to the box. The score: 7–4. Three Dodgers zombied up and out in order in their half of the ninth.

This had been a tight, gritty series until Casey's pitch and Owen's play loosened the Dodgers at the joints. In the final game, the series clincher, Tiny Bonham of the Yankees hurled a four-hitter against Whit Wyatt as Gordon, Keller, and Henrich combined to wreak significant enough havoc to sink the now subdued Dodgers 3–1. DiMaggio's series was mediocre at .263 and a mere one run driven in, but the series MVP, Joe Gordon, at .500 and Charlie Keller at .389, both with five runs knocked in, picked up the slack. Keller especially was remarkable. His ankle was so severely sprained shortly before the Series that he sported a cast extending above his knee. I asked him recently how he had managed to ready himself for the Series so quickly, and his answer was direct: "I ripped off the cast." Ducky Medwick took the Dodger team honors at the plate with a meager .235 average, and Brooklyn saw its fate reflected in the sad numbers of Pete Reiser at .200 and Dolf Camilli at .167. The Yankees in those days of modest earnings carried home $5,943.31 as their winning share; the Dodgers got $4,829.40 each for the solace of losing.

After the season and the series, DiMaggio and his wife, Dorothy Arnold, awaited the birth of their first child. Joe DiMaggio, Jr.'s, arrival on October 23 provided the great Yankee with his biggest thrill of a year in which thrills were many. DiMaggio sounded like every father when he told reporters the day after his son's birth: "You ought to see the little fellow, he has the most perfect nose. And I never saw such a pair of hands on a baby." Joe, Jr., grew up with the decade, and at ten he figured in that memorable and poignant photograph taken in 1951 at the end of DiMaggio's career, with father and son walking into the gloom of the visitor's clubhouse corridor at the Polo Grounds during the World Series, a familiar number 5 hunched on DiMaggio's back and a tender arm drooped over his boy's shoulders.

The year ran its course. A crop of movies that made 1941 one of the most brilliant in the history of American film reaped more of its harvest in later summer and fall: *How Green Was My Valley, Here Comes Mr. Jordan,* Hitchcock's *Suspicion* with Cary Grant and Joan Fontaine, even Disney's *Dumbo.* In his madcap comedy *1941,* director Steven Spielberg alluded to the currency of Disney's animated film when he had Robert Stack, as a commanding general, cry like a baby over *Dumbo* in a Hollywood movie house during an imagined Japanese invasion of Los Angeles. A much younger Robert Stack, coincidentally, was one of the rising stars in 1941; his name had even appeared on the *Sporting News*'s list of potential candidates to play Lou Gehrig in *The Pride of the Yankees.*

After the World Series, the football season kicked into full swing with notables such as Frankie Albert, left-handed quarterback for Clark Shaughnessy's radical T formation at Stanford, and Otto Graham, exceptional sophomore passer for Northwestern. Navy beat Army in mid-November 1941, 14–6, before nearly 100,000 at Philadelphia's Municipal Stadium. The game was initiated as always by the on-field procession of midshipmen and cadets. On this November day the huge crowd cheered for minutes on end, seeming to sense that the pageant of American men in uniform would soon display itself less ceremoniously in a world perilously at war.

On the professional football circuit in 1941 George Halas' Chicago Bears, with Sid Luckman doing the passing and Whizzer White, future Supreme Court justice, doing the kicking, won their division in a rugged end of the season game with Green Bay and then coasted to a championship victory over the New York Giants, 37–9. The championship game, played a week after Pearl Harbor, drew only 13,000 disconcerted fans. A few days earlier Bruce Smith, tailback for the undefeated Big Ten champions, the University of Minnesota, had given his Heisman Trophy award acceptance speech. He cut his remarks short because President Roosevelt planned a radio address to the nation at the same time that afternoon to rally the land after the shock of Pearl Harbor. Smith's few words were in a language one now recognizes as prewar Americanese: "Those far eastern fellows may think American boys are soft, but I have had, and even now have, plenty of evidence in black and blue to show that they are making a big mistake."

There was no doubt at the end of the year that America was a fighting nation. But even before Pearl Harbor and the declaration of war, the isolationist cause in America had begun to founder badly. This became more obvious as the months passed, and in an important editorial for *Life* Walter Lippmann called isolationism a "stupendous failure." By late summer and early fall Charles Lindbergh, whose appearances across the land had coincided with so many of the prominent days of DiMaggio's streak, spoke more desperately and more bitterly. Many in his own organization, America First, had deserted the troubled aviator. Things reached their sorriest level in a particularly vicious September rally in Des Moines, where Lindbergh blamed the Jews of Europe for bringing problems down upon their own heads. After Pearl Harbor, Lindbergh was a man without a cause and almost without a country. He had already quit his Army reserve rank of colonel, and Roosevelt not only refused to recommission him but withheld security clearance so that he could not work for the aircraft industry. The President finally relented when Henry Ford offered Lindbergh a job as consultant on the manufacture of the B-24 Liberator bomber. Even then Lindbergh could barely stifle his admiration for things German; he called the Ford plant at Rouge the highest creation of Faustian man.

The amazing flight of Rudolf Hess that had so startled the world near the beginning of DiMaggio's streak quieted as a story later in 1941, primarily because the British put a lid of absolute secrecy on the deputy führer's confinement. Churchill wished to keep Hitler off guard, and he also knew how furious the entire incident made Stalin. Hess' efforts to gain an English alliance against Russia rendered him a symbol of Nazi perfidy, and even if he were repentant—which he wasn't—the Russians would keep him locked up in Berlin's Spandau Castle until he died.

The military campaign along the huge Russian front in the latter half of 1941 remained the focus of the European war. Of the millions who fought, tens of thousands died; of the tens of millions who merely tried to live, hundreds of thousands were executed. Hitler's ten-week projection for taking Russia had not counted on the endless supply of manpower and the capacity of the Russian nation to endure the bitterest savagery the world had ever known. Soon the Nazi armies would find themselves bogged down in the mud and snows of the Russian plains and forests, facing the doomed prospect of having to lay in for a long siege of the two cities they had planned to capture weeks before: Leningrad in the north and Stalingrad in the south. These struggles would change the course of the European war.

It is sad testimony to the vigilance of the Western democracies that the most extreme measures of the Nazi program, the murder of civilian populations and the full-scale siphoning off of European Jewry into SS detention and labor camps, were relegated to the back pages of the news late in 1941. Editors were reluctant to give prominent space to what they fervently hoped was just rumor. Civilized nations did not dematerialize populations. What no one knew at this time, however, proved even more appalling. Hitler's lieutenant, Reinhard Heydrich, had formed an addendum of sorts to the German plans for the invasion of Russia, plotting the elimination of so-called "racially inferior" populations of the captive nations. Göring put the second piece of the puzzle in place in regard to the final solution. He cabled Heydrich on July 31, 1941, "to carry out all the necessary preparations with regard to organizational and financial matters for bringing about a complete solution of the Jewish question in the German sphere of influence in Europe."

The world would all too soon see the undeniable result of Heydrich and Göring's newly conceived horror when 33,000

Ukrainian Jews were rounded up from the lovely city of Kiev and its environs and shot in an unspeakable series of mass executions at Babi Yar. Matters would get even worse through the bone-chilling Russian winter. By year's end the casualties for the campaign, including civilians and soldiers, reached close to six million. "Never before" is the only accurate way to describe what took place along the eastern front of the European war, and the experience inured Germany for a pan-European Holocaust in regard to which much of the modern world has long intoned "Never again."

The emerging story of the war for America after DiMaggio's streak and into the fall and winter of 1941 concerns Japan, the Far East, and the Pacific theater. There had been hints throughout 1941 of more than a mere tropical storm on this horizon, but Roosevelt's and the Defense Department's hearts and minds were forever at sea in the Atlantic. A week after DiMaggio's streak ended, Japan moved its armies into Indochina. In response, the United States froze Japanese assets, as we had done to the Germans and the Italians in June. Though months earlier the Japanese had worked out the full scenario for a sneak attack on the U.S. naval installation in Hawaii, diplomatically at least Japan wished to maintain contact with Washington. America offered a nonaggression pact in return for guarantees from the Japanese for a free China. A diplomatic stall set in, continuing to the very hour when the Japanese raided Pearl Harbor.

For its issue just after the attack on Pearl Harbor, as part of a story that had been prepared earlier, *Life* magazine hit the streets with a huge picture of a bucolic teenager, starlet Patricia Peardon, in the innocent Moss Hart Broadway musical *Junior Miss*. All was sweet innocence. The next week *Life* grew somber and tense. Its cover was an image of the American flag. The war raged with the United States fully in it when Hitler's Germany joined its Japanese ally by declaring war on us before the formality of our doing so on them.

Little in a culture as various as America's probably ever was as simple as many believed (and still do) before World War II, but that doesn't lessen the feeling for the last year before our full immersion into an awful conflict, a year that both forges and closes the myth of an epoch to which Joe DiMaggio's fifty-six-game hitting streak contributes its bounty of energy, endurance, and grace.

Acknowledgments and Thanks

In addition to the authors who contributed to this book, I'd like to thank the numerous other people who helped in various ways with the research and production. My thanks to Tim Wiles, Director of Research at the Baseball Hall of Fame and to Peter Clark, Curator of Collections, Ted Spencer, Curator of Exhibits, Jeff Idelson, Exectutive Director for Communications and Education, and Bill Burdick, Senior Photo Researcher. Thanks go also to thank Del Wilber, and Micheal O'Brien of the Major League Baseball Players Alumni Association for their help, and to Tom Goldstein of *Elysian Fields Quarterly*, who recommended several of the writers appearing in this book. For his help with research on the film careers of Joe DiMaggio, Dorothy Arnold and Marilyn Monroe, I'd like to thank Dave Datta, and for their help with obtaining difficult to find books, my thanks to Marty Gallagher, Cynthia Grant, and Pat Mikkelson of the Brown County (Wisconsin) Library. Also, thanks to Lisa Steinman of the Commissioner's office for her assistance in arranging the interview with Bub Selig, and to Marty Greenberg and John Helfers of Teknobooks for their good work in the production of this project.

Richard Gilliam
July 6, 1999